The Simply Grande Gardening Cookbook

THE Simply  Grande Gardening Cookbook

Jean Ann Pollard

with Gardening Notes by
Peter Garrett

BURFORD BOOKS

To our European and Native American antecedents,

this book is dedicated

Printed in the United States of America

10 9 8 7 6 5 4 3 2 1

Library of Congress Cataloging-in-Publication Data
Pollard, Jean Ann, 1934-
    The simply grande gardening cookbook/Jean Ann Pollard;
with gardening notes by Peter Garrett.
        p.cm.
    Includes bibliographical references and index.
    ISBN 1-58080-087-4
        1. Cookery (Vegetables) I. Garrett, Peter, II. Title.

TX801.P652001
641.65—dc21
2001025552

Contents

SPRING

April–May

June

SUMMER
July

August

FALL
September

October

WINTER

November

Thanks

"We stand on the shoulders of giants."

That's an old quote but, in the case of this book, totally appropriate: The people whose cooking expertise, research, and love of history have inspired the writing of *The Simply Grande Gardening Cookbook* are giants indeed.

Thanks first of all to my mother and grandmother—cooks of the "old school" whose attention to cleanliness and fine cooking techniques pervade my kitchen. Thanks to my husband, Peter, that dedicated gardener whose vegetables thrive and satisfy our dinner plates and palates. Special thanks to all those splendid researchers of past and present who are listed in the bibliography, whose work undergirds my own, and whom I quote.

Warm appreciation to Publisher Peter Burford, who has patiently seen the book through all its trials and permutations.

And to copy editor Laura Jorstad, cheers for the careful editing that has immeasurably improved our prose.

Last, but certainly not least, thanks to this grand planet, which has nourished us since we humans first appeared in the not-so-distant past, scrabbling about in the dirt seeking sustenance in her bounty.

—Jean Ann Pollard

Introduction

In the 1600s the area of what today we call New England formed a nucleus for early European settlement. Beyond Plymouth, beyond Boston, trending northeasterly past a coastline deeply indented and decorated with thousands of islands, stretched a great, treed wilderness, its shores visited by Basque fishermen whose fish-drying racks prepared cod for faraway ports.

French fur trappers, and English settlers lured by king's grants, ultimately followed fishermen to hack farms out of the forest and river bottomlands. And soon their numbers, although nearly extinguished by desperate Native Americans who saw doom approaching, spread and prospered.

This unique cookbook, based as it is on historic and seasonal produce, and coming from central Maine (still a great, treed tract at the upper, eastern limit of the United States), can be deliciously and delightedly enjoyed by all New Englanders—in fact, by all Americans whose lives have been touched by our precocious, precarious early gardening and cooking history.

THE COOK, THE GARDENER

Up here in the "wilds" of central Maine people enjoy roastingly hot summers as well as freezingly cold winters. August temperatures, in fact, can soar into the 100s—and the peppers and tomatoes love it!

Like everything else in the North, gardening has a distinct season. The old saying is "Make hay while the sun shines." Which means that successful vegetable growing proceeds according to strict date and plan. It also means that cooking follows the seasons as produce arrives.

None of this is hard to bear. Nothing is ever boring. Instead, there's the excitement of looking forward to treats only available at certain times of the year: strawberries in June, baked beans in November. It's good training in appreciation, organization—and patience.

The Simply Grande Gardens in Winslow, Maine, consist of 1 acre of well-loved and -tilled land where the husband-and-wife team of gardener-hydrogeologist Peter Garrett and artist-writer Jean Ann Pollard plant and harvest delicious vegetables for 15 families—or about 45 people—every year. Nothing in our garden has ever seen a herbicide, or a pesticide beyond rotenone, an old-fashioned worm killer made from the pyrethrum plant. Our type of gardening is, we admit, labor intensive—the way historic Mainers proceeded for generations—and that's the way we like it.

Through the years Jean Ann has handed out recipes to match whatever vegetable has peaked with perfection. For folks meeting celeriac or cilantro for the first time, the collection has been a distinct hit.

Now it has grown. Not only are delicious recipes included, but Jean Ann has added the fascinating history of vegetable travels, while Peter has supplied gardening tips. The result is *The Simply Grande Gardening Cookbook*.

Simply Grande Gardening Basics

Following are some basic ideas and tips for gardening that have served Simply Grande Gardens well for years. They all come as hand-me-downs and through experimentation. There is no right way. But we have found that these simple methods work for us.

SOILS

Soil is a combination of mineral matter (sand, silt, and clay) and organic matter. Each contributes something. Sand makes the soil light and well drained, but can make it too dry in summer. Silt and clay are what give soil its inherent fertility, but can cause waterlogging in spring and adobe in summer. The addition of organic matter solves all these problems. It is also microscopic life in the organic matter that makes the natural fertility available for vegetables. Continual addition of organic matter is the key to the easiest garden to grow, and the best vegetables you have ever tasted. So your first job is to check out local sources of organic matter. They could include:

COMPOST. If you don't have a compost pile, it's time to start one. Very briefly, it is made by piling lawn clippings, leaves, weeds, other garden wastes and kitchen scraps in one place, and letting them rot. There are special techniques for having the job done fast (in weeks). They involve layering and the introduction of air, and conserving moisture to heat up the pile by aerobic decomposition. But don't let those details keep you from starting composting anyway. Any pile of such materials will rot slowly, and produce good compost within a year, though the pile will not have become hot enough to kill the weed seeds.

COVER CROPS. These are crops grown not for food but for improving the soil or for outcompeting weeds—some call them "green manures." The three best known are clover, rye, and buckwheat. Clover (alsike variety is best) will improve the nutrient content of the soil by converting nitrogen in the air into nitrate in the soil. Rye (annual or winter rye) is commonly sown to produce lush growth quickly in fall. Buckwheat is the best of the weed beaters—grow it in springtime, and wait until it flowers before cutting it down. In all cases the crop, once grown, should be cut before it goes to seed, and tilled under. If you can spare a piece of your garden for cover crops within your rotation (see Crop Rotation, below) you can plant cover crops in succession throughout the year, thus bringing additional benefit.

FARMYARD MANURE. Old manure (more than one year) of any kind is the best—it requires no waiting time for planting. If you only have fresh cow, horse, pig, or sheep manure, it should be spread and then tilled under as soon as possible. Wait at least 3 weeks before planting, and don't plant root crops in such treated soils unless you have 4 months prior to harvest. Chicken and rabbit manure are very high in nitrate, so use only very sparingly by themselves.

TREE LEAVES. Dead leaves are great, but some are very acidic, and some take years to decay. Chop them first with a lawn mower, string trimmer, or shredder, and mix them with other materials in a compost pile. If you bag leaves, include a shovelful of dirt, shake it up, and put the bag in the sunshine—by the following summer it should be good compost. Some towns and cities collect and compost leaves as a way to recycle municipal waste. Ask how you can get some.

LAWN CLIPPINGS. These provide heat in a properly constructed compost pile, and should be mixed with dry materials (last fall's leaves, for instance) for the best compost.

ORGANIC MULCHES (see Mulches, below).

ORGANIC FERTILIZERS. If none of the above are available, you can purchase bagged organic fertilizers from a local garden store. But be careful; some are inorganic chemicals disguised with a little organic matter. Look for the N-P-K label. Numbers represent immediately available nutrients. If any number is greater than 8, it's probably inorganic. Organic materials have slow-release nutrients with low N-P-K numbers. Also check for ingredients such as ammonium, muriate, urea, nitrate, phosphoric, or superphosphate. They are inorganic chemicals and, though remarkable for stimulating plant growth, will kill microorganisms and earthworms in the soil. Only organic matter builds soils. It is at the heart of organic gardening.

Call your local university extension service for a soil sampling kit, and follow instructions. The analysis you get back will suggest what you need to do to balance your soil for growing the best vegetables. For instance, if the pH is low, you can add lime. If nutrients are low, you can add special organic products such as blood meal for nitrogen (N), bonemeal for phosphorus (P), or greensand for potassium (K). Each of these is particularly rich in that nutrient. But there are many types of organic matter that would do just as well.

CROP ROTATION

Crop rotation is like a children's game. There is no strictly right way to play it. The important thing is to play, keeping to a general set of rules, but always observing where new rules might make it more fun as you go along. Unlike most children's games, this one begins on paper indoors in winter. It's played in real life outside in summer.

Important background for the game is the knowledge that:

➤ Different plants take different nutrients from the soil in differing amounts.

➤ Some plants give back nutrients (especially peas, beans, and clover, which manufacture nitrate fertilizer from nitrogen in the air).

➤ Different plants have different pests and diseases.

➤ Some plants are deep rooted and loosen up the subsoil.

For all these reasons, the basic rule is not to plant the same vegetable in the same place in successive years. The following is a how-to guide for the game of crop rotation of annual vegetables:

1. Measure your garden. Say it consists of four large plots, each of which is 50 feet by 20 feet. Each plot should give you the space for about 12 3-foot beds, with a 1-foot walkway between beds in each plot. That's 48 beds in all—a pretty good area for growing vegetables for a family of four for an entire year, with some left over for friends.

2. Cut slips of paper (about 1 inch by 3 inches is good) equal to the number of beds in your garden. In the example above you should cut 48 slips.

3. Divide your vegetables into family or other groups as follows:

➤ Leafy greens (lettuce, salad greens, and spinach)

➤ Cucurbits (squash, pumpkin, melon, and cucumber)

➤ Onion family (garlic, onions, scallions, and leeks)

➤ Peas

➤ Corn

➤ Potatoes

➤ Brassicas (cabbage, broccoli, brussels sprouts, cauliflower, kale, and kohlrabi)

➤ Nightshade fruits (tomatoes, peppers, and eggplant)

➤ Roots (including carrots, beets, turnips, and radishes)

➤ Beans

4. Divide the slips among the groups. For instance, you might want to grow two beds of beans, four of corn, six of potatoes, and three of tomatoes, peppers,

and eggplants together. Write those names on the slips: two bean slips, four corn slips, and so on.

5. Keep the slips with the same name in a group together.

6. Then arrange them in order—one long parking lot for paper slips across the kitchen table would be good. Have the groups follow each other approximately as in the list in #3 above.

7. Then take a group of slips out of the parking lot, keeping them in the same order, and fit them into models of your actual garden plots. Arrange the slips so that each plot is full.

8. If there are spaces in some plots, don't worry. You can fill such spaces with some small crop, perhaps a surprise that isn't on the list, like fennel or annual herbs. Alternately, there may be space enough for a cover crop.

That is your plan for the garden next summer. Draw it on paper for a permanent record. Refer to it as you plant in spring. The following year, you should move the plantings from Plot 1 to Plot 2 and on around, so that Plot 4 replaces Plot 1.

There is nothing fixed about this crop rotation scheme. Remember, it's a game. As you learn from experience and reading, you'll be able to modify it, with inclusion of succession plantings and other refinements.

Some succession plantings you might want to try are leafy greens for fall harvest after the peas are done in August. Or carrots for winter harvest after the early potatoes are dug. If at all possible, include spaces in your rotation or succession for cover crops.

BED SIZES

Your garden doesn't need beds—but they sure help. You can make them any size, but the ideal width seems to be 3 feet, which is about as wide as anyone wants to pick or weed across. It's also very useful to have a standard length for a bed, because so many accessories can be cut for use anywhere (for instance, lengths of floating row cover, or pieces of reusable plastic sheet for mulch). Twenty feet seems to be a pretty good bed length.

Raised beds are a nice idea, especially where the soil is very poor, where you want permanent beds, or when you want to bend down less. Find a type of untreated wood that rots slowly, like hemlock or black locust, and buy or cut planks for the construction. Then add topsoil.

Even without raised beds it is usually beneficial to create paths between beds, so that the place to walk is clearly marked for you and others. If you're considering the 20-foot bed length suggested above, take a flat 1-foot-wide shovel and scrape off the top 4 inches of soil between one bed and the next. That's your path, 20 feet long and 1 foot wide. Spread out that soil on the bare ground next to the path. Then measure off another 3 feet and create another parallel path. The space between is your bed. Make another. The process is simple and creates an ideal garden plan, with beds and paths all of the same length and all parallel.

WHEEL SEEDER

This tool is simply great. It actually does six things at once with hardly any effort. It makes a notch in the soil, cuts that notch to the desired depth, plants seeds, covers them, rolls the soil over them, and marks the location of the next parallel row for planting at the spacing you choose. The Earthway model is also cheap, at less than $100 including shipping. Use it for peas, beans, carrots, lettuce, and so on. Small seeds and big, it handles them all. Its particular benefits are that you don't have to bend down to plant, the planting goes fast, seed spacing is more accurate than by hand, and your plants will come up in beautiful straight rows. Because of the difficulty that cabbage family seeds pose (they're round like ball bearings), you should buy the optional seed plates for them.

Before you plant, smooth the bed with a rake. Then, with wheel seeder ready to go, stand at one end of the bed where you want to start a row, check out an equivalent point at the far end of the bed, and walk straight toward it. That will keep the row straight.

COLLINEAR HOE

The collinear or draw hoe is the perfect partner of the wheel seeder. It's a recent invention by Elliot Coleman and is a precision tool—like having a razor blade at the end of a 5 1/2-foot-long handle. You may have to hunt for it. Johnny's Selected Seeds carries it. If you plant seeds in rows 8 inches or more apart, you can follow this procedure:

About 10 days after raking and planting, on a bright sunny morning, walk alongside the row and draw the collinear hoe behind you, between or beside the rows. You should do this even if your seedlings have yet to emerge (for instance carrots, which are slow). The purpose of collineal-hoeing is to cut off the tiny weeds before they get established. The hoeing is so simple that, with practice, it can be done at a slow walking speed.

Repeat the procedure about 10 days later. Weather is crucial, because if the day is bright and dry, the weeds pulled by the collineal-hoeing lie there to die. The soil is also easier to work on such days. On wet days the hoe doesn't cut as well and the weeds can reroot themselves.

Wipe the blade clean for next time. Sharpen the blade periodically, maintaining the cutting edge on the soil (bottom) side.

MULCHES

In all parts of the country, during summer, the volume of water evaporated from soils and transpired from plants exceeds the volume of rainfall. Some summers are so dry that plants wilt. Most vegetables (except perhaps beets and carrots, with their very deep roots) do not fare well under such conditions. So you must either irrigate or mulch or both. Another good reason to mulch is to keep weeds down.

Mulches come in two basic types, organic or plastic.

Organic mulches could include hay, straw, cardboard, newspapers, shavings, and sawdust. All are great for keeping moisture in the soil, but their use has several disadvantages, each of which can be overcome:

1. They all are high in carbon relative to nitrogen, and therefore rob the soil of nitrogen as they decompose. If you use them, feed the soil with compost before you mulch, or add a high-nitrogen material (such as grass clippings or chicken manure) with them.

2. They keep the soil cool if added or left in place in springtime. It's best to apply such mulch in summer and fall. Six to 10 inches of hay mulch will keep the soil from freezing in winter, even in Maine. Such mulches are advisable for keeping perennial vegetables (such as asparagus, sorrel, bunching onions, and garlic planted in fall) in good condition until the following spring.

3. In a wet summer organic mulches provide ideal conditions for slugs. So don't use them around crops that would be damaged by slugs.

Plastic mulches are the alternative. The simplest kind is black polyethylene, which comes in sheets a few thousandths of an inch ("mils") thick. More recent inventions are red plastic mulches, which have been shown to cause earlier fruit set or root growth. Specific advantages of plastic mulches are that they warm the soil, preserve soil moisture, and prevent weed growth. They are especially good for crops that need warmth, like peppers, tomatoes, eggplant, melons, squash, and cucumbers. They are also good for potatoes, cabbages, cauliflower, broccoli, and brussels sprouts, because plastic mulches retain moisture. Their disadvantage is that they eventually tear or disintegrate until they're no longer usable, and are then a disposal problem.

To use plastic mulches for the above crops, here's what to do: Choose the size of bed you want for each crop. Then obtain or cut a piece of plastic to fit the bed. This particular piece will be designated for this crop from now on. Choose a non-windy day and spread the plastic sheet on the bed. Walk around the bed and, with a shovel, dig under the edge of the plastic, removing the sod or soil and placing it on the edge. Pull the plastic tight as you move along and the sun warms it. When all sides are secure, it will not lift off in high winds. Measure the spacing of holes for the particular crop (see directions under each vegetable), marking them if necessary before you cut. Cutting is final—there is no going back! Use a posthole digger to cut holes. It takes two strikes, one at right angles to the other, to make a hole 6 inches in diameter, which is good for planting seedlings. This size of hole, though smaller than the traditional "hill," is also good for direct-planting of seeds for squash, melons, and cucumbers.

At the end of the season remove the plastic, fold it up, and move it to the bed that you will use for that designated crop next year (check Rotation, above).

FLOATING ROW COVERS

Floating row covers are made of spun polypropylene or cotton, and are very light-weight. They let in air, rain, and 85 percent of the sun. They are very useful for extending the season by giving about 4 degrees of frost protection, sheltering the crop from wind, and keeping bugs out.

Floating row covers come in bed widths or large sheets. Sheets are best laid directly on the newly planted seedlings, to be pushed up by them as they grow. Bed widths can be laid like that too, or supported on wire hoops stuck into the ground across the bed. In either case you need to hold down the edges of the row covers with rocks, dirt, or garden staples.

To keep black flea beetles out, always use a new piece of fabric, and be very careful to seal the edges with soil all around the entire bed. To keep weed seedlings at bay within the same bed, you'll have to either use a mulch in combination or take the cover off every 10 days for a quick collineal-hoeing.

When you're done with these covers for the season, take them off carefully, dry them, fold them, and put them away for next year. Then pull up the wire hoops and store them, too.

SPRING

According to *Simply Grande* gardener Peter Garrett,
mud season—that bane of every floor washer—
represents one of six actual New England
seasons. There are, he reckons, spring,
summer, fall, the fallen season (that time of year
between blazing October and winter when skies are gray
and the land rests), snowclad winter, and the March–April
mud season—or how to keep the mud out
of the house and on the driveway!

It's also the time of year when eagles are nesting,
chickadees sing love songs, woodpeckers hammer,
and gardeners eye heavy, wet soil and think
about planting seeds—or foraging.

"Fine words butter no parsnips"
—OLD ENGLISH PROVERB

Parsnips

Familiar to every New Englander in the old days when winter waned, the big, fat, ivory-colored parsnip, *Pastinaca sativum* of the Umbelliferae (carrot) family, arrived all succulent and sugar-tender from overwintering right in the brown earth. It had been known by Greeks and Romans long before. Along with turnips, radishes, onions, leeks, and probably carrots, an undeveloped form was among the root crops commonly grown in Europe during the first millennium A.D.

But the treasure familiar to us today didn't develop until the Middle Ages. Flemish weavers, fleeing the persecution of Spain's Philip II around 1558, probably introduced it to England. And by 1597 the English botanist John Gerard was mentioning it in his book called *The Herball, or General Histoire of Plantes.*

He apparently wasn't much impressed: "There is a good, pleasant food or bread made of the roots of the parsnip, which I have myself not tried of, nor mean to."

The parsnip took its time traveling to America, finally arriving to stay when colonists brought it to New England, where it was used pretty much as the potato is today. It had actually arrived in Virginia's Jamestown Colony by 1608 or '09, but perhaps because its succulent-sweet flavor develops only after a cold winter's blessing, it became a favorite among northern rather than southern gardeners.

Says Howard S. Russell in *A Long, Deep Furrow: Three Centuries of Farming in New England,* in the Boston area settlers were planting—besides Indian corn, beans, and pumpkins—turnips, carrots, and parsnips, "all of them roots that do well in spaded ground." In fact, "The first vegetables to become of importance in the new colonies, appear to have been the roots."

Farther north in Maine, John Winter of Richmond Island in Casco Bay "paled" a field of 4 or 5 acres. "We have proved divers sorts [of crops such] as barley, peas,

PARSNIPS

CHOOSING SEEDS: There's not much variety, but choose those with known canker resistance. There are 5,000 seeds per ounce. Use 1/2 ounce for each 100 row feet. Buy new seeds every year; old seeds don't germinate well. Parsnip seeds have "wings" and are difficult to plant mechanically.

CULTIVATION: Parsnips like deep, friable soils because they have very long taproots. Plant by hand in rows 8 to 10 inches apart. Wait 3 weeks for germination, and don't let the soil dry out. Collineal-hoe between the planted rows even before you see parsnip seedlings emerge. Be ruthless in thinning to 2 to 3 inches apart. Parsnips are slow growers. Be patient.

PESTS: Deer and woodchucks love to nibble off parsnip leaves.

HARVESTING: Parsnips take a full season to grow. Harvest in late fall if you're desperate. Or go digging during a winter thaw for a New Year's treat. Or leave the plants buried until the frost leaves the ground for the sweetest parsnips of the year. Dig deep and pull. You must pull all of them before they start to sprout. If you want to save seeds, leave two plants to go to flower: Parsnips, like carrots, are biennials.

If you have too many parsnips to eat all at once, try grating and drying some for fine additions to soups later in the year.

---

pumpkins, carrots, onions, garlic, radishes, turnips, cabbage, lettuce, parsley, melons . . ." and parsnips, he said. That was in 1634.

Accolades aren't surprising. "It's possible," advises Marian Morash in *The Victory Garden Cookbook*, "to harvest parsnips anytime they've achieved any size but I prefer to leave many of them undisturbed in the ground and dig them in the spring, when I think they have reached optimum sweetness." Indeed, she calls them "garden candy." One can only imagine the joy of early settlers who knew, as winter supplies dwindled, that buried out there in the still-cold garden was good, fresh food. And as a popular song of the day put it: "For pottage and pudding and custards and pies our pumpkins and parsnips are common supplies."

Even an early Puritan waxed enthusiastic. A quotation found in the dissertation of the Reverend Francis Higginson titled *New England's Plantation, or a Short and True Description of the Commodities and Discommodities of that Countrye, Written by a reverend Divine now there resident* (published in 1630) said, "Our Turnips, Parsnips and Carrots are here both bigger and sweeter than is ordinarily to be found in England." And by 1774, as reported in his *Garden Book,* Thomas Jefferson was planting two types at Monticello.

The parsnip, which can grow to 20 inches in length yet remain tender, contains a lot of potassium in a cupful—some 587 milligrams—along with 2.3 grams of protein and 70 milligrams of calcium. And in a New England spring it yields fine eating. Planted the summer before and stored right in the garden, its sweetness is bursting as spring approaches. By April parsnips are moist, plump, and irresistible when washed well, peeled a little (if very stained), sliced into 1/4-inch disks, and simmered in just a little water or milk for perhaps 10 minutes. Topped with a sprinkling of cinnamon, they're perfect served as a side dish to any meal—especially one rich in crisp greens.

Leftovers are also fine. Says a little English cookbook called *The Healthy Life Cook Book,* published in 1915: "Cold steamed parsnips are nice fried. Sprinkle with chopped parsley, and serve."

These unusual muffins are sweet— and delicious.

Parsnip Muffins

MAKES 12 MUFFINS

Preheat the oven to 350°F.

THE DRY INGREDIENTS

In a small bowl, sift together:
  2 cups refined white flour
  OR 1 cup white flour and
    1 cup whole-wheat pastry flour
  2 teaspoons baking soda (see page 28)
  1 1/4 cups refined white sugar
  2 teaspoons powdered cinnamon

THE VEGETABLE INGREDIENTS

Into a large bowl, grate to equal:
  2 cups grated parsnips
Add:
  2 cups currants
  1/2 cup sunflower seeds
  OR coarsely chopped walnuts
  1/2 cup grated coconut
  1 apple, coarsely grated

Add the flour mixture and toss together.

THE WET INGREDIENTS

In yet another bowl, beat together:
  3 eggs
  1 cup sunflower seed oil
  2 teaspoons natural vanilla
Pour this into the flour-parsnip mix and stir together till just combined.

BAKING

Pour into 12 1/3-cup, buttered muffin tins, filling to the top. Bake in the preheated oven for 35 minutes. Cool on a rack 5 minutes and enjoy while warm.

A treat for springtime eating is parsnip pie cooked in a prebaked pastry shell.

Parsnip Pie

THE CRUST

In a preheated 450°F oven, bake:
  10-inch single-crust pie shell
    (see page 67)
Be sure the fluted rim is high.

Reduce the oven temperature to 350°F.

THE PARSNIP FILLING

Wash carefully, peel, and cut into disks 1 inch thick:

2 pounds parsnips

Place the chunks in a large pot and add:

about 1 cup cold water

Bring to a boil, then reduce the heat to medium and cook till tender—perhaps 5 minutes. Drain well in a colander.

Place the parsnip chunks in a blender or food processor and purée until smooth. You should have 3 cups of purée.

COMBINING

When the purée has partially cooled, beat in:

2 tablespoons melted butter
1/3 cup light brown sugar
1 teaspoon freshly squeezed orange OR lemon juice
1 teaspoon freshly grated, well-washed orange OR lemon rind
1/2 teaspoon powdered cinnamon
1/4 teaspoon ground cloves
1/4 teaspoon freshly grated nutmeg
1/2 teaspoon natural vanilla
2 large eggs
1 cup heavy cream

BAKING

If your prebaked 10-inch pastry shell has become cold, warm it in your oven till it feels hot—5 to 10 minutes—before filling. Pour in the parsnip mixture.

Sprinkle with:

3 tablespoons finely chopped walnuts

Bake till firm, about 40 to 50 minutes.

Many cooks feel that the best way to cook parsnips is the simplest: sautéing. Peel and thinly slice parsnips, then fry them in butter about 5 minutes till lightly browned.

If you've stored the big white roots until calendulas or nasturtiums bloom, however, an extra treat is in store. Nasturtiums, with their spicy-honey taste, are particularly toothsome here.

Sautéed Parsnips with Sunshine

SERVES 4

Wash well and peel:

1 pound parsnips

Slice into thin disks.

In a large porcelainized saucepan, combine:

1 1/4 cups freshly squeezed orange juice
1/4 cup freshly squeezed lemon juice
1 teaspoon grated rind from a well-washed orange
1/8 teaspoon powdered cinnamon
1 teaspoon maple syrup

Bring to a boil and add:

the prepared parsnips

Reduce the heat and simmer till the parsnips are tender—perhaps 10 minutes. Remove the parsnips with a wire spoon (reserve the cooking liquid) and set aside in a warm dish. Keep warm.

In a small bowl, combine well:

1 tablespoon butter
1 tablespoon unbleached white flour

Return the orange-parsnip cooking liquid to a boil and add the butter-flour mixture, whisking and cooking until the sauce is thick and smooth.

When it's thick enough, add:

a little sea salt
some freshly ground black
OR white pepper

Pour the sauce over the warm parsnips. Sprinkle with:

finely chopped parsley
fresh calendula petals
OR chopped nasturtium flowers

Serve right away with rice or baked potatoes and a great green leafy salad.

THE NEW MAINE COOKING offered a recipe for Parsnip Stew that pleased (and still pleases) parsnip lovers.

J. A.'s Parsnip Stew

SERVES 4–5

THE VEGETABLES

Purchase or dig from the garden:

7 large parsnips

Wash well, and peel if necessary. Then slice into 1/4-inch disks to measure 7 cups.

Wash well, peel thinly (if you please), and cut into 1/2-inch cubes to measure 3 cups:

'Kennebec' (or other) white potatoes

Peel and chop to measure about 1 cup:

1 large onion

COOKING

In a large pot with very little water, simmer all three vegetables together over low heat till the parsnips are barely tender—about 20 minutes.

Place 2 cups of this parsnip mixture into a blender and purée. Return to the pot. Depending on how thick you like your stew, add:

up to 2 quarts milk
sea salt to taste

Bring to a simmer and add:

1/2 cup finely chopped fresh parsley

SERVING

Serve in warmed bowls and sprinkle with:

powdered cinnamon

Fresh rolls and a green leafy salad turn this into a fine lunch.

MAPLE SWEETENING

We can't discuss parsnips without mentioning maple sugar. In New England's early days, maple syrup and sugar were the only sweeteners available. And how diligently those colonists worked to make both as light in color as possible—a silly enterprise, as every lover of maple products today would agree.

Historically, said the famous back-to-the-land pair Helen and Scott Nearing in their *Maple Sugar Book,* as far back as Virgil (around 40 B.C.) the "honey of wild bees was the chief means of sweetening and was probably the first sugar food used by men.

"The first historic mention of sugar," they continue, "is found in China in the eighth century B.C., where it is spoken of as a product of India. The sugar cane was native in Bengal and cultivated there. After the fifth century B.C. it was introduced to the Euphrates valley and to China. Fellow travelers of Alexander the Great who invaded India in the fourth century B.C. . . . brought back tales of a reed that produced honey without the aid of bees. 'Honey cane' it was called originally, and

Herodotus spoke of sugar as 'manufactured honey.'

"Pliny," add the Nearings, "describes it as resembling salt and speaks of its medicinal properties" in his *Historia Naturalis.* "Dioscorides in the same era (about 50 A.D.) in his *Materia Medica,* states that 'there is a sort of concreted honey which is called sugar, found upon canes in India and Arabia; it is in consistence like salt, and is brittle between the teeth.' The Greeks and Romans called it 'sweet salt,' 'Indian salt,' 'sweet gravel.' The Bible's Jeremiah 6:20 mentions a 'sweet cane from a far country.'"

In tracing the history of sugar, W. W. Skeats remarked that "It long continued to be regarded as a rare and costly spice, and . . . remained so up to the time of the discovery of America." And, said G. Imlay in 1792, "The articles of sugar and salt, though not absolutely necessary to life, have become from habit so essential, that I doubt if any civilized people would be content to live without them."

"It was not until the close of the seventeenth century," say the Nearings, "when tea and coffee drinking were becoming habits, that sugar came to be more generally used. By the 1800s, sugar was established as a regular part of the diet." In fact, it's been estimated that each American today consumes about 100 pounds a year.

Although Virgil wasn't to see his dream of a golden age in which sweet syrup emerged from forest trees, maple products had long been appreciated by Native

---

BAKING SODA (bicarbonate of soda) makes cooking water alkaline and was once used by certain cooks to enhance the green color in vegetables—a poor idea, because it doubtless destroyed vitamins, and it certainly made peas, for instance, mushy.

BAKING POWDER, which causes cakes, pancakes, muffins, biscuits, and quick breads to rise, contains alkaline baking soda and an acidic component such as tartaric acid. When wet, the single-acting variety releases carbon dioxide when the batter is cold; double-acting does it again in the oven.

A rule of thumb is to use no more than 1 teaspoon of baking powder per cup of flour; any more than this may increase the loss of the B vitamin thiamine, due to the powder's alkalinity. Most commercial baking powders contain sodium, lime, and aluminum salts. Aluminum, it has been suggested, may come to rest in the brain, possibly causing senility. It may also damage other vital organs. Whether it does or not, choose one free of aluminum.

You can make your own baking powder by sifting together three items: 1 part potassium bicarbonate, 2 parts cream of tartar, 2 parts arrowroot or cornstarch.

Potassium bicarbonate can be purchased at almost any pharmacy, or you can substitute baking soda (sodium bicarbonate). Potassium bicarbonate helps the body be more alkaline and stimulates a greater flow of urine; sodium bicarbonate helps retain water. Cream of tartar (potassium bitartrate) is a diuretic, a cathartic (laxative), and a refrigerant. Tartaric acid is a white powder derived from grapes and various other plants. It is rarely toxic unless taken in large doses.

Rumford Baking Powder has long been the powder of choice because it contains only calcium acid phosphate, bicarbonate of soda, and cornstarch.

Americans, who taught Europeans the secrets of producing it. French and English settlers, naturally, were avid learners. In early colonial days, write the Nearings, "it was valued because it proved, with carriage dear and distances between trading towns far, the most available and unfailing source of sweetening." Some people even looked at it as a direct act of God. Benjamin Rush, the best-known physician of his time on the American continent and a signer of the Declaration of Independence, wrote in a letter to Thomas Jefferson, "The gift of the sugar maple trees is from a benevolent Providence."

And, of course, for those people disgusted by slavery, *The Farmer's Almanac* offered another incitement. "Make your own sugar, and send not to the Indies for it. Feast not on the toil, pain and misery of the wretched."

Containers were scarce in new settlements, and it was easier to store sugar in wooden tubs, pails, or large blocks. "These cakes are of a very dark colour in general, and very hard," reported Isaac Weld in his 1799 book, *Travels through the States of North America and the Provinces of Lower Canada*. When wanted, "they are scraped down with a knife, and when thus reduced into powder, the sugar appears of a much lighter cast, and not unlike West Indian muscovada or grained sugar."

By the 1800s refined white sugar had definitely gained favor. In describing the process of making the prizewinning sample of sugar exhibited at the annual New York State Agricultural Fair of 1844, the committee that awarded the premium said they "have never seen so fine a sample, either in the perfection of the granulation, or in the extent to which the refining process has been carried; the whole coloring matter is extracted, and the peculiar flavor of maple sugar is completely eradicated."

More's the pity.

In the old days maple sugaring was carried out in February or early March, just in time to satisfy everyone's craving before the long, hot days of summer. Springtime parsnips cooked with maple syrup make a naturally sweet treat even sweeter.

Mapled Parsnips

SERVES 4–6

Trim off the thick stem and slender root ends of:

1 1/2 pounds parsnips
Peel and cut into 3/4-inch disks.

In a large skillet, combine the parsnip disks with:

2 cups water
3 tablespoons sunflower seed oil
1 teaspoon sea salt
freshly ground black pepper
Bring to a boil, then reduce the heat and simmer the parsnips, covered, till just tender, about 10 minutes. Uncover, increase the heat to high, and quickly cook down the liquid.

Decrease the heat to medium and add:

3–4 tablespoons maple syrup
Cook, stirring gently to coat, for another minute. Sprinkle with:

freshly grated nutmeg

Serve right away with a big green salad and fresh rolls.

Fiddleheads

Many old-time sayings in New England have to do with weather: "March winds and April showers bring forth mayflowers" is one, referring to the heavenly scented, ground-hugging arbutus—and May means the real beginning of the green season.

Which leads to another saying: "In spring a young man's fancy . . ."

We all know what *fancy* refers to. For country boys, however, as well as country girls, *fancy* could well involve something a city kid never heard of: ferns. To be specific, fiddlehead ferns, which dot the bottomlands of rivers and brooks each spring when water levels fall and sunlight brings them back to life from the blackened lumps they hid in all winter.

The fern Mainers call the fiddlehead is the ostrich fern, *Pteretis pensylvanica,* not the woolly-headed bracken fern, *Pteridium aquilinum*—although that, too, is edible.

Fiddleheads are easy to recognize. In late April and early May they put up dark green spirals capped by thin, rather leathery shells of golden brown. The shells slip off easily.

So amid the rusty-sounding skirls of returning redwings, the lilt of robins, song sparrows, cardinals, orioles, and the rush of water, the idea is to wander along riverbanks with a sack for collecting while studying a good guidebook for identification. One such is Lee Allen Peterson's *Edible Wild Plants;* another is Joan Richardson's *Wild Edible Plants of New England.*

Once you're certain of fern identification, pluck tightly packed spirals when they're 3 to 6 inches high. Late fronds, which begin to pop out as plants uncoil, are reputedly poisonous, although nobody known to us has ever become ill from eating them. When the fronds appear, however, the plant is growing up. So let it grow.

And be very careful not to hurt unfurling plants by trampling or overpicking. You want to ensure a trip through the ferns again next year.

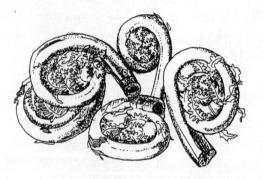

Fiddleheads can easily be ruined by over-cooking: They become slimy. Here are directions for quickly steaming them.

Steamed Fiddleheads

COLLECTING

Collect your fiddleheads from a nonpolluted stream or river. This is important.

PREPARING

Wash well, and remove all the brownish papery covering from:

a handful of fiddleheads per person

COOKING

Place the fiddleheads in a big porcelainized or stainless-steel pot without any liquid other than the rinse water remaining on them. (You might need to add a little, but no more than 1/2 inch in the bottom of the pot.)

Turn heat to high, cover, and steam the young things till just tender. This won't take long. Stir them once or twice.

SERVING

Serve on a heated platter and sprinkle with:

a few drops extra-virgin olive oil
some freshly squeezed lemon juice
perhaps a few drops of natural soy sauce

Baked potatoes or rice plus colorful carrots or winter squash are good companions.

NOTE: An alternative method, and one necessary for long-term fiddlehead storage, is to bring a big pot of water to a boil and add the prepared fiddleheads slowly, so boiling doesn't stop. Blanch for 2 minutes (at the most), then dip the fiddleheads out, drain well, and proceed with instant eating. Or you can place them into ice water to cool, drain well again, pop into plastic bags, and freeze for winter enjoyment. Fiddleheads defrost quickly and need no further cooking. The trick is to keep them crunchy.

Fiddleheads fit nicely into this scrumptious springtime quiche.

Fiddlehead Quiche

MAKES 1 9-INCH QUICHE

THE CRUST

Into a big bowl, sift together:

1 cup unbleached white flour
1 cup whole-wheat pastry flour
1/4 teaspoon sea salt

Return any sifted-out salt or wheat germ to the bowl.

Cut in with a pastry cutter or two knives:

2/3 cup butter, softened to near room temperature

Add and toss with your hands as for a salad:

6–8 tablespoons ice water

Add more water if necessary till the dough clings together. Then knead it lightly perhaps five times. Shape the dough into a firm ball and refrigerate for at least 1 hour before rolling out.

When ready, roll out the dough on a lightly floured board to approximately 1/8 inch thick. (Whole-wheat flour demands thinness.) Fold the dough over your roller and place it loosely over an inverted 9-inch pie pan. Trim it to 1 inch larger than the pan. Turn the pan over, fold the dough over your roller again, and place it in the pan. Tuck the edges under, and flute. At this point you could put the pastry in a plastic bag and freeze it for future use.

When you're ready to continue, brush the entire piecrust with the slightly beaten white of an egg (to prevent sogginess). It's ready to fill.

THE FILLING

Preheat the oven to 400°F. Into your piecrust, place:

3/4 cup thinly sliced onion
1 cup freshly grated Cheddar cheese
1/2–3/4 cup leftover cooked fiddleheads

In a small bowl, mix together:

1 cup yogurt
4 large eggs, beaten
1 cup milk
1 teaspoon dried basil OR oregano
1 teaspoon sea salt (optional)
freshly ground black pepper

Pour over the fiddleheads in the crust. Sprinkle on top:

Hungarian paprika

BAKING

Place the quiche on the middle rack in the oven and bake at 400°F for 10 minutes. Reduce the heat to 350°F and bake for about 45 minutes, or until a knife inserted into the egg custard comes out clean.

SERVING

Let the quiche sit for a few minutes, then serve it hot (or cold) with a salad of leafy greens and grated carrots, rice or another grain, and fresh bread.

MORE FIDDLEHEAD USES: Once they're cooked and cooled, fiddleheads make wonderful additions tossed into green leafy salads. Marinate them in a mixture of extra-virgin olive oil and freshly squeezed lemon juice seasoned with a little sea salt. They're also good stuffed into tacos for lunch, or used in almost any recipe that calls for spinach, such as spanakopita.

Sunchokes

(JERUSALEM ARTICHOKES)

Another winter survivor, *in vivo* as it were, is the Jerusalem artichoke—perhaps more fittingly known as the sunchoke. Along with parsnips, horseradish, and the last of the root-cellared beets, potatoes, and carrots, every New Englander with a garden (or a good eye for old cellar holes) can welcome a once popular, now mostly forgotten, springtime treat: the tubers of the native American sunflower.

Knobby and brown on the outside but crisply ivory colored inside, the oddly named Jerusalem artichoke, with a botanical moniker of *Helianthus tuberosus*—a member of the Compositae (daisy) family—is neither from Jerusalem nor an artichoke.

According to the 18th-century linguist J. H. Trumbull, the Algonquian word for it was *kaishucpenauk,* a compound of words meaning "sun" and "tubers."

Unfortunately, the word languished in America. After traveling to Europe follow-ing the voyages of Columbus, this American beauty became *girasol,* which means "sunflower" in Spain, while Italians called it *girosole,* referring, apparently, to the plants' habit of turning with the sun, as well as to certain gems. Anglicized, *girosole* became *Jerusalem*—at least according to some.

Why the word *artichoke* arose isn't much clearer, although in *How to Grow Vegetables and Fruits by the Organic Method* J. I. Rodale announced that "the name is thought to be a corruption of the Italian name, *girasoli articocco,* meaning sun-flower artichoke." And Bradford Angier, in *Feasting on Wild Edibles,* states simply that *artichoke* "stems from the fact that even centuries ago the flower buds of some of the edible sunflowers were boiled and eaten with butter like that vegetable."

What *is* certain is that the French explorer Samuel de Champlain noted the tall, bright flowers being cultivated by Abenaki Indians on Cape Cod. "We saw an abundance of Brazilian beans, many edible squashes of various sizes, tobacco, and roots which they cultivate, which have the taste of artichokes," he wrote. The date was July 21, 1605.

A little later, at what is now Gloucester, Massachusetts, he found them again, calling them "some roots which were good, having the taste of cardoons"—rela-tives of the globe artichoke.

Lawyer Marc Lescarbot, who accompanied one of his clients to New France, car-ried the first Jerusalem artichoke tubers back to the Old World when he returned from Nova Scotia with Champlain in 1607. He described them as "a certain kind of root, as big as turnips or truffles, most excellent to eat, tasting like chards [or car-doons], but more pleasant, which when planted, multiplies as it were out of spite." In France they "increased so much that today all the gardens are full of them."

We can well believe it. Sunchokes tend to take over any plot of ground where they're introduced.

At any rate, it seems that Paris was agog during the spring and early summer of 1613, not only because of sunflowers, but by the arrival of six natives of Brazil, members of a tribe known as the Topinamboux. Queen Marie de Médicis received them, her son Louis XIII played godparent at their baptism, and savvy Parisian street vendors began calling the tubers Topinamboux.

While the French also called them *artichaut de Canada* (Canadian artichoke) and *poire de terre* (earth pear), the English stuck to *artichoke* and *Jerusalem.* The question, really, is why?

According to writer Harold McGee, Redcliffe N. Salaman proposed an entirely different derivation of the name in *The History and Social Influence of the Potato*. His theory originated with friend and botanist David Prain. "Prain thought it likely that the tuber would have been introduced to England as a commodity not from Italy, but from the Netherlands, which had been supplying vegetables to England for many years. A Dutch book of 1618—four years before the first documented appearance of 'Jerusalem artichoke' in English—records that on February 28, 1613, a gardener named Petrus Hondius planted at least one shriveled tuber, and . . . was astonished by the bumper crop he harvested on November 13."

GARDENING NOTES

SUNCHOKES

START-UP: Few suppliers offer sunchokes in their catalogs, even among sunflowers, their relatives. You'll probably find them listed with onion sets, potatoes, and the like. What you'll get is a package of thumb-sized tubers. Plant them 1 to 4 inches deep, 1 foot apart, in early spring. Then stand back and watch them grow.

CULTIVATION: It doesn't matter what soil you plant sunchokes in. Clay soils and sandy soils are both just fine. Choose a patch of garden where you'd like to see 6-foot-tall ornamentals with yellow daisylike flowers. They make a nice backdrop for any garden in midsummer.

Prepare the bed by digging out all the witchgrass and dandelions you can find. Like any other plant, sunchokes enjoy a dose of good compost, but without it they'll grow anyway. Sunchokes are notorious for spreading and can easily become a weed. Burying 4-inch-wide aluminum flashing around the entire bed, with only 1 inch showing aboveground, is a good way to control their spread, contain them where you want them, and keep witchgrass out.

PESTS: Don't worry about summer pests: Sunchokes are survivors. But field mice gnaw on tubers in fall and winter. Don't worry. Leave those gnawed tubers in the ground for next year's crop.

HARVESTING: Sunchokes, like parsnips, are a spring-thaw treat. You can harvest them only when the frost is out of the ground, and then you'd better harvest immediately or they'll start growing again. Dig them up using a garden fork, and pick out the biggest ones for your kitchen, leaving the small or damaged ones in the ground for summer growth.

Prain then suggested that the sunchoke became known as the "artichoke-apple of Ter Neusen," Terneuzen being the town in which Hondius lived. When the word *terneuzen* (pronounced "ter-noozen") traveled to England, it would have meant little to London street vendors, so they transformed it into *Jerusalem.*

Regardless of its moniker, the tubers of tasty *Helianthus* were mentioned in the first cookbook to be published in America by an American. Amelia Simmons called her tome *American Cookery, or the Art of Dressing Viands, Fish, Poultry, and Vegetables, and the Best Modes of Making Pastes, Puffs, Pies, Tarts, Puddings, Custards, & Preserves, and All Kinds of Cakes, from the imperial Plumb to plain Cake adapted to This Country & All Grades of Life.* It appeared in 1796. Finding a few pages to spare after the title, she suggested recipes for Jerusalem artichokes among "cramberry" sauce, johnnycake, and other local delicacies.

As Simmons doubtless knew, the tubers we now call sunchokes—a name apparently coined by a Los Angeles specialty produce company called Frieda's Finest—could be boiled, steamed, or sautéed like potatoes. Or peeled, sliced, and nibbled raw. "Choose those that are small, firm, and without pink discoloration," says Jane Brody, giving directions to 20th-century Americans in her *Good Food Book.* "Wrap them in plastic, and store them in the refrigerator, where they will keep for about a week."

According to Brody, sunchokes "contain a type of sugar, inulin, that can be safely consumed by diabetics. They are a source of calcium, iron, and magnesium."

Harold McGee, who thinks that sunchokes should more properly be called sunroots, adds, "There was a promising period early in the twentieth century when it looked as though the starchless, glucose-poor Jerusalem artichoke could be recommended to diabetics." Physicians, however, "found that their patients couldn't tolerate the gastrointestinal side effects."

England's John Goodyer put it bluntly. "The tuber had not been grown in England until John Franqueville, who had connections with the king's botanist in Paris, received some." In 1617 Franqueville gave two to Goodyer, who described them like this: "These roots are dressed diverse ways; some boil them in water, and after stew them with sack [white wine] and butter, adding a little ginger: others bake them in pies, putting marrow, dates, ginger, raisins of the sun, sack, etc. Others some other way, as they are led by their skill in cookery. But in my judgement, which soever way they be dressed and eaten they stir and cause a filthy loathsome stinking wind within the body, thereby causing the belly to be pained and tormented, and are a meat more fit for swine, than men."

Strong words. Few Mainers ever complained of such problems, perhaps because of the season of harvest. Planted in spring like parsnips, then allowed to winter in the garden, they're dug up the following spring before first foliage, having endured the frozen white world for six months. Overwintering, which causes the sunchoke to "predigest its own carbohydrates," according to McGee, may solve the problem.

A cupful of sunchokes contains, among other items, 3 grams of protein, 12 grams of carbohydrate, 30 International Units of vitamin A, 6 milligrams of vitamin C, 21 milligrams of calcium, and a huge amount of iron—3 milligrams per 100 grams.

Crisp and crunchy, they have a nutty taste and can be enjoyed raw or cooked, hot or cold. If you find yourself the lucky recipient of a pound or two of knobby tubers, short-term storage is necessary but easy: Wash them well, pop into plastic bags, and refrigerate. A soaking in ice water restores crispness to those that refuse to cooperate.

Sunchokes can substitute for water chestnuts in any stir-fry, whether used immediately or stored in lemon water as follows. But beware: Certain of their carbohydrates may cause flatulence. Limit your intake at first.

Sunchokes Stored in Lemon Water

MAKES 1 QUART

Dig or purchase:
   1 pound sunchokes
Scrub carefully; clay will cling to all nooks and crannies. Cut off knobs as necessary to facilitate cleaning. Peel only if necessary. Slice into thin disks to equal 4 cups.

Pop into a quart-sized, glass container and add:
   freshly squeezed juice of 1 lemon
(about 1/2 cup)
   enough cold water to cover all disks

These sunchokes will keep for a month if tightly covered and refrigerated, and come out tenderly tart and perfect for any stir-fry or salad addition. (Use leftover lemon water in soups or bread dough.)

Adapted from Jean Ann's NEW MAINE COOKING, this recipe is for a stir-fry that uses the first springtime asparagus spears, pea pods, or tightly curled fiddleheads, as well as sunchokes substituting for water chestnuts.

Stir-Fry Springtime Goodies

SERVES 3–4

From your jar of Sunchokes Stored in Lemon Water (at left), measure out:
   1/2 cup sunchokes
Drain.

Pour into a hot wok seated on its ring:
   2 tablespoons extra-virgin olive oil
   OR sunflower seed oil
Add and toss together:
   3 cups asparagus spears, OR slightly
      steamed fiddleheads, sliced into
      1/2-inch bits, OR pea pods
Add:
   1/2 cup sliced mushrooms
   1 tablespoon shoyu
      (naturally fermented soy sauce)
   1 tablespoon water
   1/4 teaspoon maple syrup
Cover and simmer till the vegetables are tender—a matter of 2 to 3 minutes.

Add:

**the sliced, lemony-flavored,
well-drained sunchokes**

Toss for about 1 minute.

Serve with mounds of short-grain brown rice and fresh, whole-grain bread. A leafy green salad topped with cooked, marinated navy beans and a yogurt dressing, sprinkled with toasted sesame seeds, would provide more than adequate protein as well as trace elements such as calcium, and vitamins for good nutrition.

─────────────────

Steamed sunchokes make an interesting salad. Because of their potential power, settle for a small amount when first you try them.

Sunchoke Salad
SERVES 4

Scrub well:

1 pound sunchokes

Slice into 1/4-inch disks. To prevent browning, immediately drop them into a bowl filled with:

2 cups cold water
**3 tablespoons freshly squeezed
lemon juice OR rice vinegar**

Place a rack in a saucepan over 1 to 2 inches of water. Bring the water to a boil. Place the lemon-treated chokes on the rack, cover, and steam for about 5 minutes, or till they're just fork-tender. Remove and let cool.

In a medium-sized bowl, combine:

the cooled sunchokes
1 cup thinly sliced celery
1 cup thinly sliced red onion
2 hard-boiled eggs, diced

In a small bowl, whisk together:

1/2 cup J. A.'s Favorite Salad Dressing

(see page 256)
**2 tablespoons diced Great Cucumber
Pickles (see page 152)**
1 teaspoon Dijon mustard

Pour over the sunchoke mixture and stir well. Add:

sea salt to taste
freshly ground black pepper

Cover and refrigerate about 4 hours. Stir again. Serve sprinkled with:

1 tablespoon freshly chopped parsley

─────────────────

Boiling may reduce situations of intestinal gas when dealing with sunchokes. Try storing them for a short time, as in the following receipe, adapted from Harold McGee's CURIOUS COOK.

J.A.'s Pickled Sunchokes

Scrub well and slice thinly to measure 4 cups:

1 pound sunchokes

As you work, place the slices into a little lemon juice to prevent browning.

In a porcelainized or stainless-steel saucepan, heat:

2 cups distilled white cider vinegar
2 cups water

Bring to a boil, then add the sunchoke slices. Return to a boil for 4 minutes. Add:

1/4 cup maple syrup
1 1/2 teaspoons sea salt
**1 tablespoon Pickling Spice Mix
(see page 151)**
1/4 teaspoon hot pepper sauce
6 garlic cloves, slightly crushed

Let the mixture boil for 1 minute longer.

Spoon the sliced chokes and garlic cloves into a quart jar; pour in boiling liquid to fill; cover, cool, and refrigerate.

Recipes for sunchokes aren't common. The well-known STOCKING UP preserving book, however, has one that's hot and spicy. In the following revision, maple syrup is a sweet substitution, because Ayurvedic medicine recommends that people should not cook with honey. Tubers, naturally, should be meticulously washed and peeled. These directions are for long-term storage.

Hot Spiced Jerusalem Artichokes

MAKES 4 PINTS

Scrub well, peel, and slice into 1/4-inch disks:

1–1 3/4 pounds sunchokes

Scald four 1-pint jars. Set them on a towel on your counter so they won't break. Be careful not to get burned.

In a small saucepan of hot water, heat four metal bands and lids to just under boiling. When they're hot, drop them into a sieve (use tongs) and drain.

Into each scalded pint jar, place:

1 dried red pepper
1 bay leaf
1 large garlic clove, peeled
5 peppercorns
1/4 teaspoon mustard seeds

In a small porcelainized or stainless-steel saucepan, bring to a slow boil:

3 cups distilled white cider vinegar
1 cup light-colored maple syrup
2 teaspoons powdered turmeric

Place sliced sunchoke tubers into each jar to within 1/2 inch of the top.

Fill with the hot maple syrup–vinegar liquid.

Wipe off the rims of your filled jars. Place hot lids and bands on the jars, screwing down tightly.

Place the hot, filled jars on a rack in a big pot of hot water. Add more hot water if necessary to come at least 1 inch above the jar tops. Cover the pot, bring to a boil, and process in this boiling-water bath for 10 minutes. Measure processing time from when a rolling boil begins.

When time is up, remove the jars with tongs and let them cool on a towel-covered counter to prevent breakage. When they're completely cool, remove the metal bands, check to see that each jar is safely sealed—the metal lid will feel slightly concave when you press it—rinse gently, wipe dry, and label.

Store in a cool, dark place.

CANNING HOW-TO: If you're new to canning, study the Ball Company's *Blue Book: Guide to Home Canning, Freezing, and Dehydration*, latest edition, available from Alltrista Corporation, Consumer Products Company, Dept. PK40, P.O. Box 2005, Muncie, IN 47307-0005. The *Blue Book* probably gives the best available canning advice. Many other books are cumbersome, involved, and sometimes unclear—but when you're canning, you must be absolutely clear about the method, because botulism is a real threat.

Asparagus

According to Benjamin Watson in *Taylor's Guide to Heirloom Vegetables*, *Asparagus officinalis Eurasia*—the hardy perennial that pokes its tender spikes above-ground to warm New England's hungry heart come spring—has been a star performer since ancient times. "In fact," he says, "one of the emperor Augustus's favorite sayings was *Citius quam asparagi coquentur*, 'Do it quicker than you can cook asparagus'—an expression that proves the Romans knew how to treat this noble vegetable."

Besides enjoying it fresh from the garden, Roman chefs valued asparagus so much that they dehydrated the finest stalks and kept them on hand to use as need-ed. But the plant actually lived close by. Originally native to seashores and river-banks of southern Europe, the Crimea, and Siberia, it was cultivated as early as 200 A.D.—much to the annoyance of Pliny, who remarked, "Nature ordained that asparagus should grow wild, so that everyone may go and pick it, and now we see cultivated asparagus!" According to him, the Ravenna area was famous for aspara-gus shoots, some of which weighed 1/3 pound. This would have been a Roman pound, of course, but it does seem to represent asparagus of a remarkable size.

Reay Tannahill, whose book *Food in History*, besides being full of information, is eminently readable, reports that "A modest man like Juvenal might content him-self with dining simply, on 'a plump kid, tenderest of the flock,' with 'more of milk in him than blood'; some wild asparagus; 'lordly eggs warm in their wisps of hay together with the hens that laid them'; and grapes, pears and apples to end with."

Marcus Gavius Apicius, that great Roman gastronome whose cookbook *Of Culinary Matters*, dating from A.D. 14, is the world's first known book of recipes, instructs the cook to combine pounded asparagus tips with pepper, lovage, fresh coriander, savory, onion, wine, oil, eggs, and a fish-flavored sauce. After baking, he says, it should be sprinkled with more pepper. The dish, called a *patinae*, was served as a gratin to accompany little birds called *beccafici*.

So much for the delicate flavor of unalloyed asparagus!

But by A.D. 16 the Romans were absolutely doting on it. They considered a dinner unimportant unless asparagus was featured as an appetizer.

Historian Maguelonne Toussaint-Samat says asparagus lovers date back even farther. The Greeks, she says, discovered that wild *Asparagus officinalis* was delicious, while Egyptians seem to have offered bundles of it to their gods. She adds, "The Arabs seem to have introduced it into Spain, whence it spread to France." But whether or not people gathered it wild, "it is not

ASPARAGUS

SEEDS AND CROWNS: The best varieties now come from Rutgers University in New Jersey, the most productive of which are male only. It's usual to buy crowns (rosettes of roots with baby shoots), though you can also grow asparagus from seeds.

CULTIVATION: Choose your garden's very best soil. An asparagus bed could be your pride and joy till you're old and toothless.

If possible, start preparing the bed the fall before you plant. Dig out all witchgrass, dandelions, and other perennial weeds. Dig deep, or double-dig. Then add as much of the best compost or well-rotted manure as you can find. In spring dig trenches 1 foot wide, 18 inches deep, and 2 feet apart. (Pile the soil into the 2-foot-wide spaces between the trenches for the time being.) Place 9 inches of good compost in mounds 18-24 inches apart in the trenches. Those mounds are where you'll place the baby asparagus crowns. Separate the crowns carefully, spreading the roots over the mounds of compost. Cover with 2 inches of soil. As new, very slender shoots emerge, pile on more soil till the whole bed is level.

If you purchase seeds, start them indoors 12 to 14 weeks before your local last frost date. Then transplant into trenches as above.

PESTS AND DISEASES: The major pests for asparagus are weeds. Go through the bed a couple of times each summer, pulling out the lush undergrowth that likes rich soil as much as asparagus does. Mulch the bed heavily with hay in early summer. If you've inherited an asparagus bed, you may find that asparagus itself is its own worst enemy: Thin any plants that are crowding each other out between rows to the spacing suggested above.

Asparagus sometimes succumbs to fusarium wilt and rust diseases. If the soil is rich enough, however, such problems are unlikely.

HARVESTING: Don't harvest from your new bed in its first or second year. Only pick when the spears are as fat as or fatter than your middle finger. Leave the rest to keep growing into the beautiful, delicate, fernlike fronds that will characterize the bed all summer. If you planted seeds rather than root crowns, expect harvesting to be delayed an extra couple of years.

You may not have any spears to store. Sometimes asparagus from Simply Grande Gardens never makes it to the kitchen.

mentioned again until around 1300, when it began to be grown around Paris (always a centre for gourmets, of course), in Argenteuil, which was to become famous for it, in Bezons and in Epinay."

A long time later—by 1654—*asperge blanche,* or white asparagus, was widely cultivated in France. By 1660 it had even become popular—along with artichokes, primeurs, spinach, truffles, and mushrooms—on the tables of rich Englishmen, who didn't usually favor vegetables. Samuel Pepys noted in 1667 that he bought "sparrowgrass in Fenchurch Street, 100 spears for 1 shilling sixpence," says James Trager in *The Food Chronology.* Tradesmen continued for centuries to call asparagus "grass."

From Europe the "grass" finally reached America as early colonists brought crowns to be planted out, and it has remained—as it's called in Quebec—the "aristocrat of vegetables."

Denied formal education, early New England women naturally left few written records. In fact, no female diary exists until 1750, when Mary Holyoke, a physician's wife, began jotting down her garden's progress. She "Sowed sweet marjoram . . . pease . . . colliflower . . . six weeks beans. . . . Pulled firest radishes. . . . Set out turnips. . . ." and "Cut 36 asparagus, first cutting here."

Says David Tucker in *Kitchen Gardening in America,* "The memoirs of an Albany girl reported that her gardens were small, perhaps one-fourth of an acre." Instead of planting Indian corn, cabbages, potatoes, or roots, she enjoyed beds of flowers, kidney beans, celery, salad greens, sweet herbs, cucumbers—and asparagus.

Reay Tannahill has a fine summation of edible vegetable immigrants—as well as asparagus. "As new settlers . . . arrived in America from various Euopean countries, they . . . introduced their own traditional dishes, judiciously adapted when necessary to suit the materials available. The English brought apple pie. The French introduced chowder (from *chaudiere,* the fish kettle in which the dish was cooked). The Dutch took cookies *(Koekjes),* coleslaw *(kool:* cabbage, and *sla:* salad) and waffles. In the end, the American cuisine became a mirror of history, the names of dishes reflecting a medley of peoples, religions, wars, geographical locations, even occupations." Among others were Shaker loaf, Boston baked beans, Philadelphia pepper pot, Moravian sugar cake, Swedish meatballs, haymaker's switchel, whaler's toddy—and ambushed asparagus!

As well as being tasty, asparagus is good for you, containing 4.1 grams of protein, 4.94 grams of carbohydrates, 44 milligrams of vitamin C, 2.59 International Units of vitamin E, 28 milligrams of calcium, 404 milligrams of potassium, 160 micrograms of folic acid, and a whopping 1,201 International Units of vitamin A—all in a single cupful. It's also a super source of glutathione, an antioxidant with strong anticancer activity.

Perhaps the best way to enjoy this spring-time treat is to munch a short, succulent spear plucked fresh from the garden while listening to birdsong. Sliced into a green leafy salad with a light, lemon-flavored vinaigrette, asparagus is superb. And cooked quickly, it's fine for additional uses. As follows:

Simply Cooked Asparagus

Bend each spear while holding its ends; it will snap at approximately the point where tenderness begins. Remove and discard the woody end.

Using plain kitchen twine, tie the spears into serving-sized bundles.

Bring a large kettle of salted water to a rolling boil. Drop in the asparagus bundles. (You can also use a cooker made especially for asparagus, which is tall enough that the spears stand upright, allowing the thicker ends to cook first.) Return to a boil and blanch till barely tender—never mushy— perhaps 3 to 5 minutes. Test by biting into a spear.

Once tender, plunge the asparagus into ice water using tongs. When cool— a matter of moments—drain it and pat dry. Your asparagus is now ready for anything.

It takes a good vinaigrette to accompany asparagus spears cooked as above and chilled. This sample, and the next, are neither too acidic nor too bland.

Vinaigrette for Asparagus 1

MAKES 1 CUP

In a blender, whiz together:
1 teaspoon Dijon mustard
1/4 cup red wine vinegar
1 teaspoon refined white sugar
OR maple syrup to taste
1/2 teaspoon sea salt
1/2 teaspoon freshly ground black pepper

While whizzing, pour in until thick:
1/2 cup extra-virgin olive oil

Pour this mixture into a small bowl and add:
1 tablespoon finely minced fresh parsley AND/OR chives (optional)

Vinaigrette for Asparagus 2

In a blender, whiz:
1/2 cup extra-virgin olive oil
3 tablespoons freshly squeezed lemon juice
1/2 teaspoon Dijon mustard
1/2 garlic clove, minced
3/4 teaspoon sea salt
freshly ground black pepper

When the mixture is thick, remove it from the blender and chill.

Serve by dribbling carefully over chilled asparagus. Sprinkle with:

1 hard-cooked egg, minced

1/4 cup finely chopped fresh parsley

Soup, either hot or cold, is a superb way to enjoy full asparagus flavor.

Cream of Asparagus Soup

SERVES 4

Chop to measure 2 cups:

2 large onions

In a large pot, heat:

1/4 cup extra-virgin olive oil

Add the onions and sauté till soft and golden, stirring often. Add and bring to a boil:

1 quart Vegetable Stock
(see the sidebar)

Pick or purchase:

1 1/2 pounds asparagus

Bend each spear while holding both ends; it will snap at approximately the point where tenderness begins. Remove and discard the woody stem ends. Slice off the tips, chop small, and reserve for later. Chop the spears into 1/2-inch bits. You should have 4 cups.

Drop the asparagus into the boiling vegetable-flavored stock. Cover, reduce the heat, and simmer for 10 to 15 minutes or until the onion and asparagus bits are very soft. Pour the soup into a blender and whiz to produce a purée. (Place a towel over the blender cap; be careful not to get burned.)

Pour the purée back into your pot. Season with:

sea salt (optional)

Vegetable Stock

Stock can be made from nearly any vegetable except those of the cabbage family. Two cups of water and 2–4 tablespoons of Bragg's Liquid Aminos (see page 63) also makes a quick, usable stock. If you'd like to make your own, here's a sample recipe:

Into a large, heavy pot, pour:

1/4 cup extra-virgin olive oil

Add and sauté for 5 minutes:

4 big onions, chopped

Add and heat to boiling:

3 garlic cloves, skins and all

4 celery stalks, including leaves, chopped

4 carrots, carefully scrubbed and chopped

2 whole leeks, chopped

1 big bunch parsley, coarsely chopped, stems and all

1 teaspoon fresh thyme

1 fresh sage leaf, chopped

1 bay leaf

1 1/2 teaspoons sea salt

10 peppercorns

10 allspice berries (optional)

a little freshly grated nutmeg (optional)

4 quarts water

1 tablespoon cider, rice wine, or red wine vinegar

Simmer for 2 to 3 hours, until the liquid is reduced to 2 1/2 quarts. Strain and store in the refrigerator.

freshly ground white pepper

If the soup has cooled, warm it a bit but do not boil.

Scatter on top:
the asparagus tips
chopped cilantro OR parsley
Add:
1/2 cup cream OR buttermilk (optional)

Serve immediately. A crisp leafy salad and freshly baked rolls make this a scrumptious lunch.

Asparagus tips and bits are always fine additions to omelets, quiches, or soufflés.

Asparagus Soufflé

SERVES 3 AS A MAIN DISH

Preheat the oven to 425°F.

Prepare about 1 pound of asparagus by bending each spear while holding both ends; it will snap at approximately the point where tenderness begins. Remove and discard the woody stem ends. Cut the remaining spears into 1-inch bits to measure 2 cups.

Bring a large kettle of salted water to a rolling boil; drop in the asparagus and cook till barely tender—a matter of moments. Cool, drain, and purée in a blender. (Be careful not to get burned.)

In a heavy saucepan, heat:
1/4 cup extra-virgin olive oil
Add and sauté over medium heat until translucent:
1/2 cup finely chopped onion
Sprinkle with:
3 tablespoons unbleached white flour
Cook gently over low heat for 5 minutes, stirring constantly.

In a small second saucepan, bring to a scald:
1 cup milk
Pour the hot milk into the onion mix, whisking vigorously as it bubbles. Set over medium heat and bring to a boil, stirring constantly, for about 3 minutes.

Separate 5 eggs into two small bowls and set aside.

Remove the hot milk from the heat and gently whisk in, one at a time:
4 egg yolks

NOTE: You can save the leftover yolk to coat pie crusts before filling to prevent sogginess. See Great Pastry for Great Pies, note 2, on page 67.

Then stir in:
the asparagus purée
1/3 cup freshly grated Parmesan cheese
a little sea salt
some freshly ground black pepper
some freshly grated nutmeg

In the bowl of an electric mixer, beat until foamy:
5 egg whites
Beat until stiff by adding:
a pinch of cream of tartar
OR a few drops freshly squeezed lemon juice

Stir a third of the egg whites into the asparagus–egg yolk mixture. Then fold in the remaining egg whites.

Butter a 1-quart soufflé dish. Sprinkle with:
1/3 cup freshly and finely grated Parmesan cheese
Shake out any excess cheese and save. Pour the asparagus mixture into the dish, gently rapping it once to remove air bubbles. Sprinkle the top with any excess Parmesan.

Set in the center of your 425°F oven, immediately reduce the heat to 375°, and bake for 20 minutes. The soufflé should rise 2 inches above the rim of the dish.

Let it bake another 10 or 15 minutes, till it's brown on top.

Serve immediately with a leafy green salad, fresh rolls, and other in-season vegetables.

Horseradish

Also surviving in the New England spring garden, having experienced snow and sleet and freezing temperatures since November, are the remarkable long roots of horseradish, *Radicula armoracia*, also called *Cochlearia armoracia*, but more commonly *Armoracia rusticana*.

As noted by J. I. Rodale in his 1967 book, *How to Grow Vegetables and Fruits by the Organic Method*, horseradish is perfectly hardy, a member of the mustard family, and "well adapted for growing in the north temperate regions of the United States." Like the sunchoke, it's best grown in some out-of-the-way garden spot where it can't take over.

Originating in Europe, from the Caspian Sea area through Russia and Poland to Finland, horseradish leaves and roots were appreciated by Germans during the Middle Ages, but not till much later by other Europeans, no doubt when they discovered the plant's medicinal value.

Jean Carper, author of *The Food Pharmacy*, suggests that horseradish (along with other hot foods, such as mustard and chili peppers) is beneficial when dealing with respiratory problems. The Russians, she says, "use horseradish to cure colds." Its main active chemical—allyl isothiocyanate, or mustard oil—irritates the endings of olfactory nerves, causing tears and salivation as well as affecting the viscosity and consequent movement of mucus in the lungs, helping them clear.

Carper quotes one recipe for a sore throat remedy from Dr. Irwin Ziment, an authority on pulmonary drugs and professor of medicine at the University of California School of Medicine at Los Angeles. His advice: Grind up a tablespoon of horseradish, add a glass of warm water and a teaspoon of honey, and drink it!

April 14 was the date when the Simply Grande gardeners dug a pailful of horseradish roots in 1996. Because of a late, chilly spring, the first digging in 1997 was mid-May. It always varies. The best time is after a summer's growth in September, and all winter long if the ground hasn't frozen prohibitively.

Among other things, a cupful of prepared horseradish contains 6 calories, 9 milligrams of calcium, 5 milligrams of magnesium, and 44 milligrams of potassium. To prevent its volatile oils from burning eyes and blistering skin, you can scrub and scrape it under running water.

Basic Pickled Horseradish

Dig or purchase:

1 pound horseradish root

Wash it well, then peel and dice it.

Place it in a food processor and process until finely chopped. Add and process till the mixture is spreadable:

apple cider OR white vinegar (about 1 1/2 cups)

Then add:

1 teaspoon sea salt
2 tablespoons refined white sugar, or to taste

Store refrigerated in a capped jar.

NOTE: If a food processor isn't available, a blender will do. Chop the washed and peeled root into small bits. Whiz with just enough vinegar to process; then continue blending until fine.

___

Horseradish and cream seem to be long-standing partners, as recipes in Fannie Farmer's 1896 cookbook attest. A revised edition called the BOSTON COOKING-SCHOOL COOK BOOK appeared in 1923, and inspires the following recipe for a fine, highly caloric, spicy sauce for serving with anything that needs a springtime pickup.

Creamy Horseradish Sauce

Beat until it begins to stiffen:

1/2 cup heavy cream

While continuing to beat, gradually add:

3 tablespoons vinegar

When the mixture is stiff, add:

1/4 teaspoon sea salt
a little freshly grated white OR black pepper
2–3 tablespoons freshly grated horseradish

Let rest for 15 minutes before serving.

NOTE: To decrease calories, cottage cheese can be beaten till thick, then substituted for cream. Thick yogurt is also acceptable, but don't beat it.

___

Horseradish becomes available just at the moment when old-fashioned root cellars provide big, succulent 'Lutz' beets—even in spring. Be aware that the following recipe doesn't stint on fat or cholesterol.

Beets with Creamy Dill and Horseradish

SERVES 4

Wash well and place in a saucepan:

1 1/2 pounds beets

Cover with cold water. Heat slowly to boiling, then reduce the heat and simmer, uncovered, till barely tender—35 to 45 minutes, depending on beet size.

Drain. Remove the beet skins by rubbing them under cold water. Chop into moderate-sized chunks. You should have about 3 cups.

In a large porcelainized pot over medium heat, warm:

2 tablespoons extra-virgin olive oil

Stir in:

the chopped beets
1/2 cup whipping cream
OR whipped cottage cheese

2 tablespoons Basic Pickled
    Horseradish (see page 46)
    OR commercially prepared
    horseradish
3 tablespoons chopped fresh dill

Reduce the heat and simmer for about 4
minutes. Then add:

sea salt to taste
freshly ground black pepper to taste

Serve immediately with baked potatoes
and a "winter salad" of blanched broccoli and cauliflower florets (frozen are
fine), grated carrots, and alfalfa sprouts
tossed in a light vinaigrette.

*Another horseradish-beet combination
is a relish.*

Beet Relish

Coarsely grate:

**1 pound cooked, peeled, well-cooled
    beets (as described in the previous
    recipe)**

Add:

**1/4 cup (or more) finely grated
    horseradish**

In a capped jar, shake until well mixed:

GARDENING NOTES

HORSERADISH

ROOTS, NOT SEEDS: *The plants do not make viable seeds. You'll need to buy
root cuttings.*

CULTIVATION: *Horseradish will probably grow in any soil you give it. Choose
an area away from other beds. Horseradish loves clay, but if you want the
biggest, fattest roots, dig about 1 foot deep and work in compost or manure.*

PESTS: *Horseradish itself is a pest. The roots grow deep, to a depth of about 14
inches, like long carrots. Unlike carrots, however, they play a trick. Turning a
right angle at the bottom, they propagate sideways to come up elsewhere in
your garden. Once you've got them, you can't control them. That's why you
need to be careful where you plant.*

HARVESTING: *Harvest anytime after hard frost in fall, or in springtime before
regrowth. Using your strongest fork, deep dig, take the fattest roots, and leave
the rest for next year. You'll inevitably break off some roots in the ground. The
broken ends will sprout.*

*Store trimmed, washed roots in plastic bags or boxes in a root cellar. The
ideal temperature is 30° to 32°F.*

1/2 teaspoon Dijon mustard
1 tablespoon refined white sugar
1/2 teaspoon sea salt (optional)
freshly ground black pepper
3 tablespoons red wine vinegar

Pour this over the beet-horseradish mix and stir well. Fold in:

1 cup thick yogurt OR sour cream

Serves to perk up any bland grain or bean dish.

From Nancy Loomis, one of Simply Grande's favorite shareholders, comes this recipe for a delicious horseradish spread.

Nancy's Horseradish Spread

Chop fine (but not mushy):
2 large Red Delicious apples

Chop into tiny pieces:
1/4 cup almonds OR walnuts

Add to taste:
refined white sugar
sweet red wine
freshly squeezed lemon juice
powdered cinnamon
The result should not be watery.

Wash, peel, and slice thinly:
a bit of horseradish root

Serve by spreading a goodly amount of the apple-nut combination on matzo or crackers and topping with a thin slice of horseradish.

Horseradish adds a surprising tang to baked beans. Use any amount you fancy in this recipe, but remember to balance the sweet with the tangy.

J. A.'s Red Kidney Beans Baked with Horseradish and Maple Syrup

1 CUP DRY BEANS YIELDS 2–2 1/2 CUPS COOKED BEANS

FRIDAY NIGHT

By pouring them from hand to hand and discarding any moldy or discolored samples, stones, and dirt lumps, clean carefully:

2–3 cups red kidney (or other dried) beans

Wash them thoroughly and drain in a colander or strainer. Pour into a large bowl and cover with three times as much water so that, as the beans swell, they won't soak it all up. Soak overnight. (Soaking shortens cooking time and aids digestibility.)

SATURDAY MORNING

Into a big pot, place:
the swollen beans
enough fresh water to barely cover

Bring to a boil. Immediately lower the heat and simmer until you can blow on the skins and see them peeling. Drain the beans.

Into a large ceramic bean pot—the kind with a narrow neck and wide shoulders that slant in at the bottom (and which hopefully is well seasoned)—place, in order:

the presoaked, simmered beans
1 medium-sized onion, sliced thinly
2 medium-sized, tart winter apples,
cored and sliced
a lot of freshly ground black pepper
1 heaping teaspoon dry mustard
1 heaping teaspoon powdered ginger
1/2 cup maple syrup
2 tablespoons extra-virgin olive oil
(optional)
enough hot water to barely cover

Bake, covered, in a 300°F oven all day, adding hot water as necessary.

THE FINISHING TOUCH

Half an hour before serving, carefully stir in:

1/2 cup freshly grated horseradish

Return to the oven to heat thoroughly, if necessary.

NOTE 1: When baking beans, do not add salt: It toughens them by attracting away water. In fact, salt, fat, and molasses all prolong cooking time. Fat coats the legumes' exteriors and prevents moisture from passing readily inside it. Acid in molasses toughens the outside covering. Add sea salt only when beans are cooked and tender.

NOTE 2: On stormy days, or days when a storm is brewing, beans will "cook away"—dry up—much faster than on clear days. Watch 'em. The secret to really good baked beans is a long, slow simmering in just enough liquid to cover, not drown.

Chives and Garlic Chives

When spring "comes in like a lamb," bestowing warmth and sunshine, the last week of April at the Simply Grande Gardens sees chive clumps growing tall and thick.

When the weather is uncooperative and cold, however, May is the month for chives. Continually trimmed like a crew cut before or after blossoming, this mild member of the Liliaceae (lily) family will produce fresh green spears all summer and continue well past the first frosts.

Sometimes called by wags an "ally" of the onion, *Allium cepa*, chives have been properly latinized to *A. schoenoprasum*. They're mentioned in Chinese literature as early as 3000 B.C.; and J. I. Rodale in his 1967 book, *How to Grow Vegetables and Fruits by the Organic Method*, says they were "also used in other parts of Asia, and in Europe." He adds that "the plants are pictured, but they were not described there as a variety of perennial onion separate from other types until after the eighteenth century."

As regards cooking onions, Harold McGee suggests in *On Food and Cooking* that despite an "impressive chemical arsenal," which every weeping cook knows intimately, "the onion family is quickly subdued by cooking. Not only are its odor compounds driven off by high temperatues, but some of them appear to be converted into another complex molecule that is 50 to 70 times sweeter than a molecule of table sugar."

Mild chives, which contain 192 International Units of vitamin A in 1 tablespoon, along with 2 milligrams of calcium, 1 milligram of magnesium, and 8 milligrams of potassium, are perfect for chopping finely and scattering over salads, mincing into vinaigrettes, adding to omelets, soups, and stews, or using in any recipe that requests an oniony taste.

There's an added fillip: Their edible, lavender-colored blossoms look beautiful when topping green salads and adding a bit of oniony flavor.

For tips on growing chives and garlic chives, see page 127.

Garlic chives *(A. schoenoprasum* var. *tuberosum, A. tuberosum,* or *A. odoratum),* otherwise known as Chinese chives (gow choi), are closely related to our common chives. But there the similarities end. Where familiar chives have hollow, thin stems, garlic chives grow broad, flat leaves. And their flowers, unlike the rounded lavender balls of common chives, usually come in white, flat-headed, star-shaped sprays. *A. odoratum,* reports Geri Harrington in *Grow Your Own Chinese Vegetables,* has the scent of an old-fashioned rose. Lavender-flowered varieties are faintly garlic scented.

Garlic chives can be used exactly like common chives but taste, obviously, like garlic instead of onion. They can be substituted for common chives in any recipe, minced into salads, added to cottage cheese or yogurt, or sprinkled as a garnish over stuffed eggs.

When you're cooking with them, add during the last few minutes. They have a tendency to lose their flavor and get stringy if overcooked.

Unlike common chives, garlic chives produce bulbs, which are useful like garlic or shallots in stir-fries, or minced and scrambled with eggs. They can also be crushed, added to boiling apple or rice vinegar, and set aside for a few days to mellow.

Mild buds and blossoms are enjoyable dried, or eaten fresh as a garnish. They're delightful when added to Vichyssoise (see page 286) at the last moment.

Sorrel

Near the end of April and May's beginning, sorrel (also called sour grass) peeks through New England mud to offer tender rabbit ears of green for the picking.

Members of the buckwheat family (Polygonaceae), the sorrels, *Rumex acetosa* (sour dock) and *R. scutatus* (garden sorrel), were originally native to Eurasia. Long considered poisonous because of astringent flavor, the plants' seeds were always popular with birds and, according to Bert Greene in *Greene on Greens*, "some food snoops claim that this hardy perennial spread to Europe and the New World on the wing."

Elizabethan England loved it. So did France. Pierre François de la Varenne, who codified the evolving Franco-Italian cuisine and whose 1655 cookbook, *Le Pastissier François*, is now considered rare and valuable, recommended sauces based on meat drippings combined with vinegar, lemon juice, verjuice—the juice of sour grapes—or sometimes of sorrel.

For tips on growing sorrel, see page 231.

Yellow dock, *R. crispus*, a first cousin gone wild and considered a weed in America, is rich in protein and vitamin A, and enjoyed by foragers. The French perennial variety grown in the Simply Grande Gardens provides long, thin, lemony-tasting leaves, which add tang to salads when minced. It can also be cooked just like spinach.

And like spinach, sorrel is a superb treat. But in moderation. Swiss chard, beet greens, rhubarb, spinach, and sorrel all contain oxalic acid, which binds with calcium and iron, making those nutrients unavailable for absorption through the digestive tract (see page 90). The addition of milk, however (as Greeks and Italians seem always to have understood), reputedly offsets the binding.

Sorrel makes a fine soup to perk up winter's leftover potatoes. Since bunching onions are also surging with springtime eagerness, the combination here seems natural.

Sorrel and Bunching Onion Soup

SERVES 4–6

Wash nicely:
1 pound tender new sorrel leaves

This should equal about 12 cups of solidly packed leaves. Fold the leaves gently into little wads and slice them into thin shreds to equal 9 cups.

Thinly peel:
about 1 1/2 pounds potatoes
Cut into smallish chunks to equal 4 cups. Pour the potatoes into a 4-quart porcelainized or stainless-steel pot and add:
4 cups Vegetable Stock (see page 43)
the sliced sorrel
Cook about 20 minutes, or until the potatoes are tender.

In a 2-quart porcelainized pot, heat:

2 tablespoons extra-virgin olive oil

Sauté in it until just limp:

**1 cup sliced bunching onions,
including green tops**

Place the wilted onions in a blender, add the potato-sorrel-onion mix, and purée. (Be careful not to get burned.) Return the purée to the 2-quart pot and add:

freshly ground black pepper

Then add:

**1 cup heavy cream OR (to lower fat
content) 1 cup low-fat milk
into which you have whisked 1
heaping tablespoon cornstarch**

Reheat this thick soup—bringing it to a quick boil and stirring constantly, just until the cornstarch (if you're using it) has cooked—for only a minute. Sprinkle with:

freshly grated nutmeg

Serve hot or chilled with a dollop of yogurt or sour cream on each bowlful.

A simple version of sorrel soup without potatoes is quick and easy. Because it's rich in heavy cream, fat and cholesterol contents are high, but the oxalic component is tastily taken care of. Do note: Sorrel turns brown with cooking. Not to worry.

Simple Sorrel Soup

MAKES 5–6 CUPS; SERVES 2–3

Rinse thoroughly, then strip tender leaves from the thickest midribs, roll into wads, and chop to equal:

3 cups sorrel leaves

In a porcelainized or stainless-steel pan, heat:

2 tablespoons extra-virgin olive oil

Add the leaves and sauté till wilted.

This will result in a surprisingly small amount of wilted leaves. Add:

4 cups Vegetable Stock (see page 43)

Simmer for a minute or two.

In a small bowl, beat slightly:

3 egg yolks

Remove the hot stock-sorrel mix from heat and add:

**1/2 cup heavy cream
the slightly beaten egg yolks**

Heat again until the soup thickens slightly. Do not boil.

Garnish with finely chopped chives and serve hot with salad and fresh rolls. Sorrel soup is also good cold.

Sorrel continues to grow all summer and, if seed stalks are kept strictly cut, will produce still-tender leaves well into fall. Combined with Swiss chard, which appears in midsummer in the Simply Grande Gardens, it perks up the common custard.

Individual Sorrel and Chard Custards

MAKES 4 1/2-CUP MOLDS

Preheat the oven to 350°F.

Purchase or pick:

**1/2 pound Swiss chard leaves
2 large, tender sorrel leaves**

Slice off the stems and any thick ribs of the chard leaves, then slice off the stems of the sorrel. Roll all the leaves together into a big "sausage" and cut into 1/4-inch slices.

Set a wok on a ring, heat it, and add:

2 tablespoons extra-virgin olive oil

Add the chard and sorrel leaves and toss gently. Sorrel will turn brownish olive:

not to worry. Cover and simmer for about 2 minutes or until wilted. Uncover, increase the heat, push the greens up the side of the wok, and quickly evaporate any moisture, if necessary. Do not allow the greens to stick. Set aside to cool.

In a medium-sized bowl, whisk together:

> **3 large eggs**
> **1/2 cup yogurt**
> **1/2 cup milk**
> **1/2 teaspoon sea salt**
> **some freshly ground black**
> **OR white pepper**
> **some freshly grated nutmeg**

Butter four 1/2-cup molds. Place some of the sliced leaf combination into each one. Pour over this some of the egg mixture, and stir gently with a fork to mix.

Set the molds in a cake pan and add boiling water to come halfway up their sides. Bake in your preheated 350°F oven about 25 minutes, or till a knife inserted in the center comes out clean. Remove the molds from the water bath and let them rest a few minutes.

Run a knife around the inside of each mold and invert the custard onto a serving platter or individual plate. Serve with rice or mashed potatoes, salad, and other vegetables.

NOTE 1: Sorrel is available all summer long. Beetles love it, but don't be disturbed by evidence of their nibbles: Lacy leaves are healthfully free of pesticides.

NOTE 2: Lovage, which appears at the same time as sorrel but tastes like celery, can be substituted in the first two recipes, but reduce the amount to 1 cup of chopped leaves in the first recipe.

NOTE 3: A fresh egg has a high-standing, round yolk and a thick, translucent white. Settle for nothing less.

Dandelions

With May, the wild things appear. Maple trees put on fragile red flowers; trout lilies bloom along brook banks, as does bloodroot. Chickadees sing love songs; myrtle warblers and orioles flit from branch to branch.

At Simply Grande, while the plum trees begin to bloom and daffodils dance in every corner, peas, fava beans, and onions get planted. Bunching onions, which remain in the garden all winter long, are fat; lovage and sorrel soar; fiddleheads stand high and unfurled; and the dandelions turn golden. This will, of course, enrage certain individuals. In fact, life is hard for *Taraxacum officinale*, victim of every mowing machine and herbicide lover of a weed-free lawn. Cousin to the sunflower, marigold, and zinnia, the dandelion is a member of the Compositae (daisy) tribe. But is it a pest?

Though thousands of dollars are spent yearly all over America in attempts to obliterate it, it was once highly respected. The Cherokee have a legend:

> Every spring Shawondassee the South Wind journeyed north to warm the land. Tardy when leaving his winter cave one year, he had to travel quickly, chanced upon a meadow of lovely gentian maids, and, unable to resist, tarried for a spell to woo them. When he finally departed, he hurried faster than before.
>
> Soon he passed a field of golden dandelion maidens and was tempted to stop again. But he was late. He would return.
>
> A great distance was covered, a long time passed; and while he was away the sun discovered the beautiful dandelion maidens, casting ardent rays upon them. The maidens aged quickly from the heat; their golden hair turned snowy white. When Shawondassee finally returned to woo them, all he found were white locks scattered far and wide.

T. officinale is nearly ubiquitous, with something like 3 species in this country and 25 in the civilized world. The botanical name is derived from two Greek words, *taraxos* (disorder) and *akos* (remedy). *Officinale* indicates that the plant has been considered a medical remedy for a long time.

The Greeks used the dandelion to treat liver complaints; it was recorded by Arabian physicians in the 10th century; and in England there survives from Tudor times a recipe book containing a list of medicinal, cordial, and toilet waters for a nobleman's family. "Water of Tantelyon" is among them.

New Englanders have always revered the dandelion. Come spring Grandmother would serve up a "mess" to disperse the ills of winter. Whole families could be found digging greens while listening to birdsong. Rich in iron, copper, and vitamins C and A, the "weed" saved many a colonist from scurvy. It can still serve any family today.

DIGGING A "MESS OF GREENS"

When dandelion leaves are fresh and green, the plant barely budded but not blooming, choose large, single or double samples. (Groups of many small, entwined plants take an age to untangle.) Be sure they grow in unpolluted neighborhoods where there is no danger of pesticides or manure.

Shove a knife, or a special two-tined dandelion digger, under the plant to sever its tough, long root, placing the cut just under the whorl of leaves but not so high as to slice them off.

Then, right there in the out-of-doors, begin cleaning. Using a short-handled paring knife, scrape off any brown, leaflike material at the leaf base on the outside. Trim the root close to where leaves begin but not so close as to make the plant fall apart. Then shake out any dirt, insects, or worms hiding therein. And don't be squeamish about worms. They aerate the soil by digging little burrows, and a worm never pesticided or polluted anything!

Place your greens into a big basket or bag as you clean. Finish cleaning by dousing them several times in a lot of water until it runs clear. This may take as many as six rinsings, depending on the muddiness or grittiness of the soil.

You're ready for cooking.

The old-fashioned, high-fat way to cook dandelion greens was to place them into a kettle with boiling water and a piece of salt pork. Served with vinegar, salt, and pepper, they were scrumptious but often overcooked and full of animal fat.

A healthier way is possible.

Dandelion Greens

Place into a large kettle with wash water still clinging:

your greens

Add if necessary:

about 1 inch of water

Bring to a boil, then lower the heat and steam for anywhere from 15 to 30 minutes, depending on the age of your greens: Young means tender. Turn with a long-handled fork once or twice to prevent burning.

When the greens are tooth-tender, drain well in a colander, place them on a platter, and cut them into several "blocks" using a sharp knife. Sprinkle with:

extra-virgin olive oil
sea salt
freshly ground black pepper

Pass to each diner:

shoyu (naturally fermented soy sauce)
apple cider, balsamic vinegar,
  OR freshly squeezed lemon juice

While a lot of earth-disconnected people complain, others admire the dandelion, Grandmother's age-old medicinal cure. One of the most valuable of plants, it needs no gardening attention and will waft its puffy, silken heads into the breeze to populate waste ground once blossoming has matured. Taraxacum provides not only healthful eating from leaves but also "coffee" from dried roots, and its yellow petals make a delicious wine.

If you're a cook whose stir-fries, soups, and sauces need a touch of springtime all year long, or if you're in need of a very sweet, clear dessert libation from time to time, here's a wine to satisfy.

Simply Grande Dandelion Wine

MAKES 1 GALLON

GATHERING

On a sunny morning, right after the dew has dried, fill a big basket with fully open, bright yellow dandelion blossoms. Spread them on a sheet of white paper to reveal any insects. Taking care to discard every bit of bitter stem and green leaf (which would spoil fermentation as well as taste), hold each blossom by the stem in one hand and pull out the petals by digging into the middle with your other thumbnail. These blossoms close on rainy days and shortly after picking, so work quickly. Pluck out enough to measure:

2 quarts dandelion petals

PREPARING

Place the petals in a porcelainized, crockery, or stainless-steel container.

Add:

1 gallon boiling water

Stir with a long-handled plastic or wooden spoon. Cover the container and allow it to sit for 2 or 3 days, stirring daily.

ADDING AND COMBINING

Wash well, then peel off the rinds thinly, omitting any white pith, from:

2 lemons
2 oranges

Set the rinds aside, then squeeze and reserve the juice from the lemons and oranges.

Pour the petal-water mixture into a large stainless-steel or porcelainized pot and add the thinly peeled rinds. Place on the stove and bring to a boil. Simmer for 10 minutes.

FERMENTATION 1

Into a big crock or large food-safe, plastic container, place:

3 pounds refined white sugar

Over this, through several thicknesses of muslin or fine cheesecloth, strain your boiled petal mixture. When this is lukewarm, add the fruit juice and:

1 ounce wine-making yeast

Stir well with a long-handled plastic or wooden spoon.

Cover and let the mixture ferment in a warm room for 2 to 3 weeks. By the end the petals will have dissolved, leaving a sweet, brass-colored liquid.

FERMENTATION 2
AND INSERTION OF THE AIR LOCK

Using a nylon sieve or several sterilized thicknesses of muslin or fine cheesecloth draped over a colander, strain your liquid again into a food-safe fermentation container. A glass jug, sealable with a cork that has a hole in it suitable for the insertion of an air lock, works well.

Insert your air lock. Seal the lock by pouring into it enough boiled-then-cooled water, or Campden solution, so that the liquid rises halfway up its convolutions. Store the container in a warm room 2 to 3 weeks, at an even temperature if possible.

Transfer to a cool place for 2 weeks or longer, till little bubbles no longer rise to the surface if the container is moved.

RACKING

At this point sediment will have fallen to the bottom of the container. This is spent yeast, and must be removed by a process called racking. To do this, siphon the wine into another sterilized jug using about 4 feet of 1/2-inch plastic tubing. The easiest way to do this is to stand your wine on a table and your clean jug on the floor below. Place one end of the tube into the wine, above any sediment. Suck the other end till wine comes down the tube, then pop it quickly into your clean jug and let it flow. Be sure to leave all sediment behind!

Cap your clean jug and leave it in a cool place. Rack again as more sediment forms; and again, if necessary, till the wine remains clear for a week or so. (Clearing may take as long as 4 months.)

BOTTLING

Wash wine or champagne bottles with detergent and hot water, rinse them thoroughly, and dry them in a warm oven. (Or follow instructions for using Campden solution.)

Fill the bottles by siphoning wine into them to within 1 inch of the top.

CORKING

Soften new straight-sided corks in boiling water. Cork your bottles tightly. A cork flogger will blow the corks home without a lot of fuss.

STORING

Store bottles on their sides in a cool, dark place (or wrap them with paper) and age for about a year.

An English recipe for dandelion beer suggests it was "the drink most favoured in the past by workers in iron foundries and potteries. It is refreshing and particularly good for relieving stomach upsets or indigestion and for clearing the kidneys and bladder, and it is an enjoyable drink."

For this, you'll need a trowel or garden fork to begin: You're after plant roots.

Dandelion Beer

Loosen the soil around:
young dandelion plants
Dig up enough to weigh:
1/2 pound

Wash well (as described under Digging a "Mess of Greens") and remove the hairy roots without breaking the main taproot of each plant.

Place in a large stainless-steel or porcelainized pot:
the clean dandelion plants with their taproots
1/2 ounce gingerroot, well bashed
rind of 1 lemon (no white pith)
1 gallon water
Bring to a boil for 10 minutes.

Using a nylon sieve or several thicknesses of sterilized muslin or fine cheesecloth draped over a colander, strain the mixture into a big stainless-steel or porcelainized pot, or a large food-safe, plastic container. Let it cool. Add:
1 pound demerara sugar
1 ounce cream of tartar
Stir until the sugar is dissolved.

When the liquid is lukewarm, add:
1 ounce yeast
freshly squeezed juice of 1 lemon
Cover and let this ferment in a warm room for 3 days.

Again using a nylon sieve or several thicknesses of sterilized muslin or fine cheesecloth draped over a colander, strain to remove all sediment. Then pour into cider or beer bottles that have been washed with detergent and hot water, rinsed thoroughly, and dried in a warm oven.

Cap the bottles. Store on their sides in a cool, dark place.

This beer is ready when it hisses as the cap is loosened—about a week. It won't keep for very long.

Many herbes in the spring time there are commonly dispersed throughout the woods, good for broths and sallets, as Violets. . . . Besides many we used whose names we know not.—CAPTAIN JOHN SMITH, 1612

Violets

The *Viola* species, those lovely, little blue-violet, yellow, or white flowers nestled close to the ground in New England's May, are not only beautiful to see but also fine to eat—although some yellow species "may be mildly cathartic" according to Lee Allen Peterson in *A Field Guide to Edible Wild Plants*. The tender, bland, young leaves, which are rich in vitamins A and C, he says, "can be added to salads, boiled for 10–15 minutes to make a palatable cooked green, or added to soups as an okralike thickener."

Ten to 15 minutes would boil the life out of a violet leaf—or any other leaf, for that matter—but dried leaves can be made into tea. The English herbalist Nicholas Culpeper, writing in 1681, claimed that an infusion from dried leaves "doth purge the body of choleric humours."

Before that, a 1475 Icelandic medical manuscript supposedly written by Thorleif Bjornsson and translated by Henning Larsen in 1931 suggests that "Viola is wet and cold in the first degree. . . . If a man's head is heavy from meat or drink, then it is good to drink violets. . . . If one crushes roots of violets with vinegar it is good to apply for swelling of the feet, cools sweetly the body and gives sleep."

Furthermore, "If one has on his head a wreath of violets, it drives away vipers with its smell"!

Smell has certainly always been an important aspect of violet appreciation, as any Victorian would have agreed. Love of the fragrance traveled as far as China, where the last dowager empress imported bottles of "Violetta Regia" from Berlin.

An odd addendum comes from writer Audrey Wynne Hatfield: "The particular breath of violets . . . affects human beings by so numbing the nerves which control our sense of smell that gardeners who grow a lot of these flowers are unable to enjoy their fragrance."

Despite the Greeks, who chose the sweet violet as their symbol of fertility; the Romans, who (naturally) enjoyed sweet violet wine; or even Napoleon, who chose it as the emblem of the imperial Napoleonic party, the violet could be considered simply charming. Beautiful when eaten fresh in salads, crystallized violet blossoms can also decorate cakes, puddings, or ice cream.

For this recipe, pick the familiar five-petaled blue violet blossoms of Viola papilionacea.

Crystallized Violet Blossoms

Gather:

a handful of violet blossoms, retaining the stems

Beat until just frothy:
2 egg whites

Pick up a violet and, holding it by the stem, dip it into the beaten egg white, being sure to cover all blossom surfaces. Then gently dip each blossom into a bowl of:

superfine white sugar

Be sure all petals are sugared, top and bottom.

Line a cookie pan with waxed paper; place each violet on the paper and snip off the stem. Using a toothpick, open the petals to their proper shapes (if necessary). Sprinkle again with sugar if there are any uncoated spots.

Dry in the house if the day is warm; otherwise, place the pan into a 200°F oven for 10 to 20 minutes, leaving the door open, until the sugar crystallizes.

When the violets are fully crystallized, lift the blossoms gently from the cookie pan. Sprinkle again with sugar if they appear at all syrupy. Cool on racks.

Store in an airtight container with waxed paper between the layers.

Violet leaves are considered nutritious. Fine in salads, they also make a delicious springtime soup. This one isn't for dieters. Use Viola papilionacea.

Springtime Violet Soup

SERVES 4

Pick and remove the stems to measure:

3 cups packed, heart-shaped violet leaves

Rinse, drain well, roll into wads, and chop finely.

Chop finely to equal 1 cup:

the white part of bunching onions OR scallions

Pour into a heavy 3-quart, porcelainized or stainless-steel pot:

1/4 cup extra-virgin olive oil

Add the chopped onions and cook until translucent. Then add the violet leaves and cook over medium heat till nicely wilted, stirring often—a matter of 2 to 3 minutes. (They'll be slightly gelatinous.)

In a measuring cup, mix together with a fork:

1/2 cup cold water
1/4 cup cornstarch

Pour this into the cooked onion-leaf mixture, then add:

2 cups cold water

Over medium heat, bring the liquid to a boil, stirring constantly until it's thick.

Add:

1/2 cup heavy cream
1/2 cup milk
1 teaspoon sea salt to taste

**freshly ground black
OR white pepper to taste
some freshly grated nutmeg**

Serve warm, garnished with violet flowers.

Fresh rolls and a big salad, of course, complement this perfectly.

NOTE: If the soup is too thick, thin it with more milk.

EDIBLE FLOWERS

Calendulas, Chives, Daylilies,
Nasturtiums, Pansies, Violets

CHOOSING SEEDS: Most of these plants (chives, daylilies, pansies, and violets) grow as perennials or wild annuals. Calendulas will self-seed, so you only need to choose varieties once, or you can add new ones each year. Nasturtiums must be planted each year. Some pansies are not hardy and must be grown from seedlings.

CULTIVATION: Plant perennials anywhere you want that splash of color. Calendulas and daylilies like full sun. Others can take partial shade. Nasturtiums need poor rather dry soil for flowering. Fertile soil produces leaves aplenty. Wild pansies and violets are springtime specials.

PESTS: None. Even weeds find it difficult to compete against these vigorous plants.

HARVESTING:

Calendulas: Cut for flower arrangements. Save some to pick off the petals for salads.

Chives: Snip the blossoms off for garnish. Give chive bushes a periodic haircut for continuous fresh leaves and flowers.

Daylilies: Pluck buds for stir-fries, and flowers for salads. Eat them quickly, on the same day.

Nasturtiums: Pluck flowers and leaves. Both add spice.

Pansies and violets: Snip flowers for salads or ice cubes.

Johnny Jump-Ups and Pansies

Both Johnny jump-ups and pansies produce colorful, edible flowers—the former small and dark, the latter large and smiling. Pop them atop salads! Or freeze them into ice cubes and enjoy their color in cold drinks.

Frozen Flowers

Half fill an ice cube tray with:
  water
Into each compartment, place carefully:
  a single flower
Freeze. Cover with more water, and freeze again. *Voilà!* (Viola?)

> For tips on growing and collecting these flowers, see page 60.

This herbe for hys sweete savoure is used in bathe.
—THOMAS HYLL,
THE GARDENER'S
LABYRINTH, 1577

Love That Lovage

The mostly unknown old-fashioned herb called lovage *(Levisticum officinale)* looks and tastes a lot like celery, although it's stronger in both growth and aroma. In fact, a little lovage goes a long way as seasoning.

A native of southern Europe, it was introduced to Great Britain by the Romans and welcomed in English herb gardens until the middle of the 19th century. Writer Eleanor Sinclair Rohde remarked that it "joyeth to growe by wayes and under the eaves of a house, it prospers in shadowy places and loves running water."

This very large umbelliferous perennial with thick, hollow stems, looking something like a vast celery plant with greenish yellow flowers, soars to 7 feet tall, spreading at least 2 feet wide. According to Tom Stobart in *Herbs, Spices, and Flavourings*, one member of the family, *Ligusticum scoticum*, grows wild in the north of Britain and along the northern Atlantic coast of America. In Scotland's past it was much used cooked or raw. The Scots called it *shunis*.

Like so many other plants, lovage was brought to New England by colonists. Parkinson, writing in 1640, says of it: "The whole plant and every part of it smelleth strongly and aromatically and of a hot, sharpe, biting taste. The Germans and other Nations in times past used both the roote and seede instead of Pepper to season their meates and brothes and found them as comfortable and warming."

The Germans, naturally, learned from the Romans. Lovage is mentioned in the nearest thing to a Roman cookbook that survives today. Bearing the name of the first-century gourmet Apicius, it was compiled at least three centuries after him, and not all of the recipes can be attributed to the man himself. "Some," says Reay Tannahill in her *Food in History*, "were certainly later, and a few of these were extracted from manuals of dietetics—fortunately, since writers on diet sometimes specified quantities (a practice not adopted by food writers until the fifteenth century)."

One incredible recipe for a sauce concocted to accompany roast meat lists—in translation—"a quarter of an ounce each of pepper, lovage, parsley, celery seed, dill, asfetida root, hazelwort, cyperus, caraway, cumin and ginger, plus a little pyrethrum, 1 Imperial or 1 1/4 American pints of liquamen [best described as a fish sauce] and 2 1/2 fluid ounces of oil."

One can only marvel.

According to *Herbs for Use and for Delight*, an anthology of writings from *The Herbalist*, a 1974 publication of the Herb Society of America, lovage grew in the Herbularius or medicinal herb garden of the famous Abbey of St. Gall in England, taking its history back to the eighth century. "In New England the root used to be candied in sugar syrup . . . as a candy and a breath purifier, and was called Smallage by our grandmothers. It was very largely grown for sale at the Shaker colonies." In fact, Dee Herbrandson's compilation of *Shaker Herbs and Their Medicinal Uses* says that *Levisticum officinale* was "exported both plain and sugared for female complaints and nervousness."

Lesley Bremness in *Herbs* reveals that its leaves "used to be laid in shoes to revive the weary traveler, and at inns it was served in a popular cordial, which was flavored with tansy and a variety of yarrow known as *Achillea ligustica*. . . . A modern form of this cordial," the book adds, "is made by steeping fresh lovage seed in brandy, sweetening it with sugar and then drinking it to settle an upset stomach."

> **For tips on growing lovage, see page 127.**

Lovage leaves are often used as a celery substitute in stews. Like garlic, they can be rubbed on the inner sides of salad bowls for flavor, on chicken before cooking, or even steeped and drunk as tea. Seeds can be crushed and added to bread and pastries, or sprinkled over salads, rice, or mashed potatoes. Stems can be candied like angelica, or blanched and eaten with a white sauce; even the roots can be thinly peeled and cooked.

Why, we might ask, has lovage gone out of favor?

The following soup is a good introduction. Serve it in small bowls.

Simple Lovage Soup

SERVES 2–3

In a 2-quart porcelainized pot, heat:

2 tablespoons extra-virgin olive oil

Sauté in it gently for about 5 minutes, till translucent:

2 medium onions (2 rounded cupfuls) chopped medium fine, OR 2 cups bunching onions, including tender bottoms and tops, chopped

Add:

1/4 cup finely chopped fresh lovage leaves

2 large garlic cloves, minced

Add and cook for 1 minute, stirring constantly:

1/4 cup white flour

Gradually add:

2 cups Vegetable Stock (see page 43) OR 2 cups water and 2 tablespoons Bragg's Liquid Aminos (see the sidebar)

Cover and simmer gently for 15 minutes, stirring once or twice to release any sticking flour-onion mixture.

Then add:

1 cup milk

freshly ground black OR white pepper

Reheat slowly, being careful not to boil, and serve immediately.

NOTE: If the soup isn't thick enough to please you, whisk 1 heaping tablespoon of cornstarch into 1 cup of cold milk, then add to the pot. Be sure to bring the soup to a quick bubble for 1 minute to cook the cornstarch.

BRAGG'S LIQUID AMINOS: This product, advertised as a "delicious healthy gourmet alternative" to tamari or soy sauce, is an all-purpose seasoning from vegetable protein that contains no preservatives or alcohol, tastes similar to fermented soy sauce, is reputed to contain 16 amino acids, and is very salty.

Combined with grape leaves, lovage takes the place of celery. Canned grape leaves, available in most supermarkets and health food stores, make this recipe possible before wild ones mature. (Then it's possible to can your own.)

Stuffed Lovage and Grape Leaves

SERVES 2–4

THE GRAPE LEAVES

Collect:

28 big, young, bright green grape leaves

Rinse the leaves and lay them in a large heatproof bowl. Cover with:

boiling water

Leave for 10 minutes, drain, rinse under cold water, drain in a colander, and set aside to cool.

Collect:

4 stalks lovage leaves

Rinse the leaves and strip them from the stalks, discarding the stalks. Lay the leaves in a small heatproof bowl. Cover with:

boiling water

Leave for 10 minutes, then place in a colander to drain; set aside to cool.

Preheat the oven to 400°F.

THE STUFFING

In a 3-quart saucepan, heat:

1 tablespoon extra-virgin olive oil

Sauté in it for about 5 minutes or till soft:

1 small onion, finely chopped

Remove from the heat and add:

1/4 cup ground walnuts

1/2 cup cooked rice

1 1/2 tablespoons currants

1 teaspoon finely chopped fresh rosemary

1/2 teaspoon sea salt

freshly ground black pepper

Stir in:

1/2 pound firm tofu, crumbled

Knead it all together with your fingers.

COMBINING

Lay out on your counter, shiny-side down:

1 wilted grape leaf

Place in the center:

1 lovage leaf minus stem

Place about 1 tablespoon of stuffing on the leaf and roll it up, starting at the stem end and tucking in the sides as you roll.

Place each roll in a greased 8-inch-square or 6- by 10-inch rectangular baking dish. Continue for all 28 leaves.

COOKING

Pour over the layer of rolls until covered:

about 1 cup Vegetable Stock (see page 43)

Cover the dish and simmer in the preheated oven for 30 minutes. Remove from the oven and let rest for perhaps 15 minutes. All liquid should be absorbed.

SERVING

Just before serving, squeeze over:

juice of 1 lemon

Stuffed grape leaves make fine appetizers. Or you can serve them as accompaniments to rice, potatoes, great green salads, and other vegetables.

When tomatoes finally ripen come midsummer in New England, the following recipe will delight palates—if there are still tender young lovage leaves available.

Summertime Tomato Soup

SERVES 6

Peel (see page 197 for directions) and remove the seeds from:

2 huge red OR yellow tomatoes

Chop to equal 6 cups. In a large porcelainized saucepan placed on a wok collar, heat:

3 tablespoons extra-virgin olive oil

Over moderate heat, sauté in it till wilted:

2 cups chopped onions

1 cup chopped leeks

OR bunching onions

Add:

2 cups of the chopped tomatoes

1 cup finely sliced baby carrots

2–3 large garlic cloves, minced

1 teaspoon maple syrup

Cook together over medium-low heat, stirring, till the moisture evaporates and mixture is quite thick, 10 to 20 minutes.

Stir in and cook for 2 minutes more, stirring often:

1 tablespoon unbleached white flour

When this is thick, add:

2 tablespoons finely chopped fresh,
   young lovage leaves
the remaining 4 cups tomatoes
1/2 cup chopped walnuts
1/2 cup red lentils
3 cups nicely seasoned Vegetable
   Stock (see page 43) OR 3 cups
   water plus 1/4 cup Bragg's Liquid
   Aminos (see page 63)
freshly ground black pepper

Simmer for 20 to 30 minutes, or till
the lentils are soft. Add more stock if
necessary. Add to taste:
   sea salt (optional)

Sprinkle over the soup:

1/4 cup finely chopped parsley

Serve immediately with new bread and
a huge salad.

NOTE 1: Lovage dies back each winter,
but along with chives it is the first
perennial herb out of the ground come
spring, and it continues to burgeon
throughout the summer. The best plan,
if you grow it, is to clip it back every so
often, ensuring a steady supply of fresh,
young leaves.

NOTE 2: Because the plant dries poorly,
chopped lovage leaves can be frozen in
ice cubes to add that celery flavor to
winter soups.

Rosy-Stalked Rhubarb

A springtime treat is *Rheum rhabarbarum,* the welcome, rosy-stalked rhubarb with
its tart, mouth-puckering flavor. A member of the buckwheat family, it traveled
to America via Europe from southern Siberia and the Volga regions. It was, in fact,
cultivated in Asiatic countries for many centuries before being introduced to
Europe by about 1600, where it was valued for its roots.

Says Benjamin Watson in *Taylor's Guide to Heirloom Vegetables,* "More than
2,000 years ago, the Chinese were grinding up its dried roots to make a bright yellow powder, which they valued as a potent and effective medicine." And Professor
Tucker in *Kitchen Gardening in America* adds that it was used "as a purge . . . a cor-
rective and tonic remedy for the digestive system."

The plant's reputation in Europe remained medicinal for a long time. Rhubarb
pills were widely prescribed for rickets, scabs (probably from smallpox), itching,
leprosy, scurf, and even freckles! It's mentioned in *Macbeth,* as well as in a little
recipe book of Lady Elinor Fettiplace dated 1604. There Lady Fettiplace gives
general advice about the running of an Elizabethan or Jacobean household, along
with cookery recipes and remedies for illnesses, including one for "Ruberb Pilles."
Her remark was, "If it never woork it can not hurt."

Though rhubarb roots doubtless possess medicinal properties, the portions
prized today are the straight, thick stalks, best twisted gently away from their bases
rather than cut. These should be at least 10 inches long and 1 inch thick before

harvesting. And although they contain a lot of potassium, as well as a fair amount of iron, calcium, and vitamin A, they also harbor a small amount of oxalic acid. This is what gives that tart sensation—and can bind calcium so it's no longer available to your body. Leaves should never be eaten. They contain what can be fatal amounts of oxalic acid (see page 90) and its salts. Be sure to tell children!

Rhubarb sauce is always popular. And pies and rhubarb seem naturally to go together (whether for medicine or sheer enjoyment). Some people say no pie is

---

RHUBARB

VARIETIES: There are several varieties available, all heirloom. Though each can be grown from seed, the seeds do not always run true to type. So, in order to get a good variety, it is best to propagate from rootstock. Rhubarb roots can be bought at most garden stores. Alternatively find a friend with a good rhubarb patch and ask for a cutting. Do the job in early spring. Dig around an old plant with a shovel to expose the root mass to a depth of about 1 foot. Then cut a large chunk off the root with the shovel. The original will heal back up, and the chunk is ready for replanting.

CULTIVATION: Choose the best soil in the garden for your rhubarb patch, as for other perennial vegetables. Clay soil will not do. A rich well-drained loam in full sun is best. Dig a hole at least 18-24 inches deep, and fill the bottom with compost. Plant the root in this rich soil with the top 2-3 inches below the surface, then fill around and cover with more compost. Space plants 3-4 feet apart.

Shoots and leaves appear early in springtime. Pile more compost on top of and around the crown. Then let it emerge. Cut out the flower stalks on a regular basis as it grows. There is no need to weed the patch, because rhubarb leaves shade out any competition.

PESTS AND DISEASES: THERE are none.

HARVESTING: Forego harvesting leaf stalks in the first year or two so that the plant can become well established. When stalks are thicker than your thumb they are ready to harvest. Harvesting can be at any time from early spring through late summer. Either cut the stalks at their base with a knife, or pull stalks out with a yank. Cut the leaves off with a knife and leave them in the patch as mulch.

---

better than strawberry rhubarb. Strawberries in New England usually come along after rhubarb has peaked, but rhubarb plants will continue to produce if mature stalks are removed, allowing young ones to continue growing. You can also freeze rhubarb early on, and take it out when strawberries are ripe—or vice versa.

Stalks that are mature have a tough, stringy skin that sometimes needs to be peeled. It's an easy process. Simply catch the "strings" at their root end with a sharp knife, then pull.

The following pastry is perfect for any pie, quiche, tart, or what-have-you. Prepare it before you turn to berries and rosy rhubarb.

Great Pastry for Great Pies

MAKES 1 DOUBLE-CRUST PIE
(WITH LEFTOVERS) OR 2 SINGLES

THE DOUGH

Sift together:

2 cups unbleached white flour
2 cups whole-wheat pastry flour
2 teaspoons sea salt
1 tablespoon refined white sugar

Cut in with a pastry cutter or two knives:

1 3/4 cups solid vegetable
shortening

(Do not use oil, lard, margarine, or butter.)

In a small bowl, whisk together:

1/2 cup cold water
1 tablespoon cider vinegar
1 medium-sized egg

Pour the wet ingredients into the dry and stir quickly with a fork until combined. Form into two balls and knead lightly five or six times to make the dough cling together.

SHAPING

Handling lightly, cut each dough ball into two sections, then shape into flat, round patties. Place in plastic bags, or wrap in waxed paper, and refrigerate for at least half an hour before rolling out.

When you're ready to roll, lightly flour both sides of a patty, place it on a bread board (or marble slab) that has been lightly floured with unbleached white flour, and roll to 1/4-inch thickness. Then fold the rolled dough in half, drape it over a rolling pin or large knife, and drape over your upside-down pie pan.

FOR A TWO-CRUST PIE

Trim the edges to measure a bit less than 1 inch larger than the pan's edge. Fold the dough in half again, remove it, turn the pan over, and lay the dough within, arranging it gently to fit. It will overlap the rim. Trim off the remaining edges with a table knife.

Roll out a second patty of dough to 1/4 inch thickness for the top. Place whatever filling you're going to use into the pan. Wet the edge of the pastry already in the pan, and lay the second crust on top. Trim the edges with a knife and "glue" the two crusts together by pressing lightly all around with fork tines, making a pattern.

Proceed with cooking as your recipe directs.

FOR A SINGLE-CRUST PIE
WITH FLUTED EDGES

Roll out one patty, fold the dough in half, and drape it over a rolling pin; then place it loosely over an upside-down pie pan. Trim the edges to measure 1 inch larger than the pan's edge. Fold the dough in half again, lift it, turn the pan over, and lay the dough gently within, arranging it to fit.

Fold the edges under once (toward the outside) and flute to produce a high-standing "ruffle" all around. Then proceed with any single-crust recipe, such as quiche.

NOTE 1: For savory fillings (such as quiches), omit the sugar in the dough.

NOTE 2: For recipes demanding a single prebaked pie shell, flute the crust, prick its bottom and sides with a fork, and bake at 450°F for 15 minutes, till brown. Coating the shell with the yolk of one egg before filling helps prevent sogginess.

NOTE 3: Single unbaked crusts can be frozen in their pans and stored in plastic bags till you're ready to use them. The crust will be very crisp.

NOTE 4: Extra dough can be rolled very thin, buttered, sprinkled with cinnamon and sugar, rolled into a "sausage," cut into 1-inch bits, and baked till brown. For big and little kids.

For cooks who popped quarts of last summer's strawberries and blueberries into the freezer, springtime is the appropriate moment for combining them with fresh young rhubarb for a scrumptious treat.

J. A.'s Strawberry, Blueberry, Rhubarb Pie

THE CRUST

Prepare two patties of Great Pastry for Great Pies (see page 67) for a double-crust pie.

Line a 9-inch pie pan with pastry. Preheat the oven to 425°F.

THE FILLING

Wash well, then cut into 1/4-inch lengths to measure:
4 cups rhubarb
Place in a large bowl and add:
**2 cups frozen strawberries
(cut in half if large)
1/2 cup frozen blueberries
1 1/2 cups refined white sugar
1/4 cup cornstarch
OR quick-cooking tapioca
1/4 teaspoon sea salt**
Mix gently together. Let the mixture rest for 15 minutes to combine well; then heap it into the crust (you may have some left over) and dot with:
2 tablespoons butter, cut into small bits

BAKING

Brush the edge of the bottom crust lightly with cold water, lay on the top crust, trim the edge, and crimp together with the floured tines of a fork. Using the same fork, prick steam vents—possibly in the shape of an *R*! Brush the top crust with:

milk

Sprinkle with:

2 teaspoons refined white sugar

Place on a baking sheet (to catch any spillover) and bake in the 425°F for 30 minutes. Reduce the heat to 350° and bake for 30 minutes more, or until thick juices bubble through the cut vents.

SERVING

If your family can stand it, let the pie cool before eating.

For a rhubarb-only pie filling, try this recipe.

Rosy Rhubarb Pie

THE CRUST

Prepare two patties of Great Pastry for Great Pies (see page 67) for a double-crust pie.

Line a 9-inch pie pan with pastry. Preheat the oven to 450°F.

THE FILLING

Into a medium-sized bowl, measure:

5–6 cups young rhubarb stalks
chopped into 1/4-inch slices

In a measuring cup, mix together:

2 cups refined white sugar
3 tablespoons quick-cooking tapioca

Add this to your chopped rhubarb, mix well, and let stand for 15 minutes.

Spoon the mixture into your 9-inch pie shell and dot with:

1 teaspoon powdered cinnamon
1/4 teaspoon freshly grated nutmeg
2 tablespoons butter

BAKING

Cover the pie with a top crust, brush with milk, sprinkle with 1 tablespoon white sugar. Cut slits to allow steam to escape, and bake at 450°F for 10 minutes. Reduce the heat to 350° and continue
to bake for about 45 minutes more.

Rosy Rhubarb Custard Pie

THE CRUST

Line a 9-inch pie pan with Great Pastry for Great Pies (see page 67), making a high, fluted rim. Preheat the oven to 375°F.

THE RHUBARB

Cut into 1/4-inch slices to measure:

2 1/2 cups rhubarb

THE CUSTARD

Separate:

3 large eggs

In a small bowl, beat:

the whites of the eggs

Add gradually while beating till stiff:

1/4 cup refined white sugar

Set aside. In another small bowl, beat together thoroughly:

the 3 egg yolks
1/4 cup well-softened butter
3 tablespoons frozen orange juice
concentrate

Add and beat well again:

1 cup refined white sugar
1/4 cup unbleached white flour
1/4 teaspoon sea salt

Scoop into a medium-sized bowl.

Add to the yolk mixture and stir well:
the sliced rhubarb
Fold in the reserved egg white meringue gently, then pour the filling into the pastry. Sprinkle with:
1/3 cup chopped pecans OR walnuts

BAKING

Bake on the bottom rack of the 375°F oven 15 minutes. Reduce the heat to 325° and bake 45 to 50 minutes more, or until the custard sets. Cool before serving.

Ginger Rhubarb with fresh strawberries ladled over vanilla ice cream or white or yellow sponge cake (at right) is a dessert delight.

Ginger Rhubarb

Trim and cut into 1- to 2-inch lengths:
1 pound rhubarb
You should have 4 rounded cups. Place in a porcelainized saucepan and add:
1 cup refined white sugar
Let the mixture rest for 15 minutes. Then add:
1/2 teaspoon powdered ginger
1–2 tablespoons (or more)
diced candied ginger
Stir with a wooden spoon. Cover, turn the heat to medium, and simmer for 20 minutes or till the rhubarb is very tender.

Cool. Just before serving, slice in:
1 cup fresh strawberries

Of course, a topping of sweetened, vanilla-flavored whipped cream would be calorically as well as aesthetically enhancing.

NOTE: You *could* stir in a tablespoon or two of gin just before serving when the compote is ice cold.

This sponge cake dates from the 1940s.

Art Pinkham's Easy Sponge Cake

Preheat the oven to 325°F.

Grease and flour an 8-inch round cake pan thoroughly. Sift together:
1 cup white flour
1 teaspoon double-acting baking powder (see page 28)

In a saucepan, bring nearly to a boil:
1/2 cup milk
Add and melt:
1 tablespoon butter

In an electric mixer, beat until very light:
2 eggs
Beat in:
1/4 teaspoon sea salt
1 cup refined white sugar
1 teaspoon natural vanilla
Then beat in:
the hot milk
the sifted flour–baking powder mix

Pour quickly into the prepared cake pan and bake for about 45 minutes.

Turn the cake out onto a rack to cool, then serve with Ginger Rhubarb (at left) or sweetened whipped cream.

Leftover winter beets, kept fat and firm in country root cellars, combine well with June rhubarb. Here's a sauce for garnishing any entrée, in the same way that cranberry sauce brightens Thanksgiving.

Beet-Rhubarb Garnish

In a large stainless-steel or porcelainized pot, place:

2 cups cooked, diced beets
4 rounded cups rhubarb cut into
　1/2-inch bits
1/4 cup refined white sugar
1/2 cup freshly squeezed orange juice

Bring the mixture to a boil, then lower the heat and simmer till it's slightly thickened, stirring often, perhaps 10 minutes. Don't overcook. Remove from the heat and stir in:

zest of 1 orange (about 1 tablespoon)

Cool. Serve at room temperature, or refrigerate.

It may come as a shock to learn that tart rhubarb makes an excellent wine— but it does. And it's fine to use in stir-fries or any Oriental type of cooking that calls for saké. If wine making is new to you, don't be put off by such items as Campden tablets (a sterilizing agent), wine yeast, nutrient, cork floggers, or air locks.

These items—along with plastic tubing— are available at most health food stores or at wine supply shops.

Dry Rhubarb Wine

MAKES 1 GALLON

PREPARING

Pull from the garden or purchase:

2 pounds rhubarb stalks

Wash each stalk carefully and chop it into 1-inch chunks. Place into a large food-safe plastic, stainless-steel, or crockery container and add:

1/2 pound sultana raisins, chopped
1/2 gallon water
1 Campden tablet dissolved in
　1/4 cup warm water

In another large pot, bring to a boil, then lower the heat and simmer for 2 minutes:

1 quart water
2 pounds refined white sugar

Cool, then add this to your rhubarb-raisin pulp. Also add:

1 cup freshly made but very strong
　black tea
1 package wine-making yeast
1 teaspoon yeast nutrient
　(see page 266)

FERMENTATION 1

Pour the rhubarb mixture into a food-safe plastic, stainless-steel, crockery, or porcelainized container.

Cover loosely, then place the entire container inside a large plastic bag. Gather the plastic over the top and fasten with a rubber band. (This is a British suggestion for keeping dust and unwanted bacteria out while providing easy access for stirring.)

Let the mixture sit for 8 days at room temperature, stirring daily with a long-handled plastic or wooden spoon.

FERMENTATION 2

Using several layers of muslin or cheesecloth draped over a stainless-steel colander, strain your mixture into a bowl or crockery jar. Both the muslin and the container should have been sterilized by rinsing with Campden solution. Let stand 1 hour.

Pour into a 1-gallon glass jug (such as cranberry juice is sold in) that has also been sterilized with Campden solution. Fill to within 1 inch of the top by adding cooled, boiled water. Insert an air lock into the jug's cover. A stopper with an air-lock-sized hole in it is perfect. Seal by pouring enough boiled and cooled water, or Campden solution, into the lock to rise halfway up its con-volutions. Allow your incipient wine to ferment until little bubbles no longer rise to the surface if the jug is moved.

RACKING

At this point sediment will have fallen to the bottom of the jug. This is spent yeast, and it must be removed by a process called racking. Using about 4 feet of 1/2-inch plastic tubing, siphon the wine into another sterilized, 1-gallon glass jug. The easiest way to do this is to stand your wine jug on a table and your clean jug on the floor below.

Place one end of the tube into the wine, above any sediment. Suck the other end till wine flows down the tube. Pop the tube quickly into your clean jug and let flowing continue. Be sure to leave all sediment behind.

Cap your jug and leave it in a cool place to clear. Rack it again if necessary.

BOTTLING

Wash used wine or champagne bottles (which many restaurants will happily give away) with Campden solution. Once your wine is clear, siphon it into your sterilized bottles to within 1 inch of the top.

CORKING

Soften new, straight-sided corks in boiling water, then blow them home using a cork flogger.

STORING

Label and store the bottles on their sides in a cool dark place and let them age for about a year.

Rhubarb also makes a fine chutney.

Rhubarb Chutney

MAKES 3 PINTS

Cut into 1/2-inch bits:
   2 pounds rhubarb stalks
Peel and chop fine to measure:
   2 cups onions

Place the rhubarb and onions into a heavy porcelainized pot and add:
   1 1/2 pounds light brown sugar
   1 cup currants
   1 teaspoon white mustard seeds
   1/2 teaspoon powdered cinnamon

1/2 teaspoon ground cloves
1 teaspoon freshly ground black
   pepper
1 teaspoon powdered ginger
1 teaspoon sea salt
1/4 teaspoon cayenne powder
2 cups apple cider vinegar

Simmer gently, uncovered, stirring often, for 3 hours or till the mix is of jam consistency.

Place in hot, sterilized jam jars (as in typical jam preserving—but see page 38 if you're unfamiliar with canning procedures), cap tightly (using metal tops and rims), process for 10 minutes in a boiling-water bath, then store as usual. You could also check canning directions for Great Cucumber Pickles on page 152.

Away off in England, Peter's father is a master marmalade maker. So Peter decided to try his hand at experimenting. Being inventive, he thought of rhubarb. J. A., out of oranges, substituted grapefruit, and—voilà! Grapefruit-Rhubarb Marmalade! (Four oranges can be substituted for grapefruit.) And note that having a wok ring on which to set a pot is a marvelous burn preventive.

Grapefruit-Rhubarb Marmalade

MAKES 6 1/2-PINT JARS

Pull, wash well, and drain:
   about 4 1/2 pounds rhubarb stalks
Cut the stalks into 1-inch pieces to measure 4 pounds.

Wash thoroughly with soap and water:
   2 grapefruits

Cut the grapefruits in half, juice them (retaining the seeds), and slice the rinds into thin strips. Cut the strips into bite-sized pieces. Meanwhile, place the seeds into a little clean cloth bag and close with a string.

Into a large stainless-steel or porcelainized pot, place:
   the 4 pounds cut-up rhubarb
   2 1/2 pounds light brown sugar
   the thinly sliced grapefruit rinds
   2 tablespoons powdered ginger
   1/2 cup grapefruit juice
   the little bag of seeds

Put a wok ring on your stove, place the pot on it, and cook slowly over medium-low heat till the marmalade is thick and brown. This will take 4 to 6 hours. Stir once in a while, especially at the end, to be certain there is no burning on the bottom.

Once the marmalade is thick and yummy, remove the bag of seeds, ladle the marmalade into hot, sterilized jam jars, and process in a boiling-water bath for 10 minutes. (See page 38 if you're unfamiliar with canning procedures.)

NOTE: You could also ladle marmalade into jelly jars, pour melted canning wax onto the surface of the hot marmalade, and cover with the traditional thin metal caps.

JUNE

Free for the Asking

Milkweed

From almost any New England field, and in any vegetable or flower garden where it particularly likes to plant itself, the weed called milkweed represents free, delicious food. As well as beauty.

The First Americans knew it long before Pilgrims arrived. According to David M. Tucker's *Kitchen Gardening in America,* each spring women gathered poke, yellow dock, burdock, and milkweed, which were "among the more than 175 wild foods that eastern American Indians gathered, while they cultivated fewer than 9."

Those ladies knew a good thing when they saw it. From the first spears to thrust through the ground in May, to the four to six leaves standing upright like sentinels on the plant's main stalk in June, to the golf-ball-sized flower-head buds in July—even to the first tiny, tightly wrapped cocoons of incipient milkweed seeds—the plant is a legacy of good eating.

It's also difficult to overlook. But be sure you identify it correctly. Roger Tory Peterson's *A Field Guide to the Wildflowers of Northeastern and North-Central North America* states that the milkweed family, Asclepiadaceae, consists of plants with "thick, milky juice." "This thick sap," according to Joan Richardson's description, "neither tastes good nor is it at all good for you." Moreover, there are from 30 to 37 species "in our area"—meaning New England—down to the Carolinas and west to some of the central states, depending on whose botany book you use.

The name *Asclepias syriaca* originates from that great observer Carolus Linnaeus, who labored under the impression that it, or something like it, came from Syria. It is, however, very much a native of America, and Richardson, in her *Wild Edible Plants of New England: A Field Guide,* gives, I think, its best description. "With young leaves held close against the sturdy green stems, the shoots look much like asparagus stalks with leaves. The young leaves have a broad paddle shape, a promise of their mature form and will already be thick for their size. A most important identification feature is the dense white nap on the lower surfaces of the leaves, even when young. . . . The poisonous dogbanes have somewhat similar stalks with paddle-shaped leaves; dogbane, however, is not at all fuzzy, and quickly branches, which milkweed never does."

Do not, she cautions, confuse it with other milkweeds or dogbane. And "Don't look for milkweed in damp meadows . . . ; this is the habitat of the purple milkweed" *(A. purpurascens),* which is "unknown as to edibility."

Key to the easy identification of New England's edible milkweed are:

➤Its leaves, which, even when young, show a dense white nap on their lower surfaces.

➤Its large, dusty rose flower heads.

➤Its mature, warty pods, which appear in late summer after it flowers.

Now that we've shared these precautionary remarks, rest assured that cooking the big, rosy-flowered plant, though often said to be "laborious," is straightforward. That great wild-food gatherer Euell Gibbons suggests in *Stalking the Wild Asparagus* that you place the shoots, leaves, buds, or pods into a pot, cover with boiling water and boil for 1 minute, then drain and repeat the process three times before finally boiling for 10 minutes. His reason, he states, is to reduce bitterness.

To the Simply Grande palate, nothing seems outrageously bitter in milkweed, and so much boiling would produce mash. Another forager, however, agrees with Gibbons's directions: Billy Joe Tatum suggests that we "Bring a large pot of water to a boil and keep it boiling. Put the milkweed in a smaller pot and pour in boiling water to cover. Boil for 1 minute, then pour off the water. Again add boiling water to cover and again boil for 1 minute. Repeat . . . until all bitterness is gone— taste to make sure. . . . Remember to keep the supply of water boiling, otherwise the bitterness tends to 'set' in the plant." Then cook for 10 to 20 minutes.

Like Gibbons, this excellent forager also seems to suggest mash.

Here are our own suggestions for respectfully cooking milkweed.

Milkweed Shoots

When shoots are 4 to 6 inches tall, identify carefully, then blanch them once, steam like asparagus, and serve with a lemon-flavored sauce.

When the plant is taller come June, and the four to six tiptop leaves cupped about the stem are about 1 to 1 1/2 inches long, serve in place of spinach.

Milkweed Leaf "Spinach"

Identify your milkweed, then pluck off the top four to six leaves and about 2 inches of tender stalk.

Wash quickly, pop into a large pot in which an inch of water is already boiling, and simmer for 8 to 10 minutes, turning once with a long-handled fork.

Drain and serve immediately with slices of lemon, sea salt, and freshly ground black pepper, or with a sprinkling of extra-virgin olive oil and shoyu (naturally fermented soy sauce).

NOTE: If you find the flavor bitter, as Euell Gibbons and Billy Joe Tatum suggest, simply repeat blanchings. Vitamins and minerals, of course, are lost when cooking water is poured off.

When milkweed flower buds look like small, knobbly, round balls wobbling at the top of the plant, they can be steamed and served like broccoli.

Steamed Milkweed Buds

Identify your milkweed and pluck off the smallish bud clusters with their one or two attendant leaves.

Rinse quickly, pop into a large pot in which an inch of water is already boiling, and simmer till tender, perhaps 8 minutes, turning once with a fork.

Drain well and serve with slices of lemon, sea salt, and freshly ground black pepper, or with extra-virgin olive oil and shoyu.

Milkweed flower-bud clusters can also be dipped in batter and deep-fried to the oohings and aahings of surprised guests. Japanese tempura batter works perfectly, as does a slightly heavier beer batter.

Deep-fried Milkweed in Whole-Wheat Beer Tempura

About 4 cups bud clusters

In a medium-sized bowl, whisk until light and fluffy:

    2 eggs

Into another bowl, sift together:

    1/4 cup whole-wheat pastry flour
    OR unbleached white flour
    2 tablespoons cornstarch

Sift the flour mixture into the eggs and add:

    2 tablespoons light beer
    1/2 teaspoon sea salt

Whisk well again.

Dip the milkweed-bud clusters into the batter, allow them to drip a little, then refrigerate about 30 minutes.

Set a wok on its collar, add peanut oil to a depth of 3 inches, and heat to 350° to 375°F. (You could also use some other highly saturated oils that won't break down at the high temperatures necessary for such frying.) When the oil is hot but not smoking, gently insert your "battered" buds and deep-fry till golden.

When the buds are golden, remove them quickly from the hot oil and drain well on a rack and/or paper towels.

Serve immediately.

As with all battered vegetables, rice or noodles are good accompaniments, along with pickles and other vegetables.

NOTE 1: When milkweed pods are young, firm, and not at all spongy feeling—and you know that fall is on the way—they, too, can be batter-dipped and deep-fried, or simply stir-fried with other vegetables Oriental style.

NOTE 2: A good way to use leftover cooked milkweed greens or flower buds is to chill them and serve with freshly squeezed lemon juice, extra-virgin olive oil, and a sprinkling of shoyu (naturally fermented soy sauce).

Daylilies

When June arrives, sunshine seems to drown the earth. And to welcome it, the throats of *Hemerocallis,* otherwise known as daylilies, open to drink it in.

The first of the family to appear in northern gardens is a big yellow blockbuster, and, peeking around it, the antique, slimmer, lighter-colored cousin called the lemon lily. Soon follow aunts and uncles in shades of yellow, orange, rust red, green, nearly white, pink—and who knows what hybridizing will produce next?

In fact, with more than 35,000 registered cultivars, modern daylilies have come a long way from the familiar so-called wildflower that slipped out of colonial gardens to grace fields and roadsides. Almost endless selections of color, shape, foliage habit, size, and length of blooming season have been created by amateur and professional breeders, and heights can range from 7 inches to several feet. The flowers stay open for 1 day only—thus the name—but abundant blossoming occurs throughout the season, and different varieties produce at different times, so color and scent proceed all summer.

According to *The New Encyclopaedia Britannica,* daylilies can be described as "any plant of the genus *Hemerocallis* of the family Liliaceae, consisting of about 15 species of perennial herbs distributed from central Europe to eastern Asia. Members of the genus have long-stalked clusters of funnel- or bell-shaped flowers . . . fleshy roots [called rhizomes], and narrow, sword-shaped leaves that are grouped at the base of the plant."

Native to the Orient, these travelers moved westward in caravans via the famous Silk Road to eastern Europe, eventually making it to England and Holland and finally to the United States, where they escaped. According to W. H. Duncan and L. E. Foote in *Wildflowers of the Southeastern United States,* the tawny daylily, *H. fulva,* is now the most widely distributed daylily in the world. This is even more remarkable because it's a sterile form, which means it journeys by root movement alone.

Although fragile looking, these lilies-of-the-day are robust. Adapting to almost any site that provides at least 6 hours of sun, they spread rapidly in either wet or dry conditions and choke out weeds without becoming invasive themselves. Heat tolerant, they also grow well in cool regions. Insects and diseases don't bother them.

For more tips on growing daylilies, see page 60.

As if beauty weren't enough, with their swordlike leaves and gorgeous blossoms, daylilies are edible from tip to toe. Shoots are fine added to salads. Blossoms are stuffable. Even the roots can be eaten.

In the Orient the most esteemed portion has always been the bud. Exquisite if lightly stir-fried with other vegetables, buds can also be prepared tempura style or added to soufflés. Strung on a heavy thread and hung up to dry, they become crunchy, taste slightly tart, and make interesting additions to winter soups. The Chinese call these dried lily buds *kim jim*, or "golden needles." When offered in the form of pressed, golden cakes, they can be sliced, soaked in warm water for 30 minutes, squeezed dry, then cut to the same size as accompanying meat and vegetables and stir-fried.

A Chinese cook might combine mushrooms, shredded chicken, chopped scallions, and water chestnuts with the buds. The ingredients would then be stir-fried in order from toughest to tenderest. Soy sauce, cornstarch, sugar, and a little toasted sesame oil for flavoring would be added, along with a small amount of stock. Covered and simmered for 2 or 3 minutes, the dish would accompany rice.

This Japanese version of lily buds simply sautés them to produce a condiment or side dish. Remember that in Oriental-style cooking, previous preparation is a must.

Sautéed Daylily Buds
SERVES 4

When your daylily buds are from 1 to 1 1/2 inches long, still tightly closed and yellow green, go into the garden just before mealtime and pick about a handful per person. Be sure that you've identified the daylily—*Hemerocallis.* Never confuse it with the true lily, which grows from bulbs, not rhizomes,

and isn't edible. It's easy to tell the difference.

Wash, if necessary, in cool water, and gently pat dry.

Prepare all the other ingredients listed in this recipe before you begin to cook.

When you're ready, place a wok on its collar over high heat and, when it's hot, pour in:
 1 teaspoon sunflower seed oil
Add and toss lightly to coat:
 1/2 cup shallots cut into 1/2-inch bits
 2 1/2–3 cups daylily buds

Add:
 2 tablespoons water
 1/2 teaspoon minced fresh thyme
Cover, reduce the heat to moderate, and steam for 1 minute.

Add and toss lightly:

3–4 drops toasted sesame seed oil

Serve immediately, scattered over heaps of steaming rice with other vegetables and sprinkled with natural soy sauce for seasoning.

Another way to enjoy daylilies is with the following rather esoteric recipe that produces six individual omelets. A blossom is buried in the center of each one—perfect for luncheon with the ladies. A tossed salad and cooked grain match well.

Please note that you're going to mix up more stuffing than necessary. Save it to enjoy in tomorrow's crêpes or enchiladas.

Individual Daylily Omelets

SERVES 6

THE STUFFING

Blanch, drain well, squeeze dry in a towel, and chop:

1 1/2 pounds fresh spinach
OR lamb's-quarters

In a skillet, heat:

2 tablespoons extra-virgin olive oil

Add and sauté until limp:

3 tablespoons diced onion
1 garlic clove, minced
1 cup chopped button mushrooms

Add and stir for about 1 minute:

3 tablespoons white unbleached flour

Stir in:

3 cups hot milk

Simmer until moderately thick. Then add:

1 tablespoon dry white wine

1 cup freshly grated Cheddar
OR feta cheese
1/2 teaspoon sea salt (optional)
freshly ground black pepper
1/4 teaspoon freshly grated nutmeg

Blend well.

Place the chopped spinach in a bowl and add:

1 cup cottage cheese
1 large beaten egg
only enough sauce (above) to bind nicely

You're aiming for a burger-type consistency.

THE DAYLILIES

When ready to make your omelets, collect:

6 daylily blossoms

Remove the stamens, chop them, and add to your stuffing (above). Into each blossom place:

a thin 2- by 1/2-inch bit of feta cheese
1 tablespoon of the spinach stuffing
a tiny bit of hot jalapeño pepper (optional)

THE EGGS

In a medium-sized bowl, beat together until they form soft peaks:

6 large egg whites
1/8 teaspoon cream of tartar

In another bowl, beat together until creamy:

6 large egg yolks
1/4 cup unbleached white flour
1 1/2 tablespoons cold water
1/4 teaspoon sea salt

Fold the yolk mixture into the whites.

COOKING

In a heavy-bottomed skillet, heat:

a small amount of sunflower seed oil
OR butter

In it place:
    **1/2 cup of the egg mixture,
        making a mound**
Push into the mound:
    1 stuffed blossom
Enclose it completely by topping with:
    1/4 cup or more of the egg mixture
Cook for 2 to 5 minutes or till golden brown on one side. Turn gently and cook till just set.

SERVING

Serve to the first lucky diner immediately. A little Hot Tomatillo Salsa (see page 230) would be just the right condiment.

NOTE: Oil the pan between omelets.

Summer Salads

Since daylily varieties bloom at different times, blossoms are available all summer for salads. Following are some ingredient suggestions for an entire summer. Gold on green is exemplary. Pink on green is exquisite.

Bloomin' Summer Salads

PRELIMINARIES

If you're lucky enough to have access to a garden, gather flowers and greens just before dining. Deep green leaves contain greater concentrations of vitamins and minerals than any other type of fresh food, so handle them gently and with respect. Wash quickly in cold water. Drain for a few moments. Swing in a wire basket or bag, or dry on a towel by patting lightly. Cover and chill in the refrigerator for half an hour. Then dress and serve immediately.

Vegetables such as string beans and broccoli florets should be washed equally as quickly in cold water. Store them in the refrigerator, or at least in a cool place, before adding to any salad.

PREPARATION

Place in a large wooden bowl (whose insides you may rub with a peeled clove of garlic to liberate its flavor) any of the following greens torn into bite-sized pieces, as well as the following vegetables cut into cubes, or into matchsticks (julienned), or shredded moments before serving:
    lettuce (loose leaved, oak leaved, bibb, romaine or cos, crisphead, etc.)
    mâche (corn salad)
    endive
    escarole (Batavian endive)
    radicchio (see the sidebar)
    arugula (roquette)
    amaranth
    cress
    young dandelion leaves
    OR Italian dandelion

sorrel

spinach

Chinese cabbages

the leaves of new beets, carrots,
    radishes, turnips

mustard greens

parsley (flat-leaved Italian or regular
    curly leaved), finely chopped

alfalfa (and other) sprouts

new celery, diced

bunching onions or scallions,
    sliced finely

red or green cabbage, shredded

asparagus, sliced moderately finely

radish, sliced or grated

carrots, shredded

beets, boiled and marinated
    or shredded raw

green beans, snapped into bite-sized
    pieces

cauliflower, bite-sized florets,
    sometimes sliced thin

broccoli florets, steamed slightly,
    perhaps marinated

kohlrabi, peeled and sliced paper thin

sunchokes, peeled, dipped in lemon
    juice, and sliced thin

cucumbers, sliced or diced,
    sometimes salted and left to drain
    for half an hour to remove excess
    liquid

young zucchini, in thin slices

small summer squash, sliced thinly

green and red bell peppers, diced

tomatoes when available: peeled,
    seeded, and chopped, or simply
    sliced

uncooked or cooked peas

slightly steamed and chilled
    small pea pods

onions, sliced thinly
    (red Bermudas are mild),
    OR chives, minced

Anything else you can think of, such as:

julienned celeriac

thinly sliced fennel

raw, julienned turnip

raw potato, dipped in lemon juice
    and cut into thin strips or stars

Scatter thinly on top:

cooked and marinated dry beans
    (navy, black, and garbanzo
    are best)

water chestnuts OR sunchokes,
    thinly sliced

sunflower seeds, pumpkin seeds,
    sesame seeds

tofu, cut into cubes (sometimes
    marinated in shoyu, deep-fried,
    drained well, cooled, and used
    as croutons)

croutons of whole-wheat bread,
    sautéed briefly in olive oil,
    garlic, and oregano

cheese (almost any kind), cubed or
    crumbled, especially Cheddar,
    panir (see page 111) or feta

RADICCHIO has only recently been introduced to America. A traditional winter green of the Venice region, cultivated for centuries in Italy and highly prized by ancient Romans, it's a true chicory *(Cichorium intybus)* of the same species as Belgian endive. 'Verona' grows into tightly closed little heads, which look like small lettuce heads but of a deep blood red. Other types include 'Rossana', 'Giulio', and 'Sugarloaf' varieties, which are green rather than red. Torn into bite-sized bits, red radicchio complements the greens of any salad. For tips on growing radicchio, see page 231.

hard-boiled eggs, crumbled or sliced
olives, sliced or whole, green or ripe
anchovies (if you please)

Fresh herbs turn the "ordinary" into
the "superior." Collect the tips of:
chives and their flowers
cilantro
chervil
dill
basil
mint
tarragon
salad burnet
thyme
marjoram
anise
lovage
oregano
fennel

Use three different kinds at once.
Bruise them with your fingers,
discard all large stems, and toss 1
or 2 tablespoonfuls into your salad.

Finally, chop and dot your salad with
three or four big, bright:
nasturtium, violet, or
daylily blossoms

Serve any of the above ingredients
immediately, chilled, with any dressing
you fancy.

J. A.'s Simple Vinaigrette 1

Shake together in a small jar
until well combined:

2/3 cup extra-virgin olive oil
1/3 cup vinegar of your choice
1 teaspoon sea salt
1 tablespoon any finely chopped
herb of your choice

J. A.'s Simple Vinaigrette 2

Shake together in a small jar
until well combined:

2/3 cup extra-virgin olive oil
1/4 cup shoyu (naturally fermented
soy sauce)
2 tablespoons umeboshi vinegar

DILL, derived from the old Norse *dilla*, meaning "to lull," is a member of the
Umbelliferae family and always a choice herb. The Middle Ages thought *Anethum
graveolens* protected people from witchcraft. Drayton's *Nymphidia* says,

Therewith her Vervain and her Dill,
That hindereth Witches of their Will.

It can even make an unusual pesto; see "Perspicacious Pesto" on page 123 and
substitute dill for oregano. For tips on growing dill, see page 126.

LETTUCE

CHOOSING SEEDS: The choice is bewildering. Below, to help you, are the major types, each of which has several varieties in green, red brown, or some mixture of colors.

Leaf lettuce: Does not form tight heads. Examples include 'Grand Rapids', 'Lollo', and 'Oakleaf.'

Summer crisp: Thicker leaves form a loose head. Tolerant of hot weather.

Romaine or cos: These have long, broad, upright leaves. The lettuce of Caesar salad.

All the above are good for snipping off as baby leaves for salad mixes.

Butterhead and Boston: Ruffly outer leaves and a soft, folded heart.

Bibb: Small, compact bunched rosettes.

Iceberg: Tight, large firm heads, mild in taste (some would say tasteless). Not frost tolerant.

Most lettuce seeds are dormant at soil temperatures above 75° to 85°F. Choose heat-tolerant types for midsummer plantings, or buy pelleted seeds. There are 25,000 seeds per ounce. A package should suffice.

CULTIVATION: Plant early (as soon as the ground can be worked), plant often (every 2 to 3 weeks), keep planting (through late summer). Lettuce is an ideal crop for spring and fall, growing well in cool, damp weather (use floating row covers to speed growth at the beginning and end of season).

Almost any soil will do, but lettuce needs plenty of nitrogen throughout the season. To get a jump start, plant indoors 3 to 4 weeks before transplanting out. Harden seedlings before taking them outside by reducing water and temperature.

Transplant on a cool, rainy day. Alternately, snip off the larger leaves for a salad, and plant seedlings with all the root but almost no shoot. Soak each seedling with water from a dribbling hose as you go. Space lettuce plants 8 to 12 inches apart—closer for cos and bibb types, wider for leaf, summer crisp, and iceberg types.

For field planting, seed one row per 3-foot-wide bed and collineal-hoe until the seedlings are 2 inches tall. Then follow the transplanting directions above to fill the bed.

Weed between the plants until they take over and prevent weed growth.

PESTS: Lettuce has few or no pests.

HARVESTING: Young lettuce, if grown in rows that haven't been thinned, can be snipped to within an inch of ground level for baby leaf salad mix. Snip again the following week.

Leaf lettuce: Harvest leaf by leaf, early in the day when leaves are crisp.

Head lettuce: It's best to wait till these are fully mature. Then cut them off with a knife at ground level.

When lettuce bolts, leaves become bitter, so pull it up and take it to the compost pile. Lettuce will survive frost, but after frosty nights harvest at midday.

This is not a recipe for the health minded.

J. A.'s Dressing for Greens
Decorated with Daylily Blossoms

In a blender, place:
  1 (10 3/4-ounce) can tomato soup
  1/2 cup sunflower seed oil
  1/3 cup apple cider vinegar
  a pinch of sea salt
  1 garlic clove, minced
  2 tablespoons cold water

Whiz, then add and whiz well:
  1 cup granulated white sugar

This dressing is useful on chilled or just-cooked greens and vegetables.

Seed Sauce

Whiz in a blender until smooth:
  1 cup sunflower seeds
  1/2 cup hulled sesame seeds
  1 cup extra-virgin olive oil
  OR sunflower seed oil
  1/2 cup rice vinegar
  **1/4 cup shoyu (naturally fermented
    soy sauce)**
  1/4 cup water

Adjust the texture by adding more water.

Spinach

S pinach, as everyone knows, grows best in cool, moist weather. So spring and fall in New England are prime times for enjoying the two main horticultural types: round seeded and prickly seeded, of which luckily a few strains still exist, their delicious, arrow-shaped leaves remaining tasty even when the plants begin to bolt.

Along with beets and chard, *Spinacia oleracea* var. *inermis,* a member of the Chenopodiaceae family that came to America with European settlers. But it originated in southwestern Asia, was first cultivated in what is now Iran, and, according to James Trager's *Food Chronology,* was introduced into Sicily by the Saracens in A.D. 827. They called it *isfanaj.* "True spinach," says historian Susan Campbell, "was introduced to Moorish Spain from Persia and Afghanistan by the Arabs in the eleventh century, and may have reached Italy by 1305, as the cultivation, comparisons and description of spinach made by the Italian writer, Pietro de'Crescenzi, tally with the real thing." Did it really take that long, we wonder, to travel from Sicily to the mainland?

Not surprisingly, spinach was brought to New England by English colonists, whose kitchen gardens had enjoyed it for a long time. In fact, in England the kitchen garden already had a long history, as reported in Campbell's charming book *Charleston Kedding: A History of Kitchen Gardening.*

"The medieval kitchen garden," she reports, "was known either as the 'curtilage' or as the 'leac-garth' or the 'leac-tun' from the Anglo-Saxon 'leac' (leek) and 'garth', 'geard,' 'zeard' or 'tun' (yard or enclosure). Americans still call their back gardens backyards, which shows how closely the language of the earliest, Elizabethan colonists was linked to the Anglo-Saxon of their ancestors. The use of the term 'kechyngardyn' or 'kechengardyn' is quite late; it is thought to have first appeared in English in the Bishop of London's account rolls for the manor of Stepney of 1383–84 and 1395–96."

Those early gardens produced many vegetables familiar to us. "A late-medieval kitchen garden like the Bishop of Stepney's would have grown broad beans, collards, kale, beets for their leaves, mustard for its spicy seed, garlic, chibols (known as Welsh or winter onions) and scallions which could also be taken to mean chibols, or shallots, or any young onion eaten green. These plants were usually made into a kind of soup or 'porray' (pottage or purée), thickened with bread, oatmeal or dried pulses (field-peas, vetches and beans), and enlivened with a choice of cress, mint, parsley, sage, hyssop, dittander and fennel." You may be reminded of the old New England poem "Pease porridge hot . . ."

"There are also frequent mentions of 'spynach'," she continues, but there is some doubt as to whether the true spinach *(Spinacia oleracea)* was grown in

England before about 1500; "plants previously called 'spinach' in English were likely to have been orach or orage *(Atriplex hortensis)* and were even more likely to have been fat-hen or Good King Henry *(Chenopodium bonus-henricus)*, or one of the other edible goosefoots." Which we call lamb's-quarters.

A rich source of vitamin A and folic acid, high in vitamin C and potassium, spinach contains more protein than do most green vegetables, as well as anti-

---

GARDENING NOTES

SPINACH

CHOOSING SEEDS: Some seed catalogs list two types of spinach, smooth and savoyed (textured). But there are many gradations. For spring plantings, choose varieties that are bolt resistant. New Zealand spinach is actually a different type of vegetable altogether (called Tetragonia) that looks and tastes a bit like spinach and grows well in summer.

Several weed species can be harvested and cooked like spinach in spring-time. Try lamb's-quarters, milkweed, redroot, stinging nettle, and galinsoga. Spinach has about 2,600 seeds per ounce, enough to plant 150 to 200 row feet.

CULTIVATION: Spinach is a spring and fall crop. Sow as early in spring as you can get onto the soil. For continuous harvest, sow every couple of weeks, though not in the hottest part of summer. Expect to harvest the first leaves 35 to 40 days after planting. For a fall crop, sow in July and August. To over-winter and for earliest harvest, sow from September until the ground freezes.

Amend soils with plenty of nitrogen fertilizer—but don't add fresh manure or nitrogen shortly before harvest, because spinach concentrates nitrogen in its leaves.

Sow in rows 12 inches apart, about 10 to 12 seeds per foot. Collineal-hoe between rows. For full-sized spinach leaves, thin to 2 inches apart. Seedlings can be transplanted in the bed with care and lots of water. If you're preparing for a small-leaved salad mix, do not thin.

PESTS: Heat is the worst spinach pest. It will cause the whole row to bolt.

HARVESTING: For a salad mix, snip off the larger leaves as they come. For full-sized plants, cut off thinned plants just below the root attachment.

---

oxidants that reportedly help block cancer-causing substances and processes. Its oxalic acid content, however, can interfere with the body's absorption of iron and calcium (see page 90). As cooks throughout the ages seem to have known, this is easily rectified by cooking spinach with calcium-rich dairy products.

The easiest and perhaps the tastiest way to enjoy spinach is in a salad with other greens. Or alone.

Spinach Yogurt Salad

SERVES 2

Wash well and remove the stems from:
3 cups spinach
Rinse, trim off the stem ends, and slice:
8 mushrooms of your choice
Slice into rings:
1/2 large red onion

In a small skillet, brown lightly:
1 tablespoon sesame seeds

Toss the spinach, mushrooms, and sesame seeds together in a bowl; top with the red onion rings, and pour on Yogurt Dressing (below).

Yogurt Dressing

In a blender, combine till thick:
1/4 cup rice vinegar
1/2 cup extra-virgin olive oil
1/2 teaspoon Dijon mustard
1 small garlic clove, chopped

Remove the mixture to a bowl and whisk in gently:
1 cup low-fat yogurt
1–2 tablespoons freshly minced parsley

Refrigerate in a capped jar.

Another way to enjoy spinach is by way of a pizza.

Spinach Pizza

MAKES 2 12-INCH PIZZAS

THE DOUGH

In a 2-cup measuring cup, stir together quickly with a fork:
1 1/4 cups lukewarm water
1/2 teaspoon refined white sugar
2 tablespoons dry baking yeast

After 5 to 10 minutes, when the yeast is bubbling nicely, pour the mixture into a large bowl and stir in:
2 tablespoons extra-virgin olive oil
2 1/2 cups whole-wheat pastry flour
1 teaspoon sea salt (optional)

Turn the dough out onto a lightly floured board and knead for about 5 minutes. Mix in enough unbleached white flour to make a stiff, but not hard, dough. It should be firm and quite elastic, although dough made with whole-wheat flour (and especially pastry flour, which lacks the gluten of bread flour) is never as elastic as that made with white flour.

Form the dough into a ball and place it in a large oiled bowl. Turn it once to coat with oil, cover with a damp tea towel, and let it rise for 1 hour or till doubled in bulk.

Punch it down and divide in half.

Using white flour to lightly dust your bread board, roll out one half of the dough to form a 12-inch disk.

Grease a cookie sheet or round pizza pan with butter and sprinkle with:

1 tablespoon finely ground cornmeal

Carefully lift your dough onto the pan. Repeat (in a second pan) with the remaining half of the dough.

THE TOPPING

Remove the thick stems from:

1 pound well-washed fresh spinach

Place the leaves in a big pot. Cover and steam in their own wash water, along with 1/2 cup more water, till just wilted —3 or 4 minutes.

Remove the spinach to a colander, let it drain and cool, then squeeze out as much water as possible by pressing inside a dish towel. You will have about a cupful of spinach. Chop it fine.

In a large skillet, heat:

2 tablespoons extra-virgin olive oil

Add and sauté for several seconds:

1 large, freshly minced garlic clove
1 medium-sized onion,
finely chopped

Add and stir for another minute:

the squeezed, chopped spinach

Remove from heat and set aside.

COMBINING AND BAKING

Preheat the oven to 475°F.

In one pan, spread onto your already prepared dough:

a layer of Simply Grande Garden Tomato Sauce (see page 196)
1/2 the garlic-onion-spinach mixture
paper-thin tomato slices
sliced mushrooms
some chopped green bell pepper

some chopped red bell pepper
some small, sliced black olives

Sprinkle with:

1 teaspoon sea salt (optional)
freshly ground black
OR multicolored pepper
2 teaspoons crumbled, dried oregano
OR 4 teaspoons finely chopped fresh oregano

Drizzle with:

1–2 tablespoons extra-virgin olive oil

Top with:

1 cup shredded Cheddar
AND/OR mozzarella cheese

Brush oil on any exposed crust edge.

Place a pizza on the bottom shelf of the oven and bake for 15 to 20 minutes or till the crust is golden and cheese is melted.

Repeat the whole process with the second pizza, varying the toppings if you like.

SERVING

Cut each pizza into eight portions and serve with a tossed green salad in which you include grated carrot.

The moment New World maize met Old World cooks, it was taken to heart. An Italian dish to enjoy with spinach is polenta made with cornmeal.

Spinach Polenta

SERVES 4

THE SPINACH

Pick or purchase:

1 pound fresh spinach

Rinse it, trim off the stems, and place the leaves in a medium-sized pot.

Cover and steam the spinach in its own wash water, plus 1/2 cup more water, till just wilted. Fork it over once to avoid burning.

Turn the spinach into a colander, drain well, and cool slightly. Then place it in a tea towel and squeeze dry. You should have 1 cupful. Chop it coarsely. Put it in a bowl and stir in with a fork:

1 large garlic clove, minced

1 tablespoon extra-virgin olive oil

1/8 teaspoon freshly grated nutmeg

Spread this mixture in the bottom of a well-buttered 1 1/2-quart baking dish, either round or rectangular.

THE DAIRY-CORNMEAL MIXTURE

Pour water into the bottom half of a double boiler and bring to a boil. In the top half of the double boiler, pour:

1 1/2 cups milk

1/2 cup stone-ground yellow cornmeal

Place over the boiling water and cook, 20–30 minutes, stirring occasionally, until the cornmeal is thick. Stir in:

1/2 teaspoon sea salt (optional)

freshly ground black pepper

Remove from the heat and whisk in:

1/2 cup finely minced onion

1/4 cup freshly grated Cheddar cheese

2 eggs

COMBINING

Preheat the oven to 350°F.

Spread the cornmeal mixture over the spinach in your baking dish to a depth of about 1 inch. Sprinkle on:

2 tablespoons freshly grated Parmesan cheese

paprika

BAKING

Place the dish on the middle shelf of the oven and bake for 20 to 25 minutes or till hot and lightly browned around the edge.

SERVING

Serve with beans, a big green salad, and other in-season vegetables.

NOTE: Swiss chard, kale, lamb's-quarters, or any other green can be substituted for the spinach.

The Middle East, probably the most profound center of plant and animal domestication in the distant past, offers this spinach and nut dish. Pine nuts are best; walnuts may substitute. And, if necessary, Swiss chard can substitute for the spinach.

Spinach with Raisins and Nuts

SERVES 3–4

Wash well and trim the stems from:

2 1/2 pounds fresh spinach

Place in a large pot with only the wash water that's still clinging to it. Cover and cook over medium heat for about 5 minutes, turning once or twice, until the spinach wilts. Remove it to a colander, drain well, and cool slightly. Then drop it into a towel and lightly press out the excess liquid. Chop finely and set aside.

In a small bowl, soak together for 15 minutes:

1/3 cup currants

warm water to cover

In a medium-sized porcelainized pot, heat:

1/4 cup extra-virgin olive oil

Add and cook for a few moments:

1–2 minced garlic cloves

Then add:

1/3 cup pine nuts (the best)
OR coarsely chopped walnuts
the drained currants

Cook for about 2 minutes, stirring.

Reduce the heat and add:

the chopped spinach
sea salt to taste
freshly ground black pepper
freshly grated nutmeg

Cook till hot, 4 to 5 minutes.

Serve right away with rice or baked potatoes, a big salad, and other in-season vegetables.

THE TROUBLE WITH OXALIC ACID: In his *On Food and Cooking,* Harold McGee explains why oxalic acid in foods can be a concern: "The oxalic acid in certain plants, notably spinach, and phytic acid in the outer layers of whole grains, both form insoluble compounds with calcium ions, thereby binding the minderal in a form that cannot cross the membranes of intestinal cells. . . . In any case, severe calcium deficiency is rare, and usually involves a shortage of vitamin D as well."

Radishes

Especially welcome after a long Maine winter, the radish is often one of the garden's first delights. A member of the Cruciferae (mustard) family and cousin to all the cabbage tribe, it arrived early in New England.

But its history is ancient. Nor has it always resembled the small, familiar red globe garnishing today's salad or crudité platters. Protected in the earth from the worst ravages of weather, root vegetables must always have been important to hungry humans. Along with turnips, a large type of radish probably dates back to prehistoric times in Europe. And varieties have certainly been grown for many centuries in China and Japan, where they've played an important role as food plants. In fact, every part has been used at one time or another. Historians Rodale and Heiser report that one Chinese radish was grown for the oil in its seeds; Egyptians grew another for its green tops; and yet another variety, the rat-tail, has edible seedpods that may reach lengths of 2 feet and can be pickled.

Japanese samples have enormous roots, sometimes reaching 65 pounds. They can be stored for the winter, and, used as a cooked vegetable, treated much like turnips. In fact, almost every dish in Japan contains or is served with some type of radish.

As long ago as 479 B.C. the great Chinese philosopher Confucius (K'ung-Fu-tzu), who died at age 72, left behind writings that his followers collected in the *Analects*, in the *I Ching (Book of Changes)*, and in songs that give a picture of agriculture in Chou times. He mentioned at least 44 food plants (the Old Testament mentions only 29), including radishes.

Benjamin Watson, whose *Taylor's Guide* lists valuable heirlooms, assures us that though radishes came from China, they apparently spread to the Mediterranean area at a very early date where they were cultivated in ancient Egypt, Greece, and Rome. The Greeks, he says, "offered up radishes made of beaten gold to the god Apollo."

By A.D. 1551 meat-eating Western missionaries and traders reached Japan but were not impressed by the local diet, which consisted mostly of radishes, millet, wheat noodles, rice, seafood, and seaweed.

Raphanus sativus, however, was destined to populate the Americas, but via a circuitous route. Raymond Sokolov's *Why We Eat What We Eat* tells us that after banqueting with the Hispaniolan king on December 16, 1492, Columbus reported "on the results of some horticultural experimentation done with seeds brought from Europe. Spring melon, cucumber, Old World squash, and radishes flourished."

Soon after—along with stolen gold and silver—Spanish galleons carried tomatoes, potatoes, and string beans to Europe. In return came pigs, cattle, pomegranates—and radishes. In fact, Sokolov states, "By 1600, Europe and the Americas (and to a lesser but not inconsequential extent Africa and Asia) had exchanged the fundamental ingredients and ideas of their cuisines."

While a state of religious and political upheaval during the 1600s encouraged Pilgrim fathers and mothers to begin a new life at Plymouth, Massachusetts, Lady Elinor Fettiplace of Appleton Manor in Oxfordshire, England, was calmly writing down recipes—an unusual occupation at a time when few women could read or write. The result was a small, stout, handwritten book, bound in leather and stamped in gold, with endpapers made from odd scraps of medieval Latin manuscripts and an inscription in the front reading LADY ELINOR FETTIPLACE 1604. Like later New Englanders, she took pride in her kitchen garden and appreciated the crucially important seasonality of foods. Her salad calendar included radishes. She wrote, "Radish prove best that sowen a day after the full [moon] in August."

Boston's Puritans found the radish valuable: Along with cucumbers, coleworts, and cabbages, it is mentioned in William Bradford's odd poem, "A Descriptive and Historical Account of New England in Verse." And Fearing Burr Jr., in his 1863 classic, *Field and Garden Vegetables of America*, says that "The excellence of a Radish consists in its being succulent, mild, crisp, and tender." He lists 28 varieties in colors from red to black.

RADISHES

CHOOSING SEEDS: Radishes are available round like a ball or long, and in several colors, principally red and white. All are crunchy and spicy.

Small round radishes: These come in white, red, and purple. Most are short season—25 days.

Long, fat Japanese daikons: These are mostly white and long season.

Specialty radishes: Some are long, some round; most are red or white.

Radishes have 2,500 seeds per ounce; 1 ounce will plant 100 row feet.

CULTIVATION: Choose a bed where the soil is as loose and well drained as possible. Radishes grown in clay soils tend to be deformed.

Small round and specialty types: Plant as early as the ground can be worked. Sow in rows 8 inches apart. Cover the bed with a floating row cover to keep flea beetles off, removing this only to collineal-hoe for weed control. Thin seedlings in the row by pulling out the mature small round radishes. Plant succession crops every 3 weeks through spring, and then again in late summer for fall harvest.

Daikons: Plant in rows 18 inches apart. Thin to 6 inches apart and keep weeding. If the plants start going to seed, pinch the tops to keep the growth in the root.

Radishes grow fast with plenty of moisture. Hot, dry weather makes them tough and pithy.

PESTS: Radishes' worst enemies are flea beetles, which can ruin a good crop before it starts. Prevent this with floating row covers, or treat with rotenone or pyrethrum.

HARVESTING:

Small varieties: Harvest as soon as the roots are ready. They don't stay prime for long, except those planted in summer for fall harvest.

Daikon: The roots are brittle. Harvest carefully, undermining the roots rather than lifting them. Cut the leaves 2 inches above the crown, then wash and store.

Perhaps the best way to enjoy the red globe so familiar to us is to eat it raw. Sliced and sprinkled with or dipped into sugar it's— well, a treat. Marinated, it's also fine.

Marinated Raw Radishes 1

Pull or purchase:

2 radishes per person

Wash well, trim off the root and stem ends, and slice into a bowl.

Pour over the radishes:

a little rice OR apple cider vinegar

Sprinkle with:

refined white sugar

Allow each person to consume what seems necessary!

Here's a more involved variation on the basic recipe above.

Marinated Raw Radishes 2

In a medium-sized bowl, marinate together for 1 hour:

4 cups trimmed, sliced radishes
1/4 cup vinegar
OR freshly squeezed lemon juice
2 teaspoons refined white sugar
1 tablespoon sea salt

In another bowl, marinate together for 1 hour:

4 cups small cucumber slices
1/4 cup vinegar OR lemon juice
2 teaspoons white sugar
1 tablespoon sea salt

After they've marinated, drain the radishes and cucumbers well. Pat them dry with a towel, then toss them together in a large bowl.

Add and combine gently:

1–2 cups thick yogurt
finely chopped red onion (optional)
any finely chopped fresh herb
such as dill, parsley, or cilantro

If time allows, radishes cut into flowers make pretty, edible garnishes.

Radish Flowers

Cut off the radish root and trim the stem end, leaving a few leaves. Starting at the root tip, slice down to 1/4 inch from the stem, carving out five or six "petals." Don't detach the skin.

Cut a second layer of petals if you please, starting at the root tip again and spacing between the first cuts.

Chill in ice water for a few hours to enable the petals to open and curl.

Surprisingly enough, radish leaves produce a soup with just a hint of spiciness. Fall radishes and thick leeks make a perfect combination.

Radish Leaf Soup

SERVES 4–6

In a large saucepan, heat:

1/4 cup extra-virgin olive oil

Add and cook till golden (about 5 minutes):

1 1/2 cups chopped onions
OR thinly sliced leeks, including
some green tops

Wash well and trim the stems from:

8 cups loosely packed tender young radish leaves

Stir these into the onions and add:

1/2 cup water

Cover and simmer over low heat till wilted, about 8 minutes. Fork over several times to prevent burning.

In the meantime, pour into a large pot:

3 cups water
OR Vegetable Stock (see page 43)
1 teaspoon sea salt (optional)

Add and cook till soft:

2 cups peeled, diced potatoes

Add and simmer, covered, for 5 more minutes:

the onion–radish leaf mix

Pour into a blender, place a towel over the blender cover, and whiz to make a fine, smooth purée. (Begin slowly and be careful not to burn yourself.)

Return the mixture to the pot and whisk in:

1/2 cup cream (optional)

Season with:

sea salt (optional)
freshly ground black
OR multicolored pepper

Garnish with:

freshly grated nutmeg

Serve hot as a first course, or for lunch with fresh bread and a barley salad, perhaps including sliced tomatoes and grated carrots.

The large Japanese white radish known as the daikon can grow to nearly any length. One measuring 14 inches and weighing 5 pounds is more than adequate. With its crisp, mildly pungent flavor, it's a ubiquitous, versatile ingredient in Japanese cuisine—where it appears grated as a garnish (daikon-oroshi), as an addition to stews and soups, or cooked by itself as a side dish. It's also good for stir-frying and pickling.

The following recipe offers daikon as a vegetable valued for itself. Saké or rice wine promotes good flavor; white Western radishes or Chinese white radishes can be substituted if daikon is not available.

Simmered White Radish

SERVES 1–2

Pull from the garden or purchase:

1 daikon (2–3 inches in diameter)

Wash it well and cut off an 8-inch section. Peel and slice into rounds about 1/2 inch thick.

In a large skillet, heat:

1 tablespoon extra-virgin olive oil

Add and sauté for about 2 minutes:

the daikon slices

Turn over with a spatula and sauté the other side for 1 minute more.

Add:

1 tablespoon refined white sugar

1 tablespoon saké

Reduce the heat and simmer for
5 minutes.
Then add:

**1 1/2 tablespoons shoyu (naturally
fermented soy sauce)**

Turn the slices again and simmer for
perhaps 5 minutes.

Turn the slices once more, cover, and
simmer until all the liquid is absorbed.
Remove before they become too soft.

Garnish with tiny slices of chili pepper
and serve as a side dish to rice and other
vegetables.

*Heidi Kim, one of Simply Grande's
shareholders, offers a quick daikon relish
to perk up rice or potato offerings.*

Heidi's Daikon

Dig or purchase:

1 daikon (2 inches in diameter)

Peel about 10 inches of this and shred
it, piling the shreds in a bowl.

Add and toss together:

2 tablespoons rice wine vinegar

1 tablespoon refined white sugar

red pepper flakes to taste

OR 1/4 teaspoon cayenne powder

1/2 teaspoon sea salt

Serve as a condiment at any meal.

Lamb's-Quarters

Lamb's-quarters! Pigweed! Fat-hen, goosefoot, bacon weed, dirty dick, muck hill weed. . . . Despite numerous, often odoriferous monikers—and this little list is only partial—*Chenopodium album* is a delicious, nutritious forager's delight, and an early-summer treat nobody should miss.

In fact, you can hardly ignore it. Magically popping up amid beets and radishes —anywhere that bare earth appears in any garden plot—it's eager to produce edible greens till frost. And it's considered a "weed" only because nobody has decided to sell the seeds and make it sound domesticated.

It wasn't always so.

Once upon a time lamb's-quarters greens received more respect. Their ancient name was *all good*, and "all good" they are. Containing more iron and protein than either raw cabbage or spinach, they offer more calcium than raw cabbage, more vitamin B_1 than raw cabbage, and more vitamin B_2 than either cabbage or spinach.

According to Joan Richardson's guide to *Wild Edible Plants of New England*, the lamb's-quarter "even outclasses spinach as a storehouse of protein, calcium, phosphorus, iron, vitamin C, and great amounts of vitamin A, not to mention all the minerals pulled out of the earth by its strong taproot." It also lacks the "puckishness" of spinach, caused by oxalic acid.

Ancient people, of course, revered the plant. English writer Audrey Wynne Hatfield in *How to Enjoy Your Weeds* says that lamb's-quarters were "once the most valued vegetable for human beings and fodder for their animals. . . . It lost favour only after its relative, the novel spinach, was introduced [to England] from Southwest Asia in the sixteenth century." It grew so profusely in some areas that settlements were named for it.

Hatfield adds, "We find this plant . . . growing in Britain in the Late-glacial and the Post-glacial periods. It was in the accustomed diet of the Neolithic, Bronze Age and early Iron Age people; and it was much used by the Romans and later diners."

Angrily thrown out by most gardeners today, lamb's-quarters were originally introduced to America by settlers from Europe. Both have since run rampant.

No wonder. By puberty the human female has something like 400,000 eggs in place, while a single plant can produce at least 75,000 seeds. Of course gardeners (who don't view a "weed" as the archenemy) are apt to cheer: They don't have to purchase seeds, plant them, or coddle seedlings to get a healthy crop. Not all seeds are this easygoing!

Identifying lamb's-quarters is straightforward. Euell Gibbons's amusing classic *Stalking the Wild Asparagus* is fine, but Joan Richardson in *Wild Edible Plants of New England* gives, I think, the clearest clues: "The shape of its leaves and, especially, the talcum-powdered appearance of the young growing leaves gives it away.

This mealy powder, most noticeable on the undersides of the leaves as the plant gets older, repels water, but disappears upon cooking. The leaves themselves are bluish-green, delicate to the touch. The stem is fleshy, tender when young."

And as it matures, "The leaves of the upright, well-branched plant are alternately placed. While the upper leaves may lack teeth, the lower ones are roughly triangular in shape and coarsely, roundly toothed. The plant may stretch to three or more feet in height."

She warns, "There is one caution to be observed when you first go after this plant: If, when you have crushed and sniffed a leaf, it smells like turpentine, you've not found lamb's-quarters, but an inedible relative. Leave it alone."

And be sure, she adds, to pick it "from ordinary untreated soils or from areas whose history is known to you."

Such caution is true for any foraging.

Lamb's-quarters can be prepared like any other green. And like many another green, they shrink when cooked, so a large quantity is needed. This never proves a problem, however: Great clumps provide easy plucking. Steamed lamb's-quarters provides a delicious side dish for basmati rice, a bean salad, and colorful vegetables such as carrots or sliced tomatoes.

Simply Steamed Lamb's-Quarters

Pluck 2 inches of tender lamb's-quarters tops shortly before dinner. Gather twice what you imagine you'll need. They shrink a lot.

Rinse them gently and pop them, still dripping, into a big pot with an additional 1/2 inch of water.

Cover and steam over medium heat, turning occasionally, for 5 to 10 minutes (depending on the amount) or till barely tender.

Drain well in a sieve.

Place the greens on a hot dish and, using a sharp knife, cut them into large cubes for easy serving. Pass extra-virgin olive oil, shoyu (naturally fermented soy sauce), and a freshly cut lemon for each diner to season at will.

Lamb's-quarters also make a remarkably good salad, whether chilled or warm.

Wilted Lamb's-Quarters Salad

SERVES 2–3

THE GREENS

Gather, wash, and chop coarsely:

> **4 cups lamb's-quarters top leaves and tender stems (packed)**

THE SAUCE

In a medium-sized skillet, heat:

> **3 tablespoons extra-virgin olive oil**

Sauté in it till limp:

> **1 small onion, diced**
> **2–3 garlic cloves, minced**

Add and bring to a simmer:

> **1/4 cup vinegar**
> **OR freshly squeezed lemon juice**
> **1/4–1/2 teaspoon sea salt**
> **freshly ground black pepper to taste**

Add:

> **2 dried water chestnuts,** soaked for

half an hour in boiling water, peeled and chopped finely (optional, but good for their smoky flavor); you can substitute finely chopped sunchokes if available (see page 36).

Pour the sauce over raw greens and toss.

SERVING

Serve warm or chilled with pasta, rice, or potatoes and other vegetables.

Far from being a nuisance, leftover cooked lamb's-quarters or other greens form the basis for many delicious offerings, such as the following main-dish custard.

Green Leaf Custard

SERVES 6–8

THE ONION-MUSHROOM MIXTURE

In a skillet, heat:
   1 tablespoon sunflower seed oil
Sauté in it till limp:
   1 large onion, chopped finely
   1 heaping cup sliced button
   OR portobello mushrooms

Spread this mixture over the bottom of a buttered 7 1/2- by 11-inch lasagne pan (or a 10-inch pie pan).

THE GREEN MIXTURE

Drain well and pat dry:
   4 cups chopped fresh lamb's-quarters
Mix your greens with:
   1 cup small-curd cottage cheese
   OR crumbled soft tofu
   1 cup thick plain yogurt
   1/2 teaspoon dried thyme
   1 teaspoon dry mustard

THE EGG MIXTURE

Beat till fluffy:
   6 eggs
Add:
   1 teaspoon sea salt (optional)
   freshly ground black pepper

COMBINING AND BAKING

Preheat the oven to 325°F. Combine the greens and egg mixture. Spread over the onion-mushroom layer. Bake, uncovered, for 30 minutes.

Sprinkle with:
   freshly grated Cheddar cheese

Continue baking till the cheese is melted and the custard is set in the center — a few more minutes. Let stand for 10 minutes before cutting into squares.

SERVING

Serve with a vegetable salad and sliced tomatoes, or for lunch with fruit and hot yeast rolls.

If you're a dedicated forager, still searching—as did early New Englanders— for what the wilds offer by summer's end, lamb's-quarters remain your choice.

Lamb's-Quarters Flour

Choose a dry fall day when all the leaves have fallen from the tall lamb's-quarters plants and their little pods are filled to bursting with hard little black seeds. Knock them into a container.

Spread the seeds on a cookie sheet and bake for 1 hour in a 300°F oven.

Cool. Run them through a coffee mill or blender till fine. Mix into regular flour for pancakes, muffins, breads, or biscuits in the same proportion as you would buckwheat.

Writer and weed lover Audrey Hatfield offers an interesting English soup with French overtones.

Lamb's-Quarters Soup

"For soup," she advises, "wash a good handful of the leaves and their small stalks and put them into a pan with a pint of cold water, a little salt and a tablespoonful of ground rice. Cook with the lid on until the greenery is tender; then strain the liquid into a basin and rub the solids through a sieve to make the purée. Thin this down to the desired consistency with the liquid and some milk, add a dash of nutmeg and pepper and return to the pan to reheat with a good chunk of butter. Beat with a whip as it simmers until it is blended. It must not boil. When it is sufficiently heated and blended, remove the pan and add a little thick cream or top milk. And to bind the soup in true French manner, pour it into the tureen containing the yolk of an egg beaten with a little of the cooking liquid."

Grape Leaves

The Norse tale of Leif Eriksson's epic voyage across the Atlantic to "Vinland" circa A.D. 995–996 reports that the adventurers found vines and grapes in North America. The saga also reports that "No frost came in winter and the grass withered only a little."

So where did they land?

According to Farley Mowat in *Westviking*, "The determination of Leif's actual landfall on the eastern coast of North America is a complex procedure requiring the analysis of much data." While others argue for points farther south, Mowat's choice is Newfoundland's Baccalieu Island at the entrance to Trinity Bay.

Newfoundland seems a bit northerly for grapes, argue some scholars. But the Norse were traveling during the so-called Little Climatic Optimum—a period between A.D. 1000 and 1200 "when vineyards in western Europe were being cultivated . . . farther north than their present limits"—and, according to Mowat, "It is a widespread misapprehension that Newfoundland has a cold, even subarctic climate. The truth is that the average winter temperatures of the southern and eastern coastal regions of the island are much higher than those of any other place in eastern Canada, and even of most parts of the New England states as far south as northern Massachusetts."

Wherever the Vikings found grapes—and some folks favor the coast of Maine—they would be prized. According to J. I. Rodale in *How to Grow Vegetables and Fruits by the Organic Method*, "Some type of grape is native to almost every portion of the temperate and many of the subtropical portions of the world." Several varieties were found in America by settlers on the eastern seaboard. But though they tried for many years to grow the grapes they brought with them from Europe, they found it couldn't be done "except in greenhouses or under the most artificial conditions." Only when they gave up the attempt to grow European grapes and turned to native species did American grape growing became successful.

The variety of grape encountered in New England was *Vitis labrusca*, the eastern American or fox grape. It's a Concord type, with slip skins and a comparatively short ripening period. This grape is tart: It's splendid for jelly or wine making; and—as anyone from the Middle East knows—its leaves are fine for stuffing. In fact, they're extolled by wild-food forager Bradford Angier for their "delicate acid savor." To use them for cooking, he advises, they "should be gathered in the spring when they have achieved their growth but are still tender."

June and early July in northern New England can still be "springy," so it's a good time to proceed with some Lebanese-style cooking.

Sadie's Walnut-Stuffed Grape Leaves

THE LEAVES

Gather:

50–60 large, tender, wild grape leaves

Cut off the stems close to the leaf itself. Rinse with cold water, blanch quickly in boiling water by dipping in and out, and drain well.

THE STUFFING

In a large skillet, heat:

1/2 cup extra-virgin olive oil

Add and sauté over medium heat till soft and transparent:

1 large onion, finely chopped

Add and toss in the oil to coat:

1 cup basmati rice

Then add:

1/2 cup chopped walnut meats
1/3 cup currants
2 teaspoons chopped fresh dill

1/2 teaspoon powdered cinnamon
1/2 teaspoon sea salt
a lot of freshly ground black pepper

Remove from the heat and let cool.

COMBINING

Drizzle the bottom of a heavy, 2-quart casserole with:

extra-virgin olive oil

Line it with a single layer of grape leaves.

To stuff the remaining leaves, place each leaf, vein-side up, on a cutting board. Onto the center of each leaf place:

1 heaping tablespoon of the rice-walnut mixture

Tuck the bottom of the leaf over the filling, fold the sides over the center, and roll up into a tight, neat packet. Stack the stuffed leaves, folded-side down, in a single layer in the casserole. Arrange a second layer at right angles to the first.

COOKING

Mix together and pour over the stuffed grape leaves:

1/2 cup freshly squeezed lemon juice
2 cups boiling water

Place an inverted heatproof dinner plate over the layers to hold them in place during cooking. If necessary to reach the top of the plate, add:

more boiling water (up to 1/2 cup)

Cover and simmer over medium-low heat till the rice is tender (about 45 minutes). Drain the liquid and cool.

SERVING

Serve at room temperature garnished with lemon wedges. Offer slices of pita bread to mop up the juices. Rice, pasta, or potatoes and a leafy salad are good accompaniments.

While bottled grape leaves are purchasable in any supermarket, they can also be stored for winter by the well-worn method of canning. When you gather and can them yourself, you're sure of no contamination from pesticides or other chemicals. And the use of an acid such as vinegar protects against botulism. As Nicols Fox remarks in SPOILED: THE DANGEROUS TRUTH ABOUT A FOOD CHAIN GONE HAYWIRE, "The inherent guarantee of acidic foods . . . explains the many recipes for pickled foods in old cookbooks. Okra and green beans were safer when pickled. Chutneys with vinegars and spices were a safe medium for a mixture of vegetables."

Canned Grape Leaves

MAKES ABOUT 2 QUARTS

Collect:

75–85 large, tender, new grape leaves
Trim the stems to 1/2 inch with scissors.

In a porcelainized saucepan, combine:

10 cups water
1/2 cup canning salt
Bring to a boil. Blanch the grape leaves in this briefly—about 5 seconds.

Then place them in a colander and drain thoroughly.

In a canning kettle, bring a lot of water to a boil over high heat and sterilize two widemouthed quart canning jars by boiling for 5 minutes.

Once the grape leaves are cool enough to handle, place them shiny-side up in stacks of 12, with the largest leaves on the bottom. Roll up each set of 12 stem-first, and tie with string. Pack vertically into your hot canning jars and tuck in:

several slices of well-washed lemon

In a porcelainized saucepan, bring to a boil:

2 cups water
2 cups cider vinegar
OR white distilled vinegar

Pour this over your leaves, tucking them down at the top, making certain they're covered but leaving 1/2 inch of headroom. If you need more liquid, mix more water and vinegar in equal proportions. Remove air bubbles by poking gently into each jar along the sides with a chopstick.

Meanwhile, in a small saucepan of hot water, heat metal bands and lids to just under boiling. When they're hot, drop them into a sieve and drain.

Wipe off the rims of your grape-leaf-filled jars. Place the hot lids and bands on the jars, screwing the bands down tightly. (At this point you can cool your jars of grape leaves and refrigerate them for up to 6 months. For longer storage, proceed with canning.)

Place your hot, filled jars on a rack in a big pot of hot water. Add more hot water if necessary to come at least 1 inch above the jar tops. Cover, bring to a boil, and process in this boiling-water bath for 15 minutes. (If you haven't canned before, see page 38.) Measure processing time from when a rolling boil begins.

When time is up, remove the jars with tongs and let them cool on a towel-covered counter to prevent breakage.

When the jars are completely cool, remove the metal bands, check to see that each jar is safely sealed—the metal lid will feel slightly concave when you press it—rinse gently, wipe dry, and label.

Store in a cool, dark place.

Rinse leaves briefly before using.

NOTE: If you're using commercially canned grape leaves, drain them and soak in cold water for about 30 minutes. Drain and rinse again until all the salt is removed. Squeeze gently to remove moisture. Cut off the stems when you're ready to cook.

SUMMER

Hot weather arrives with July in central Maine, and the
Simply Grande Gardens enjoy roasting days and cooler nights,
which cause the string beans, cucumbers, corn, zucchini, peppers,
and tomatoes—along with weeds—to flourish.

Someone once said that you can hear the corn growing if you
listen carefully enough. Certainly the raccoons do. They know when
an ear is ripe before a gardener does. Moreover, they actually
giggle when tearing down stalks to get at succulent ears.

At Simply Grande the summer's largesse brings awe
along with hard work and harder muscles:
truly a great way to stay in shape.

pease: PLURAL.
ARCHAIC OF PEA.

Peas–Mostly Shell

According to Professor Charles Heiser of Harvard, peas and lentils were among the very early cultivated plants of the Near East. *Pisum sativum,* the pea, has two main varieties, he says: "the field pea, now used mostly for forage and dried peas, and the garden pea with its high sugar content, considered by some to be the aristocratic food plant of this family."

But the Far East seems to have known it first. In 1970, reports Reay Tannahill, "a University of Hawaii expedition at 'Spirit Cave,' near the Burmese border of Thailand, found the seeds of beans [surely the Old World fava bean], cucumbers, water chestnuts, and peas 'that might have been cultivated.'" Carbon dating to roughly 9750 B.C. put them almost 2,000 years before agriculture began in the Near East or Central America.

Professor Jared Diamond, writing later, suggests that techniques of radiocarbon dating have improved, and errors from the 1960s and 1970s have been adjusted. Southwest Asia, he points out in *Guns, Germs, and Steel,* has the earliest definite dates for both plant domestication (around 8500 B.C.) and animal domestication (around 8000 B.C.). It also "has by far the largest number of accurate radiocarbon dates for early food production." He adds, "Dates for China are nearly as early."

Easily dried and stored peas, in any case, early took to traveling. They've been found in debris left by people who inhabited the Languedoc region of southern France in the seventh millennium B.C., along with chickpeas, vetches, broad beans, and lentils. These seem to have been cultivated. Alternately, the place could have been occupied only seasonally, at the time for harvesting the seeds. According to Christie White, a horticulturist at Old Sturbridge Village in Massachusetts, carbonized samples dating from 7000 B.C. have been found as far north as Switzerland.

By 2300 B.C. the people of Harappa and Mohenjodaro, the two great cities of India's Indus valley, grew the field pea. Later, peas became a standby of Egyptians, Greeks, and Romans. Roman Legions gathered them from the sands around their camps in Numidia and Palestine to supplement their rations of flour, oil, and salt meat.

Our word *pea*, in fact, is from the Latin *pisum*, itself derived from the Greek *pison*. The Old English term *pise*, becoming *pease* a little later, was misunderstood as a plural, so the singular *pea* was coined.

The form in which peas were mainly eaten in Roman and medieval times was dried. Historian Maguelonne Toussaint-Samat notes in *History of Food* that the satirist Rabelais (circa 1483–1553) enjoyed dried peas cooked "with a good piece of bacon—'cum commentato' (with a gloss), as he explained."

Medieval cooking was pretty basic. Iron cauldrons filled with whatever vegetables and meats were available hung permanently over the fire in peasant hut and lordly manor alike, probably representing the original stockpot, or *pot-au-feu*. Only for the meatless weeks of Lent were they cleared out.

Savory puddings as well as stews could be cooked in such cauldrons, if "tied in a flaxen cloth and suspended from a pot hook." According to Reay Tannahill, "Pease pudding, that mess of dried legumes which went so well with the boiled salt meat that was the commonest flesh food of the Middle Ages, may have been cooked in this way," giving rise to the old rhyme:

Pease pudding hot, pease pudding cold,
Pease pudding in the pot, nine days old.

Both iron cauldron and "pease" made it to New England. Waverly Root and Richard De Rochemont stated in *Eating in America* that "In 1607 colonists devoted to the English Establishment founded Jamestown, Virginia, and in 1620 colonists hostile to the English Establishment founded Plymouth, Massachusetts." Within a single generation, they say, New England became a farming community able to take care of itself.

It wasn't easy. After the first year when Pilgrims, unaccustomed to the heat of American summers, planted peas too late, they practically burned up on the vines.

While dried peas were an important food in Europe during the Middle Ages, fresh peas weren't enjoyed until the 16th century. Then, according to Harold McGee in *On Food and Cooking*, they became a great delicacy and luxury at (naturally) the French court. "Both the wife of Louis XIV and the mistress of Louis XV recorded their infatuation with this innovation," he says.

"Green peas, or *petits pois*, made their entrance into French gastronomy some 60 years after the *mange-tout* or sugar pea, which had come from Dutch market gardens in the time of King Henri IV," suggests Maguelonne Toussaint-Samat. "In January 1660, on his return from Italy where he had been on a confidential mission (learning how to make liqueurs), the Sieur Audiger brought a hamper of green peas back from Genoa and presented it to Louis XIV in front of all his eminent courtiers. 'All declared with one voice', Audiger reported proudly, 'that nothing could be better or more of a novelty, and that nothing like them, in that season, had ever been seen in France before.'

"On the King's orders, Audiger entrusted the cooking of this wonderful new Italian vegetable in the French manner to the Sieur Baudoin, whose office it was to attend to such matters. 'There was a little dish of them for the Queen, another for the Cardinal, and the rest were shared between his Majesty and Monsieur' [the king's brother]. No sooner had news of the green peas spread than they became a positive craze: everyone wanted to eat them, at Versailles, in the outlying districts, in the world of finance and the Church. Mme de Sévigné hurried to her writing desk to tell her daughter all about them—while the King indulged himself in indigestion on a royal scale, and his head gardener, La Quintinie, worked miracles to raise young green peas in the glasshouses of Versailles."

England, ever slow to rhapsodize over food, heard *petits pois à la française* accused of toxicity by Oliver Goldsmith in the next century. The French way of cooking them, according to Goldsmith, made them practically inedible. And for once English cooking does seem superior. Green peas flavored only with mint leaves, instead of the onion and lettuce of the French tradition, are truly delicious.

Although today we tend to think of the peas eaten by our forebears as being of the dry variety suitable only for pea soup, according to Christie White the fresh green variety was popular in England at the time of our colonial period. Even ediblepod varieties are mentioned in old books, she reports: "They're not as recent as one usually imagines."

Peas have a significance beyond taste and nutrition: Gregor Mendel, the Austrian monk who discovered the laws of genetics, used them in his little garden for his famous experiments. Says Jean Carper in *The Food Pharmacy*, "Very soon after Mendel's forgotten discoveries had been brought to light again by a Dutch botanist in 1900, an American named George Harrison Shull began Mendelian researches into corn." The rest, as they say, is history.

The Fourth of July has always been considered "pea day" in Maine, the legumes served along with poached salmon to celebrate. And although the building of dams on the Kennebec and other rivers where fabulous anadromous fish used to spawn destroyed nearly all of Maine's salmon fishery in the 1800s, with the fight to restore that fishery remaining an uphill struggle, peas at least are still solidly on the menu.

Well they should be. Among other nutrients, a cupful contains 7.9 grams of protein, 3.2 grams of fiber, 934 International Units of vitamin A, 58.4 milligrams of vitamin C, 3.1 International Units of vitamin E, 36 milligrams of calcium, and

357 milligrams of potassium. Loaded with soluble fiber that stimulates the body to reduce its LDL cholesterol, peas are said to help control blood sugar, and are therefore an excellent food for diabetics. They may even lower blood pressure and help prevent certain infections and cancers.

Here's something to meditate on: According to Carper, "green peas . . . contain well-known antifertility agents." "The population of Tibet has remained stationary for the last 200 years and the staple of the diet of the Tibetans consists of barley and peas," reported Dr. S. N. Sanyal of the Calcutta Bacteriological Institute in 1949. In a world swarming with over six billion people as of October 1999, peas might be better news than anyone suspected.

At any rate, don't forget to enjoy their taste.

GARDENING NOTES

PEAS

CHOOSING SEEDS: There are four types:

Shell peas: The traditional pea. These need to be removed from the pod, which is tough and inedible.

Snow peas: Served in Chinese restaurants, these peas are small, and their pods are flat and edible when ripe.

Snap peas: Fat peas in edible pods.

Dry peas: The traditional pea for splitting and soup.

You can choose either dwarf types, which need no trellis, or climbing types, which need strong support.

Seeds come treated or untreated; the untreated kind are more susceptible to rotting in prolonged cold, wet weather. There are 110 seeds per ounce; 1 pound sows 100 feet of double row.

CULTIVATION: Choose a well-drained soil or use raised beds, and prepare as early in spring as possible. Sow thick (10 to 12 seeds per foot) in two parallel rows 6 inches apart. Separate double rows by 3 feet for dwarfs, or 5 to 6 feet for climbers. (This space can be used for early potatoes or other crops.) For increased yields, sow bacterial inoculants with the seeds, or shake them on the ground afterward.

Collineal-hoe between the rows every 2 weeks until peas start spreading. Be careful not to cut off the delicate pea stalks.

You'll need to build a strong support structure for climbing peas. It could be branches stuck in the ground, chicken wire spread between metal stakes, fishing net hung from a top bar on poles, or a homemade string arrangement. Some climbing types grow to 7 feet tall, but after they reach about 2 feet, all peas need weekly attention with baling twine to keep the vines from flopping over.

To keep weeds down and the soil cool and moist, mulch generously between the rows.

DISEASES: Fusarium (pea root rot) causes browning and drying of the foliage from the ground up. Choose disease-resistant varieties and rotate your crops.

Powdery mildew causes a white powdery mold on leaves, stems, and pods in hot weather. Expect it, or choose resistant varieties.

HARVESTING: For a special treat, harvest some small stems and leaves as salad greens. Harvest pods early in the morning for the best-tasting peas, and to slow the development of powdery mildew.

Shell and snap peas: Wait till the peas are really fat in their pods.

Snow peas: Harvest when the peas and pods are small to medium sized. Harvest two or three times per week.

Dry peas: Wait until the pods have dried.

Snow and snap peas develop strings along the pod suture that should be removed, along with the attachment to the stem, before cooking.

Fourth of July Jewels

Shell out:
   1 pound fresh peas per person
You should end up with 1 cup of peas per person.

Place in a heavy-bottomed saucepan with:
   about 1 inch milk
Add:
   a few fresh mint leaves

Bring almost to a boil, remove from the heat, and let rest, covered, until the peas are *just* tender, about 15 minutes. Don't allow the milk to burn!

Once the peas are *al dente*, remove the mint leaves and serve as is with a light sprinkling of:
   sea salt
   some freshly ground black pepper

The milk makes a thin "sauce" to be eaten with the peas, wasting no nutrients —a traditional New England attitude.

NOTE: Cold peas (cooked in water) can be marinated in a little oil and vinegar or freshly squeezed lemon juice and served as a salad by themselves. Or try sprinkling them over leafy greens with tomatoes and other crudités.

For generations the Fourth of July's new peas accompanied fresh-caught *Salmo salar*, the gorgeous Atlantic salmon. Poaching is perhaps the best cooking method to retain the salmon's natural moisture and tenderness. But how to bake, poach, or broil a truly large specimen, timing it correctly so that it emerges from the pan barely done, beautifully firm and juicy, is the challenge.

One prescription for odorless cooking and tender flesh calls for baking the fish in a preheated 300°F oven. The use of a meat thermometer and removal from the oven when internal temperature reaches 145° to 150°F ensures perfection.

Poaching necessitates the use of a stock or, as the French call it, a court bouillon (court is French for "short"). This recipe first appeared in Jean Ann's NEW MAINE COOKING. It works to perfection.

Fourth of July Poached Salmon

SERVES 6–8

THE COURT BOUILLON

In a large pot, combine:
   3 1/2 quarts water plus 1 cup cider vinegar OR 3 cups dry white wine or saké plus 2 quarts water
Add:
   1 medium-sized onion, minced
   2 garlic cloves, smashed
   1/2 cup chopped celery with leaves

OR 1/4 cup lovage leaves
1 bay leaf
1 teaspoon black peppercorns
1/2 lemon, thinly sliced
1 tablespoon sea salt
1 sprig fresh dill weed OR thyme
1 whole clove
Simmer for about 15 minutes, till the flavor permeates the liquid.

POACHING

Clean and gently wipe with a cloth:
   1 (7- to 10-pound) absolutely fresh, prepared salmon
Wrap it in cheesecloth, leaving the ends free. Fold the ends over the top. (Once the fish is done, the ends can be grasped to lift it out of your baking pan easily.)

Place the salmon on a rack in a fish poacher or large baking dish. If you have no rack, line the bottom of the pan with coarsely shredded lettuce leaves to act as a buffer before introducing the fish. (Lettuce also adds a subtle flavor.)

Gently pour in hot court bouillon (above) to cover, adding more hot water if necessary. Bring to a boil over high heat, reduce the heat immediately, and simmer for 10 minutes per inch of fish thickness (measured at its thickest part).

Once the flesh begins to flake easily along the backbone, lift the salmon out immediately. Drain it well and place it on a hot platter.

SERVING

Garnish with lemon slices and chopped fresh parsley or watercress and serve immediately.

NOTE: To serve your salmon cold, let it cool on a rack before unwrapping it. In the meantime, boil down the court bouillon to half, then use it to make a clear gel with unflavored gelatin per directions on the box.

Spoon a layer of gel gently over the fish. Arrange paper-thin slices of carrot flowers, thinly sliced pimiento-stuffed olives, and flat sprigs of parsley on it for decoration. Wash with another thin layer to provide luster.

A simple recipe for cooking peas is derived from the French. It's perfect with any of the season's first tender lettuce leaves, such as cos or oak leaf.

French Peas

SERVES 2–3

In a medium-sized pot, heat:
3 tablespoons extra-virgin olive oil
Add:
4 cups freshly shelled peas
Cover with a moderately thick layer of:
lettuce leaves

Cover tightly and steam very slowly over very low heat for about 15 minutes. Check often to see when pea tenderness peaks. Don't overcook.

Serve with the wilted lettuce if you please—possibly sliced into strips.

A more complex recipe for enjoying fresh, green peas is influenced by traditional Indian cuisine. In fact, nothing tastes better than a pea curry with spices sautéed in hot oil, buttermilk, or stock, and vegetables simmered till just tender, all served over hot rice with an array of condiments. In this recipe tofu can be substituted for panir—an easy-to-make yogurt cheese. But panir is best.

Pea, Tofu, and Tomato Curry with Panir

SERVES 6

THE PANIR

Into a large double boiler, pour:
2 quarts milk
Bring to a scald and remove from the heat.

In a small bowl, combine:
1/2 cup yogurt
2 tablespoons freshly squeezed, strained lemon juice
Stir into the scalded milk thoroughly. Curds will immediately begin to solidify and separate from the whey.

Line a stainless-steel colander with a large square of double-thickness cheesecloth. Pour in the curds and whey. Tie the cloth ends together to form a bag, and hang it from a hook over a bowl to drain. (Save the whey for soups or bread making.)

When the whey has drained from the curds, twist the cloth to squeeze out any excess liquid. Then place the still-wrapped cheese on a slightly tilted board, set a 15-pound weight on top, and let drain until the cheese is firm and compact—perhaps 6 hours.

Once it's firm, unwrap and refrigerate, covered, until you're ready to use it.

THE CURRY

Drain well and cut into 1/2-inch cubes:
   panir to equal 1 1/2 cups

Set a wok on its ring, then add and heat to 370°F:
   3 cups peanut oil
Deep-fry the well-dried panir cubes quickly till golden. Drain them on a rack and set aside.

Pour out the oil and wipe your wok. Replace it on its ring and add:
   2 tablespoons extra-virgin olive oil
Sauté for 30 seconds:
   2 tablespoons minced fresh
     gingerroot
   1 tablespoon minced garlic
Add and cook together over moderate heat, stirring occasionally, till limp:
   1 cup finely chopped onion
   1 teaspoon sea salt
Stir in:
   1/4 cup water
Add and blend well:
   1 teaspoon powdered turmeric
   1/4 teaspoon cayenne powder
     (optional)
   1 teaspoon ground coriander
   1 tablespoon Simple Garam Masala
     (see the sidebar)
Stir in and bring to a boil over high heat:
   3/4 cup water
   2 cups finely chopped fresh tomatoes
   OR 2 cups canned tomatoes, well
     drained
Reduce the heat and simmer, partially covered, for 10 minutes, stirring occasionally. Then add:

   1 1/2 cups fresh green peas
     (about 1 1/2 pounds unshelled)
     OR pea pods OR snap peas cut
     into 1/2-inch sections
   1 teaspoon maple syrup
Simmer for 3 minutes uncovered. Add:
   the panir cubes
   1 tablespoon finely chopped fresh
     cilantro
Heat through for 2 more minutes.

SERVING

Serve in a large hot bowl, garnished with 2 more tablespoons of chopped fresh cilantro or parsley, to accompany rice or another whole grain. Offer small side dishes of raisins, yogurt, grated coconut, nuts, banana or apple slices (dipped in lemon juice to prevent browning), and chutneys from which people may serve themselves.

Garam masala differs from cook to cook, each one making adjustments for the dish at hand.

Simple Garam Masala

Combine and store in a tightly covered jar:
1 tablespoon powdered cardamom
1 tablespoon powdered cinnamon
1 teaspoon ground cloves
1 teaspoon powdered cumin
1/2 teaspoon freshly ground black
   pepper

Other Kinds of Peas

Besides the little green jewels traditionally popped from their pods before eating, there are snow peas and snap peas, grown primarily for their pods.

Snow peas, for instance, were apparently developed in England during the 19th century, but were so instantly adopted by the Chinese that they became known as Chinese snow peas. These should be harvested before pods fill out.

Snap peas, on the other hand, taste sweetest when the pods are completely filled. It would be a mistake to pick them too soon. Their history is fascinating. Sugarsnap varieties had apparently once been familiar, according to Fedco Seeds, but "they had been lost and almost forgotten when breeder Calvin Lamborn first got interested in them in the late 1960s. When Lamborn released his tall variety in 1978 he created a sensation, and his cultivar won the gold All-America Award. A few years later it was voted the #1 all-time All-America selection."

According to Johnny's Selected Seeds of Albion, Maine, unlike the flatter snow peas, snap pea pods "develop tightly around the peas, so the pods are round and firm." As they grow toward good snapping stage—which means plump and snappable like a fresh green bean—"strings" develop along the suture of the pod. These should be stripped before cooking—a great job for kids. Start at the stem end and pull the first string away from its concave edge. When snapping into bite sizes, remove lesser strings from the convex sides as well. It takes seconds but improves eating quality.

Snow pea pods and snaps are always fine raw. But even the tops of young Sugarsnaps can be harvested for greens. They're good in mesclun or lightly sautéed.

As with all Oriental dishes, vegetable preparation before cooking is mandatory and cooking is brief. Half a pound of Sugarsnaps is enough for two people.

Curried Sugarsnap Stir-Fry

SERVES 2

Place a wok on its collar over medium heat and warm it. Pour in and heat:

2 tablespoons extra-virgin olive oil

Add:

1 heaping teaspoon hot curry powder
1/2 large onion, chopped

Cook till the onion is very tender and beginning to brown.

In the meantime, "string" (as described above) and snap into bite-sized pieces:

2 cups Sugarsnap peas

Add them to the tender onion mix along with:

freshly ground black pepper
sea salt to taste (optional)
a little water, as necessary to permit
steaming

Steam for 4 to 5 minutes or till barely tender.

Serve with rice or new potatoes and a tossed leafy salad for a simple meal.

Stir-Fry with Sugarsnaps and Carrots

SERVES 2

"String" each plump Sugarsnap pod as described on page 113, and snap it into bite-sized bits to measure:

2 cups Sugarsnap pods

Drain and slice:

1 cup water chestnuts
OR fresh sunchokes (optional)

In a small saucepan, bring to a boil:

1 cup water

Slip in and cook for 3 minutes:

1 small carrot, cut into thin slices

Drain and set aside to cool.

Warm a wok, then heat in it:

2 tablespoons extra-virgin olive oil

Add and let sizzle for a few seconds:

1 large garlic clove, crushed

Discard the garlic. Place in the garlic-seasoned oil:

1 heaping cup bok choi OR joi
choi, cut into 1-inch pieces,
OR any chopped green in season
(such as Swiss chard)

Stir-fry for about 1 minute. Add:

1/2 teaspoon sea salt
1/2 teaspoon maple syrup

Stir in the carrots and sunchokes or water chestnuts. Toss a few times, then mix in quickly:

1 tablespoon shoyu (naturally
fermented soy sauce)
the prepared snap peas

Steam for approximately 1 minute.

Serve immediately with rice or barley and a tossed salad.

Turnip Greens

New England colonists brought turnips to the New World with them. In 1634 Englishman William Wood described provisions to be taken for the sea journey, as well as "the quantity necessary to ensure enough food for a year and a half after landing." He noted that "The ground afford very good kitchin Gardens, for Turneps."

For tips on growing turnips, see page 313.

Turnip greens are an old New England favorite, providing not only nutritious eating but also a way of thinning the thickly planted roots to provide space for the big, round critters that will appear come fall.

According to J. I. Rodale, "the tops are an excellent source of A and C vitamins and of calcium"—women, take note. A cup, in fact, contains 4,180 International Units of vitamin A, 33 milligrams of vitamin C, 105 milligrams of calcium, and 163 milligrams of potassium, among other nutrients.

While tender turnip tops may be eaten raw in salads, or lightly steamed (serve with extra-virgin olive oil and freshly squeezed lemon juice, as you would spinach) before the bulbous roots appear, the following recipe is especially fine for gardeners, since it depends on freshly picked, small, sweet turnips as well as their tops.

Turnip Greens with Baby Turnips

SERVES 4

THE "NEEPS"

Purchase or pull from the garden:

16 small, 1-inch turnips

Cut off the leaves and set them aside. Trim, wash, and dry the turnips well. Peel thinly if you please.

In a large skillet, heat:

3 tablespoons extra-virgin olive oil
OR sunflower seed oil

Add the turnips in one layer and sauté for 5 minutes or until lightly browned all over. Reduce the heat, cover, and cook till tender but still crisp, about 6 minutes. Season with:

sea salt
freshly ground black pepper

Remove from the pan and keep warm.

THE GREENS

Cut large leaves into diagonal slices. In the same pan, heat:

2 tablespoons extra-virgin olive oil
OR sunflower seed oil

Add the greens, stir to coat well, and wilt for about 3 minutes.

SERVING

After seasoning to taste, arrange the two aspects nicely on a platter—perhaps the neeps over the greens—and serve immediately with new potatoes or rice, and a leafy salad.

Beet Greens

Mid-July in New England means a plethora of greens—or potherbs as colonists called them—including those of beets.

Beets have apparently been on the menu since prehistory. Native to a wide swath of Eurasia from Britain to India, they were appreciated in Roman times mainly for their greens. A first-century Roman agriculturist named Columella felt that the garden variety was "curious" and that it "owes its name, *Beta Vulgaris*," to its "physical resemblance to the second letter of the alphabet."

We seldom see beet roots growing in the form of a *B* (have we missed something?), even when thickly planted, so it's difficult to translate what Columella meant. Nor, apparently, could other Romans. In fact, they simply preferred the leaves.

Pliny the Elder, whose *Natural History* remained an authority on scientific matters up to the Middle Ages, referred to beet roots as "the crimson nether parts," relegating them to pharmacists, surgeons, and soothsayers while choosing the red-veined outer leaves for salads.

According to chef Bert Greene in *Greene on Greens*, this plucking had historical significance, because "the habit of picking the leaves created a swollen and juicy root, which was to provide future tables with one of the tenderest comestibles that grows."

I'm not sure that leaf plucking would produce swollen roots, but it's an intriguing thought. Greene adds, "It took close to a millennium before some trencherman had the good sense to consume a plateful drenched with butter and a jot of lemon juice."

Which is a very good idea.

An amusing recipe comes to us from 14th-century France. Guillaume Tirel, known as Taillevent, cook to Charles V, included only one vegetable dish in his group of recipes for Lent, and it sounds very Arabic: a purée of white beets and cress "fried and boiled in almond milk."

BEETS AND BEET GREENS

CHOOSING SEEDS: Many people don't care for beets or beet greens.
Commercial beets have a funny aftertaste, and beet greens in most stores are
small, limp, and insipid. Organic beets, however, grown in good soil, are so
sweet and tasty that kids and adults drool.

Choose several varieties just for fun. Some, such as 'Bull's Blood', with deep
red leaves, complement any mesclun. 'Forono' is good for pickles because it's
cylindrical and easily chopped into handy slices. 'Lutz' is the keeper of choice.
Many others—pink, golden, white, or with multicolored rings—provide a
visual or taste treat.

A 1/2-ounce packet sows 100 row feet. The seeds keep well.

CULTIVATION: Beet seeds are actually pods containing several viable seeds.
Plant through springtime, in rows with a wheel seeder. Space rows 10 inches
apart for small beets, and 14 inches apart for big storage beets. Sprinkle the
ground with borax—about 1/4 teaspoon per 20-foot row.

When the leaves first appear, collineal-hoe between the rows, and repeat
10 to 14 days later. When you start thinning for beet greens, pull out all the
weeds within the beet row. Your beet bed should be virtually free of weeds
from then on.

Irrigate beets in hot, dry weather.

PESTS AND DISEASES: Beets get scab, like potatoes, especially in alkaline soils
and in dry summers. The borax treatment should prevent internal hollows or
browning in hot weather.

Deer and mice love the sweetness of beets. Deer will go for both the greens,
which they pull up in springtime, and the roots, which they graze on in fall.
You may need an electric fence around beet beds. Mice also nibble at the
fattening roots in fall, especially if the beet bed is surrounded by hay mulch.

HARVESTING: Beet greens can be harvested when the plants are more than
about 6 inches tall. The idea is to thin the remaining beets in the row until
they're spaced just right to allow for full maturity of the root in summer. For
'Lutz', which are big beets when mature, you should leave at least 4 inches
between remaining plants. For others, 2 inches is plenty. When thinning,
choose big young beets for maturation. Pull out the remaining plants, top and

root and all. Cut up for three separate vegetables: leaves for beet greens, stalks for stir-fries, and baby beets. If you're careful, you can string out the beet green season over 3 or 4 weeks, and each week the greens become bigger and better.

Don't delay harvesting full-sized beet roots in fall: Their flavor deteriorates if roots are left in the ground after maturity. Break off leaves until only a stub of leaf bases remains. These leaves are still good for greens. Try freezing them for a winter treat. Keep the beets moist in storage—drying them out softens them quickly.

An interesting phenomenon is that the leaves of root vegetables are often more nutritious than the roots themselves. Beet tops are a good source of potassium and calcium, not to mention some 2,308 International Units of vitamin A per cupful.

Steamed Beet Greens

SERVES 4

Pull or purchase:
1 1/2 pounds beet greens
Trim away the tiny roots and wash the rest well.

Steam the young things quickly in a porcelainized pot without any other liquid than the water in which they've been washed. Fork them over often to prevent burning.

When the greens are tender, drain them well, slip them onto a warmed platter, and, using a sharp knife, cut them into wedges or squares.

Offer diners a choice of extra-virgin olive oil, some freshly squeezed lemon juice, and a little shoyu (naturally fermented soy sauce) to sprinkle on top.

Beet greens are also fine when sautéed.

Sautéed Beet Greens with Garlic

SERVES 4

Pull or purchase:
1 1/2 pounds beet greens
Trim away the tiny roots and wash the rest well.

In a skillet or wok, heat:
2 tablespoons extra-virgin olive oil
Add and sauté briefly:
several fat garlic cloves, minced

Add the clean greens and toss till they're wilted and tender—perhaps 4 minutes.

Sprinkle with:
sea salt
freshly ground black pepper

Serve immediately on a warmed platter.

An Old World Favorite Fava or Broad Beans

While few Americans have heard of them, the English and other Europeans, as well as Mexicans, Brazilians, and the people of India and the Mediterranean, all love broad beans—those fat, lima-bean-like dollops native to the Old World. They're also called faba or horse beans, English beans, and windsor beans.

Vicia faba probably originated in southeastern Afghanistan, central Asia, and the Himalayan foothills before traveling to other places. According to Harold McGee in his book *On Food and Cooking,* the fava bean had been domesticated by 3000 B.C. The Sumerians, for instance, were largely vegetarians, beans being one of their staples. But some writers put bean culture even farther back—to 8000 B.C. Some even push its origin to Thailand.

Ultimately arriving in ancient Greece, at any rate, the fava became one of the crops that Greeks plowed into their light soil as a green manure. Leaves added humus, and roots provided nitrogen. They were also used as ballot papers in election procedures, and were eaten green, in their pods. Herodotus, however, reporting in 484 B.C., remarked that Egyptian priests regarded the fava as unclean, while Pythagoras blamed it for insomnia and bad dreams. In fact, McGee tells us, Pythagoras forbade his followers to eat favas, "on the grounds (it is thought) that beans contained the souls of the dead."

When the fava arrived in Rome, the Romans felt differently. Served at funeral banquets as an important part of the offering made to dead relatives, it was mentioned by Cato as one of the vegetables on which the living largely survived. Cakes of meal called *lomentum* made from dried beans were eaten when there was a grain shortage. Roman Legions, of course, took favas traveling. After they left Britain late in the fourth century, standby vegetables were leeks, cabbages, dried peas, and broad beans.

While soy and mung beans are native to Asia, and peanuts, lima beans, and common beans (navy, kidney, black, pinto, and many others) came from the Americas, lentils, broad beans, peas, and chickpeas basically arrived from the Fertile Crescent of the Near East. On average, says Harold McGee, these legume seeds are twice as rich in protein as grains, and especially well stocked in iron and the B vitamins.

He adds, "A remarkable and as yet unexplained sign of their status in the ancient world is the fact that each of the four major legumes known to Rome lent its name to a prominent Roman family." *Lentulus* came from the lentil,

Piso from the pea, *Cicero*—the most distinguished of them all—from the chickpea, and *Fabius* from the faba bean. "No other food group," he exclaims, "has been so honored."

In New England favas are planted as early as peas, and the big pods with their few succulent, enclosed seeds are usually harvested at the same time. They're good additions to soups.

For more tips on growing fava beans, see page 134.

Basic Favas

Once fava pods are big and fat, shell out:

a handful of beans per diner

Place them in a heavy saucepan and add:
about 1 inch of water
sea salt
freshly ground white pepper
2–3 garlic cloves, crushed (optional)
Bring to a boil then cover tightly, turn down the heat, and simmer for about 30 minutes or till the beans are very tender. Check the water for evaporation and add more if necessary.

Serve well cooked and hot.

The English like favas with a white sauce of some kind. This Lebanese yogurt recipe works well.

Laban

In a small saucepan, combine:
1 cup yogurt
1 egg white
1 tablespoon cornstarch
1/2 teaspoon sea salt

Using a whisk, cook over high heat, stirring gently and constantly *in one*

direction only till the mixture begins to bubble. Lower the heat and continue to cook, stirring constantly, till smooth and creamy—about 2 minutes.

Season with a little white wine (optional) and a lot of freshly chopped parsley (also optional).

Dilled Fava Bean Sauté

SERVES 4–6

Place a wok on its ring, heat it, and when it's hot pour in:
2 tablespoons extra-virgin olive oil

Add:
2 pounds tender, well-cooked
fava beans
Sauté, stirring constantly, for about 3 minutes.

Add and mix in:
1/4 cup freshly squeezed lemon juice
Sprinkle with:
1/4 cup chopped fresh dill
sea salt to taste
freshly ground black pepper

Serve right away with potatoes or rice, a green leafy salad, and other vegetables.

FAVA CAUTION: Harold McGee's *On Food and Cooking* notes that "People of Mediterranean background may suffer from favism, a serious anemic condition that results from eating undercooked broad beans or inhaling the plant's pollen. The disease appears to involve a genetically determined sensitivity to the fava bean toxin vicine, which causes oxidative damage to the red blood cells of susceptible individuals." One key, of course, is to cook the beans well.

Basil

Remarks Helen Noyes Webster in a book called *Herbs for Use and for Delight,* "Almost as precious as the Bible to the early settlers were their herbals of Tusser, Culpepper, and Coles, which contained all that was necessary for the housewife to know about . . . herbs. . . . Sweet basil is one of the herbs mentioned before 1806 in colonial garden records."

Basil had taken a long time traveling to New England. According to Tom Stobart in *Herbs, Spices, and Flavourings,* "Basil probably came from India to Europe overland via the Middle East. It arrived in Britain in the sixteenth century and reached America in the seventeenth, so its use in the West is comparatively recent."

"The ancient Greeks knew it," agrees Jill Norman in *Salad Herbs: How to Grow and Use Them in the Kitchen,* "and Virgil mentions it." In fact, the basils are mentioned from the old Greeks and Romans through Dioscorides, Theophrastus, and others.

In its birthplace, however, basil was considered more than a culinary plant of strong aroma and tempting, spicy foliage. A 1936 book titled *A Garden of Herbs* by Eleanour Sinclair Rohde tells us that "in the East there is no herb with more sacred associations. Tulasi" *(Ocimum sanctum L.),* sometimes spelled *tulsi,* "is a holy herb to the Hindoos, and is grown near every temple and dwelling that it may protect those who cultivate it from misfortune, and guide them to Heaven. It is sacred to Vishnu, and 'propitious,' 'perfumed,' 'devil-destroying,' are only a few of the epithets applied to it. . . . When an Indian dies they place on his breast a leaf of tulasi; when he is dead they wash the head of the corpse with water in which flax-seeds and tulasi leaves have been dropped. . . . Good fortune awaits those who build their house on a spot where tulasi has grown freely, and there is no forgiveness in this world or the next for any one who wilfully uproots it. It must never be picked at all except for some worthy purpose, and this prayer is said: 'Mother Tulasi, be thou propitious if I gather you with care, be merciful unto me, O Tulasi, Mother of the world.'

"It is curious," she adds, "that among Western nations one of the oldest associations with basil is hatred and abuse. The ancient Greeks believed basil must be sown with words of abuse or else it would not flourish, and to this day the French have the proverb, 'semer le basilic'—slandering. Both amongst Western and Eastern nations basil is associated with death, and in Crete the plant is associated with the Evil One. Yet in Western Europe it is regarded as of sovereign power against witches! The Italians say basil engenders sympathy between those who wear it; and to Moldavians it is an enchanted flower of such potency, that a man who accepts a sprig from a woman will love her for ever. Bacon records the curious superstition that if basil is exposed too much to the sun it changes into wild thyme, and nearly every old herbalist assures us that rue and basil will never grow near each other.

"The very earliest reference, to my knowledge," she says, "is where Chrysippus, about 250 B.C., declares that 'Ocimum exists only to drive men insane.'"

In *Herbs,* editor Lesley Bremness assures us that "Basil was found growing around Christ's tomb after the resurrection, so some Greek Orthodox churches use it to prepare the holy water, and pots of basil are set below church altars."

In England it was one of the old strewing herbs, and English literature abounds with allusions to it. "Read any of the Tusser editions of *Five Hundred Points of Husbandry* since 1557," advises Rohde with amusement, "turn to his directions for May and then go stroke your basil, as he bids, that 'It may grow and multiply' the better for your sympathy."

There are many varieties of basil, and not all came from India. Says Helen Noyes Webster, "Before 1848, when DeCandolle made his long list of *Ocimum* species and varieties from all over the world, the early herbalists seemed to content themselves with these three 'Sortes,' the Great Basil, the Medium Basil, and the Lesser Basil, and this naive classification is common in herbals up to the eighteenth century. Exactly to what modern species some of these might be compared we can only conjecture."

Bush basil, according to Bremness, is a South American native. "In Haiti, it belongs to the pagan love goddess Erzulie, as a powerful protector, and in rural Mexico it is sometimes carried in pockets to return a lover's roving eye."

For tips on growing basil, see page 126.

Whatever species we choose to identify or grow today, *Ocimum,* either dried or fresh, is a kitchen partner *par excellence.*

When dried, suggests Helen Noyes Webster, the large wrinkled leaves and short spikes of crowded flowers of curly basil (probably a French agricultural variety of so-called lettuce leaf) make "the best herb pepper when in combination with costmary, savory, and marjoram."

Maine herbalist Madeleine H. Siegler of Monks Hill Herbs remarks in a pamphlet called *Growing Herbs in New England* that "Sweet Basil *(Ocimum basilicum)* dries well, if your seed is 'lettuce leaf variety.'" She also suggests that you "chop and freeze the leaves as they tend to turn black during drying."

Although John Evelyn, writing in the late 1600s, advised that basil "must be used very sparingly, and for salads, only the tender tops," today the strong, lovely flavor is tantalizing in any vinaigrette for greens, or sprinkled on tomato slices with scallions and an olive oil vinaigrette. Tom Stobart would agree. "Where I lived on the Italian Riviera," he says, "the common snack consisted of a crusty roll split and filled with sliced tomato, salt, olive oil, and a few leaves of fresh basil—no butter of course—just squashed to make the oil and juice impregnate the bread."

"Perhaps the most delicious use of basil," he adds, "is in *pesto Genovese,* which in various forms is found all along the Riviera coast from Genoa to Provence (where it is called *pistou*). The basis is always basil, with garlic, salt, olive oil, Parmesan and sardo (hard Sardinian sheep's milk) cheese, pine nuts and often skinned walnuts—all pounded together to a thick sauce."

Pistou is used to flavor soup; in Italy pesto with plenty of olive oil makes a sauce for spaghetti or trenette.

Pesto/Pistou

**MAKES ENOUGH FOR
1 POUND COOKED PASTA**

Place in your blender or food processor and whiz to a paste:

> **2 cups freshly picked, washed, and dried basil leaves (no stems)**
> **2–3 garlic cloves, crushed**
> **1/2 teaspoon sea salt**
> **freshly ground black pepper**
> **1/4–1/2 cup extra-virgin olive oil**

Add and continue processing until thick and creamy:

> **1/2 cup pine nuts OR walnuts**
> **3/4 cup grated Parmesan AND/OR Romano or Pecorino cheese**

Serve at room temperature with pasta, vegetables—even on toast!

NOTE: You can adjust the amount of oil, basil leaves, and cheese to suit your taste. Pesto freezes well in small amounts if the cheese is left out to be added later.

Tom Stobart shares a recipe for preserving basil leaves in oil in HERBS, SPICES, AND FLAVOURINGS. "If the leaves are dirty, wash and dry; otherwise pack . . . into a clean dry jar, sprinkling a good pinch of salt over each layer. When the jar is full, fill up with olive oil to cover. Close well. This will keep indefinitely in a cool store cupboard or refrigerator and preserves most of the fresh flavour, even though with time it will blacken." The oil will give a flavor of basil to any dish it is used in. Preserved in this way, it's also fine for making pesto.

Basil in Olive Oil

Place in a widemouthed glass jar:

> **a large handful of basil leaves**

Cover with:
extra-virgin olive oil

Cap, and store in a cupboard for a month before using.

Basil in Vinegar

Fill a large, widemouthed glass jar with:
about 2 ounces basil leaves

Cover with:
1 pint red wine vinegar

Let steep for 2 to 3 weeks, then strain off the vinegar into bottles. Put a fresh sprig of herb into each bottle and cap. Store in a dark place.

PERSPICACIOUS PESTO! Pesto doesn't stop with basil. As any bright cook will tell you, experimentation is what makes the kitchen joyous. Parsley can produce a good pesto. So can oregano.

Origanum vulgare, also called wild marjoram, comes to us from Greece, where it covers summer hillsides, giving us legends and the name *oros ganos* (joy-of-the-mountain).

There are several varieties. *Origanum majorana,* or sweet marjoram, apparently was introduced into Europe in the Middle Ages. Ladies put it into sweet bags, nosegays, and washing waters. According to Lesley Bremness in *Herbs,* "Its leaves were also rubbed over heavy oak furniture and floors to give a fragrant polish. In thundery weather, dairymaids would place marjoram by pails of fresh milk" in the belief that it "would preserve its sweetness."

A member of the *Mentha* (mint) family, oregano spreads in the garden like— well, like a weed. Snip it into vinaigrettes along with dill, basil, cilantro, chervil, and other herbs. Tomato sauce, of course, finds it absolutely necessary. But here is . . .

Oregano Pesto

Place in your blender:
1 1/2 cups firmly packed fresh oregano leaves
1/2 cup firmly packed fresh parsley
1/2 cup freshly grated Parmesan OR Romano cheese
1/2 cup extra-virgin olive oil
1/4 teaspoon sea salt
3 freshly peeled garlic cloves
1/4 cup pine nuts, walnuts, OR sunflower seeds

Blend until smooth, adding more oil if necessary. Store in a capped jar in the refrigerator. As with basil pesto, this can be frozen: Add cheese later.

More Herbs

The harvesting and drying of herbs has been and still is an important, time-honored method of preserving summer's bounty and adding zest to winter fare. According to "Harvesting Herbs," an article by Elizabeth B. Neaville appearing in *Culinary Herbs*, the handbook of the *Brooklyn Botanic Garden Record*, it also offers "aesthetic, satisfying pleasure."

In colonial times a woman's kitchen garden always contained herbs, for she was not only the cook but also the font of medicinal lore. Without her ministrations, many a fevered brow would have remained fevered, and such plants as boneset (*Eupatorium* spp.) and eyebright (*Euphrasia* spp.) received their names for obvious reasons. Says Ann Leighton in *Early American Gardens*, "Ladies who arrived from manor houses in England well versed in the arts of distilling and fermenting and brewing, seething and drying, and making waters and spirits and pills and powders, found themselves as busy as any apothecary in England."

When drying herbs, says Neaville, "The goal is to harvest the leaves when they contain the optimum amount of essential oils, that is, oils that volatilize at room temperatures, on which the flavor of the herb depends, and to retain during the drying process the color of the fresh leaves."

To accomplish this, she advises poetically, "herbs ideally are cut soon after the dew has evaporated on a fair day which has been preceded by two full days of sunshine. They should also be cut when the flower buds are just beginning to open, except for mint, which has the most oil in its leaves when in full bloom."

A perennial herb can be cut back one- to two-thirds of its height, and an annual down to 3 or 4 inches.

Since essential oils are fleeting, very little time should elapse between cutting and drying. Herbs "should be collected quickly but gently in an open-weave basket. Stacking them, or stuffing them into plastic bags, generates heat and causes rapid deterioration."

Remove any undesirable material, she continues; wash in warm water, never cold or hot; and, when clean, remove the herbs at once and place them on a bath towel. Pat gently dry.

The next step, of course, is complete drying. If you don't have an electric food dryer, "A clean dark well-ventilated room with an evenly warm temperature ranging from 70–90°F" is needed. "Racks with wood frames covered with muslin, cheesecloth or nylon net"—even "metal window screens with muslin or cheesecloth laid on top"—should be elevated so air can circulate under and around them. A rack atop stacked books on a table is also suggested.

ANNUAL HERBS

Basil, Cilantro, Cutting Celery, Dill, Fennel, Parsley

CHOOSING SEEDS:

Basil: There's plenty of variety to choose from. The standard 'Sweet', 'Genovese', or 'Italian' germinate best and are just great. For size try 'Mammoth', for color try one of the purple varieties, and for something exotic try a spicy or Thai basil.

Cilantro: All varieties are good.

Cutting celery: Try 'Alfina' for an early start, or 'Par-Cel' to grow like parsley.

Dill: 'Bouquet' is the standard, but 'Fernleaf' is slow to bolt.

Fennel: 'Bronze Fennel' is fabulous in mesclun. 'Zeta Fino' is also good for its bulbs.

Parsley: There are two types—curly and plain leaved. Grow both. Plain-leaved parsley is preferred for tabouli.

There are 18,000 seeds per ounce for basil. A package should be all you need of any of the above herbs.

CULTIVATION: All annual herbs benefit from fertile soil and moisture throughout the summer, unlike the perennial herbs (see next page). Plant basil only after the danger of frost is gone. Cilantro and dill both go to seed, so seedlings will probably come up next year wherever you plant them this year. Mulch all of these herbs with hay or grass clippings to keep weeds to a minimum and retain moisture.

Basil, cilantro, and dill: Plant in rows 12 inches apart. Collineal-hoe the bed as soon as you can see where the seedlings are germinating. Then keep hoeing the weeds out until the bed is well established. When the plants are about an inch tall, you can thin to 2 to 4 inches apart for maximum plant size. Use thinned plants to fill out the bed in extra rows if you wish.

Fennel: Replant from flats, or sow seeds directly. Mulch growing fennel well or give it plenty of water. Replanting sometimes causes bolting, as does insufficient water.

Cutting celery and parsley: Plant indoors in March, then transplant 8 inches apart in rows 12 inches apart.

PESTS: Fusarium wilt is basil's worst pest—it's best to ensure that your seeds are fusarium tested. Nothing much bothers the other herbs.

HARVESTING

Basil: Snip or pinch off the top four leaves. This will encourage the growth of buds lower on the stem, discourage bolting, and increase your total harvest. Harvest everything before the leaves turn black in late summer, before the plants bolt, and certainly before the first frost.

Cilantro and dill: Snip the leaves off as long as you can. Then let both go to seed for coriander and dill seeds, respectively.

Cutting celery and parsley: Keep snipping through late fall. Parsley will not bolt. It's a biennial and will, if you cover it with hay to overwinter, produce seeds the second year.

Fennel: Snip leaves off for a tasty licoricelike addition to salads. 'Zeta Fino' bulbs can be twisted off the root, and the tops can be eaten, too.

PERENNIAL HERBS

Chives, Garlic Chives, Lovage, Mint, Oregano, Rosemary, Sage, Thyme

PLANTS, NOT SEEDS: Instead of choosing seeds, visit a nursery and choose a baby plant or two of each herb. Better yet, visit a friend with an herb garden and get a rooted cutting of each.

CULTIVATION: Plant these starters in moderately poor but well-drained soil with plenty of access to sun. It doesn't matter if the soil dries out in summer. That's what these mostly Mediterranean plants are used to. All you need do is weed around them a few times each year.

Chives and garlic chives grow as bunches. It's best to have at least two bunches of each for a home garden.

Lovage is huge. Expect plants to top 7 feet, so put one only on the north side of your garden.

Mint and oregano can take over a bed if they're not contained. One way to contain them is to cut a tire along its middle tread, bury it, and plant your oregano or mint in it. The roots won't escape through the rubber.

Rosemary isn't hardy. Keep it in a pot and take it indoors each winter.

Sage and thyme die back in winter. Cut off the dead branches in midspring.

PESTS: *Oregano in particular will get black patches on some leaves as summer progresses. Cut such stems back to within a few inches of the ground, and let new growth replace them.*

HARVESTING FOR FRESH USE:

Chives: Snip off about 6 inches of the thin cylindrical leaves. Periodically cut one clump back to 2 inches above ground level and let it grow again.

Garlic chives: Loosen the soil beneath the bunch and pull the chives, roots and all, leaving two or three in the ground for next time.

Lovage: Snip off the leaves when you want them.

Mint, oregano, rosemary, sage, and thyme: Snip off the leaves or the top few inches of stem.

HARVESTING FOR DRYING *(all except chives and garlic chives): Snip off the best-looking tops of the herbs when they're in their prime, and before they show flower buds. This will be midspring for most. Cut off about 6 inches of stalks for drying, then go back to the herb bed and cut the remaining stalks to within a few inches of the ground to encourage new growth of fresh leaves.*

HARVESTING FOR FREEZING *(chives and garlic chives): Harvest as for fresh, then chop the herbs fine to freeze.*

Certain herbs are dried before stripping; others are stripped before drying. After they're washed, basil, celery, dill, lemon balm, lemon verbena, lovage, (but see page 62) mint, parsley, sage, and French tarragon leaves should be stripped from their stems and placed in a single layer on each rack. Marjoram, oregano, rosemary, the savories, and the thymes are dried first and then stripped, being sure that all stems are removed.

Racked herbs will dry in 3 or 4 days, particularly if turned daily, says Neaville. But "In humid weather," she warns, "drying takes longer, and crisping is necessary as a final step. Herbs spread sparsely on a cookie sheet and placed in an oven at 125°F will become crisp and ready for immediate storage in a few minutes."

Herbs also dry well if they're tied in small bunches and hung by string in the drying room. This method takes longer—about a week. A particularly pleasing, clean technique is to hang bunches of herbs, stem-base uppermost, inside brown paper bags in which a few holes have been cut. This allows air circulation while keeping out dust.

Once your herbs are thoroughly dry, store them in glass jars with airtight screw tops to retain crispness and prevent mold.

Dried herbs are three times stronger than fresh ones, and leaves stored whole retain flavor longer than those crumbled or powdered. The flavor should last at least a year.

Chives should be frozen, because they don't dry well. But even flowers can be dried. Harvesting in most cases should occur at the moment when they have just come into full bloom, then process and store them in the same manner as herb leaves. Calendula blossoms, for instance, snipped from their stems and dried are fine in salads, soups, and stews. And daylily buds, called golden needles in China, are an ancient favorite.

AN HERB BY ANY OTHER NAME: *Culinary Herbs* tells us that until 1475 the word "was erb, both in spelling and pronunciation. It came to England from the Latin herba, through the Old French herbe or erbe. At the beginning of the sixteenth century the Latin *h* was re-attached to the word, but it remained mute until 1800. Since then pronunciation of the *h* has come into use; herb is correct in England. American usage still clings to the historical erb."

Calendulas

During July and August the bright orange and yellow blossoms of *Calendula officinalis*—or pot marigold, a native of southern Europe—continue to appear everywhere in the flower borders once they've been planted. In fact, they self-sow and sometimes have to be weeded out!

Called "hardy annuals" (which they certainly are), calendulas have blossoms that are, according to the catalog of Johnny's Selected Seeds, "rich in carotenoid for use as dye, for antiseptic tinctures, and healing skin ointments." The plant is also recommended for edibility, and is "the sunniest flowering herb with a long blooming period."

The botanic Latin name—*Calendula*—"reflects the belief that it was always in bloom," according to *Herbs*, edited by Lesley Bremness. The French today enthusiastically call it *tous les mois* (all months). "Ancient Egyptians valued it as a rejuvenating herb. Hindus used it to decorate temple altars, and Persians and Greeks garnished and flavored food with its golden petals."

The Complete Book of Herbs by Emma Callery adds that dried petals were sold "from barrels by spice merchants in the Middle Ages for culinary and medicinal use."

What a picture! Added to custards, yogurt, soft cheese, butter, rice, or omelets, the bright petals give a saffron color and tangy flavor. They're also amusing added to cakes and sweet breads, sprinkled over salads, or—doubtless most often in medieval times—popped into stews, hopefully at the last minute.

> **For tips on growing calendulas, see page 60.**

Like dandelion blossoms, but possibly with less bother, fresh calendula flowers make a fine wine.

Yeast nutrient, like campden tablets and other supplies, are availabe at wine-making supply stores and some health food stores.

Marigold Wine

MAKES 1 GALLON

GATHERING

On a warm, sunny day, being careful to choose *C. officinalis* only, gather enough blossoms to measure:

2 quarts petals

PREPARING

Place the petals in a large porcelainized, crockery, or stainless-steel container and pour over them:

1 gallon boiling water
Then stir in:
1 Campden tablet, crushed
Stir with a long-handled plastic or wooden spoon. Cover the container and let it rest for 24 hours.

ADDING AND COMBINING

When the time is up, wash well and peel thinly the rinds of:

3 oranges
1 lemon

Be sure to leave the pith behind. Place the rinds in a porcelainized or stainless-steel pot, then draw off and add to the pot:

1 quart petal liquid
Heat to the boiling point. Immediately pour over and stir until dissolved:

5 3/4 cups white sugar
Leave to cool to blood temperature. In the meantime, squeeze the peeled oranges and reserve the juice.

When it's cool, pour the sugar-rind liquor into the bulk of the original liquid (3 quarts) together with:

the reserved citrus juice
1 1/4 cups white raisins, finely chopped
1 ounce wine-making yeast
1 teaspoon yeast nutrient (see page 266)

Stir well with a long-handled plastic or wooden spoon.

FERMENTATION 1

Cover and leave the wine to ferment in a warm room for 5 days, stirring twice a day.

FERMENTATION 2
AND INSERTING THE AIR LOCK

Using a nylon sieve or several sterilized thicknesses of muslin or fine cheesecloth draped over a colander, strain your liquid into a food-safe plastic fermentation container—the kind that has a tight lid suitable for the insertion of an air lock. Insert your air lock. Seal the lock by pouring into it enough boiled-then-cooled water, or Campden solution, so that the liquid rises halfway up its convolutions. Store the container in a warm room for 2 to 3 weeks, at an even temperature if possible.

Transfer the wine to a cool place for 2 weeks or longer, till little bubbles no longer rise to the surface if the container is moved.

RACKING

At this point sediment will have fallen to the bottom of the container. This is spent yeast, and it must be removed by a process called racking. To do this, siphon the wine into sterilized jugs using about 4 feet of 1/2-inch plastic tubing. The easiest way to do this is to stand your wine on a table and your clean jug on the floor below. Place one end of the tube into the wine above any sediment. Suck the other end till wine

flows down the tube, then pop it quickly into your clean jug and let it flow. Be sure to leave all sediment behind!

Cap your jug and leave it in a cool place. Rack again as more sediment forms; and again, if necessary, till the wine remains clear for a week or so.

BOTTLING

Wash wine or champagne bottles with detergent and hot water, rinse them thoroughly, and dry in a warm oven. (Or follow instructions for using Campden solution.) Fill the bottles by siphoning wine into them to within 1 inch of the top.

CORKING

Soften new straight-sided corks in boiling water. Cork your bottles tightly. A cork flogger will blow the corks home without a lot of fuss.

STORING

Store the bottles on their sides in a cool, dark place (or wrap them with paper) for at least 6 months before tasting.

AUGUST

Napoleon's Delight
String Beans

*P*haseolus vulgaris, otherwise known as the bush bean, string bean, snap bean, French bean, kidney bean, and haricot bean, has been an American staple since Siberian explorers, having crossed the Bering Strait, learned to grow it among patches of squash and corn. It seems, in fact, to have been cultivated at least 5,000 years ago in Mexico.

Before that it was domesticated in Peru. Chef Bert Greene remarks enthusiastically that the Incas grew the string bean "not so much for flavor as for theology." They were sun worshipers, he says, and his reasoning was that "A green bean will climb any vertical surface, notably a pole, twisting and turning in its search for the light." Chewing the pods, therefore, "was seen as an act of sacrament."

Phaseolus traveled extensively, as observed much later by the Florentine explorer Giovanni Verrazano when he explored the Atlantic coastline. In a 1524 letter to his wife he described the foods that Native North Americans ate: "They grow slender pods born on bushes with bright green leaves. These have the virtue of a good flavor but require long and careful chewing even after a long stay in the cook pot." He must have been describing dried rather than fresh string beans!

At any rate, Columbus was probably one of the first Europeans to see a New World bean, finding it near what is now Nuevitas in Cuba. No doubt he brought it back to Spain with him, as he did with all the new foods he found in America. But it made little impression, suggest Waverly Root and Richard De Rochemont in *Eating in America,* since "the name eventually given it in Europe, 'haricot,' comes from the Aztec ayacotl, which suggests that it did not receive recognition until it arrived from Mexico, where the conquistadores who entered that country in 1519 discovered it."

Spaniards at first enjoyed it merely as a flowering plant with red-to-pink blossoms known as *pincel*—"paintbrush." This continued for about 50 years until, legend has it, someone mistakenly cooked a few pods in a pot of soup, which led to exclamations and lip smacking.

It was taken to France in 1533 by cooks attending 14-year-old Catherine de Médicis, on her way to marry the French dauphin, Henri of Valois, who became Henri II in 1547. According to Greene, French cooks took it to their culinary hearts. "They called the dried seeds of the beans *haricots,* because they put them in *ragouts* or *haricots* of mutton. The young pods, eaten whole, were called *haricots verts,* and the shelled beans, eaten extravagantly young, became known as flageolet beans—the name is a corruption of the Latin *phaseolus,* and also relates to the fact that the French imagined the bean resembled a flute known as a flageolet. The dried, mature beans were called *haricots jaunes.*"

People seem to disagree over the name's origin. James Trager reports that *Oudin's Dictionary* of 1640 introduced the word *haricot* for the fagioli beans brought to France by Catherine. *Haricot,* says the dictionary, is derived from *héricog,* "used at least since the 14th century and probably derived from a Germanic word, *harigoté* or *aligoté,* meaning a stew or ragout of meat and vegetables, usually turnips."

Maguelonne Toussaint-Samat, writing in 1987, notes that Jean-Henri Fabre, author of a study on insects, quoted the Cuban poet and author José Maria de Heredia as more proud of his discovery of the etymology of the word *haricot* than of writing his famous sonnets. "The word haricot was unknown in France until the seventeenth century. . . . Thirty varieties of haricot were cultivated in Mexico before the conquest. They are called *ayacot* to this day, especially the red haricot, with black or violet spots."

Other evidence for ascribing *haricot* to Mexican roots comes from Geronimo de Aguilar, shipwrecked off the coast of the Yucatán in 1511. Escaping his Mayan captors, he reported that the beans he had eaten with them were called *avacotl,* a word the Spanish turned into *habichuela,* and the French into *haricot.*

By 1749, at any rate, haricot beans were planted extensively for the first time in France, and near Soissons they soon replaced favas. Napoleon, it is rumored, was so fond of them that when he was imprisoned he ate haricot bean salad every alternate day.

In England the first *haricot vert* apparently arrived with fleeing French Huguenots, who presented some as a gift to Queen Elizabeth I for allowing them religious freedom in her land. The queen found green beans "much engaging to the royal taste." Planted in the garden at Hampton Court, they appeared shortly thereafter all over the island. English farmers, naturally, changed the name to the Elizabeth bean, but when Elizabeth died and James took over, they reverted to "Frenchies."

String beans began to be raised commercially in the United States after 1836. The very first crop was harvested by an enterprising truck farmer outside Utica, New York, says Bert Greene. "He reportedly mortgaged his family home to import the seeds from France. Ten years later, they say, he was so filthy rich that he moved his family to the Riviera."

This may be apocryphal. Still, by the late 1800s, Greene continues, "string beans were so fashionable that they were marketed by vegetable distributors as 'The Ninth Wonder of the World.' Eventually lawyers for P. T. Barnum, who had coined the phrase, threatened legal action and the legend was amended to read: 'The Wonder of the World [and in smaller type] of Food!'"

In New England, string beans burgeon with August. The beauteous 'Purple Pod' turns green when cooked, and the wax variety is sunny yellow. Cut into small bits and served raw in a leafy, green salad, the combination is an artist's delight. Nor do string beans shrink with cooking. What you pick or purchase is what you get. Moreover, since 1894, hybridizing has produced a stringless bean—certainly a boon to the cook.

From string to dried, beans provide a lot of nutrition. A cupful of green beans contains 2 grams of protein, 735 International Units of vitamin A, 17.9 milligrams of vitamin C, 41 milligrams of calcium, and 230 milligrams of potassium, along with other nutrients. While dried beans are absolute storehouses of nutrients, green beans are about 92 percent water, and contain a few more than 30 calories in a cooked cupful.

GARDENING NOTES

BEANS

BUSH, POLE, SHELL, DRY, LIMA, FAVA, SOY

CHOOSING SEEDS: String beans are edible, pod and all. Most varieties sold today, however, are stringless, or almost so. That is, they have no "string" (like dental floss) along the backbone of the bean, which used to make preparation for eating so time consuming. Most varieties are green; some are yellow or purple. Most are bush type. Others (pole) grow on vines that need staking. Some grow fat or long, while others need to be harvested at the slender stage. Black beans generally germinate better. A 2-ounce packet sows 25 row feet. One pound will sow 100 feet of double row. Seeds store well.

Shell beans grow like bush beans, but have larger seeds best eaten when they're fat and shelled from the pod. Fava, lima, and soybeans are special

---

varieties of shell beans that represent different species. Fava beans take different cultivation. Dried beans are shelled and stored dry.

CULTIVATION:

Fava beans: Plant as early in spring as possible—with peas. Lay out a string along the row and push the big seeds 1 inch deep and 5 inches apart in rows 24 inches apart.

Bush varieties (except fava): Don't plant till the soil has warmed to at least 60°F. The wheel seeder was made for bush beans. Use it to space double rows 4 to 6 inches apart. Seeds should be 3 to 4 inches apart and 1 inch deep. Separate each double row from the next by a 3- or 4-foot harvesting path. For a continuous supply of beans, plant rows successively every 2 to 3 weeks.

Pole beans: Use a sturdy frame, or push branches into the ground in the middle of the double row. Some pole beans grow to 16 feet or more. Their vines are very strong.

For bigger plants of all bean types, along with higher yields and soil enrichment, use an inoculant of beneficial bacteria. Either shake this with the seeds before sowing, or shake it on the ground before or after seeding.

Collinear-hoe between the rows at least twice while the beans are emerging. Then individually pull weeds that survive within the bean rows. Once bean plants are established, they take over the job of weed prevention.

PESTS: Beans are subject to several fungi, especially in damp weather. Don't get into the bush bean bed after rain, and avoid harvesting while dew is still on the plants. Mexican bean beetles can be controlled with pyrethrum or rotenone. Deer will pull plants right out of the ground, so an electric fence is a must.

HARVESTING:

Fava beans: Harvest when the pods are very fat. Remove the pods for composting.

Stringless beans: Harvest on dry days when slender (for French fillet treat), or when the pods are full but barely bumpy with the growing seeds. Harvest often to keep beans coming.

Shell beans: Harvest when the bean is fat and the pod soft. Shell out immediately.

Dried beans: Cut the plants from their roots when pods are full and rather dry. Dry some more in the sun or shed, and shell out later.

Although simmering in a pot of boiling water is time tested, the following technique for basic bean cooking retains more nutrients.

Simple Green String or Yellow Wax Beans

Buy or pick:

as many handfuls of beans as you have eager eaters, one brimming handful per person

String them and snap into bite-sized pieces.

Place a layer of snapped beans into a large heavy-bottomed saucepan. Sprinkle with:

a little sea salt

Put down another layer, add more salt, and continue till all the beans are used up. Then add:

about 1/2 cup cold water

Cover your pot tightly. Turn the heat to high and bring the beans to a boil, then reduce it to medium low and let the beans steam till they're *al dente*. Uncover the pot and evaporate what little water remains. Beans should be tender but never mushy.

Serve the beans as is, marinate and chill them for a salad, or proceed with the following recipe.

String Green or Yellow Wax Beans with Herbs

Place a wok on its ring and heat it over high heat. When it's hot, add:

3 tablespoons extra-virgin olive oil
1–2 garlic cloves, minced
1 small onion, finely chopped

Sauté over medium heat till the onion is limp.

Add your cooked beans (above) and toss gently. Remove the wok from the heat and add:

1/2 teaspoon freshly gathered and finely chopped rosemary OR 1 teaspoon freshly chopped summer savory, sage, OR marjoram

Serve immediately with any cooked grain or new potatoes, other vegetables, and a big salad.

Simply Grande shareholders Deb Norden and Frank Bright suggest heading East (should people in New England say "West"?)—to the Orient for a treat.

Spicy Hot Green Beans

SERVES 2–3

Place a wok on its collar, heat, and add:
2 tablespoons sunflower seed oil
When the oil is warm, reduce the heat to medium and add:
2 garlic cloves, minced

When these are lightly browned, stir in:
**1 tablespoon red chili paste
(see the sidebar)**
**1 tablespoon refined white sugar
OR maple syrup**
**shoyu (naturally fermented soy sauce)
to taste**
Continue stirring for about 30 seconds till blended and aromatic. Taste. Adjust the sweetening and chili paste as desired.

Add:
**1 pound green beans, snapped into
1-inch lengths**
You should have 4 cups. Stir-fry for about 2 minutes, till the beans are crisp-tender.

Serve hot.

RED CHILI PASTE: Chili paste is made of chili peppers, vinegar, garlic (sometimes), and spices. It's a hot sauce available where Oriental foods are sold. Commercially, it's often bottled as chili curry.

"The wax or yellow bean is nothing more than a string bean that has been cultivated for its lightened (and some consider more appealing) color," says chef Bert Greene. "In the process of hybridization a jot of folic acid . . . is lost, but the flavor and texture are otherwise indistinguishable. In France, wax beans are known as mange-tout, which roughly translates as wholly edible . . . !" Cold, cooked string beans of any color make wonderful salads.

String Bean, Walnut, and Feta Cheese Salad

SERVES 3–4

In a skillet, toast until browned:
1 cup walnut meats
When they're toasted, chop them coarsely and set aside.

Bring to a boil:
a large pot of salted water
Pour in and blanch till just tender (a matter of 4 or 5 minutes):
**4 cups string beans, snapped into
1-inch lengths**
Drain well. Cool.

In a salad bowl, place:
the 4 cups cooked, cooled string beans
**the 1 cup toasted, chopped walnut
meats**
**2/3 cup feta cheese, cut into small
cubes**

In a blender, whiz together:
1/2 cup extra-virgin olive oil
1/4 cup freshly squeezed lemon juice
1 large garlic clove, minced
1/4 teaspoon sea salt

freshly ground black pepper to taste
Add and mix well:
   1/2 cup finely chopped fresh mint

Just before serving, pour the vinaigrette over your bean-nut mixture and toss gently. This is very good heaped in lettuce leaves. Leftover vinaigrette can be saved for other salads.

Many cooks laboriously slice string beans vertically and call them "Frenched." It's really not necessary. Tender young beans are invariably fine if snapped. And there are always the beautiful, pencil-thin 'Maxibels'.

Lemony Green Beans

SERVES 4

Pick or purchase:
   1 pound tender string beans
Remove the strings, if present. Cut or snap into 1-inch lengths. You should have 4 cups.

Bring to a boil:
   a large pot of salted water
Pour in the beans and blanch till just tender—a matter of 4 or 5 minutes. Drain well and place in a warm serving dish.

In a small bowl or jar, mix together with a fork:
   3 tablespoons extra-virgin olive oil
   1/2 teaspoon sea salt
   1/4 teaspoon freshly ground black pepper
   1 tablespoon minced fresh parsley
   3 tablespoons freshly squeezed lemon juice
Pour this dressing over the hot beans and serve immediately.

Green beans make a pleasing light soup for hot days. Cryptotaenia canadensis grows wild in North America and is sometimes known as wild chervil. Native Americans enjoyed it, and the Swedish plant explorer Peter Kalm wrote that the French in Canada were inordinately fond of it in soup. Italian parsley or cilantro would substitute very well.

The Simplest Green Bean Soup

SERVES 4

Pick or purchase:
   a handful of beans per diner
String them (if necessary) and cut into 1/4-inch pieces to equal 3 cups.

Pour the beans into:
   4 cups well-flavored, simmering Vegetable Stock (see page 43)
Add:
   1 tablespoon grated lemon rind
   1 teaspoon freshly grated gingerroot
   a few leaves chopped fresh wild chervil, cilantro, or Italian parsley

Cook the beans till they're barely tender and serve immediately in warmed bowls. Fresh bread or rolls should accompany.

With many months of cold and snow, then early springs and falls, old-time New Englanders found many ways to store summer harvests for winter. Before the advent of glass canning jars, big crocks were used to pickle produce such as cabbage and cucumbers, to store porkfat in thick layers of salt, or to store eggs in waterglass (see page 141). Later, with the coming of commercial canning in actual metal cans and then the invention of heat-resistant glass, shelves of see-through jars lined on cellar shelves would be brilliant with the reds and greens and golds of summertime.

Home canning today is easy but takes attention. If you're new to it, the "bible" to study is the Ball Company's BLUE BOOK, latest edition, published in Muncie, Indiana. (See page 38.)

Be sure that your work areas, hands, and produce are as clean as possible to avoid contamination and potential spoilage from soil organisms, which are omnipresent. In the case of highly acidic fruits and vegetables, and everything pickled with vinegar, a boiling-water bath is fine for processing. For nonacidic vegetables, however, only processing in a pressure cooker will protect your family from possible botulism poisoning. Here is the classic recipe for canning string beans.

Classic Canned String Beans

MAKES 7 QUARTS

Pick or purchase:

young, tender, crisp string beans

Wash quart jars in hot soapy water. Rinse and let the jars rest in hot water until needed.

Trim the ends from the beans, remove any strings, and cut or snap into pieces about an inch long.

Place the beans in a large pot and cover with:

boiling water

Boil for 5 minutes. Drain, saving the water. Return it to a boil.

Place one of your hot jars on a towel-covered countertop and add:

1 teaspoon canning salt

Pack in your beans, leaving 1 inch of headroom. Cover with boiling water. Remove any air bubbles by poking gently into each jar along the sides with a chopstick. Continue with all seven jars.

Meanwhile, in a small saucepan of hot water, heat seven metal bands and lids to just under boiling. When they're hot, drop them into a sieve and drain.

Wipe off the rims of your bean-filled jars with a clean cloth. Place hot lids and bands on the jars, screwing down the bands tightly.

Place your hot, filled jars on a rack in a big pressure canner that contains 2 to 3 inches of hot water. (If pressure cooking is new to you, be sure to check the directions for your pressure cooker before using it.) Place the canner over high heat and lock on the cover per the manufacturer's instructions. Leave the vent open until steam escapes steadily for 10 minutes; then close the vent, bring the pressure up to 10 pounds, and keep it steady for 20 minutes by adjusting your stove. Watch carefully. Measure processing time from when the pressure reaches 10 pounds.

When time is up, remove the canner from the heat and let the pressure fall to zero. Be certain the pressure is all the way down. Wait 5 minutes, then open the vent. Unfasten the cover and slide it toward you, allowing steam to escape, then hold it tipped away from your face to prevent any possible burn. Place on a shelf. Let the jars rest for 10 minutes before removing them with tongs.

Place on a towel-covered counter to cool and prevent breakage. Don't let the jars touch each other.

Allow the jars to cool completely—perhaps overnight. When they're completely cool, unscrew the metal bands, check to see that each jar is safely sealed—the metal lid will feel slightly concave when you press it—rinse gently, wipe dry, and label.

Store in a cool, dark place.

While processing in a pressure cooker is mandatory for nonacidic foods, a boiling-water bath is fine for highly acidic fruits and vegetables, and for everything pickled with vinegar. Home-canned dilled beans are a longtime favorite. Best results are always obtained from freshly picked produce. Again, if you're new to canning, refer to the Ball Company's BLUE BOOK mentioned on page 38.

J. A.'s Dilled String Beans

MAKES 7 PINTS

Purchase or pick:

4 pounds tender, young string beans

Wash well and drain. Remove the stem ends, string the beans if necessary, and trim a handful to come an inch below the rim of a pint canning jar, all lengths being equal.

Pack the beans, standing upright, into seven widemouthed pint jars that have been sterilized by boiling. (A towel underneath them will prevent breakage if countertops are cold. Be careful not to get burned.)

To each jar of beans, add:

3 peppercorns
4 tablespoons dill seeds
OR 1 fresh dill head
1/4 teaspoon cayenne powder (optional)
1 garlic clove

In a large porcelainized saucepan, combine and heat to boiling:

3 cups white distilled vinegar
3 cups 5 percent cider vinegar
6 cups water
2/3 cup canning or kosher salt

Pour this over the beans to within 1/2 inch of each jar's rim. Remove air bubbles by poking into each jar along the sides with a chopstick.

Meanwhile, in a small saucepan of hot water, heat metal bands and lids to just under boiling. When they're hot, drop them into a sieve and drain.

Wipe off the rims of your bean-filled jars. Place hot lids and bands on the jars, screwing down the bands tightly.

Place your hot, filled jars on a rack in a big pot of hot water. Add more hot water if necessary to come at least 1 inch above the jar tops. Cover, bring to a boil, and process in this boiling-water bath for 10 minutes. Measure the processing time from when a rolling boil begins.

When the time is up, remove jars with tongs and let them cool on a towel-covered counter to prevent breakage.

When they're completely cool, remove the metal bands, check to see that each jar is safely sealed—the metal lid will feel slightly concave when you press it—rinse gently, wipe dry, and label.

Store in a cool, dark place.

WATERGLASS EGGS: When the waterglassing of eggs began is difficult to determine. It was fairly common, however, during the 1800s and before electricity brought refrigeration to New England. Sodium silicate, used today to seal concrete floors (among other tasks), is purchasable from building supply companies. It's a rather syrupy mixture, and, according to *Putting Food By,* "fills the pores of the eggshells, thus preventing moisture loss from the inside or air damage from the outside."

Hens tend to stop laying when days grow short and light diminishes with summer's end, so Jean Ann's Maine parents put down big crocks of the last eggs in the dirt- and ledge-floored cellar every fall. Carefully removed from their waterglass covering as needed during the winter, these stored gems might have been worthless for meringue or boiling, but they were fine for cakes and similar products.

Here's how to waterglass your eggs: Select only nest-fresh eggs with perfect shells; discard any dirty eggs. Wipe them clean. Do not wash them, as this removes their natural protective coating. Place them in a ceramic crock. Cover with diluted water- glass (sodium silicate)—1/3 cup of waterglass per quart of water—to 3 inches above the top layer. Store in a cool cellar (under 40°F). When you remove an egg, wash it well before you break it.

New Potatoes

When summer truly arrives, the first tender, baby potatoes *(Solanum tuberosum)* are ready for harvesting. Is anything more delicious? Could the Incas have given the world a better gift?

Of course, the people of the Andes grew many more varieties than went to Europe in the 1500s, which is one reason behind the tragedy of Ireland's later Potato Famine. A million Irish died of starvation in the 19th century, either on land or at sea attempting to emigrate, while another million who did reach other countries further decimated the home population. It's said that such a large pop- ulation loss had not been seen since the Black Death of the 14th century.

As with many tragedies, the etiology of this one was complex. Of the few pota- to varieties introduced into Europe in the 1500s, none were resistant to *Phytopthora infestans,* the late potato blight. Irish farmers, taxed heavily by Britain, were forced to export other food crops, and had come to rely almost entirely upon spuds for subsistence—especially 'Lumper', a high-yielding variety. The average Irishman, it was said, ate between 6 and 12 pounds of potatoes a day. Between 1845 and 1851, however, the crop failed and starvation arrived.

According to the United Nations Food and Agriculture Organization, lack of genetic diversity was a big factor in the devastation, along with a lack of "clean seed," poor crop rotation, and ideal weather conditions for *Phytopthora.*

Nor did Maine escape. Historian Clarence Day tells us that "Potato rot from various causes had not been unknown, although it had seldom caused appreciable damage; but in 1843 notices began to appear in the *Maine Farmer* that potatoes were rotting badly in New York for some strange, unknown reason. The next year the disease was serious throughout New England. . . . In some places in Maine nine tenths of the crop rotted in the ground or in the cellars after they were stored." In 1849 the potato crop was less than one-quarter that of 1839.

"Nearly twenty years elapsed before the real nature of the trouble was finally demonstrated by Speerschnieder and confirmed by Kuhn and De Bary in Germany," says Day. Today, although the pathogen still exists worldwide, agricultural inspection keeps a constant watch to ensure that the seed is clean. Potatoes remain too precious a crop to lose.

For tips on growing new potatoes, see page 320.

'Norland' has always been an early-summer favorite in New England. With its red skin and white flesh, it's perfect for boiling and early eating, especially if tossed gently with extra-virgin olive oil and freshly chopped parsley, chives, or cilantro.

Then there are fingerlings—longer and thinner than most potatoes, and sporting colorful flesh and skin colors. The 'French Fingerling', for instance, has a glistening, smooth, rose-red skin and yellow flesh slightly splashed with pink. The 'Peanut' or 'Mandel' has yellow flesh and a tan, lightly russeted skin. 'Rose Finn Apple' has a buff skin with a rose blush, and bright yellow flesh hidden underneath. Baked simply in a pan with whole garlic cloves, olive oil, sea salt, and some freshly ground black pepper, it's an artist's choice!

Choose potatoes with firm textures for this recipe. Medium-sized 'Russian Banana', with its yellow skin and waxy yellow interior, would be superb.

Fingerling Fantasy

Pick or purchase:
   a handful of small fingerling
   OR very new potatoes per person
Wash carefully and pat dry but do not peel.

In a heavy skillet, heat:
   2–3 tablespoons extra-virgin olive oil
Add the potatoes and roll them around in the pan to coat them. Cover and cook over low heat till they're tender, perhaps 15 minutes. (You may need to precook them if they're at all big.)

Add and cook a few moments longer, stirring occasionally:
   1–2 garlic cloves, minced
   freshly chopped rosemary
   OR herb of your choice

While the potatoes are still firm, sprinkle in:
   sea salt to taste
   freshly ground black pepper

Serve herbed and hot with a green, leafy salad and other summer vegetables.

The people of the Russian north depend on potatoes today, and no one cooks them better. They're grown, in fact, just 4 degrees below the Arctic Circle—a continent and hemisphere away from their South American origin. Simply Grande gardeners know all about the great Russian love of potatoes through firsthand experience. During a 1991 visit to the city of Kotlas—Waterville's sister city in what was then the U.S.S.R., situated on the big, north-flowing Dvina River (which enters the sea at Archangelsk)—samples, always delicious, never tiresome, were offered.

Small new potatoes make splendid hors d'oeuvres for a party. With caviar.

Party Potatoes

Choose:

1 1/2- to 2-inch new, waxy-fleshed potatoes

Wash well but do not peel.

Bake them in a 400°F oven for 20 minutes or until tender. Remove from the oven.

When they're cool enough to handle, split the potatoes carefully in half. Arrange them on a tray and top with:

sour cream
caviar

Offer to happily surprised guests.

While visiting Kotlas, New Englanders also learned to hanker after those warm, Russian-style potato salads enhanced with dill. 'Caribe', with its purple skin and waxy, white flesh is superb for this dish, although any new potato with a firm flesh will do.

Kotlas Potato Salad

SERVES 4

Choose:

8 medium-sized, waxy-fleshed potatoes

Wash them thoroughly, place in a large pot, cover with water, and add:

1 teaspoon sea salt

Bring the water to a boil over high heat, reduce the heat to medium, and simmer until the potatoes are easily pierced by a fork.

Don't let them overcook or crumble. Drain and set aside.

When they're cool enough to handle, peel the potatoes if necessary (and if there are unsightly spots), cut them into smallish chunks, and place in a medium-sized bowl.

In a tightly capped jar, shake together vigorously:

2 tablespoons apple cider vinegar
1/2 teaspoon sea salt
1/8 teaspoon freshly ground black pepper
1/3 cup sunflower seed oil

Pour this vinaigrette over the potatoes and toss gently with:

a lot of chopped fresh dill weed

Serve right away.

SUNFLOWER SEED OIL: Please note that sunflower seed oil comes from the native American sunflower. One of the largest daises of the family *Compositae*, the sunflower was collected by Spanish explorers. By 1580 it was a common garden flower in Spain; then English and French explorers introduced it to England and France. From there it spread along the trade routes to southern Europe, Egypt, Afghanistan, India, and China.

It's said that the Tsar Peter Great introduced it to Russia on his return from the West, and that it soon became a major source of food oil. It's also reported that the tsars fed their soldiers 2 pounds of sunflower seeds a day as a staple. With all the current discussion about what oil is best for us, processed, polyunsaturated sunflower Seed oil may have to take a back seat to monounsaturated, especially for cooking. Olive oil would be a reasonable substitute.

Kohlrabi

Head cabbage, cauliflower, kale, broccoli, brussels sprouts, and the odd-looking kohlrabi are all varieties of one species, *Brassica oleracea*, family Cruciferae. Kohlrabi seems to have been mentioned earliest by ancient Rome's Pliny, who described it as "a Brassica in which the stem is thin just above the roots, but swells out in the region that bears the leaves, which are few and slender."

Benjamin Watson, who describes so many vegetables so well, seems to disagree by saying, "kohlrabi has not been around very long. No clear mention of it exists before the 16th century, when it first appeared in Italy and from there spread to central Europe." James Trager reports that the 1554 *Cruydeboek* of Dutch botanist Dodonaeus (Rembert Dodoens) made the first mention of kohlrabi as well as brussels sprouts.

At any rate, several varieties, both open pollinated and hybrid, have been introduced in recent years, but the basic color types—with green, white, or purple skins—have remained essentially the same.

The name of this member of the cabbage family is German, derived from *kohl* (cabbage) and *rabi* (turnip), possibly because the enlarged stem resembles a turnip, and the leaves taste like cabbage.

Says Watson, "With its swollen globe-shaped stem that squats just above the ground and looks like a small green apple, kohlrabi certainly is an odd vegetable. In fact, the only indication of its membership in the cabbage family are the small leaves that stick straight up from the sides of the bulbous stem."

For tips on growing kohlrabi, see page 313.

Nutritionally, a cupful of kohlrabi contains 50 International Units of vitamin A, 86.8 milligrams of vitamin C, 34 milligrams of calcium, and 490 milligrams of potassium, along with other vitamins and minerals.

Regardless of looks, kohlrabi has a crisp sweet nuttiness that is best eaten raw and julienned into salads.

"Summertime and the livin' is—" Cucumbers

In New England, at least, summer livin' is busy! August brings a bounty of harvesting, particularly in the cucurbit line. Cucumbers *(Cucumis sativus),* along with gourds and squashes, are members of the cucurbitaceae family. Possibly cultivated for 4,000 years, their original home isn't certain, although cook and cookbook writer Bert Greene says they probably came from the region of Pakistan "where the overflowing Indus River makes the land muddy and fertile and the warm wind off the Sulaiman mountains blows the tiny seedlets for thousands of miles every spring."

They've since gone everywhere. Travels began early. Remains have been found at Spirit Cave, near the Burmese border of Thailand. The Sumerians grew cucumbers along with lettuce, cress, and mustard by 3000 B.C. In the Sumerian epic *Gilgamesh,* the first known written legend (which tells of a great flood in which people were saved by building an ark), caper buds, ripe figs, grapes, several edible leaves and stems, honey, meat seasoned with herbs, bread—a kind of pancake made of barley flour mixed with sesame seed flour and onions—and wild cucumbers were mentioned.

Egyptians enjoyed them at every meal, usually dipped into bowls of salted water. The Old Testament tells us that Moses' one regret after the Red Sea parting was the fact that he hadn't brought a peck of cucumber seeds into the desert. Ancient Greeks mixed the pulp with honey and snow for festive occasions. And Romans served them every day of the week when possible—but highly flavored and practically unrecognizable with pepper, vinegar, garum, and silphium (see page 146).

"The first serious appraisal of cucumbers in Europe," announced one writer, "occurred in France during the reign of Pepin the Wise at the end of the eighth century." Called *concombres* in his gardener's record books, it was 50 years before Pepin's son, Charlemagne, decided to eat them for sheer pleasure! Then according to Greene, it was, "only as dessert, in sweet tarts and custards."

Fortunately, someone suggested that savory was better than sweet, and the idea prospered. But the vegetable didn't get to England until the 14th century. And from the Middle Ages to the 18th century it was considered unhealthful.

It fared better in the New World. After banqueting with the Hispaniolan king on December 16, 1492, Columbus reported the results of horticultural experiments in a letter: Cucumber seeds that he'd brought from Europe flourished.

In 1535 explorer Jacques Cartier mentioned seeing large cucumbers being grown at what is now Montreal, and in 1539 Hernando DeSoto found Indians in Florida growing cucumbers that were "better than those of Spain."

Centuries later that inveterate gardener, Thomas Jefferson, maintained an interest in horticulture even in his last year. "When an Ohio newspaper reported cucumbers growing four feet long in a Cleveland garden, Jefferson wrote an old friend there for seed. 'Altho giants do not always beget giants,' he wrote, 'yet I should count on their improving the breed, and this vegetable being a great favorite of mine, I wish to take the chance on an improvement.'" Dividing the seeds, he planted his and sent the other nine to a gardening friend "to multiply the chances of a cucumber success."

GARUM AND SILPHIUM: According to historian Maguelonne Toussaint-Samat in *History of Food*, garum was "one of the great gastronomic passions of Rome, the basic seasoning used in its cookery, the supreme condiment." Each seaport had its own secret recipe, some more famous than others. "Garum was a sauce made of the intestines of mackerel or anchovies, macerated in salt and then left out in the sun until the mixture had completely decomposed, or rather had digested itself by the action of the fish's own intestinal microbes. Carefully calculated amounts of concentrated decoctions of aromatic herbs were added. Then a very fine strainer was plunged into the vessel containing the mixture to collect the syrupy, strongly flavoured liquid. The garum was ladled out and left to mature. The residue or *alec* . . . was not thrown away. Poor people used it to season and enrich their cereal porridges. Garum could command fantastic prices—the price of caviar is nothing by comparison."

Silphium was "a kind of wild carrot which has disappeared so completely that we cannot now account for its amazing popularity." One historian of Libya suggested that it prevented pregnancy.

Cucumis sativus has been a New England standby from early days, although some folks found it bitter. According to Marian Morash in *The Victory Garden Cookbook*, "Bitterness in older cucumber varieties was caused by the so-called bitter gene." She adds, "Almost all the research devoted to cucumbers has been aimed at removing this gene. As a result, the new hybrid varieties contain very little bitterness."

CUCUMBERS

CHOOSING SEEDS: Don't be fooled by the usual division of cucumber varieties into "pickling" and "slicing." Many varieties are very good for both. Choose several varieties, based on your preferences in length of season, ease of growing, color, length, and taste. There are 1,100 seeds per ounce. You'll need 1/2 ounce to plant a 100-foot row.

CULTIVATION: Seeds may be sown indoors 4 to 5 weeks before the weather becomes warm and settled. Use pots or plugs. Keep the soil above 70°F to germinate. When you're transplanting, don't disturb the roots, but water well at first. For direct-seeding, wait until the soil is warm, at least 2 weeks after the last frost. Because the productive life of any cucumber plant is only a few weeks, you may wish to sow seeds in succession throughout the season.

Any well-drained fertile soil will do, but cucumbers will do best when you dig in compost or dried manure where they'll be planted. First you must choose whether to grow in rows or in hills. There are advantages to each. For row planting, your next choice is whether to let the vines spread over the ground or climb on trellises. Trellises save space and are a must for the long, straight European slicing cucumbers, which then grow clean, undeformed, and straight. For hill planting, your choice is whether or not to use mulch. Six-mil black plastic mulch has the advantage of keeping the soil warm, moisture in, and weeds under control. Cut 6-inch-diameter holes for hills, spaced 3 feet apart in rows 6 feet apart.

Cucumbers need lots of water, so either irrigate regularly or use mulch.

PESTS AND DISEASES: Cucumber beetles (striped or spotted) are the worst enemies. They nibble at the leaves and spread diseases. Either cover your cukes with a floating row fabric before the seeds germinate, or dust the plants with rotenone or pyrethrum when the beetles appear. Be persistent (every day) with the dusting if beetles appear early. You may need to plant a second time if you lose the battle.

Cucumbers are subject to many viral and fungal diseases. Choose disease-resistant varieties, rotate crops, and be sure to remove all vines from the field and compost them at the end of the growing season.

HARVESTING: Once your plants are bearing, pick daily. Cucumbers grow fast.

Moreover, there's a trick for removing bitterness, one long accepted by down-Maine cooks. The trick is to slice off 1 inch of the stem end and peel the entire skin, since the bitter taste seems concentrated there. Scoring with a fork creates pretty as well as sweeter slices.

More than 95 percent water, a cupful of cucumber contains 46 International Units of vitamin A, 4.8 milligrams of vitamin C, 8.4 International Units of vitamin E, 14 milligrams of calcium, and 156 milligrams of potassium, among other nutrients.

Cucumbers are superb when served as the Persians must have done—as a side dish or cold soup.

Persian Cucumber Yogurt

SERVES 2–3

In a medium-sized bowl, mix together till smooth:

2 cups thick yogurt
4 cups finely chopped cucumbers
1 shallot, finely chopped (tops and all)
1 teaspoon freshly chopped mint leaves
1 teaspoon freshly chopped basil leaves
2 tablespoons dried currants
2 tablespoons finely chopped walnuts
1/2 teaspoon sea salt

Serve as a side dish to any meal, or as a dip with strong cos lettuce leaves, celery stalks, or julienned carrots.

NOTE: If cucumbers are mature and watery (and to remove any bitterness if there is any), slice lengthwise or crosswise and sprinkle with salt. Then let them drain in a colander for about an hour before using.

This classic salad combines cucumbers, tomatoes, and the brined cheese called feta.

Cucumber, Tomato, and Feta Cheese Salad

SERVES 2

Slice:
7–8 small, firm, ripe tomatoes
Peel, cut in half lengthwise, remove the seeds from, and slice:
2 medium-sized cucumbers
Remove the seeds from and slice:
1 green pepper
Cut into bite-sized bits. In a large salad bowl, toss the vegetables together with:
1/2 pound feta cheese, crumbled
10–12 black olives

In a small bowl, whisk together until smooth:
1/4 cup extra-virgin olive oil
juice of 1/2 lemon
2 tablespoons rice vinegar
OR umeboshi vinegar
1 garlic clove, minced
Stir in:
3 tablespoons freshly and finely chopped mint leaves
1/2 teaspoon sea salt (omit if using umeboshi vinegar)

freshly ground black or white pepper

Pour the dressing over the vegetables and serve right away.

Chilled soups are a novel way to use summer's overproduction—especially when it comes to cucumbers. What follows is a revised version of Simply Grande shareholder Winnie Kierstead's Chilled Cucumber Soup for two.

Winnie Kierstead's Chilled Cucumber Soup

SERVES 2

Purée together in blender:

3/4 cup Vegetable Stock (see page 43)
1 medium-sized cucumber, peeled, seeded, and chopped
1 small garlic clove, minced
1/8 teaspoon hot pepper sauce
1 teaspoon curry powder

Pour into a small bowl and whisk in gently until smooth:

1 cup plain yogurt

Cover and chill. Just before serving, stir in:

1 medium-sized cucumber, peeled, seeded, and finely chopped

Serve in chilled glasses or bowls garnished with:

3 or 4 paper-thin, unpeeled cucumber slices
a sprinkling of paprika

Allow each diner to add sea salt if desired.

This cucumber soup leans toward dill for seasoning and is very quick to make.

Dilled Cucumber Soup

SERVES 2

Grate:

2 medium-sized, nonbitter cucumbers, peeled and seeded
1 small red
OR sweet Walla Walla onion

Stir in:

4 cups buttermilk
3 garlic cloves, minced
3 tablespoons minced fresh dill
sea salt (optional)
freshly ground black or white pepper

Serve chilled and garnished with more finely chopped dill or parsley.

Cucumbers can be cooked. To be specific, they can be baked, especially if they're disappointingly overgrown (which often happens). The result is fine. Keep in mind that, in New England, new potatoes are "in" when cukes appear, so the following recipe is seasonally appropriate.

J. A.'s Baked Oversized Cukes

SERVES 2–4

Preheat the oven to 350°F.

Cook until tender:

3–4 new potatoes

In a porcelainized or stainless-steel saucepan, bring to a boil:

3 cups water

1/2 teaspoon sea salt
2 teaspoons apple cider vinegar

Halve and seed:
**2 very large (6- to 8-inch) green
cucumbers**

Add them to the boiling mixture and simmer for 3 minutes. Remove and drain well. Place them, hollow-side down, on paper towels until you're ready to stuff.

Mash your cooked potatoes; you should have 2 cups. In a medium-sized bowl, whip together:
**the mashed potatoes
2/3 cup plain yogurt
1 tablespoon chopped fresh dill
OR chives
1 teaspoon freshly minced thyme
sea salt to taste
freshly ground black pepper
a little freshly grated nutmeg**

Turn the cucumbers right-side up and pile the potato mixture into their hollows.

Place the cukes in a buttered lasagne pan and sprinkle with:
**grated Parmesan
OR Fontinella cheese**

Bake for about 35 minutes and serve immediately with a big salad.

The English word gherkin, like the related German Gurke (used for cucumbers and gherkins alike), comes ultimately from Greek aggourion. "The first written mention of gherkins is not found until 1549 when it occurs in the work of Robert Estienne, although cucumbers (and gherkins are only a small variety of rough-skinned cucumber) had been very popular in Europe in classical times," reports Maguelonne Toussaint-Samat. Picked before they ripen, gherkins have been eaten in India for more than 30 centuries with salt or lemon juice. They came to Europe during the Renaissance as a truly exotic import.

Historically, New England gherkins always referred to tiny cucumbers pickled in honey. These were splendid accompaniments to baked beans and brown bread on Saturday night.

Summer Gherkins

MAKES 10 PINTS

THE CUCUMBERS

Wash well and remove the spines as necessary from:
6 pounds 1 1/2- to 2-inch cucumbers
Place in a large bowl and cover with:
**ice cubes
cold water**
Chill for 5 hours. Drain.

THE SPICES

Tie into a little cheesecloth bag:
**2 teaspoons celery seeds
2 teaspoons Pickling Spice Mix
(see the sidebar)
4 cinnamon sticks, broken into 1-inch
bits
1/2 teaspoon fennel seeds**

In a large porcelainized or stainless-steel pot, combine:

the drained cucumbers
6 cups 5 percent apple cider vinegar
1/2 teaspoon powdered turmeric
1/2 teaspoon powdered ginger
the bag of spices
Bring to a boil. Remove the cloth bag and add:
2 cups honey
Bring to a boil again.

Meanwhile, sterilize widemouthed pint canning jars by plunging them into boiling water. Remove them with tongs and place on towels to fill. Be careful not to get burned. (A towel underneath them will prevent breakage if counter-tops are cold.)

In a small saucepan of hot water, heat metal canning bands and lids to just under boiling.

Pack the drained cucumbers into the hot jars, leaving 1/4 inch of headroom. Cover with the boiling vinegar-honey liquid, again leaving 1/4 inch of head-room. Remove air bubbles by poking gently into each jar along the sides with a chopstick.

Wipe off the rims of the filled jars with a clean towel. Drop hot lids and bands into a sieve and drain. Then place them on the jars, screwing the bands down tightly.

Place the hot, filled jars on a rack in a big pot of hot water. Add more hot water if necessary to come at least 1 inch above the jar tops. Cover, bring to a boil, and process in this boiling-water bath for 5 minutes (pint jars) or 10 minutes (quart jars). Measure processing time from when a rolling boil begins. (If you're new to pickling and canning procedures, see page 38.)

When time is up, remove the jars with tongs and let them cool on a towel-covered counter to prevent breakage.

STORING

When the jars are completely cool, remove metal bands, check to see that each jar is safely sealed—the metal lid will feel slightly concave when you press it—rinse gently, wipe dry, label, and store in a cool, dark place.

It's possible to purchase commercial pickling spice. But you can fashion your own for use in many recipes.

Pickling Spice Mix

Crush and place in large bowl:
4–5 bay leaves

With a mortar and pestle, pound cardamom pods to extract the seeds. Add to the bowl:
1 tablespoon cardamom seeds

Break into small bits and add to the bowl:
1 cinnamon stick

Break into small bits and add to the bowl:
1 whole, dried chili pepper

Add to the bowl:
2 tablespoons white mustard seeds
1 tablespoon whole allspice
1 tablespoon coriander seeds
1 teaspoon whole cloves
**1 tablespoon black AND/OR
    multicolored peppercorns**

Store in a tightly capped jar.

Pickling is, of course, the method of choice for preserving summer's cucumber harvest. The following recipe is based on a classic New England hand-me-down and is a favorite.

Great Cucumber Pickles MAKES 8 PINTS

THE CUCUMBERS

Buy or pick:

6 pounds small, fresh cucumbers (about 4 inches long)

Wash them thoroughly but do not peel. Remove both ends and cut the rest into 1/4-inch slices.

THE ONIONS

Remove the skins from:

1 pound onions

Rinse well if necessary, and cut into 1/8-inch slices to measure 3 cups.

PROCEDURE

In a large stainless-steel or ceramic bowl, combine:

the cucumbers and onions

Add:

4 large, peeled garlic cloves, crushed
1/3 cup canning salt OR kosher salt

Mix thoroughly. Cover with:

2 trays of ice cubes

Let stand for 3 hours. Drain completely and remove the garlic (optional).

PROCESSING

In a large porcelainized pot, place:

4 1/2 cups refined white sugar
1 1/2 teaspoons powdered turmeric
1 1/2 teaspoons celery seeds
2 tablespoons Pickling Spice Mix (see page 151)
3 cups white vinegar

Bring nearly to a boil and add:

the drained cucumbers and onions

Heat over high heat for 5 minutes.

Meanwhile, in a small saucepan of hot water, heat metal bands and lids to just under boiling.

Ladle out hot pickles and juice into clean, hot, widemouthed canning jars, leaving 1/4 inch of headroom. Be sure the juice covers the pickle slices. Wipe off the rims of your pickle-filled jars. Remove air bubbles by poking into each jar along the sides with a chopstick.

When the bands and lids are hot, drain them in a sieve. Then place hot lids and bands on the jars, screwing the bands down tightly. Place the hot, filled jars on a rack in a big pot of hot water. Add more hot water if necessary to come at least 1 inch above the jar tops. Cover, bring to a rolling boil, and process in this boiling-water bath for 5 minutes (pints) or 10 minutes (quarts). (And see page 000 if you're new to canning procedures.) Measure processing time from when a rolling boil begins.

When time is up, remove the jars with tongs and let them cool on a rack or a towel-covered counter to prevent breakage.

STORING

Let the jars cool completely. When they're cool, remove the metal bands, rinse the jars gently, wipe them dry, label, and store in a cool, dark place.

NOTE: Fresh grape leaves added to pickles result in more crunch. To each quart, add 1 or 2 well-rinsed leaves. One 3-inch chunk of horseradish does the same thing.

Green Tomatoes

Tomatoes, discovered in Central America by marauding Spaniards, were immediately transplanted to southern Europe. They ran rampant. Where would Italian cooking be without them? Orientals decided to grow them in the 1700s.

A member of the nightshade family and related to potatoes, peppers, and eggplant —and thought at first to be poisonous—they've proved to be delicious, nutritionally valuable, and easy to prepare in thousands of ways. Vitamin loss through cooking is minimal. They may even lower the risk of cancer.

Because of hot summers, New Englanders grow gorgeous tomatoes—but the season can be brief, depending on location and soil type. If your tomatoes survive the first frosts come September (usually covered with bedsheets!), they'll thrive during Indian summer.

But there are always many big, green leftovers. These can be carefully packed in baskets or boxes and left to ripen for later enjoyment. Or—perhaps a better choice—they can be eaten right away.

For tips on growing tomatoes, see page 192.

Venetian Petrus Matthiolus remarked in 1544 that green tomato slices would be good "fried in oil with salt and pepper." Mainers have always relished fried tomato slices, and, whether due to short seasons or healthy taste buds, they have always fried them green.

Fried Green Tomatoes

SERVES 2–3

Cut into 1/2-inch-thick slices, omitting the stem and blow ends of:

3–4 large green tomatoes

In a small bowl, mix together:

about 1 cup stone-ground yellow cornmeal

a lot of freshly ground black OR white pepper
3/4 teaspoon sea salt
1 teaspoon dried oregano, well crumbled

Dredge each green tomato slice in the cornmeal-herb mixture.

Pour enough extra-virgin olive oil into a hot, cast-iron skillet to coat it to a 1/8-inch depth. Heat, but don't let the oil smoke. Reduce the heat to moderate and sauté the dredged tomato slices until they're golden brown on one side. Flip gently and fry the other side.

Serve immediately with new potatoes, a green leafy salad, and (hopefully) barely steamed corn on the cob.

*In a northern clime where tomatoes some-
times refuse to ripen before first frosts,
there's a way to preserve green tomatoes—
or at least their essence—for winter. This
soup can be made in quantity and freezes
well. It appeared in THE NEW MAINE
COOKING.*

Green Tomato Soup

SERVES 4

In a 6-quart pot, heat:
6 tablespoons extra-virgin olive oil
In it, sauté until translucent:
**3 large onions, coarsely chopped
(about 5 cups)**

Then add, cover, and simmer briefly
until soft, 30 to 40 minutes:
**10–12 coarsely chopped green
tomatoes (about 12 cups)**

Pour in:
**1 1/2 cups Vegetable Stock (see page
43) OR water**

When the soup is cool enough to
handle, purée appropriate-sized batches
of the tomato-onion mixture in a
blender at low speed, and turn into a
large stainless-steel or porcelainized pot.

Into a 2-cup measuring utensil, pour:
1 1/2 cups milk
Add and mix well:
2 heaping tablespoons cornstarch
Pour into the tomato-onion purée.

Place the pot on the stove and bring just
to a boil, stirring constantly with a
whisk, being very careful not to let it
burn. When the soup is hot, season it
with:
**1 teaspoon sea salt
some freshly ground black
OR white pepper**

2 tablespoons maple syrup, or to taste
Adjust the seasoning. You're reaching
for just the right balance between savory
and sweet.

Serve hot or cold, plain or with a
spoonful of fresh yogurt on each
serving. Garnish with:
**chopped fresh chives, parsley,
OR dill weed**

*Another method of preserving tomato
goodness, especially for long periods, is to
make "mincemeat"—without the meat.*

Green Tomato Mincemeat for Tarts and Pies

MAKES 10–12 PINTS

THE CANNING JARS

Wash 10 pint jars in hot soapy water.
Rinse and let the jars rest in hot water
until needed.

THE TOMATOES

Wash, drain, and coarsely chop enough
green tomatoes to equal:
2 quarts green tomatoes
Grind up the tomatoes in a stainless-
steel meat grinder, pouring them into a
stainless-steel or ceramic dish. Sprinkle
with:
1 tablespoon sea salt
Let stand for 1 hour. Drain through a
sieve. Cover with boiling water for 5
minutes and drain again.

ADDITIONS

Wash well, grate the rind, and chop the
pulp of:
1 orange

Wash well, core, peel, and measure enough chunks to equal:

10 cups chopped apples

Put the fruit into a large porcelainized or stainless-steel pot and mix well with:

1/2 pound (1 1/4 cups) seedless currants
1/2 pound (1 1/4 cups) seedless white raisins
3 1/2 cups packed brown sugar
1/2 cup cider vinegar
2 teaspoons powdered cinnamon
1 teaspoon freshly grated nutmeg
1 teaspoon ground cloves
1/2 teaspoon powdered ginger (optional)

COOKING

Heat the mixture of tomatoes, orange pulp, apples, and spices till it's boiling hot.

CANNING

Meanwhile, in a small saucepan of hot water, heat metal bands and lids to just under boiling. When they're hot, drop them into a sieve and drain.

Place hot canning jars on a towel-covered countertop. Pour your hot tomato "mincemeat" into the hot jars, allowing 1 inch of headroom. Poke with a chopstick to remove air bubbles. Wipe off the rims with a clean cloth. Place the drained, hot lids and bands on the jars, screwing the bands down tightly, and process for 25 minutes in a pressure cooker at 10 pounds pressure for pints or quarts, according to the Ball company's *Blue Book* (see page 38) and your pressure cooker instructions.

When they're processed completely, remove the jars with tongs and let them cool on a towel-covered counter to prevent breakage.

STORING

When the jars are completely cool, remove the metal bands, rinse the jars gently, wipe dry, label, then store in a cool, dark place.

Euell Gibbons, that expert on wild-food gathering, once described a Dill Crock— a crock stuffed full of summer vegetables thrown in rather haphazardly, allowed to cure in brine for several weeks, then processed in the usual manner for winter keeping. It closely resembles many a crock put down by New England women through the years. This one includes tiny green tomatoes. The recipe first appeared in ORGANIC FARMING AND GARDENING magazine, and later in STOCKING UP. It's been revised slightly.

Euell's Layered Dill Crock

In a 1-gallon ceramic crock, place:

3 fresh dill heads
OR a handful of dill weed

Add:

3 big garlic cloves, peeled
3 hot chili peppers, washed, slit, and seeds removed (see page 201)

Wash carefully, slice into 1/2-inch disks, and place atop the chili pepper layer:

1 pound sunchokes, sliced

Add:

3 more fresh dill heads
OR a handful of dill weed

Slice into bite-sized bits and place on the dill:

6–7 scallions

Add a layer of:
cauliflower florets
Add another layer of:
**whole green sting beans, stems and
strings removed**
Place on top:
3 more fresh dill heads
Then add layers of:
**3 carrots, sliced into bite-sized disks
3 celery stalks, sliced into bite-sized
half moons
a handful of small pickling onions
some small green tomatoes**
Place on top:
**3 more fresh dill heads
OR a handful of dill weed**

In a bowl, mix together until dissolved:
**8 cups distilled white vinegar
1/3 cup kosher OR canning salt**

Pour over the ingredients in the crock. Be sure the vegetables are well covered. Weight with a saucer.

Let the crock rest on your kitchen counter for 5 days, then refrigerate. It will keep for a week. For longer keeping, process in a boiling-water bath as described above.

Gibbons's advice for processing was this: Drain the vegetables, reserving the liquid. Pack the vegetables into hot, scalded quart jars with some fresh dill. Strain the brine through cheesecloth, bring to a boil in a stainless-steel pot, then pour over the vegetables, leaving 1/2 inch headroom. Seal the usual way, and process in a boiling-water bath for 15 minutes.

Cherry Tomatoes

In New England's short growing season, tomatoes often struggle to ripen. Tiny cherry varieties, however, manage it before larger varieties can.

This recipe uses these little jewels and is a favorite of one Simply Grande shareholder. She reports that it originated at a restaurant of forgotten name, and was adapted. It has been adapted again.

Cherry Delights with Pasta

SERVES 6

THE TOMATOES

Pick or purchase:
**20–25 red cherry tomatoes
20–25 yellow cherry tomatoes**
Slice them in half.

In a blender, whiz together:
**1/2 cup extra-virgin olive oil
1 cup loosely packed fresh basil
leaves, chopped
4 big garlic cloves, minced
2 teaspoons balsamic vinegar
1/2–1 teaspoon sea salt
some freshly ground black
OR white pepper**

Pour into a bowl and, an hour before mealtime, add the tomatoes to marinate.

THE PASTA

In a large pot, bring to a boil:
  4 quarts water
Add:
  1 teaspoon sea salt
Carefully add:
  1 pound fresh spinach linguine
  OR other pasta

Cook till *al dente*. Drain. Rinse the pasta if necessary, then steam it in a colander set over boiling water till it's hot again.

When you're ready to serve, toss the pasta in a heated bowl with the tomato mixture.

Add:
  1/2 cup toasted pine nuts
  OR walnut halves
  1/2 cup black olives
  1/2 cup freshly chopped basil
  AND/OR parsley leaves

SERVING

Pass to each diner to sprinkle on:
  1 cup freshly grated Parmigiano
  OR Romano cheese

Serve immediately with a big tossed salad and fresh rolls.

Summer Squash and Zucchini

"The pumpkin and squashes (genus *Cucurbita*) are all of American origin," reports Harold McGee in *On Food and Cooking: The Science and Lore of the Kitchen*. Many "thrive in the arid climates of the southwestern United States and northern Mexico. Some of the 25 species have been cultivated for 9000 years."

Adds Reay Tannahill, "By some time between 7000 B.C. and 5000 B.C. . . . it is clear that the inhabitants of a group of caves in the Tamaulipas mountains of Mexico, although they still gathered wild plants in the form of runner beans and the agave, or American aloe, had begun to domesticate a number of others. Among these was the summer squash, which provided both a flesh and a seed food. . . ." Professor Jared Diamond would correct these dates to only 3500 B.C.

Harvard's Charles Heiser says that five different species of squash or pumpkin were domesticated in the Americas. "Since the wild cucurbits have little or no flesh in the fruit, it has been postulated that they may have been domesticated for their edible seeds—'pepitas,' or pumpkin seeds, are still eaten. Mutant types with fleshy fruits then appeared, according to the theory, and their deliberate selection has produced the thick-fleshed varieties now widely cultivated." Following the European discovery of America, pumpkins and squash were soon introduced into Europe and Asia, and today they're important in many parts of the world not only for human food but also for livestock. The largest fruit in the plant kingdom, says Heiser, comes from a squash *(Cucurbita maxima)*. Some weighing nearly 700 pounds have been reported. And since his book, pumpkins have reached 1,140 pounds, according to Gail Damerow in *Perfect Pumpkin*. The Old World, too, furnished food plants from the Cucurbitaceae, including cucumbers, melons such as cantaloupe and cassaba, and the watermelon. The cucumber and melons come from different species of the genus *Cucumis;* the watermelon belongs to the genus *Citrullus.*

Professor David M. Tucker, in *Kitchen Gardening in America,* suggests that the first seasonal vegetables from Native American gardens were yellow crookneck squash and green beans. Squash were roasted in the fire by covering them with a blanket of ashes and then heaping on hot embers for a slow bake.

It's all fascinating. And nutritious. A cupful of summer squash contains 530 International Units of vitamin A, 29 milligrams of vitamin C, 1.25 International Units of vitamin E, 36 milligrams of calcium, and 263 milligrams of potassium, among other vitamins and minerals. Yellow squash may lower the risk of cancer, especially of the lung.

The concern of Northeast gardeners during short, hot summers, however, is what to do with all those summer squash that thrive here—especially, perhaps, the ones with which we're not totally familiar, such as patty pan.

Patty pan is shaped like two pie plates with scalloped edges stuck together. Light green or yellow in color, they're rather handsome nestling amid yellow blossoms and the thick, spiny stems of parent plants. Five- to 6-inch sizes are best for eating, although larger will suffice for stuffing.

Like young green zucchini and the yellow crookneck varieties, patty pans can be cut into chunks (in this case, into wedges) and quickly pan-simmered in a little extra-virgin olive oil with sliced onions, chunked tomatoes, minced garlic, bits of freshly plucked basil and oregano, freshly ground black pepper, and a little sea salt.

GARDENING NOTES

SQUASH

CHOOSING SEEDS: Each of the major types below has dozens of varieties:

Summer squash: Zucchini, straightneck, crookneck, Mideast, patty pan (scallop), spaghetti, and more. They all taste similar, so base your choice on pleasing color and shape.

Winter squash: Acorn, buttercup, butternut, delicata, hubbard, pumpkin, and more. Choosing one from each type would be more than a home gardener could want.

Squash seeds are large (about 120 to 480 per ounce) and edible.

CULTIVATION: Prepare the bed with low mounds ("hills") of the best soil along with compost or manure. Hills should be about 1 foot in diameter and at least 4 feet apart. Use black plastic mulch around the hills to warm the soil, or hay mulch to keep weeds down and soil moist. Plant seeds when the soil is warm, four to six seeds per hill. Push them down about 1 inch. Thin to the two or three best plants per hill. Alternately, plant seedlings for an early first harvest of summer squash.

Weed once or twice until squash take over the hill.

PESTS AND DISEASES: There are lots. If cucumber beetles (small and quick, with yellow and black stripes) arrive early, they can devour the first leaves, and at any time will carry bacterial wilt. Squash bugs (big, gray, and slow) bring disease to fruits. Vine borers kill plants at the base. Sprinkle rotenone and pyrethrum powders on the leaves and around the base of the plants. Gummy stem blight (black rot) causes black sunken spots on fruits in storage, and tan scabs on butternuts in the field. Downy mildew may kill leaves in cool, damp weather. Powdery mildew may kill leaves in hot, dry weather and late summer. Rotate squash beds with other crops. Remove and compost or bury all infected squash vines.

HARVESTING:

Summer squash: These should be harvested when they're small and tender. Watch the bed daily. If some get away to produce vegetable baseball bats, use them for zucchini bread, or stuffing and baking. Spaghetti squash can be left to get big.

Winter squash: The first frost will kill leaves and can thus facilitate harvest, because fruits become visible. Pull the fruits off the vine before the next frost and cure them (to toughen their skins) in the sun for a week, covering the cache if another frost is likely. Store them in low humidity and moderate temperatures in a place where you can watch them. Pull any that show signs of rot; eat the good parts and discard the rest.

*Stuffed, patty pans become grand—
or Simply Grande.*

Simply Grande Stuffed Patty Pans

SERVES 4

THE SQUASH

Cut in half horizontally across the
widest part:

2 5- or 6-inch patty pan squash

Slice off the stem and a little piece of
skin so the scalloped disk will lie flat.
Scoop out seeds and some pulp, leaving
a 1/2-inch rim all around. Reserve the
pulp.

THE STUFFING

In a medium-sized bowl, mix together
well:

    the squash pulp, chopped fine
    1 large onion, diced, OR equal
        amount of bunching onions, sliced
    2 garlic cloves, minced
    2 large eggs, beaten
    3/4 cup crumbled feta cheese
    2–3 tablespoons finely chopped fresh
        parsley
    1/2 cup diced whole-grain bread
        crumbs
    freshly ground black pepper

BAKING

Preheat the oven to 375°F. Pour 1/2
inch of hot water into a well-buttered
lasagne pan.

Pile the stuffing mixture into the squash
"bowls," mounding slightly, and place
them in the pan. Cover tightly, and bake
till the bowls are tender and the stuffing
is firm.

SERVING

Serve immediately with a salad, new
potatoes, and hot rolls.

NOTE: You can substitute 3 medium-
sized, straight, yellow summer squash
for the patty pans.

---

*Another version of baked summer squash
uses a large, cylindrical type: 'Costata
Romanesca,' a striped, ridged variety that
grows without much of a curve and is
tender even when very mature. It's perfect
for company banquets.*

    *This recipe is a suggestion only:
Adjust the amounts of everything to
your own taste.*

Baked Company Costata

SERVES MANY

Preheat the oven to 375°F.

Purchase or pick:

    one whopping big Costata
    (perhaps 14 inches long,
    with a 6-inch diameter!)

Wash it well. Slice off the top 2 or 3
inches horizontally, and set this aside to
use as a cover while baking. With a big
spoon, scoop out all the seeds from
inside the squash body and cover, leaving a thick wall of "meat" all around.

If the seeds aren't too big, chop all of
the scooped innards finely and place in a
bowl. You'll have several cupfuls.

Mix together (in approximate amounts):

    3 cups chopped squash innards
    2 cups cooked basmati rice OR barley
    1 cup chopped fresh button
        mushrooms

1 cup finely chopped walnut meats
2 tablespoons freshly chopped parsley
1 tablespoon freshly chopped mint
    leaves
1 tablespoon freshly chopped oregano
1 teaspoon grated (well-washed)
    lemon rind (optional)
1–2 teaspoons sea salt
freshly ground black pepper
3–4 lightly beaten eggs

Pour about 1 inch of water into a large lasagne pan and place the squash boat in. Pile the stuffing into the boat, heaping it smoothly. Sprinkle with:

**a lot of freshly grated Parmesan
OR Romano cheese**
Place on the cap.

Cover and bake until the stuffing is done and squash walls are soft but not mushy. This may take 45 minutes. Prick with a long-tined fork to check. Allow to cool slightly before serving.

Serve by cutting 2- or 3-inch slices per person. A green leafy salad with fresh, sliced red tomatoes makes a complete meal.

---

*Simply Grande shareholder
Sandy Hussey presents this tasty
recipe for green zucchini.*

Sandy Hussey's Amazing Zucchini

SERVES 4–6

Cut in half lengthwise and slice again several times to result in long, thin strips like spaghetti:

2 pounds young, tender zucchini
(If a zucchini is large, cut it to equal 6-inch sections, then cut each section

in half lengthwise, slice thin, and slice again several times to result in "spaghetti.") Place the strips in a colander and sprinkle with:

1 tablespoon sea salt

Toss to distribute the salt and let this rest for 15 or more minutes. Rinse well, drain well, and gently squeeze dry in a tea towel.

Heat a wok and pour in:
1 tablespoon extra-virgin olive oil
When the oil is heated, add and stir-fry for 4 minutes:

**1 tablespoon minced fresh gingerroot
1 tablespoon minced garlic
2 tablespoons freshly chopped
    cilantro
2 tablespoons chopped green scallions
the zucchini strips**

Sprinkle with:
a few drops of toasted sesame seed oil

Serve hot with rice or new potatoes, and sliced red tomatoes. The dish can also be enjoyed at room temperature.

---

*Shredding zucchini or yellow summer
squash is easy, and enlarges the number
of ways they can be cooked.*

Zucchini-Walnut Patties

SERVES 2–4

Shred:
**1 young, 10-inch zucchini
1 young, 10-inch yellow summer
    squash**
Place in a colander set over a medium-sized bowl and sprinkle lightly with:

1/2 teaspoon sea salt

Toss to mix and let drain for 30 minutes.

Pile the squash onto a tea towel and squeeze out as much moisture as possible. You should have about 2 cupfuls of quite dry, shredded squash.

Place the squash in a medium-sized bowl and add:

5 medium-sized eggs, beaten
1/2 cup minced onion
1/2 cup finely chopped walnuts
1 tablespoon chopped fresh oregano
1 tablespoon chopped fresh parsley
freshly ground black pepper
2 tablespoons white flour

Mix well together.

Oil a skillet and drop in the zucchini mixture by rounded tablespoons or more. Cook over medium heat for 2 to 3 minutes until golden, turning once.

Serve for brunch, or for dinner with new potatoes, corn on the cob, sliced cucumbers and tomatoes, and a green leafy salad.

When August brings an absolute surfeit of summer squash, it's time to plan how to preserve that goodness for the long white season ahead. One way to do so sweetly is to make zucchini bread and freeze it—lots of it. You'll need a grater. When grating zucchini for this recipe, keep going. And going. Shredded zucchini needs no peeling or blanching before freezing. Pop it into containers, mark well, and freeze for winter soups. Or more bread.

Of course, everyone has a favorite version of zucchini bread. These loaves are very sweet; in fact, they're cake.

Zucchini Bread

MAKES 2 LOAVES

Preheat the oven to 350°F.

Sift together:

2 cups white unbleached flour
1 cup whole-wheat flour
1 teaspoon double-acting baking powder (see page 28)
1 teaspoon baking soda
1 teaspoon sea salt
2 teaspoons powdered cinnamon
1/2 teaspoon freshly grated nutmeg

If there's any wheat germ left in your sifter, return it to your flour mix.

In a large bowl, beat together until smooth and creamy:

3 eggs
1 3/4 cups refined white sugar
1 cup sunflower seed oil
1 1/2 teaspoons natural vanilla

Gradually beat the dry ingredients into the wet ingredients. Then stir in:

2 cups coarsely grated zucchini
OR other summer squash

Add:

1 cup currants (optional)

3/4 cup chopped walnuts (optional)

Spoon the batter into two well-greased, 8 1/2- by 4 1/2- by 2 1/2-inch loaf pans, and bake in your preheated 350°F oven for 60 minutes. Let the loaves rest for a minute or two, then turn them out onto racks to cool before slicing.

Here's another, less sweet version of zucchini bread. It's really bread, not cake, perfect with soups for summer.

Green Zucchini Bread

MAKES 2 LOAVES

Wash well, trim off the ends, and coarsely grate:

2 pounds green zucchini

Place in a bowl and sprinkle with:

1 tablespoon sea salt

Toss with your fingers, let rest for about 30 minutes, drain in a colander, and gently squeeze dry in a tea towel. You should have 2 cups grated zucchini.

Preheat the oven to 350°F.

Into a bowl, sift together:

1 3/4 cups unbleached white flour
1 cup whole-wheat flour
1 1/2 teaspoons double-acting baking powder (see page 28)
1 teaspoon baking soda
1/2 teaspoon powdered cinnamon

In a large bowl or the bowl of your electric mixer, beat together:

3 medium-sized eggs
1 cup refined white sugar
1/2 cup sunflower seed oil

Beat in:

1 tablespoon freshly squeezed lemon juice

1 teaspoon natural vanilla
the flour mixture

Stir in:

the grated rind of 1 well-washed lemon
the grated, drained zucchini
1 cup chopped walnut meats

Grease well and flour two 8 1/2- by 4 1/2- by 2 1/2-inch loaf pans. Pour in the bread mixture, thump each pan once to release air bubbles, and bake on the middle shelf of your oven for 50 to 60 minutes, or until a toothpick inserted into the browned loaf top comes out clean.

Zucchini also makes a truly fine, bright green soup. This one is not for weight watchers.

Green Zucchini Soup

SERVES 2

Remove the peel from and chop to measure:

1 cup finely chopped onions

Wash and slice both ends from:

about 1 pound green zucchini

Finely chop the zucchini to measure 2 cups.

Trim off the stems and finely chop to produce:

3/4 cup fresh parsley
1/4 cup fresh cilantro (including berries if green)

Into a medium-sized porcelainized pot, pour:

2 tablespoons extra-virgin olive oil

Add, cover, and cook over low heat, stirring occasionally, till tender:

the finely chopped onions

Add and bring to a boil:

1 1/2 cups Vegetable Stock (see page 43) OR 1 1/4 cups water to which you've added 1/4 cup Bragg's Liquid Aminos (see page 63)
the 2 cups zucchini

Reduce the heat and simmer till very tender, perhaps 10 minutes.

Remove the onion-zucchini mixture from the heat and add:

the parsley-cilantro mix

Cover and let the mixture rest and cool slightly. Then pour it into a blender and purée till smooth. (Place a towel over the blender top as you purée to prevent burning.) Return to the porcelainized pot and add:

1/2 cup heavy cream
Season with:

freshly ground black pepper
1 tablespoon freshly squeezed lemon juice (optional)

Reheat if necessary (but do not boil), and serve right away.

NOTE: This recipe is easily doubled.

One other rather odd squash deserves attention: the spaghetti. This big, tan oval, which looks so uninteresting in the garden, turns into a magical moment on the table. It originated in Italy as a light green squash with dark green spots, but around the turn of the 19th century a Japanese group began experimenting and, after 70 years, came up with today's vegetable.

It's as easy to prepare as any other squash. Only the spaghetti's surprising interior is different.

Summertime Spaghetti Squash
SERVES 4–6

Pick or purchase:
1 mature spaghetti squash

Fill with water a kettle big enough to hold the whole squash and bring it to a boil. When the water is boiling, gently lower in the squash. Cook for 20 to 30 minutes, till a fork pricks through the skin easily. Remove and let cool.

When the squash is cool enough to handle, split it lengthwise and remove the seeds; then, using a fork, rake the flesh. The "spaghetti" will pull off in long strands.

Serve immediately topped with:
Simply Grande Garden Tomato Sauce (see page 196)

Cooked and raked squash can also be refrigerated for later. Sauté the "spaghetti" in garlic-flavored, extra-virgin olive oil and sprinkle with freshly chopped parsley.

Endive

E ndive, *Cichorium endivia,* is a hardy annual or biennial herb of the Compositae family—otherwise known as daisies. This family is the second largest of the flowering plants, yet contributes only a few food varieties.

Native to the East Indies and possibly also to Sicily, "it was known early to the Egyptians and Greeks as a salad herb" writes J. I. Rodale in *How to Grow Vegetables and Fruits by the Organic Method.* Harold McGee says endive was native to India, and known to the Romans.

Today there seem to be two developed varieties. One has narrow, curly, finely cut leaves and is usually called endive, although some folks call it chicory, and others refer to it as frisée when it's young. The other variety is broad leaved and popularly known as escarole. Both varieties belong to one of the two main species of chicory grown for greens.

True chicory, *C. intybus* (for those interested), is what most people call Belgian endive, or *witloof.* "The white, boat-shaped leaves, called *chicons,* grow on parsnip-like roots that are marginally edible but most commonly employed as an admixture to coffee," advises Raymond Sokolov in *Why We Eat What We Eat.* "In the mid-nineteenth century someone noticed that chicory root left in the dark produces white leaves. The head horticulturist at the Brussels Botanical Gardens, a certain M. Brezier, perfected the new vegetable. The first box was sent to the United States in 1911."

Since the 19th century Americans have also noted true chicory in a wild form that produces blue flowers along roadsides. Adds Sokolov, "You certainly shouldn't try to use their seeds to grow true endive." It belongs to the same genus but is quite different.

For tips on growing endive, see page 231.

C. endivia is particularly rich in vitamin A. A cupful contains 1,026 International Units of it, along with 3.2 milligrams of vitamin C, 26 milligrams of calcium, 58 milligrams of potassium, some B_1, B_2, and B_6, and a little protein, among other nutrients.

Elizabeth Eames of Winslow, Maine, a delightful lady who for many years taught French to lucky high school students (and whose family home with its fireplaces and big 18-inch corner beams was completed in 1775 by Joel Crosby, who served and died in the American Revolution), once shared this recipe for endive and red kidney beans: an old Maine mainstay. We've revised it slightly.

Elizabeth's Red Kidney Beans and Endive

SERVES 3–4

THE NIGHT BEFORE

Pick over, rinse quickly, and soak overnight:

1 cup red kidney beans

IN THE MORNING

Place the soaked beans in a pot and add boiling water to barely cover. Then add:

2 garlic cloves, smashed
1 small onion, chopped finely
1/4 green pepper, chopped finely
3 inches celery stalk, chopped finely
freshly ground black pepper
1 teaspoon fennel, powdered in your blender (optional)
1/2 teaspoon dried thyme
2 bay leaves
1 teaspoon dried summer savory
1 teaspoon crumbled dried oregano
1 teaspoon crumbled dried basil
1 teaspoon dried thyme
1/4 teaspoon cayenne powder

Simmer the beans till they're tender, 2 to 3 hours. Add hot water as necessary.

At this point you can store your beans, covered, in the refrigerator for use later, or continue with the recipe.

DINNERTIME

Heat in a big porcelainized or stainless-steel pot:

1 tablespoon extra-virgin olive oil

Sauté in it:

1 cup chopped onion
3 large garlic cloves, minced

Add:

1 quart Vegetable Stock (see page 43)
3 cups of the cooked and drained red kidney beans
freshly ground black pepper
1 teaspoon kelp powder
OR crumbled kelp (optional)
1 teaspoon sea salt (optional)

Simmer till well blended. Add:

2 cups rinsed, coarsely chopped endive

Simmer for 15 minutes more.

SERVING

Serve hot with whole-wheat or corn bread, a small tossed salad, potatoes, and fall vegetables such as carrots or beets.

With its hint of bitterness, endive is, of course, perfect for salads.

Endive Salad

SERVES 4

Rinse well, spin dry, and allow to chill in your refrigerator until crisp:

1 head curly endive
1 small head romaine
OR other lettuce
a few bright bits of radicchio

Rub the interior of a wooden salad bowl with:

a cut garlic clove

Tear your crisp greens into bite-sized pieces, focusing on the tender, inner leaves while discarding many of the tough, outer ones.

Heap the greens in the bowl and toss with a simple dressing of:

1 part balsamic vinegar

2 parts extra-virgin olive oil

Scatter thickly on top and toss again:

sunflower seeds lightly toasted in shoyu (naturally fermented soy sauce)

Serve immediately.

NOTE 1: The shoyu-toasted sunflower seeds yield just enough saltiness without adding more.

NOTE 2: Thinly sliced, small, ripe tomatoes and cucumbers (particularly 'Boothby Blond', a Maine heirloom available from Fedco Seeds) add flavorful enjoyment.

Escarole, the broad-leaved version of what Mainers like to call endive, holds its texture well in a soufflé.

Escarole Soufflé

SERVES 4

THE SOUFFLÉ DISH

Butter a 1 1/2-quart soufflé dish. Sprinkle with:

1/4 cup freshly and finely grated Parmesan cheese

Knock out any excess cheese and save, then refrigerate the dish till you're ready to use it.

THE OVEN

Preheat the oven to 375°F.

THE ESCAROLE AND ONIONS

Wash well, remove the stem end, and weigh out:

1/4 pound escarole

Chop the leaves to equal 2 cups.

Set a wok on its collar and heat. Add:

1 tablespoon extra-virgin olive oil

Sauté in it till limp:

3 tablespoons chopped bunching onions OR scallions

Add, cover, and cook over low heat for about 4 minutes or till wilted:

the chopped escarole

Remove the cover and cook over low heat till all moisture is evaporated. You should have 3/4 cup of the escarole-onion mixture. Remove from the wok and set aside.

THE EGG SAUCE

Separate the yolks from the whites of 5 large eggs. Beat together till stiff:

the 5 egg whites

a pinch of cream of tartar

Set aside.

In a medium-sized bowl, whisk well:

4 egg yolks

(Save the fifth yolk for pastries; see Great Pastries for Great Pies on page 67.)

In a heavy porcelainized pot, heat:

2 tablespoons butter

Stir in and cook for about 3 minutes:

2 1/4 tablespoons unbleached white flour

Whisk in:

1 1/4 cups milk

Bring to a boil, whisking, then reduce the heat and boil for 1 minute.

COMBINING

Whisk a small amount of the hot milk-egg liquid into the beaten egg yolks to warm them, then pour the rest of the yolks into the hot mixture and whisk together. Stir in:

the escarole-onion mixture
1/4 cup grated extra-sharp
   Cheddar cheese
1/2 teaspoon Worcestershire sauce
1/8 teaspoon cayenne powder
sea salt to taste
freshly ground black pepper

Let this cool slightly.

Gently stir in one-quarter of the stiff egg whites, then fold in the rest of the whites.

Pour the batter into your prepared soufflé dish, thump lightly once to release air bubbles, and sprinkle with:

the leftover Parmesan cheese

Bake in the preheated 375° oven for 30 minutes, or till the top is browned.

Serve at once with lemon-flavored rice, a green salad with ripe tomatoes, and other vegetables.

Swiss Chard

B eta vulgaris, or Swiss chard, reports that inveterate organic gardener and plant historian J. I. Rodale, "is the beet as it was cultivated by the Greeks and Romans, long before the thick fleshy root we now known as beet was developed. Use of chard spread to China in the Middle Ages and is now almost universal. It is found growing wild in the Canary Islands and around the Mediterranean."

It's also found growing in America, carefully husbanded by gardeners. "Swiss chard is a hardy biennial vegetable that also goes by the name of spinach beet or silver-leaf beet," remarks Benjamin Watson's *Taylor's Guide to Heirloom Vegetables.* "Native to southern Europe, chard is apparently much older than the large-rooted forms of beets and may have developed from the wild beet more than 2,000 years ago. Aristotle mentions a red-stalked chard around 350 B.C., and white, yellow, and dark green forms have apparently been known since ancient times."

Chard was originally a corruption of the French word for "cardoon," *carde.* Its name was Swiss cardoon, a misnomer that can be likened to another famous misnomer, the Jerusalem artichoke.

Fearing Burr Jr., an unusual early New England horticulturist (who sometimes got his facts wrong) and the first American to publish excellent descriptions of vegetable varieties in his book *Field and Garden Vegetables of America,* agreed that "The Leaf-Beet, or Swiss Chard, also called Sicilian Beet, or White Beet . . . is a native of the sea-coasts of Spain and Portugal. It is a biennial plant, and is cultivated for its leaves and leaf-stalks.

"This species of Beet—for, botanically considered, it is a distinct species from *Beta vulgaris*, the Common or Red Beet—is cultivated exclusively for its leaves," he continued, "whereas the Red Beet is grown for its roots. These leaves are boiled like Spinach, and also put into soups. The midribs and stalks, which are separated from the lamina of the leaf, are stewed and eaten like Asparagus, under the name of 'Chard.'" In this instance Burr was quoting Charles McIntosh from an even earlier work, *The Book of the Garden,* published in Edinburgh and London in 1855.

Again quoting from McIntosh, Burr said "The largest and fullest grown leaves should be gathered first; others will follow. If grown for Spinach, the leaves should be rinsed in clean water, and afterwards placed in a basket to drain dry; if for Chard, or for the leaf-stalks and veins, these should be carefully preserved, and the entire leaves tied up in bundles of six or eight in each."

Burr's book, referred to by most students of horticultural history today, is rather a mystery. We can't know for certain why he decided to write it, says Professor Robert Becker in the introduction to the 1994 reprint. "It was surely not a spur-of-the-moment decision, for he must have spent a considerable period of time evaluating, comparing, and writing descriptions for the hundreds of varieties that are included."

Apparently it was a necessary job. "Nineteenth century American seedsmen," Becker continues, "obtained seed from three basic sources: abroad; their own farms; and market gardeners. Reports from the period indicate that seed quality was not always high. Germination and vitality often were low, and seed sometimes lacked varietal purity. . . . The Shakers became so disenchanted with the quality of the seed they were purchasing that they decided to sell only seed which they themselves had produced.

"When Burr began to write *The Field and Garden Vegetables of America,* the number of vegetable varieties being marketed far exceeded the number available only twenty to thirty years earlier. Fierce competition existed between seedsmen, and each endeavored to introduce new varieties to the gardening public. Frequently, the 'new' introductions were simply selections made from older varieties. . . . Some were older varieties that had just been renamed. . . . Often a single variety had more than one name, and, on occasion, dissimilar varieties carried identical names."

As a seedsman, Professor Becker concludes, "Burr was certainly aware that there was an ever-increasing number of varieties being introduced in the trade, resulting in much confusion. By reviewing the merits and demerits of each, he could help the uninformed gardener choose the appropriate variety for his need."

Fearing Burr listed chard varieties with varicolored stalks: white, bright purplish red, and bright yellow—and we have them today. Nor have cooking directions changed much. Among other nutrients, a cupful of chard contains 1,188 International Units of vitamin A, 10.8 milligrams of vitamin C, 18 milligrams of calcium, and 136 milligrams of potassium.

Possibly the tastiest way to enjoy Swiss chard is the easiest: sautéed. A mix of white- and colored-stemmed chard will do.

Simply Sautéed Swiss Chard

SERVES 2

In a large skillet, or a wok set on its collar, heat:

2 teaspoons extra-virgin olive oil

Over medium heat, add and sauté for about 3 minutes:

2 garlic cloves, minced
1/2 cup sliced leeks (the white part)
OR 1 small onion, sliced thinly
2/3 cup thinly sliced celery

Remove the ribs from:

8–10 large Swiss chard leaves

Roll them into a "sausage" and chop coarsely to equal 4 cups. Add this to garlic-leek mixture along with:

1 tablespoon water or
   Vegetable Stock (see page 43)

Season with:

sea salt to taste
freshly ground black pepper

Toss well, cover, and steam over low heat for about 5 minutes, or until the chard is wilted.

Just before serving, sprinkle with:

freshly squeezed lemon juice
some hot pepper sauce

Offer with new potatoes, sliced tomatoes and cucumbers, and corn bread.

GARDENING NOTES

SWISS CHARD

CHOOSING SEEDS: There are spectacular heirlooms of this vegetable—look for 'Fordhook' and 'Ruby Red'—and equally spectacular new varieties such as 'Bright Lights' and 'Bright Yellow'. Though Swiss chard is a close relative of beets, it doesn't have the acidic aftertaste typical of beet greens. There are 2,000 seeds per ounce; 1/2 ounce sows 100 row feet.

CULTIVATION: Direct-seed in rows 18 inches apart, 6 seeds per foot. As with beets, Swiss chard seeds are actually seedpods, so you should thin to 6 inches apart for full-sized leaves. For mesclun salad mixes, thinning is less important. Collineal-hoe between the rows until weed control is taken over by the Swiss chard forest.

PESTS AND DISEASES: None, except deer.

HARVESTING: For full-sized leaves and all the stalk you can get, twist the leaf off at its base. You can also cut with a knife or snip with scissors. For salad mix, start snipping about 5 weeks after planting.

NOTE: Swiss chard ribs—especially of the white-stemmed kind—can be sliced into 1-inch bits and added to any clear soup, as you'd do with bok choi.

Eggs and Swiss chard are a long-standing friendly combination. And wok cooking makes everything easy. With its slanted-in sides and rounded interior, it's perfect not only for stir-frying but also for cooking any vegetables—including the chard in this recipe. Use chard with thick, white stems.

Swiss Chard Custard

SERVES 6

THE VEGETABLES

Place a wok on its collar and warm over medium-low heat:

3 tablespoons extra-virgin olive oil

Add and cook for 2 minutes:

1 large onion, finely chopped
to equal 1 cup

While the onion cooks, rinse quickly and slice the ribs off:

6–8 big Swiss chard leaves

Roll the leaves into a "sausage" and chop to equal 2 cups. Chop the stems finely to equal 1 1/2 cups.

Stir the chopped stems into the onion and cook, covered, till tender, perhaps 5 minutes. Stir in the chopped Swiss chard leaves and cook, covered, till tender, perhaps 3 minutes more. Increase the heat to medium high and remove the cover. Cook, tossing, till any liquid has evaporated. The chard bits and onion will have turned golden. Set aside in a large bowl to cool.

THE CUSTARD

Preheat the oven to 325°F.

In a medium-sized bowl, lightly beat:

5 medium-sized eggs

Add to the cooled chard-onion and mix well with:

1/4 cup milk
1/2 cup heavy cream (or milk)
1/2 teaspoon sea salt
1/4 teaspoon freshly ground black, white, OR multicolored pepper
2/3 cup fresh bread crumbs
1/2 cup grated sharp Cheddar cheese

Pour into a buttered 1 1/2-quart soufflé dish.

BAKING

Place the soufflé dish in a shallow baking pan and add boiling water to come halfway up its sides. Bake for about 45 minutes, or till an inserted knife comes out clean.

SERVING

Remove the dish from the oven and let it rest for 10 minutes. Serve from the soufflé dish, or run a sharp knife around the inner edge and invert onto a serving platter. Cut into wedges or squares.

A tomato salad with grated carrots and sliced cucumbers, plus some freshly baked bread, make good accompaniments.

Eggplant

The Solanaceae (nightshade) family has provided humans with some interesting critters, among them the potato, tomato, and pepper; tobacco; the hallucinogenic jimsonweed; deadly nightshade, which grows along the brook at Simply Grande—and the eggplant, or as the French say, *aubergine.*

Ripening in Maine gardens by August, these purple, pendulous fruits first appeared in India. In A.D. 642 invading Arabs met them in Persia, and by 1274, when China's Kublai Khan was trying unsuccessfully to invade Japan (he was stopped only by a typhoon, which sank more than 200 Mongol ships along with the 13,000 sleeping men aboard), the Japanese were shopping at the markets of Edo, Kyoto, and Nara for, among other items, *aubergines.*

Says Harold McGee, "Arab traders introduced it into Spain and northern Africa in the Middle Ages, and its use was established in Italy in the 15th century, in France by the 18th."

Like the potato, it was regarded with suspicion when it first reached Europe. One name for it was *mad apple:* It was thought that eating it would lead to insanity.

James Trager's *Food Chronology* lists its adventures. A 1520 Spanish cookbook, *De guisades manjares y potages* by Ruperto de Nola, gave recipes for *berenjenas*—eggplant. Trager then says something unusual: "Mentioned in the Ebers papyrus of 1552 B.C., the vegetable was known in the Andean valleys of South America as guinea squash before it appeared in Europe."

One hardly knows what to make of such a statement.

At any rate, in 1587 a small, light brown, egg-shaped sample was introduced into England, but the English botanist John Gerard remained unconvinced of its value even 10 years later when he stated that eggplant had "a mischievous qualitie." In 1806 it arrived in the United States. American gardeners initially grew it mainly as an ornamental plant—and it *is* beautiful.

Eggplant, besides being decorative and tasty, is good for people. Among other nutrients, a cupful contains 58 International Units of vitamin A, 408 milligrams of vitamin C, 30 milligrams of calcium, and 180 milligrams of potassium. According to Jean Carper's *Food Pharmacy,* "constituents in eggplant inhibit rises in human blood cholesterol induced by fatty foods such as cheese." It also contains protease inhibitors, which disarm viruses, and it may be a cancer preventive.

EGGPLANT

CHOOSING SEEDS: Eggplants are ornamental vegetables and have more variations in color and shape than any vegetable fruit. They can be the traditional black as night, or white, green, orange, pink, deep purple, or striped. All are glossy. Some are long and skinny, some round like a ball, and others have the familiar elongated pear shape.

A few are short-season producers (50 days from transplanting), most are midseason (60 to 70 days), and a few will come really late in the season (80 to 90 days).

There are 6,000 seeds per ounce. Purchase a tiny packet.

CULTIVATION: Sow in flats indoors 8 weeks prior to planting outdoors. Keep very warm (80° to 90°F) for germination, and warm (70°) for early growth. When the first leaves form, transplant to plug trays. Harden before transplanting outdoors by dropping the temperature to 60° and reducing water.

Growing eggplant is a challenge in the variable summers of Maine. Transplant them outdoors when the summer weather has settled, 18 inches apart in holes in black plastic mulch. Cover the bed with a floating row cover to give the plants a temperature boost and keep insects at bay.

Prune periodically by cutting off leaf node branches. Tie big plants to stakes for earlier, larger, straighter fruit.

PESTS: Flea beetles attack newly set transplants. Prevent the attacks with floating row covers, or control with a dusting of rotenone or pyrethrum. Colorado potato beetles attack older plants; use floating row covers, or control with Bt insecticide.

HARVESTING: Pick fruits as soon as they're glossy and full. Cut the fruit stem with shears. Pick regularly to encourage more fruit development.

Simply Fried Eggplant and Summer Squash

SERVES 2–4

An hour before dinner, peel and cut in half lengthwise:

1 small eggplant

Cut into 1/4-inch slices to equal 3 cups. Place the slices in a large bowl.

Peel only if skins are tough, and cut in half lengthwise:

3 small (2-inch-diameter) zucchini or yellow squash

Cut into 1/4-inch slices to equal 3 cups. Add to the eggplant in the bowl.

Sprinkle the eggplant-squash mixture with:

1 tablespoon sea salt

Toss well with your fingers. Put the vegetables in a colander and set aside for 1 hour to drain.

At dinnertime pat the eggplant and squash dry with paper towels. In a large skillet, heat:

1/4 inch peanut oil

When oil is hot but not smoking, fry the eggplant and squash slices over medium heat till golden, perhaps 3 minutes. Drain on a rack or paper towels.

Place the slices on a warm platter and garnish with:

chopped fresh parsley

Offer with Garlic-Tahini Sauce (at right).

Garlic-Tahini Sauce

Whisk together until smooth and thick:

1 cup sesame tahini
1/4 cup cold water
2 garlic cloves, minced
1/4 cup freshly squeezed lemon juice
1/2 teaspoon sea salt
freshly ground black OR white pepper

NOTE: You can increase the amount of water if you'd like a thinner consistency.

Ratatouille is a specialty of the Provence area in France, but it has its own version in New England—especially when August arrives and all the garden produce is peaking. It can be enjoyed hot as a main dish, or cold as an appetizer.

Eggplant Ratatouille

SERVES 4

Rinse and peel:

1 1/2-pound eggplant

Cut into 1/2-inch cubes to equal 2 cups. Place them in a big bowl.

Wash and cut into 1/2-inch cubes to equal 2 cups:

1 1/2-pound summer squash (from zucchini to 'Zephyr')

Add to the eggplant. Sprinkle the veggies with:

1 tablespoon sea salt

Toss well with your fingers, place in a colander, and let drain for 30 minutes. Pat gently dry in a towel.

Meanwhile, set a big pot of water over high heat. Once it's boiling, dip in (in small batches) for about 1 minute:

1 pound tomatoes

Remove and plunge into cold water to cool. The skins should start to peel. Peel, squeeze gently to remove seeds, and set aside.

Slice to equal 2 cups:
1/2 pound onion
Cut into 1/2-inch bits to equal 1 cup:
1 green OR red bell pepper

Quarter:
the peeled, seeded tomatoes

Set a wok on its collar and add:
1 tablespoon extra-virgin olive oil
When the oil is hot, sauté in it over medium heat until wilted:
the 2 cups sliced onions
the 1 cup bell pepper
Add:
the tomatoes
3 large garlic cloves, minced
Cover and cook for about 3 minutes, then uncover, increase the heat, and cook briskly till the juices evaporate, being careful not to burn.

Season with:
sea salt (optional)
freshly ground black pepper
Combine gently with the sautéed eggplant and squash. Cover and simmer for 5 to 10 minutes more. Uncover and cook till the juices are reduced, if necessary.

Sprinkle with freshly chopped parsley and serve hot or cold with a green leafy salad, rice or potatoes, and in-season vegetables.

NOTE: Ratatouille also makes a fine pasta or pizza topping.

Baba ghanoush (baba means "father" in Arabic, and ghanoush or ghannuj means "cute"), is, of course, a classic Lebanese dish. It's fine for a dip with slices of pita bread (see page 273).

Baba Ghanoush

MAKES 2 CUPS

Preheat the oven to 400°F.

Pick or purchase:
1 1/2-pound eggplant
Rinse it, prick it all over with a fork, place it in the hot oven on a shallow baking pan, and bake till the flesh is tender—perhaps 40 minutes. Check for softness by pricking with a fork. Once it's very tender, remove the eggplant, let it cool enough to handle, then cut it in half and scoop out the flesh. Pour off any darkened liquid and remove any large clusters of seeds: Both may impart a bitter taste. You should have about 2 cupfuls.

Place the eggplant in a blender and whiz until smooth along with:
3 tablespoons freshly squeezed
  lemon juice
1 teaspoon sea salt
1 teaspoon minced fresh garlic
3 tablespoons sesame tahini
Scoop out into a flat bowl.

When the mixture is cool, stir in:
1/4 cup minced parsley
Drizzle with:
2 tablespoons extra-virgin olive oil
1/2 cup toasted pine nuts OR
  chopped walnuts (optional)

Serve with pita bread wedges.

NOTE 1: If you like, you can gently mix into the eggplant mixture:

1 cup peeled, seeded, chopped
    tomatoes
1/2 cup finely chopped onion
1/4 cup finely chopped red bell pepper
additional parsley

NOTE 2: Or you could add to the egg-plant mixture:

1 cup pitted, finely chopped black
    Greek olives
chopped fresh parsley

Eggplant moussaka can be prepared ahead of time and baked just before serving. Put it together, refrigerate it, then place it in the oven to bake—a bit longer than when cooked immediately.

Moussaka

SERVES 4–6

THE EGGPLANT

Oil a 2-quart casserole dish. Pick or purchase:

**1 2-pound eggplant OR several
    smaller eggplants**

Wash, peel, and cut crosswise into 3/8-inch slices. Put the slices in a bowl, sprinkle them with salt, toss with your fingers, and let drain for 30 minutes.

Pat dry. Brush the slices with extra-virgin olive oil and broil till they're lightly brown on each side. Set aside.

THE FILLING

Place a wok on its collar and heat:

1 tablespoon extra-virgin olive oil

Add and cook until soft and lightly browned:

**1 cup chopped onion
3/4 pound firm tofu, cut into tiny
    cubes
3 garlic cloves, minced**

Add:

**2 cups peeled, seeded, and chopped
    tomatoes
1 teaspoon minced fresh rosemary
2 teaspoons minced fresh dill weed
1 teaspoon sea salt
freshly ground black pepper
1/2 teaspoon powdered cinnamon**

Cook over medium heat until reduced and thick. This may take half an hour.

THE BÉCHAMEL

In a small saucepan, melt:

3 tablespoons butter

Stir in and cook for about 1 minute:

1/4 cup unbleached white flour

Whisk in:

1 1/2 cups milk

Bring to a boil, reduce the heat, and simmer, whisking, until smooth. Whisk in:

1/4 cup freshly grated Romano cheese

ARRANGING IN THE CASSEROLE

Preheat the oven to 350°F.

Sprinkle the greased casserole with:

1/2–1 cup fine bread crumbs

Put in half of the broiled eggplant. Layer with half of the tofu filling. Layer in the remaining eggplant. Finally, top with the last half of the tofu filling.

FINISHING TOUCHES

In a small bowl, beat:

2 eggs

Stir a little hot béchamel sauce into the eggs, then whisk the eggs into the remainder. Pour this sauce over the eggplant and tofu filling. Sprinkle with:

paprika

Bake in the preheated oven for about 50 minutes.

Serve right away with a green leafy salad and boiled potatoes sprinkled with parsley.

Historian Reay Tannahill says that "The true Indian curry bears very little resemblance to the parodies of it so frequently served in the West today. . . . A single *brinjal* (aubergine, or eggplant), with a couple of onions or a handful of lentils (*dal*), would be cooked in a little *ghi* or vegetable oil, flavored with spices (among them cardamom, coriander, cumin and turmeric for a mild blend, white pepper and mustard seed for a hot one), and diluted with coconut milk or the soured-milk product *dahi*, to make a traditional curry which, with rice and *chapatis*, provided a substantial meal for several people."

In a footnote she adds, "Only in the sixteenth century were chili peppers and cayenne introduced to India from their native tropical America. These are the searing ingredients that give character to hot curries today."

Aubergine Curry

SERVES 6

Rinse:

2 medium-sized eggplants
(1 1/2–2 pounds total)

Peel, quarter, then slice into 1-inch-thick bits. Place in a big bowl and sprinkle with:

1 tablespoon sea salt

Toss with your fingers. Let the eggplant rest in a colander for half an hour, then place in a tea towel, press out the excess water, and cut the slices into smaller cubes.

Wash well and cut into cubes to equal 3 cups:

3 large potatoes

Cut into 1/2-inch cubes:

2 red or green bell peppers

In a large stainless-steel or porcelainized pot, heat:

1/2 cup extra-virgin olive oil

Add and sauté for several seconds:

1 teaspoon powdered ginger
1 teaspoon powdered turmeric
1/2–1 teaspoon cayenne
1/2 teaspoon powdered cinnamon
1/2 teaspoon ground coriander
1 teaspoon white mustard seeds
1 teaspoon powdered cumin
1 1/2 teaspoons sea salt
2 large garlic cloves, minced

Add and toss till evenly coated with spices:

the eggplant
the potatoes
the green peppers

Add:

2 1/2 cups water

Cover the pan and simmer the vegetables for about 20 minutes, stirring occasionally. Remove the cover and simmer for 15 more minutes, stirring often.

Cut into small chunks and add:

4 big, firm, red tomatoes

When the tomatoes are heated through, serve with rice and condiments such as a small bowlful of currants, banana slices, a banana raita (page 178), a cucumber raita, and/or plain yogurt.

NOTE: This is superb served the next day, when flavors will have combined and enhanced one another.

Banana Raita

SERVES 6

Heat in a skillet:
1 teaspoon extra-virgin olive oil

Add and stir together quickly:
1 teaspoon powdered cumin
1/4 teaspoon powdered cardamom
1/4 teaspoon ground coriander
1/4 teaspoon cayenne powder

Add and stir in quickly:
2 cups mashed ripe bananas
Remove from the heat and stir in:
2 cups plain yogurt

Scoop into a serving dish and chill well before serving.

Fennel

Relatively unknown in New England but long esteemed in the Mediterranean region (it's called *finocchio* in Italian), Florence fennel is a licorice-flavored relative of parsley and carrots.

According to several food writers, fennel was widely used in ancient Greece, and much esteemed by the Romans. Hippocrates recommended fennel tea to stimulate milk production in nursing mothers. But its popularity goes back even farther. Cultivated by the Egyptians, and with a name referring to a kind of fragrant hay, it was mentioned in a papyrus dated 1500 B.C.

During Europe's Middle Ages fennel was considered beneficial as both food and medicine. The 17th-century herbalist Nicholas Culpeper used it to treat kidney stones, gout, and liver and lung disorders, not to mention as an antidote to poisonous mushrooms! But it wasn't mentioned as arriving in America until 1806, when it appeared in Bernard McMahon's *American Gardener's Calendar.* After that it escaped from gardens, and in some places ran amok.

Longtime organic gardening authority J. I. Rodale reports that Florence fennel *(Foeniculum vulgare dulce)* belongs to the same species as common or wild varieties. Bitter fennel, the wild type, he says, is a perennial springing to 6 feet tall with feathery leaves, coarse stalks, and aromatic seeds used mainly as seasoning and in liqueurs.

Of the sweet type, two varieties are grown as annuals. If planted as a perennial, *F. v. dulce* reverts in four or five years to a wild state. The other sweet variety, *F. v. piperitum,* is commonly called carosella. No bulb expands for this variety, but the young stalks are picked before flowering to use like celery.

Some very old recipes using fennel are extant. Back in 1387 England's King Richard II invited his country's rich barons to dine with him. Two hundred cooks were employed to feed 2,000 guests, and this is what they consumed: 1,400 oxen lying in salt, 2 freshly killed oxen, 120 sheep's heads, 13 calves, 12 boars, 1,110 marrow bones, 200 rabbits, 150 swans, 210 geese, 1,200 pigeons, 144 partridges, 720 hens, and 11,000 eggs.

His cooks also prepared a meat paste called *mortewes*, which contained broth, ale, bread crumbs, egg yolks, salt, and spices. The diners enjoyed it to the tunes of minstrels and court musicians. Seated on backless benches called banquettes, they also consumed gilded peacock, roasted boar, and venison off oaken planks set on trestles, using half loaves of bread as trenchers. Fennel, anise seeds, borage, garlic, leek, mint, nutmeg, parsley, purslane, rosemary, rue, saffron, sage, and watercress flavored and colored the dishes, including salad and a pie of *smale briddes*—small birds.

Beverages, as you might expect, included ale, claret, Rhenish wine, malmsey, mead, and fermented ciders made of apples, pears, and raspberries.

And finally, dessert was a marzipan castle 4 feet square and 3 feet high, surrounded by a moat with two drawbridges made of hardened dough.

Oh, the groans there must have been afterward!

A recipe for King Richard's amazing *salat* sounds like this: "Take parsel, sawge, garlec, chibollas [scallions], oynons, leek, borage, myntes, porrectes [young leeks], fenel, and ton tressis [cress], new rosemarye, purslarye [purslane]; lave, and waishe hem clene; pike hem, pluck hem small with thyn honde, and myng hem wel with rawe oile. Lay on vynegar and salt, and serve it forth."

"Pike hem," and "pluck hem small with thyn honde" are particularly appealing directions.

For tips on growing fennel, see page 126.

Harold McGee tells us in his *On Food and Cooking* that only a few other plants have such strongly scented oils as does fennel. The Umbelliferae (carrot) family to which it belongs includes 3,000 species and contributes anise, caraway, coriander, cumin, dill, and parsley to the spice rack, while the 3,200 species of the Labiatae (mint) family give us basil, mint, marjoram, oregano, rosemary, sage, and thyme. Of the incredible 19,000 species of the daisy family or Compositae—the largest family of plants outside of orchids—only tarragon and, for herbal tea drinkers, chamomile result.

As Benjamin Watson puts it in a little book called *Taylor's Guide to Heirloom Vegetables, F. v.* var. *azoricum*— more popular in Europe than America—"is an odd but very appealing vegetable with a mild, sweet, anise-like flavor. The fleshy white bases of the overlapping leaves form an above-ground bulb, called the 'apple.' The plant's short stalks are light green and look much like celery ribs; these stalks have a stronger flavor than the bulb and are sometimes added to soups and stews. The feathery top leaves resemble those of dill and make a good herb for seasoning fish, chicken, shellfish, and other delicate dishes."

Fennel leaves, according to food writer Jane Brody, are rich in vitamin A. The stalks, she advises, can be eaten raw or cooked (steamed or simmered for 5 to 10 minutes if cut up, 10 to 15 minutes if left whole). Moreover, fennel is high in potassium, and 1/2 pound totals only 56 calories.

If you're lucky enough to get a bulb of tender fennel, wash, dry, and trim it to form a neat package. Save the fronds.

A simple way of cooking it is to steam thin slices till they're tender. Then let them cool and serve sprinkled with freshly squeezed lemon juice. This makes a tender addition to any green leafy salad once chilled.

Baking with Parmesan cheese is possibly the next best way.

Parmesan Fennel

SERVES 4

Pick or purchase (to weigh a total of 2 pounds):
 2–3 large fennel bulbs

Wash and trim the bulbs, leaving a thin layer of core at the base of each, and trim the stalks to 1 inch. Place the bulbs in a big pot of rapidly boiling water and blanch till they're tender but still firm, 20–40 minutes. They should be fork-tender but far from mushy. Let them cool.

Preheat the oven to 400°F.

Oil a baking pan with:
 extra-virgin olive oil OR butter
Cut each bulb into quarters, retaining the thin base as you cut. Arrange the quarters in the pan, cut-side up, with the bases pointing in one direction and the tips slightly overlapping the bases.

Top with:
 a lot of freshly grated Parmesan cheese
Dribble on:
 extra-virgin olive oil

 1–1 1/2 teaspoons sea salt
 a lot of freshly ground black pepper

Bake for 20 minutes or till the cheese is browned.

Serve right away with any grain, other in-season vegetables, and a green leafy salad.

Fennel soup—with its faint flavor of licorice—is satisfying when enriched with egg and cream. This is not for weight watchers.

Rich, Creamy Fennel Soup

SERVES 4

Pick or purchase:
 2–3 large fennel bulbs
Wash and trim the stalks to 1 inch. Save a handful of the upper feathery leaves for garnish.

Cut each bulb into quarters. Then chop finely, cutting out the tough bottom cores.

Chop to equal 1 cup:
1 medium-sized onion

Pour into a 4-quart pot and heat:
1/4 cup extra-virgin olive oil
Sprinkle on and cook, whisking, for about 2 minutes:
2 tablespoons refined white flour
Add and stir in:
3 cups seasoned Vegetable Stock (see page 43)
Bring to a boil, lower the heat, and simmer for about 10 minutes. It will thicken. Remove from the heat.

When the soup is cool enough to handle, whiz it in a blender until it's smooth. (Place a towel over the blender top as you purée to prevent burning.) Return to the 4-quart pot.

In a small bowl, whisk together:
1 egg yolk
1/2 cup cream OR low-fat milk plus 1 tablespoon cornstarch
Whisking all the time, dribble 1/4 cup of the hot fennel-onion-stock mixture into the egg-cream mix to warm it. Then, whisking all the time, add the egg-cream mixture to the rest of the soup. Return to the stove and heat over a low flame till it just begins to bubble. Add:
sea salt
freshly ground white OR multicolored pepper

Serve right away garnished with:
finely chopped fennel leaves
finely chopped parsley

With new rolls and fresh salad, this soup is fine for lunch, or as the start of an elegant dinner.

Bread becomes impregnated with a faint licorice scent when seasoned with fennel.

Fennel Bread

MAKES 1 LOAF

THE VEGETABLE BEGINNING

Trim the bottoms and stems from:
2 small fennel heads
Finely chop the fronds to equal about 1/2 cup and set aside.

Chop the bulbs. Place them in a medium-sized saucepan with:
1 small, unpeeled potato
Add:
1 cup water
1 teaspoon sea salt
a lot of freshly ground black pepper
Heat to boiling, reduce the heat, and simmer, covered, till tender, about 45 minutes. Drain, reserving 1/4 cup liquid.

Purée the vegetables and the 1/4 cup of liquid in a blender. Pour into a large bowl and stir in:
2 tablespoons finely chopped fennel fronds (no stems)
1 tablespoon fennel seeds (optional)

THE DOUGH

In a small bowl, combine by mixing quickly with a fork:
1/4 cup warm water
1 tablespoon dry baker's yeast
1 teaspoon refined white sugar
Let this bubble, then pour it into the bowl of fennel purée.

Add and mix well:
2 3/4 cups whole-wheat bread flour
1/4 cup sesame seeds
This will seem very stiff at first, but then it'll all mix together.

Sprinkle a bread board lightly with:

1 cup unbleached white bread flour

Place your bread on the board and knead till it's smooth. Add more white flour if necessary—up to 1 cup more.

Place your kneaded dough into a large, well-oiled bowl, turn once to coat it all around, then cover it with a damp tea towel and let it rise till doubled in bulk.

Once it's doubled, punch it down and knead briefly again. Then knead a bit more, form the dough into a loaf, and place it in a buttered 9- by 4- by 4-inch bread pan.

Cover with a tea towel and let rise for about an hour or till doubled.

BAKING

Preheat the oven to 375°F. Brush the risen loaf with melted butter and sprinkle it with sea salt (optional).

Place a pan containing 1 inch of water on the bottom rack of your oven; place the loaf on a middle shelf, and bake till it's golden brown and hollow sounding when tapped—perhaps 45 minutes. Remove from the pan and cool on a rack.

Corn

In 1768 Benjamin Franklin, in London to plead the cause of the colonies, wrote to his daughter, begging her to send foods from America for which he was homesick. Listed were apples, cranberries, dried peaches, buckwheat flour—and cornmeal. He apparently tried to show the English women in his kitchen how to make corn bread and corn cakes. We can't help but wonder how successful he was, since "corn" as we know it was definitely foreign to the English.

Remarks Margaret Visser in *Much Depends on Dinner,* the word *corn* in English "denotes the staple grain of a country." Wheat, for instance, is "corn" where wheat bread is the staple. "When Europeans arrived in America," she says, "they saw that . . . maize was the basic food, so the English-speaking newcomers called it 'Indian corn.'"

It took a while for the sweet variety—so beloved when lightly steamed, slathered with butter, and oohed and aahed over each August—to arrive in the hands of New England colonists. Before that, its form was largely of the hard dent or flint variety—fine for cakes later called pones, and pottages called hominy. Grown by the Pilgrims, corn was mostly the low-growing, flint variety with ears of white kernels in eight rows.

A Cooperative Extension Service publication of Cornell University called *The Heirloom Vegetable Garden* says, "It is believed that the first sweet corn [probably "mutated from either dent or flint corn or from both types"] was brought to New England from the Susquehanna River Valley by one of the officers of the Sullivan Expedition in 1779." In 1828 it was listed by an American seedsman for the first time, and from 1850 to 1880 several varieties had been developed. "By the end of this period sweet corn was well established as an important item in the diet." Almost all of the early varieties had white kernels, and it wasn't until 'Golden Bantam' was introduced in 1902 that yellow varieties were considered fit for human consumption.

Francis Higginson, arriving in Salem in 1629, explained in his posthumously published *New England's Plantation* that "There is not such great and beautiful eares of corne I suppose anywhere else to be found but in this Countrey, being also of various colours, as red, blew, yellow, etc."

To Native Americans, of course, corn represented survival. They referred to it as "Our Mother," "Our Life," "She Who Sustains Us." And sustain them she did. Only when they were unable to grow and harvest their gardens did New England tribes falter in their final bid to oust Puritans and other interlopers from Massachusetts and the Connecticut valley during the so-called King Philip's War of 1675–76.

Captain John Giles, a prisoner among the Malecites on the St. John River from 1689 to 1696, described preparations for storing the flint varieties. "To dry corn when in the milk, they gather it in lage ketles and boil it on the ears, till it is pretty hard, then shell it from the cob with clam shells, and dry it on bark in the sun. When it is thoroughly dry, a kernel is no bigger than a pea, and would keep years, and when it is boiled again it swells as lage as when on the ear, and tastes incomparably sweeter than other corn."

Cooking methods were varied. "In addition to hominy, . . . the coarse part of the kernel broken in a stone or wooden mortar, they had 'samp,' whole corn hulled in scalding water with lye leached from maple ashes; 'nokehike,' corn parched and pounded and perhaps mixed with maple sugar; 'suckatash,' corn in the milk boiled together with shell beans; 'upaquontop,' broth made of boiled bass heads thickened with hominy. . . ."

Father Rasle at Norridgewock, Maine, on the Kennebec River stated that parched corn sweetened with maple sugar was his principal food.

By the mid–18th century corn was a New England staple for breakfast, lunch, and supper. Flat cornmeal cakes cooked on a stone or griddle, so handy to take on journeys, became johnnycake. Hoecake was reputedly baked in an oven on a greased iron hoe blade! American soldiers captured in Canada in the War of 1812 and imprisoned at Halifax, Nova Scotia, found corn an absolute necessity. "Their cry for 'mush and milk' was incessant," wrote the superintendent of the camp.

When it reached Europe, corn, along with potatoes, became food for the poor. Today it remains a favorite. For everyone!

According to David M. Tucker in *Kitchen Gardening in America,* "Indian women took great pleasure in announcing the arrival of green corn. Corn-on-the-cob time marked the peak of the garden season and typically called for a Green Corn Festival to celebrate. . . . Pulled fresh from the stalk and laid, still enclosed in its green husk, under cold ashes topped with hot embers, baked corn-on-the-cob delighted all. Every woman also had half a dozen other green corn recipes, including an excellent porridge in which the corn boiled with meat, pumpkin, beans, chestnuts, and maple syrup. Large amounts of green corn could even be harvested and preserved as insurance against possible crop disaster. When broiled and parched the green corn stored even better than mature shelled corn."

In the past colonial American mothers used to husk every ear carefully, remove every bit of silk, then pile the golden "logs" into a big pot in which only an inch of water (and sometimes milk) was bubbling. Simmering for 10 minutes was the rule.

Genetic tampering has made sweet corn sweeter than ever. Today the best cooking is still quick and simple.

GARDENING NOTES

CORN

CHOOSING SEEDS: Sweet corn comes in normal-sugar, sugar-enhanced, and supersweet types. All have yellow, white, and bicolor varieties. There are varieties that mature in short season (65 days), midseason (75 days), and long season (90 days). For maximum span of harvest, choose one of each.

Dry field corn and ornamental corn come in a rainbow selection of colors in different varieties. All are long season.

Popcorn comes in different colors and is long season.

Corn has 150 seeds per ounce. You'll need 4 ounces for 100 row feet.

CULTIVATION: Fertilize the soil well in preparation for corn. If you're growing the supersweet kind, plan on separating the plot by 25 feet from other corn plots; the same goes for popcorn. Alternately, stagger planting dates by more than 12 days to maturity. Otherwise you'll get tough, starchy kernels where you don't want them. All corn plots should be at least four rows wide to assure good pollination. Or you can cut the pollen tassels off and shake them over the silks by hand.

For early planting you must use treated seeds; these have been coated with fungicide. If you use untreated seeds, either wait until the soil temperature rises above 60°F or start the plants indoors. Plant 1 foot apart in rows 3 feet apart. If you're pushing the temperature range, plant 3 per foot, then thin if necessary.

Rototill or hoe to keep weeds down, or interplant with clover (to give corn extra nitrate) or winter squash or pumpkins. Plant the latter a week or two later to give the corn a head start.

PESTS: Use either bird-scaring balloons or floating row covers to keep crows from pulling up seedlings. Of many insect pests, earworms can sometimes be prevented by interplanting corn with pumpkins, or applying a few drops of mineral oil to the silks. Remove and compost all corn remnants after the season is over.

To keep raccoons from harvesting the nearly ripe ears, try playing a radio, planting corn near a doghouse, interplanting with pumpkins, or sprinkling cayenne on the silks.

HARVESTING:

Sweet corn: Harvest ears when the silks turn brown and dry, indicating that the kernels are full and "milky." This is usually 18 to 24 days after the date when half the plants show silk.

Ornamental and field corn: Harvest when the husks begin drying. This is normally after several frosts.

Popcorn: Harvest when the kernels are hard and glossy, again after several frosts.

Corn on the Cob

Select:
1–3 ears per person
Remove the husks.

In a big pot, bring to a boil:
about 1 inch water
Introduce the ears into the boiling water and let them steam for 3 to 5 minutes. Using tongs, remove the ears from the pot and pile them onto a big platter.

When they're cool enough to handle, serve with:
butter OR 4 parts extra-virgin olive oil shaken in a capped jar with 1 part lime juice
sea salt
Diners can each season their own ears.

NOTE: Since eating corn on the cob means holding the ear by hand, little "picks" inserted into both ends ease what is basically a hot, messy, delicious business.

Fresh corn fritters have always been a favorite, best served—as Native American mothers observed long ago—with maple syrup.

Corn Fritters

SERVES 4

Using a sharp knife, cut and scrape the kernels from:

5–6 ears sweet corn

You should have 2 3/4 cups.

Into two small bowls, separate the whites from the yolks of:

2 large eggs

Beat the whites until stiff peaks are formed. Lightly beat the yolks.

In a large bowl, combine:

the corn
the 2 lightly beaten egg yolks
2 tablespoons white unbleached flour
1 tablespoon refined white sugar
    (optional)
1/4 teaspoon sea salt
some freshly ground black pepper
1/8 teaspoon cayenne powder
    (optional)

Fold the whites quickly but gently into the corn mixture.

In a large skillet over high heat, warm:

2 tablespoons butter
AND/OR sunflower seed oil

When this is hot, drop in the corn batter by the tablespoonful. Reduce the heat to medium and brown the fritters on one side, about 2 minutes. Turn and brown the other side. Do not overcook.

Serve immediately with:

Maine maple syrup

New potatoes, a green leafy salad, and summer vegetables complement fritters.

A very old-fashioned dish is still going strong in New England. Made with kernels fresh from the field, or creamed and canned, it's perfect for lunch. This recipe first appeared in THE NEW MAINE COOKING.

J. A.'s Maine Corn Chowder

SERVES 4–6

In a heavy-bottomed saucepan, simmer together till barely tender:

1 cup water
2 large onions, chopped finely
3 large potatoes, cubed

In another heavy-bottomed saucepan (preferably porcelainized, which can be set directly on the table to serve), bring to a scald:

1 quart rich milk

Add and heat:

2 cups whole-kernel corn
OR canned, cream-style corn
sea salt to taste
freshly ground black pepper

Then add:

the cooked potatoes and onions
a dash of Angostura Bitters

Serve hot, with a sprinkling of finely chopped fresh parsley. This is wonderful with biscuits, rolls, or whole-wheat bread, and a large tossed salad complete with grated carrots, marinated beans, and herb combinations.

Cornmeal ground by big stones as in the old days makes a delicious bread— as every settler understood. It's best, of course, cooked in an iron skillet on an iron woodstove.

Skillet Corn Bread

THE DRY INGREDIENTS

Preheat in the corn batteroven to 450°F.

Measure out:
**1 cup plus 2 tablespoons yellow
stone-ground cornmeal**
Set aside the 2 tablespoonfuls.

Sift together into a medium-sized bowl:
**1 cup cornmeal
2 teaspoons double-acting baking
powder (see page 28)
1/2 teaspoon baking soda
1/2 teaspoon sea salt
1/4 cup whole-wheat OR rye flour
1 tablespoon nutritional yeast
(optional but good)**
Return any sifted-out bran to your bowl.

THE WET INGREDIENTS

Stir in:
1 1/4 cups buttermilk
Add:
2 large eggs, lightly beaten

BAKING

Heat a 10-inch cast-iron skillet over high heat for 1 minute. Then add:
2 tablespoons sunflower seed oil

Heat for about 15 seconds. Sprinkle with your 2 tablespoons of set-aside cornmeal and let this brown slightly. Spoon in the batter.

Bake in the upper third of your oven for 10 minutes, or until the bread is firm in the center and pulls away slightly from the sides of the pan.

Serve with a sense of history.
NOTE: If you find yourself lacking buttermilk, you can substitute 1 1/8 cups of milk and 1 tablespoon of cider vinegar. Allowing it to "work" for half an hour will usually sour it before you lose patience.

Mexico, where corn was domesticated, also offers a flat bread of unsurpassed delight. Early New England hoecakes—or corn bread cooked on a hot blade in the ashes of an open fire—came closest.

Corn Tortillas

MAKES 12 6-INCH TORTILLAS

THE DOUGH

Mix together:
**2 cups masa harina
(dehydrated masa flour)
1 1/4–1 1/3 cups warm water**
Use enough water to hold the dough together well. Using your hands, shape the dough into a ball. Roll into a log and divide into 12 equal pieces. Roll these into balls.

SHAPING WITH A PRESS

If you have a tortilla press, place a square of waxed paper on the bottom half of the press, place one ball of dough on the paper—slightly off center, toward the edge farthest from the handle—then flatten it slightly with your palm. Cover with a second piece of waxed paper, lower the top half of the press, and flatten until the tortilla measures about 6 inches in diameter. Stack paper-covered tortillas till you're ready to use them.

SHAPING WITHOUT A PRESS

If you lack a press, you can use a rolling pin. Dip two cloths into water, and wring dry. Flatten a ball of dough slightly and place it between the cloths. Roll with light, even strokes until the cake is about 6 inches in diameter. Pull back the cloths, trim if necessary, sandwich between two squares of waxed paper, and stack until ready for use.

COOKING

Carefully peel off the top piece of waxed paper. Turn the tortilla over and place unpapered side onto a preheated, ungreased, medium-hot griddle. As the tortilla becomes warm, the second paper will peel off easily. Cook for 1 1/2 to 2 minutes, turning frequently. The tortilla will puff up briefly. It should be soft and lightly flecked with brown specks.

SERVING

You can use the tortillas when they're still warm or cooled. Store in an airtight wrap in the refrigerator. Freezing also works.

Enchiladas made with fresh corn in fresh tortillas are a superb treat. First, though, it's necessary to make chili tomato sauce. You could substitute a tomatillo sauce, such as Smooth Tomatillo Salsa (see page 228), or canned Hot Tomatillo Salsa (see page 230).

Quick Chili Tomato Sauce

MAKES MORE THAN ENOUGH
FOR 12 ENCHILADAS

Heat in a skillet:
  2 tablespoons extra-virgin olive oil
Add and cook over medium heat until limp:

1 medium-sized onion, chopped
Add and whisk gently together:
  3 1/2 cups tomato purée
  2 garlic cloves, minced
  2 to 3 tablespoons chili powder
  1/2 teaspoon powdered cumin
  1 teaspoon freshly chopped oregano
  1 teaspoon sea salt
Cover and simmer for 30 minutes, stirring frequently.

It's interesting that today we never think of enchiladas without cheese, yet dairy cattle were only introduced into Mexico by Columbus and his followers in the late 1400s.

Fresh Corn Enchiladas

MAKES 12 ENCHILADAS

THE STUFFING

Pick or purchase:
  6 ears corn
Cut off the kernels to equal 2 1/2 cups.

Set a wok on its collar and heat it. Then add and heat:
  2 tablespoons extra-virgin olive oil
Add and cook, stirring over medium heat until limp:
  2 cups finely chopped onions
Add:
  the corn kernels
  1 teaspoon powdered cumin
  1/4 cup water

Cover and simmer over medium heat for about 5 minutes, stirring occasionally. Remove the cover and cook over high heat, stirring all the time, until the liquid is gone.

Remove from the heat and stir in:
  1 cup sour cream
  1 cup shredded extra-sharp Cheddar OR jack cheese

4 ounces canned green chili peppers,
    chopped (seeds and pith removed)
sea salt to taste

Check the seasoning and chilis for hotness.

THE TORTILLAS

Purchase or prepare:
    12 corn tortillas

In a 10-inch skillet, heat over a medium flame:
    1/4 inch sunflower seed oil

Dip each tortilla into the oil and fry for a few seconds, just until it begins to blister and grow limp. Don't let it become firm or crisp. Remove with tongs and drain briefly on paper towels. Continue with all 12. These are stackable. Pat off any oil before using them.

COMBINING

Pour into the bottom of a 9- by 12-inch lasagne pan:
    1/3 of the Quick Chili Tomato Sauce
        (see page 188)

Into the center of each tortilla spoon:
    a scant 1/3 cup corn–sour cream filling

Roll to enclose. Set the enchiladas seam-side down in the sauce-covered pan, side by side. Pour most of the remaining sauce over the top.

Sprinkle evenly over the enchiladas:
    2 cups shredded jack
    OR Cheddar cheese

(At this point you can cover the dish and chill it for later baking.)

BAKING

Bake, covered, in a preheated 375°F oven for 15 minutes, or until bubbling. (Bake for 30 minutes if chilled.) Remove the cover and bake for an additional 10 or 15 minutes.

SERVING

Roll into a "sausage" and chop to equal:
    2 cups lettuce
    OR crinkle-leaved endive

Arrange a band of lettuce down the center of the enchiladas. Spoon over:
    1 cup sour cream OR 1/2 cup yogurt
        mixed with 1/2 cup sour cream

Garnish with:
    1–2 tablespoons freshly
        chopped cilantro

Sprinkle with:
    freshly squeezed lime
    OR lemon juice

Serve right away.

Ripe Tomatoes

"At a time when Columbus discovered America, the Indians were using two thousand different foods derived from plants, a figure Europe could hardly have matched," say Waverly Root and Richard De Rochemont in their 1976 book *Eating in America*. In fact, in Mesoamerica as well as the Andes, dense populations were supported by intensive agriculture and a sophisticated food distribution system.

The Americans first met by Columbus, it's been noted, were well built, strong, and without paunches! Moving north, where winters dictated (and still dictate) a strict adherence to a short growing season, people were still remarkably healthy—and all this at a time when Europe faced a period of semistarvation yearly, that awful wait between the depletion of the previous year's food supply and new harvests. France, for instance, suffered 13 famines in the 16th century. And Lord Thomas William Coke, who shared farming expertise with colonials such as Thomas Jefferson (not to mention Russia's Peter the Great), was one of the earliest English lords to practice crop rotation and, along with Turnip Townshend, the growing of turnips to tide cattle over the winter months. This was in the late 1700s.

Along with sunflower seeds, blueberries, potatoes, chili peppers, squash, haricot beans, corn, and hundreds of other items, America offered Europe the tomato. Think what Italian cuisine would be without it! Yet it arrived only after Columbus stumbled ashore in 1492.

Andrew F. Smith, in *The Tomato in America: Early History, Culture, and Cookery,* remarks that "The issue of where the tomato plant originated was not resolved until the mid–twentieth century." *Lycopersicon lycopersicum,* he says, originated in the coastal highlands of western South America, and "wild tomato plants can still be found in the coastal mountains of Peru, Ecuador, and northern Chile." However, "No evidence has been uncovered indicating that any indigenous South American group cultivated or even ate tomatoes prior to the Spanish Conquest."

Somehow, the intrepid tomato migrated to Central America. But early tomatoes would hardly be recognized today. Again according to Andrew Smith, "The wild tomato was two-celled. A genetic mutation occurred, producing a multi-celled fruit, which was large and lumpy. . . . Today's large, smooth-skinned fruits are mainly crosses between the large, lumpy-skinned mutations and the smooth-skinned cherry tomato."

A late addition to the food supply of Central America, the mutation was nurtured and developed by Mayan and other Mesoamerican farmers and used in their cookery. The Aztecs readily adopted tomatoes, "probably because of their similarity to the *tomatl (Physalis ixocarpa)* a plant believed to be native to the Mexican highlands." The Aztecs named the new plant *xitomatl,* or large *tomatl.*

The Spanish first encountered tomatoes after Hernán Cortés began his conquest of Mexico in 1519. After that they were shipped to Europe, but acceptance came slowly. The first known European comment, Smith says, came in 1544 when "an Italian herbalist, Pietro Andrae Matthioli, published a reference to *mala aurea,* or 'golden apples,' which he described as 'flattened like the melrose [a sort of apple] and segmented, green at first and when ripe of a golden color." The name *pomi d'oro,* or "golden apples," continues to be used in Italy to this day. Matthioli also mentioned a red variety.

Although Matthioli (also known as Petrus Matthiolus) remarked that slices would be good "fried in oil with salt and pepper," Pietro Antonio Michiel in the later 16th century growled that "If I should eat this fruit, cut in slices in a pan with butter and oil, it would be injurious and harmful to me."

It wasn't until 1635, in Antwerp, that J. E. Nieremberg suggested tomatoes could be pickled, although Dominicus Chabraeus listed them as malignant and poisonous!

Eventually, however, acceptance came. In the United States the first reference appeared in William Salmon's *Botanologia,* dated 1710; by 1782 Thomas Jefferson was growing samples in his garden. Robert Gibbon Johnson was reputedly declared a hero when he ate a tomato on the courthouse steps in Salem, New Jersey, in 1820, although Smith declares that the story is apocryphal; as late as 1845 the editor of the *Boston Courier* compared the fruit to "rotten potatoe-balls."

However, by the first decade of the 19th century fresh tomatoes were sold by market gardeners in several states; during the 1820s tomato cookery had increased throughout the nation; and by the late 1830s and 1840s "tomato mania" had struck: Cultivation and enjoyment took over from Maine to California.

In *Kitchen Gardening in America* Professor David M. Tucker writes that by 1847 Robert Buist's *The Family Kitchen Garden* "could report that the tomato was universally grown by gardeners, occupied as much garden space as cabbage, and was served on every table from July to October, raw, stewed, stuffed, or fried. A new variety, Large Red, could grow to eighteen inches in circumference."

Today—after three centuries of wandering and hybridizing with human carriers —the tomato's popularity is rampant. According to Raymond Sokolov in *Why We Eat What We Eat,* this plant has traveled farther and wider, and changed the face of more cuisines, than any other New World food. Consumption of fresh tomatoes in the United States alone runs to 12 or 13 pounds per person per year, while tomato products total over 20—more than half in the guise of ketchup and chili sauce.

It's not hard to see why. Besides pleasing the palate, a cupful of tomato paste offers 8,650 International Units of vitamin A, 128 milligrams of vitamin C, and 2,237 milligrams of potassium, along with other nutrients. And a cupful of sheer tomato provides some protein, carbohydrate, fiber, 1,394 International Units of vitamin A, 21.6 milligrams of vitamin C, 254 units of potassium, and additional goodies.

Although hardly remembering Petrus Matthiolus and his slices "fried in oil with salt and pepper," Mainers have relished fried tomato slices from early days. In fact, despite a certain movie that made them famous, Mainers have always fried them green (see page 153). Still, there's nothing like a juicy, ripe, red (or yellow!) "love apple."

Ripe tomatoes dipped into boiling water for 1 minute to remove their skins then sliced onto white plates to exhibit their color and drizzled with extra-virgin olive oil, minced fresh basil, thinly sliced red or sweet onion (such as Walla Walla), a sprinkling of freshly squeezed lemon juice, a sifting of sea salt, and some freshly ground black or white pepper produce an unforgettable summer salad.

TOMATOES

CHOOSING SEEDS: Have fun with tomatoes. The number of heirloom and hybrid varieties is now bewildering. So get away from the standard 3- or 4-inch round red tomato and live it up with types that delight your eye and tongue. For instance, choose less acidic yellow tomatoes, or fruity striped ones. Kids love cherries, which now come red or yellow, round or pear, large and small. Some people like the meatiness of paste tomatoes, which are also ideal for salsa, sauces, and drying. Be sure to choose some early tomatoes (ripening in less than 60 days) to satisfy your tomato cravings when they're at their peak. Then choose for taste; read between the lines of seed catalogs with a drooling cloth in hand. Ask your friends for their favorites.

Tomato seeds come 9,000 to the ounce, so you need only the tiniest package to start your taste trials.

CULTIVATION: Sow indoors 5 to 6 weeks before the last possible frost date. When the date approaches, place seedlings outside on sunny days, or in a cold frame, to harden them.

Plant in fertile soil, adding a generous quantity of compost or manure in the hole before planting. Because tomatoes like warm, moist soil, you may wish to use black plastic mulch. If so, use a posthole digger to make holes in the plastic, 3 feet apart, and to dig a 6-inch-deep hole for the plant. Bury the plant so that only the top rosette of leaves and about 2 inches of shoot are showing; buried leaf nodes will grow roots. Ring the shoot at ground level with a paper collar to keep off cutworms. Keep a dribbling hose handy while you're planting so that one seedling can be soaked while you plant the next.

Tomatoes are either determinate or indeterminate. Determinate means that the plant has a predetermined adult size, usually small, that you can count on. Allow such plants to grow in standard-sized tomato cages, and prune only the most vigorous plants. Indeterminate plants are climbers and produce a tangle of branches that should be pruned. Grow them on stakes, train their vines along trellises, or keep them in large cages made from 6- by 6-inch steel reinforcing mesh (from the lumberyard). Prune by pinching off most of the side branches that emerge in the crotches of the main leaf stems. Such pruning encourages upward growth and earlier ripening of larger fruits.

PESTS AND DISEASES: Diseases such as blossom-end rot and blight can be prevented by ensuring sufficient moisture. The best solution is to use mulch; it keeps the weeds down, too. Pests (not bad) include flea beetles (see Cabbages, page 244), CPBs (see Potatoes, page 320), and hornworms (caterpillars).

HARVESTING: You already know how to pick tomatoes. When the first light frosts threaten in fall, cover the plants at night with any kind of fabric or cover, removing it during the day. When heavy frosts threaten, either pull the vine to hang upside down in a shed for the fruits to ripen, or pick all the fruits, wrap them individually in newspaper, and store them in a cool place to ripen through November.

Gazpacho

SERVES 4

Peel, gently seed (see the sidebar), chop into small bits (what can be comfortably spooned into the mouth), and place in a large bowl:

4 large, ripe, red tomatoes

Wash, peel, chop into small bits, and add to the bowl:

2 8-inch nonbitter cucumbers

Wash, chop into small bits, and add to the bowl:

1 large green bell pepper

Wash, slice thinly, including the tops, and place in the bowl:

12 scallions OR 8 bunching onions

In a blender, whiz until smooth:

3 large garlic cloves
1 tablespoon freshly chopped basil
1/2 teaspoon sea salt

1/4 cup red wine vinegar
1/3 cup extra-virgin olive oil

Pour over the tomatoes (et al.) in the bowl.

Add and mix well:

3 cups tomato juice
1/2 cup cold Vegetable Stock (see page 43) OR water (optional)
hot pepper sauce to taste
1 tablespoon Worcestershire sauce
freshly ground white pepper

Chill.

Adjust the seasoning and serve in chilled bowls garnished with:

a very thin cucumber slice,
chopped parsley, OR cilantro

Hot rolls always make a good accompaniment.

NOTE: For a smooth soup, purée in a blender and top with a dollop of sour cream.

SEEDING TOMATOES: Seeding tomatoes is easy if you cut them in half horizontally —around the circumference—rather than longitudinally. Fingers are appropriate for pressing out seeds.

Nothing is easier to can for winter feasting than tomatoes. And nothing comes in handier for making soup. All you have to do is add chopped onions, potatoes, carrots, maybe some lentils or barley, some dried oregano, sea salt, and freshly ground black pepper to that jarful of glowing red goodness.

Although in the old days tomatoes were packed cold into canning jars and then processed in a hot-water bath, recent recommendations from the U.S. Department of Agriculture suggest a procedure called hot-packing—which means bringing your tomatoes to a boil before ladling them into jars.

Some tomatoes are borderline acidic, and the addition of vinegar and salt has been a means of providing safety even with cold-packing. But pressure canning ensures it. (Be sure to check the directions for using your pressure cooker if it's new to you, and see page 38.)

Pressure-Canned Red, Ripe Tomatoes

MAKES 8 PINT OR 7 WIDEMOUTHED QUART JARS

UTENSIL PREPARATION

Wash jars in hot soapy water. Rinse and let them rest in hot water until they're needed. Place lids and bands in a small pan covered with water and bring to a simmer.

THE TOMATOES

Pick or purchase:

ripe (but not overripe), blemish-free tomatoes

Rinse carefully.

Bring a large pot of water to a boil. Drop in the tomatoes in small batches and let them rest for about 30 seconds, or until the skins begin to peel. Remove and plunge into cold water immediately. When the tomatoes are cool enough to handle, cut out the cores, peel off the skins, and trim away any blemishes.

Place a hot canning jar on a towel-covered countertop and add:

1 teaspoon canning OR kosher salt
1 tablespoon 5 percent cider vinegar

Using a widemouthed funnel, pack in your tomatoes. Press with a wooden spoon to squeeze out juice until the jar is filled to within 1/2 inch of the top with tomatoes and juice. (Overflowing juice can be saved for immediate drinking.) Remove air bubbles by poking into each jar along the sides with a chopstick. Continue for all seven or eight jars.

Wipe off the rims of your jars with a clean cloth. Drop your hot lids and bands into a sieve and drain. Place the lids on the jars, screwing the bands down tightly.

PROCESSING

Using tongs, place your hot, filled jars on a rack in a big pressure canner that contains 2 to 3 inches of hot water. Place the canner over high heat and lock on the cover per the manufacturer's instructions. Leave the vent open until steam escapes steadily for 10 minutes; then close the vent, bring the pressure up to 10 pounds, and keep it steady for 20 minutes for quarts, or 15 minutes for pints, by adjusting your stove's heat. Watch carefully. Measure the processing time from when the pressure reaches 10 pounds.

When time is up, remove the canner from the heat and let the pressure fall to zero. Be certain the pressure is all the way down. Wait for 5 minutes, then open the vent. Unfasten the cover and slide it toward you, allowing steam to escape, then hold it tipped away from your face to prevent any possible burn. Place on a shelf. Let the jars sit for 10 minutes before removing with tongs. Place on a towel-covered counter to cool and prevent breakage. Do not allow the jars to touch each other.

Let the jars cool completely—perhaps overnight. When they're cool, unscrew the metal bands, check to see that each jar is safely sealed—the metal lid will feel slightly concave when you press it— rinse gently, wipe dry, and label.

STORING

Store in a cool, dark place.

NOTE: Recommendations are to boil canned tomatoes, even pressure-canned tomatoes, for 15 minutes in an open, porcelainized or stainless-steel saucepan before using.

Stuffing tomatoes is an old idea; adding anchovies to the stuffing allies it to southern France. Crusty, white French bread works well in this recipe, although whole-wheat bread, minus crusts, is tasty. Fennel Bread (see page 181) is a good choice.

Stuffed Tomatoes

SERVES 4

THE STUFFING

Preheat the oven to 475°F.

In a small bowl, mix together:
1/2 cup milk
2 cups finely cubed bread bits

Soak for several minutes, then squeeze the milk out of the bread with your hands—like making a snowball.

In a medium-sized bowl, combine the squeezed bread with:
2 garlic cloves, minced
1 tablespoon finely chopped
fresh parsley
1 tablespoon finely chopped
fresh chives
1 teaspoon finely chopped
fresh tarragon
1 teaspoon finely chopped
fresh chervil
6–8 canned anchovies,
finely chopped
(optional but splendid)
1 tablespoon extra-virgin olive oil
1 teaspoon freshly squeezed
lemon juice

THE TOMATOES

Cut in half horizontally:
4 ripe, firm tomatoes
Scoop out the pulp, leaving the meaty walls. Sprinkle the insides with:
sea salt
freshly ground black, white,
OR multicolored pepper

COMBINING

Place the tomato "bowls" into a lightly oiled lasagne pan. Scoop some stuffing mix into each tomato. Sprinkle the tops with:
1 teaspoon fresh thyme
a few fennel seeds (optional)
some sea salt
freshly ground black pepper
Drizzle each with:
extra-virgin olive oil

BAKING

Place the pan in your preheated oven and bake for about 15 minutes, or until the tomatoes are tender but not mushy.

Sprinkle each tomato with more finely chopped fresh parsley and serve hot with potatoes or rice, a leafy green salad, and in-season vegetables.

Originally from Jean Ann's aunt—always a good source—this recipe also appeared in THE NEW MAINE COOKING. Adding baking soda to tomatoes before combining them with milk prevents curdling.

Aunt Mae's Famous Tomato Soup

SERVES 6

THE MILK

Peel the rind from:

1/2 well-washed lemon

In the top of a double boiler over rapidly boiling water, bring to a scald together:

3 cups milk
the lemon rind
1 very small onion, peeled

Measure out:

1 cup cold milk

Whisk into it:

1 heaping tablespoon cornstarch

Pour into the scalded milk and cook, stirring, until thick. Remove from the heat.

THE TOMATOES

In the meantime, pour into a medium-sized porcelainized pot:

1 quart home-canned tomatoes

Bring to a boil and then simmer for 10 minutes. Add:

1/4 teaspoon baking soda

The tomatoes will foam.

COMBINING

Remove the onion and lemon peel from your thick, scalded milk. Pour the hot milk into the simmering tomatoes and add:

1 teaspoon (or more) maple syrup
1 teaspoon sea salt
freshly ground black pepper

SERVING

Ladle the soup into warm bowls and serve with a leafy green salad and fresh rolls for lunch.

When late summer's largesse arrives with its peppers and onions and huge ripe tomatoes, it's absolutely necessary to prepare tomato sauce for winter survival!

Although some directives call for canning with a boiling-water bath, given the addition of nonacidic vegetables and the threat of botulism we prefer processing in a big pressure cooker. That old Maine saying of "better safe than sorry" holds.

Simply Grande Garden Tomato Sauce

MAKES 7 QUARTS

JAR PREPARATION

Wash your jars in hot soapy water. Rinse with scalding water and let the jars rest in it until they're needed.

THE TOMATOES

Pick or purchase:

40–50 ripe, firm, blemish-free tomatoes

(Paste tomatoes grown especially for sauce are best, because they're meatier and cook down quicker.) Wash carefully.

Bring a large pot of water to a boil. Drop in the tomatoes for about 30 seconds, or until their skins begin to peel. Remove and plunge into cold water immediately. When they're cool enough to handle, cut out the cores, peel off the skins, and trim any blemishes.

COOKING

Place a big porcelainized or stainless-steel pot on a wok collar, pop in your tomatoes, and get ready to simmer over low heat for hours.

ADDITIONS

(The amounts here are suggestions only; use what you please.) Prepare and add to the pot:

2 well-washed and trimmed green OR red bell peppers, chopped
4 medium-sized onions, chopped
3 well-washed and trimmed celery stalks, chopped leaves and all
1 carrot, shredded
3–4 garlic cloves, minced
4 teaspoons sea salt
a lot of freshly ground black pepper
a handful of fresh oregano leaves, finely chopped
3 tablespoons finely chopped fresh parsley

When the sauce has cooked down (perhaps overnight over low heat) and is beautifully thick, add:

1 cup red wine (optional)
1/2 cup sugar
OR 1/4 cup maple syrup (optional)

Cook a bit more if necessary to attain your desired thickness. Test for seasoning.

CANNING

Place a hot quart canning jar on a towel-covered countertop and add:

1 tablespoon 5 percent cider vinegar

Using a widemouthed canning funnel, pack in your tomato sauce. Remove air bubbles by poking into each jar along the sides with a chopstick. Continue for all seven jars.

Meanwhile, in a small saucepan of hot water, heat your seven metal bands and lids to just under boiling. When they're hot, drop them into a sieve and drain. Wipe off the rims of your sauce-filled jars with a clean cloth. Place hot lids and bands on the jars, screwing down the bands tightly.

Place your hot, filled jars on a rack in a big pressure canner that contains 2 to 3 inches of hot water. (Be sure to carefully read the directions for your pressure cooker before using it.) Place the canner over high heat and lock on the cover per the manufacturer's instructions. Leave the vent open until steam escapes steadily for 10 minutes; then close the vent, bring the pressure up to 10 pounds, and keep it steady for 20 minutes for quarts, 15 for pints, by adjusting your stove's heat. Watch carefully. Measure the processing time from when the pressure reaches 10 pounds.

When time is up, remove the canner from the heat and let the pressure fall to zero. Be certain that the pressure is all the way down. Wait for 5 minutes, then open the vent. Unfasten the cover and slide it toward you, allowing steam to escape, then hold it tipped away from your face to prevent any possible burn. Place on a shelf. Let the jars rest for 10 minutes before removing them with tongs. Place on a towel-covered counter to cool and prevent breakage. Do not allow jars to touch each other.

Let the jars cool completely, perhaps overnight.

When they're completely cool, unscrew the metal bands, check to see that each jar is safely sealed—the metal lid will feel slightly concave when you press it—rinse gently, wipe dry, and label.

STORING

Store in a cool, dark place. Always test a jar's seal before using it.

Hot and Sweet Peppers

THE HOTS

When Christopher Columbus accidentally discovered America, he also accidentally answered the prayers of many a European cook—not to mention diner. Though he failed to find a direct route to the Indies and the berries of *Piper nigrum*, that seasoning we grind today in our pepper mills and the spice all European merchants lusted after, what his eyes, nose, and tongue discovered in the New World were members of the Solanaceae family—fat, meaty, sometimes hotter-than-hot peppers of many colors!

In fact, after sampling a dish offered by local Indians (who were doubtless promptly murdered), he had the hold of one entire ship stocked with chilis for a return to Spain. While the date of arrival is really unknown, Jean Andrews, who has devoted many years to the study, culture, and painting of capsicums, suggests 1493, which is when the *Pinta* reached landfall at Bayona, Spain.

The journal of Christopher Columbus provides the first mention of the chili as being "better spice than our pepper *(mejor que pimienta nuestra)*." Columbus had described the island of Hispaniola (subsequently Haiti and the Dominican Republic) in his entry dated January 15, 1493. Writing that the natives called the fiery plant *aji* (pronounced "ah-hee" and transcribed into Castilian Spanish as *aji* or *axi*), he christened it *pimiento* after the spice pepper *(pimienta)* that he'd been seeking in the East Indies. *Pimiento*, grammatically masculine, apparently seemed better and stronger than *pimienta*!

People, of course, had been growing and eating peppers for thousands of years in tropical America. "Archaeologists have found evidence of chilies at the very earliest levels at Tamaulipas and Tehuacan in Mexico, which date back to around 7000 B.C.," says Benjamin Watson, although Jared Diamond would bring the date forward to around 3500. In fact, "The Aztecs had at least seven different words for hot peppers, including *guauchilli, zenalchilli,* and *chiltepin,*" from which the generic term *chili* is derived. "Among the Incas of Peru, peppers even became a form of currency, a practice that was at once so convenient and so well established that as late as 1900 (A.D., that is), one could still go shopping in the plaza at Cuzco carrying only a handful of peppers."

In their tropical and subtropical homeland, these members of the nightshade family are perennial plants. By far the most important species to North American gardeners is *Capsicum annuum*, which is comprised of a wide range of sweet and hot peppers including sweet bell, cayenne, jalapeño, and other well-known types.

Hot chili peppers are long or rounded fruits varying from the size of a fingernail to the size of a hand. They turn red as they ripen but never become mild. The species *C. frutescens* includes the pepper used in making Tabasco brand hot sauce, while lesser-known species such as *C. baccatum, C. chinense,* and *C. pubescens* remain popular in South America.

Dried chilis keep well, but the sweet (bell) pepper, cherished by most northerners, withers and rots with aging, which probably explains why Columbus took home a shipload of chilis. At any rate, in 1493 a courier to the British king was able to report that Columbus had brought back to Isabella "a pepper more pungent than any fruit from the Caucasus." For people without refrigeration, moreover, its seasoning power supposedly hid the taint of food spoilage. And it was rumored to preserve. Both are probably good reasons why hot chilis became prized in Bermuda when English settlers bound for Jamestown were shipwrecked there in 1609.

The chili pepper is also nutritious. Half a cupful contains 578 International Units of vitamin A, 182 milligrams of vitamin C, 13 milligrams of calcium, other minerals, and about 255 milligrams of potassium. Jean Carper advises that 10 to 20 drops of red-hot chili sauce in a glass of water daily, or a hot spicy meal three times a week, can help keep airways free of congestion, preventing or treating chronic bronchitis and colds. "Two teaspoons of jalapeno pepper," she adds, "can rev up the blood-clot-dissolving mechanism, protecting against heart disease and stroke."

Whether used for (questionable) preservation or simple enjoyment, all of these mild and hot nightshade relatives change color when ripe—either yellow, brown, purple, or red. Today's cherished big green bells are simply unripe.

While most hot peppers are varieties of two species, *C. annuum* and the often smaller, hotter *C. frutescens,* their pungency is derived from the alkaloid capsaicin. They must be handled with caution: Capsaicin is a general irritant that can "burn" skin. No wonder it's used in antidog and antimugger sprays. It may also perform as an antibacterial, aid digestion, and "is now consumed in larger quantities by more people in the world than any other spice," according to Harold McGee.

PEPPERS

CHOOSING SEEDS: There are hundreds of varieties of peppers. Prepare to choose among:

Bells (sweet): Big boxy fruits, some in gorgeous colors when ripe.

Ethnic sweet peppers: Mostly conical, sweet peppers with subtle tastes. Ripening red and yellow.

Chilis: Hot peppers in a variety of shapes, sizes, and colors. Smaller are generally hotter.

Ornamentals: Usually very hot, small, colorful fruits that set abundantly.

If yours is a short season, choose early varieties for harvests all summer long. Seed packets have about 30 seeds—more than enough for home gardeners who like variety. Seeds remain viable for years.

CULTIVATION: Germinating seeds and growing seedlings is tricky. Prepare to be finicky or leave it to the professionals. Sow seeds about 8 weeks prior to your transplant date. Germinate at 80° to 90°F, and when the first leaves show, grow at 70° (day) and 60° (night).

Choose a well-drained, fertile soil with abundant calcium and phosphorus in a location that isn't too windy. Don't add manure or nitrogen fertilizer in preparation. Lay black plastic mulch to warm the soil, keep weeds down, and keep moisture in. Cut holes with a posthole digger 18 inches apart.

Transplant your peppers when the soil is warm and the weather settled. Wrap seedling stems with brown paper to keep out cutworms, and irrigate thoroughly at first. Add rock phosphate to encourage high yields. Cover seedlings with a slitted row cover or floating row fabric supported by wire hoops. Remove when the plants bump up against it.

Weed around the growing plants. Don't use nitrogen fertilizer—it grows leaves but not fruits. In droughts provide regular water. In very hot, dry weather expect blossoms and young fruit to drop, but to return with more humidity.

PESTS AND DISEASES: Prevent cutworms at the seedling stage (see above). Adult plants have few pests. If necessary, you can control flea beetles, tarnished plant bugs, and aphids by sprinkling on rotenone or pyrethrum.

Several diseases such as bacterial spot and Phytopthora, and other problems such as poor fruit set, can be caused by ignoring the cultivation practices described above. Poor set can also be caused by extremely hot or cold temperatures during the flowering period.

Rotate your pepper plot annually.

HARVESTING: Pluck peppers promptly when they reach full size (to encourage others). Most colored bells can be picked green for a larger harvest. Left to ripen, they will be thicker, sweeter, more flavorful, and gorgeous to look at in their hues of red, yellow, brown, and more.

This wonderfully old recipe, doubtless widespread in the Caribbean, is an example of pepper usage as (hopefully) a preservative as well as a seasoning. It comes from Miss Lucy Blackburn of Bermuda.

Bermudian Pepper Pot

Miss Lucy advises, "A clay pot, a wooden spoon and fork. No metal ones must ever be used. Good sense and scrupulous cleanliness are most essential in preparing and keeping this food.

"Ingredients: 2 or 3 pounds fresh pork, salt, little thyme, fresh peppers, cassareep (a flavouring made from Cassava).

"Fry the pork till cooked right through and nicely browned; cut in pieces suitable for helping; bones may go in too.

"Put meat in pot, all the gravy and dripping.

"Add cassareep about 3 or 4 tablespoons, peppers cut open, thyme, salt and enough water to cover.

"Put pot on stove and bring to boil. Simmer slowly about one hour. It is best after several days.

"Cooked beef and poultry must be added, and the pot boiled every day for about 10 minutes. Always keep top on the pot. Set back to cool. Do not keep on stove. Add cassareep, meat, chicken, peppers, gravy or water when required. Cut meat into pieces and cook before putting in. Never put kidneys or anything with onion in it.

"Let the gravy come to a boil each day; should it become too greasy, remove fat when pot is cold."

Flavored oils have always been esteemed.

Hot Pepper Oil

Over low heat, slowly simmer together till the peppers blacken:

1 quart sesame seed oil
3–4 dried chili peppers

When the peppers are black, remove and discard them.

Store in a capped bottle, and sprinkle onto grains or beans lacking fervor.

PEPPER CAUTION: Hot peppers take special handling. They can be charred exactly as sweet peppers (see the recipe on page 202), but never rub your eyes—or anything else, for that matter—once your hands have touched the red-hot critters.

THE SWEETS

The sweet or bell pepper is one of the few mild members of the pungent *Capsicum* genus, and, like all the other natives of tropical America, was domesticated long before Europeans took it traveling.

It wasn't immediately noticed. "In the eighteenth century," says Maguelonne Toussaint-Samat in *A History of Food*, "a large and much milder variety, known in French as *poivron*, from Provencal *pébroun*, began to make its way into the cookery of southern Europe, eaten as a vegetable either cooked or raw. . . . Until after the Second World War [in France], in fact, cookery books scarcely ever condescended to mention sweet peppers except as a condiment pickled in vinegar."

They didn't know what they were missing. One cupful contains 530 International Units of vitamin A, 128 milligrams of vitamin C, 196 milligrams of potassium, as well as fiber and other valuable nutrients.

Always fine when sliced raw into salads, if it's charred, peeled, and marinated the bell pepper reaches gastronomic heights barely imagined.

Charred, Marinated Sweet Red and Green Bell Peppers

MAKES ABOUT 1 QUART

THE PEPPERS

Preheat the broiler. Rinse, drain, and place on a broiler pan:

8 firm, fat red or green bell peppers

Broil, rotating with tongs or a long fork every 2 to 3 minutes till all sides are charred and blistered. This may take 20 minutes.

When charred all over, place the peppers into a brown paper bag and close it tightly. Let them steam for 15 minutes. When the skins have begun to separate and the peppers are cool enough to handle (in 20 to 30 minutes), remove them from the bag, peel off the loosened skin with a paring knife, slit each pepper in half, open it up, and discard its seeds, ribs, and stem. Slice the peppers into strips and place in a bowl.

THE MARINADE

In a large bowl, whisk together:

1/3 cup extra-virgin olive oil
2–3 tablespoons freshly squeezed lemon juice
1/2 cup chopped bunching onions OR scallions
1 garlic clove, minced
1/2 teaspoon sea salt
freshly ground black pepper

Add the soft, skinned pepper strips and mix gently to coat. Cover and marinate for at least 3 hours.

SERVING

Serve at room temperature to liven up sandwiches, or salads. Store for up to a week, covered, in the refrigerator.

Perhaps the classic way to cook and enjoy big bell peppers is to stuff them.

Baked Stuffed Bells

SERVES 4

THE PEPPERS

Pick or purchase:
4 big red or green bell peppers
Rinse gently. Cut off about 1/2 inch of flesh at the stem end as you would a Halloween pumpkin. Set aside. Remove the seeds and pith from each pepper, being careful not to split it.

OPTION

To reduce cooking time, place the peppers in a colander atop a pot of boiling water and steam for 8 to 10 minutes. Be careful not to overcook. You merely want to tenderize them.

THE STUFFING

In a skillet, heat:
2 tablespoons extra-virgin olive oil
Sauté in it over medium heat till limp:
1 medium-sized onion,
    chopped finely

Under a heavy weight, such as an iron skillet, press for 10 minutes:
3/4 pound firm tofu

Crumble the tofu into the onion and sauté till golden. Add and mix together:
1 cup hot, cooked basmati rice
1 small tomato, chopped
the pepper tops (minus stem),
    chopped small
1/4 cup finely minced fresh parsley
    and cilantro
1 teaspoon sea salt
    freshly ground black pepper
Taste for seasoning (you might want to add cayenne powder). Then mix in:

2 big eggs, beaten lightly

BAKING

Preheat the oven to 375°F.

Stand the peppers upright in a lightly oiled lasagne pan and stuff with the tofu-rice mixture. Sprinkle with:
extra-virgin olive oil
Top with:
freshly grated Romano
OR Parmesan cheese

Pour 1/2 inch of water into the pan, cover, and bake for 30 to 40 minutes or until the peppers and stuffing are hot. You can check by piercing with a fork: The peppers should be tender but not falling apart.

Uncover and continue baking till the cheese is browned. Then serve right away with more rice, fresh bread, and a green leafy salad.

A peck of pickled peppers is no joke despite Peter Piper, so the following recipe shares a serious procedure for preserving summer's bounty. When winter arrives, you can take out a pepper or two, rinse well, cut off the caps, clean out the seeds, and stuff as you would fresh peppers.

One tasty stuffing mixture consists of bread crumbs, grated Romano or Parmesan cheese, an egg, chopped fresh parsley, plus freshly minced oregano and freshly ground black pepper to taste. A few moistened currants make a good addition, sweetening the result.

Pickled Peppers

Wash carefully:
as many peppers as you please,
    any size or shape, hot OR sweet

Be certain that none of them has any rotten spots.

Sterilize a crock, or a glass container and accompanying cap, with a lot of hot soap and water to which you've added a tablespoon of Clorox. Rinse well.

Make a brine of:
2 cups cold water
2 cups 5 percent apple cider vinegar
1/4 cup pickling OR kosher salt

Bring to a boil. (You can double or triple the amount of brine, if needed, to cover all of your peppers.)

Layer the peppers in your crock or glass container and add:
garlic cloves (as many as you please)
fresh mint leaves (a handful per layer, rinsed and stems removed)

Pour over to cover the peppers:
the boiling brine
Cover and set aside to rest in a cool place for at least 2 weeks before using.

Rinse each pepper well before use.

NOTE: If you're using a glass container, heat it and set it on a towel for filling to prevent breakage.

PAPRIKA

Discovery of the New World produced none of the spices that helped stimulate the voyages in the first place. Once met, however, capsicums helped revolutionize global cooking. Of the two classifications, the large sweet type and the smaller chili, a semisweet variety familiar to most Americans as a mild, powdered rust usually sprinkled on casseroles for decorative purposes is paprika. But ripe and red, dried and powdered, it isn't always mild.

Mild paprika is made from seeds only; strong paprika, darker in color, is ground from the whole, dried fruit. Interestingly, its name of origin in Europe was Polish—*pierprzyca*—but Hungarians adopted it as their national spice when they made it a basic ingredient of goulash.

Raymond Sokolov offers a look at certain pepper travels in his *Why We Eat What We Eat*. The Portuguese, he says, brought "capsicums to India and China through their colonies at Goa and Macao, making possible hot Indian and Sichuan food as we know it, but the first red capsicums to enter northern Europe came from the Balkans, imported by the Ottoman Turks." Speculation is that "the Ottomans had latched on to chilies as early as 1513, during their siege of the Portuguese colony at Hormuz in the Persian Gulf. From the Balkan fringe of the Ottoman empire the peppers spread naturally into neighboring spheres of influence, to the German-speaking part of the Holy Roman empire (1543), to the vast territories of the former Byzantine empire, and to Russia. Hungarians, in the middle of this *mitteleuropaisch* pepper pot, started talking about paprika as early as 1569. The Magyar word *paprikla* is a variation on a Slavic term for pepper: *peperke, piperke,* or *paparka*."

But while paprika for appreciative Hungarians is not the nearly tasteless red dust Americans buy in supermarkets—instead coming in several grades from sweet to fiery hot—even Hungary was slow to embrace paprika as part of its everyday cuisine. And the rest of northern Europe never assimilated truly hot spices.

Too bad. According to Jean Carper, "Hot paprika made from hot chili peppers is high in natural aspirin." In fact, the capsaicin in chilis is a potent painkiller, "alleviating headaches when inhaled, and joint pain when injected."

Cauliflower Paprika

SERVES 2–3

Preheat the oven to 400°F.

Pick or purchase:
**1 large cauliflower head weighing
1–1 1/2 pounds**
Rinse and break it into florets. Place these in a bowl and pour over them:
**2–3 tablespoons extra-virgin olive oil
1 teaspoon sea salt
freshly ground black
OR multicolored pepper**
Toss to coat thoroughly.

Place the oiled and seasoned florets in a 6- by 10-inch lasagne baking pan.

Add:
2–3 tablespoons water
Cover, place on the middle shelf of your oven, and bake until the stems are fork-tender—25 to 45 minutes, depending on the age of the cauliflower.

When it's done, remove the cauliflower to a bowl, leaving any liquid behind, and toss again with:
**1 teaspoon sweet paprika
OR (if you're brave) a combination
of sweet and hot
2 tablespoons finely chopped
fresh parsley**

Serve right away with a green salad, other in-season vegetables, and pasta or rice.

Shell Beans

What an odd name is *shell bean*. Yet it refers to one of the tastiest morsels ever to grace a plate.

Unlike the snap or string varieties—which, when eaten, are simply immature pods—shell beans mark a more mature phase when the seeds are plump and still moist, but before final maturity and drying. They should be picked when the bean bodies are clearly discernible within the pods, but the pods have not yet begun to turn limp or dry.

The variety, however, makes a big difference in texture and taste. Northern gardeners often prefer an old standby called Vermont cranberry—again, like *Jerusalem artichoke*, an odd name—also known as Roman beans. As described by the Johnny's Selected Seeds catalog, this "Oldtime Northern New England variety" has bright red mottled pods "borne on large upright plants. The shelled beans are oval, medium-size, plump, red and pink streaked. Produces very large beans for soup and baking. Mild taste."

Another type of bean enjoyed fresh is the lima bean, *Phaseolus lunatus*, little known in the early years of colonial settlement (although they've been found growing wild near old Indian garden sites in Florida). A native of tropical America, lima beans require hot days and warm nights over a 3-month period to come to maturity—an impossible attainment in New England, especially during a time when low temperatures were common.

Cultivated in Peru since 5000 or 6000 B.C., says Harold McGee, the lima bean's common name comes from that country's capital city. Spanish explorers brought it home then took it to the Philippines, Asia, Brazil, and Africa, where it's now the main legume. The species ancestors of our modern lima, however, came from Guatemala, where several types had been cultivated long before Europeans arrived.

For tips on growing shell beans, see page 134.

Like other beans, green limas are nutritious, being rich in vitamin A and a moderate amount of vitamin C, both of which are lost in drying. Limas also contain protein, calcium, and potassium.

Shell beans need to be "shelled." That is, they need to be popped out of their pods by pulling down the string and squeezing the pod at the end or between seeds, until the seam splits open. The moist, very alive gems can then be easily removed. Shelling lima beans is easy if you slice a thin strip along the inner edge of the pod; the beans will pop out.

Unlike dried beans, shell beans need no rehydrating before they're cooked.

Hot Vermont Cranberries

Remove cranberry beans from their pods and place in a pot. They won't swell: What you measure is what you'll get. For this recipe, you'll need 4 cups, but the amounts can easily be halved or doubled.

Barely cover the beans with:

water

Add:

1 tablespoon extra-virgin olive oil
1 teaspoon fresh summer savory
2 garlic cloves, smashed
1 small onion, diced
1/4 cup diced celery stalk
OR three lovage leaves
freshly ground black pepper
a little sea salt (optional)

Bring to a boil. Then lower the heat, cover, and simmer till the beans are just tender. It won't take long, depending on bean size.

Serve with the bean liquid—which will have turned into gravy—mashed potatoes or grain, and a big salad.

According to most sources, succotash— that tasty combination of new beans and corn—was an early American favorite created by Natives and adapted by New England colonists. Although limas are the beans of choice today, in colonial times any fresh or, indeed, dried bean was included along with corn, potatoes, even turnips. Chicken and corned beef were ingredients as well.

Succotash remains a favorite— especially if it's cooked the creamy Maine way. If you like your succotash clear, be careful to cut corn kernels only two-thirds of the way to the cob. If you like your succotash creamy, as in this recipe, scrape the cobs after cutting off the kernels, releasing the "cream," and add to your dish.

Succotash

SERVES 3–4

THE CORN

Boil 2 or 3 ears of corn (depending on their size) for 5 minutes. Cut kernels from the cobs to equal:

2 cups kernels

Scrape the "cream" from the cobs and save.

THE BEANS

In a medium-sized pot, simmer in 1 inch of water for about 20 minutes or till barely tender:

2 cups small, freshly shelled lima beans

Test with a fork.

OPTION

Or cook Hot Vermont Cranberries (at left) and measure out:

2 cups shelled, cooked, drained cranberry beans

COMBINING

In a large saucepan, warm:

2 tablespoons extra-virgin olive oil

Add and sauté till just wilted:

1 large onion, chopped finely
1 big red bell pepper, chopped

Add and simmer until the corn is barely cooked through:

the 2 cups cooked beans
the 2 cups corn kernels with their "cream"
sea salt to taste
freshly ground black pepper
1/4–1/2 teaspoon cayenne powder (optional)

SERVING

Sprinkle with:

chopped fresh parsley

Serve immediately with new potatoes and a heaping green leafy salad.

NOTE 1: You can substitute canned corn kernels or canned cream-style corn if fresh corn isn't available.

NOTE 2: You can also substitute dried baby limas, cooked as follows:

THE NIGHT BEFORE

Soak in cold water to cover:

2 cups dried lima beans

IN THE MORNING

Drain the beans. Pour them into a large pot, add water to cover, and cook, uncovered, for 30 to 60 minutes or till just tender. Drain.

Season with:

sea salt (optional)
freshly ground black pepper
extra-virgin olive oil

FALL

It's fall and, soon to come, the "fallen season"—
that time of year when days seem to
spiral down, down, down into the
darkest depths of winter. But it's a
time of feasting. From late broccoli
and cauliflower to splendid greens and
Chinese cabbage, not to mention apple treats
and fat potatoes, gardeners all over the Northeast
rejoice at the changing season, blessing the hot,
hard days of summer just past, looking
forward to a bit of rest and all
the scents of autumn.

It's a time of plenty. A time of thanksgiving.
And a time of putting the garden lovingly
to bed.

SEPTEMBER

Broccoli

B roccoli—that big, green-headed member of the mustard or Cruciferae family—may not be our 41st president's favorite vegetable, but it certainly is for many other people, and has been for a long time.

One of the cole crops, according to historian Charles Heiser broccoli's ancestor was native to the Mediterranean region. Human tinkering, however, put emphasis on different parts of the family, eventually producing a diversity of cultivated cousins. For instance, plants valued for their leaves became kale and cabbage, specialized buds turned into brussels sprouts, enlarged stems became kohlrabi, and flowering shoots resulted in cauliflower and broccoli.

"Other species of *Brassica*, originally native to either Europe or Asia, account for a number of other vegetables," adds Heiser. "These include plants grown for their roots—the turnip and rutabaga—and a great number whose leaves are eaten, collectively designated as the mustards. Two of these, brown mustard and black mustard, have seeds that are widely used in the preparation of the condiment mustard, which after black pepper is the most widely used spice in the United States."

Brassica oleracea botrytis cymosa "is believed to be the *cyma* referred to by the Romans," reports J. I. Rodale. They "knew it as the flowering shoots developed by cabbage plants when they were allowed to stand two years in the field."

It took a while to invade the rest of Europe.

When 14-year-old Catherine de Médicis arrived in France from Florence in 1533 to marry the heir to the French throne, Henri of Valois, duc d'Orleans (who became Henri II in 1547, and who was also 14), she took with her a number of Italian chefs and pastry cooks. Says historian Reay Tannahill, "They, and the staff of Marie de Medici, who went to France at the end of the century as the bride of Henry IV, introduced not only the new Italian style of cooking to that country, but also such vegetables as artichokes, broccoli, and savoy cabbages.

"Nevertheless, in 1577, the Venetian ambassador to Paris still could not bring himself to enthuse about French food. The people, he reported, were quite immoderate, eating four or five times a day as and when they felt inclined, consuming very little bread or fruit, but a great deal of meat. 'They load the table with it at their banquets,' he said. They 'ruin their stomachs and bowels by eating too much, as the Germans and Poles do by drinking too much.'"

By the mid–17th century, however, things had changed, and the Franco-Italian cuisine that had been slowly evolving was codified by Pierre François de la Varenne.

Broccoli didn't fare as well in England. Introduced early in the 17th century, probably from Cyprus—some 70 years after the "Italian asparagus" became popular in France—it was still reported in Florence Daniel's 1915 *Healthy Life Cook Book* as "a rather coarser variety of cauliflower."

And it didn't arrive in the United States until the 20th century. Says Rodale, "Sprouting broccoli, also known as Italian asparagus broccoli, has been grown widely in American gardens only since 1900. Another kind, the heading type, looks so much like cauliflower that it is sometimes marketed for such." Consumption has been significant only since World War II.

Eating broccoli is a healthful thing to do. This big, green-headed member of the cabbage family—so bursting with goodness that it's called an anticarcinogen—boasts only 24 calories in a cupful while containing 1,356 International Units of vitamin A, 62 milligrams of vitamin C, 42 milligrams of calcium, 286 milligrams of potassium, and some iron and protein, among other nutrients.

It's not only the head that's nutritious. Broccoli leaves, so often thrown away, are also sky high in vitamin A (something like 30,000 units in 3/4 cup), as well as containing 90 milligrams of vitamin C and some of the B vitamins. In fact, they contain much more vitamin A than the buds. The stalk, for about 3 inches below the florets, is also edible if peeled and sliced.

Other creatures besides people enjoy broccoli. But if you meet any little green worms, don't complain. Harboring a few visitors means that broccoli is free of dangerous pesticides. If it's good for worms, you know it's good for you. If they give you the shivers, however, handling them without a qualm is easy. As follows.

Before serving broccoli cold in salads, adding it to other dishes, or serving it as a dish unto itself, bring a big pot of water to a boil. Break and cut your broccoli head into bite-sized florets and place them in a tall, straight-sided colander. Plunge the colander into the boiling water for 1 or 2 minutes. Little pests will turn light green and float away.

Lift your colander out of the hot water, drain well, and either plunge the florets into cold water to chill for salads, or continue with another recipe.

BROCCOLI AND CAULIFLOWER

CHOOSING SEEDS:

Broccoli: Choose short-season, heat-tolerant varieties for summer, or grow long-season varieties for a fall crop. Some seed companies offer a broccoli mix so that some variety will be maturing at all seasons. At least once in your lifetime try 'Romanesco' for its beauty.

Cauliflower: There are early- and late-season varieties. They also come in a range of colors—white, cream, green, and red.

Broccoli has 7,000 seeds per ounce. A 5-gram packet should sow 100 row feet. Cauliflower has 8,000 seeds per ounce. A 4-gram packet should sow 100 row feet.

CULTIVATION: Start seedlings indoors in plug flats for early-spring planting. Seed the flats about 2 months before your last frost. Plant out just after the last frost. Broccoli and cauliflower like a very fertile soil, so add compost or manure to the bed before planting. They also like plenty of moisture, so plan to irrigate or mulch with hay, or plant in 4-inch holes in 6-mil black plastic sheeting to keep the soil and roots moist.

Space the plants about 36 inches apart to allow for adult expansion. When you plant seedlings, wrap the stems with strips of brown paper bags to keep cutworms away. Have the end of a dribbling hose handy, and place it at the base of every seedling while you plant the next one.

For a fall crop, plant in rows spaced 30 inches apart with a wheel seeder. Use the special cabbage wheel that picks up the little ball-bearing-sized seeds one at a time. Collineal-hoe to remove weed seedlings. When the broccoli or cauliflower seedlings are large enough, thin them to a 30-inch spacing.

PESTS: Prevent cutworm damage to seedlings by wrapping their stems (see above).

Even healthy seedlings of broccoli and cauliflower are susceptible to black flea beetles in springtime. To prevent infestation, use floating row covers sealed all around the edges with dirt. Or sprinkle on rotenone.

To keep caterpillars away, interplant with tomatoes, or use Dipel spray. You can also go around the garden plucking off the caterpillars (if you can see them).

Easy Broccoli Salad

SERVES 2–4

Blanch:
about 4 cups broccoli florets
Use the process described on page 212, which will rid the florets of any little visitors. Plunge them into cold water to chill. Once they're cold, drain well. Refrigerate until mealtime. Broccoli should be slightly cooked but still crunchy.

Mix up a vinaigrette by shaking vigorously in a covered jar or whizzing in a blender:
1/2 cup extra-virgin olive oil
3 tablespoons freshly squeezed lemon juice
1/2 teaspoon Dijon mustard
1/2 garlic clove, minced
3/4 teaspoon sea salt
freshly ground black pepper
(If the taste of olive oil is too strong for you, substitute half sunflower seed oil.)

Immediately before serving, pour the vinaigrette over your broccoli. Then add and toss lightly:
3 hard-cooked eggs, chopped
2 tablespoons grated Parmesan cheese (optional)

NOTE: If the initial, quick blanching fails to tenderize your florets enough, simply drain and blanch them again until you're satisfied.

Phil Learned, executive (and award-winning) chef of the Balsams Grande Resort Hotel in Dixville Notch, New Hampshire, complimented Simply Grande's J. A. by introducing one of her broccoli recipes to his menu. Here it is.

Broccoli Pasta

SERVES 6

THE PASTA

Place a large kettle containing about 2 gallons of water over high heat. Add:
1 tablespoon sea salt
1 tablespoon oil
(to prevent too much foaming)
Bring to a boil and add slowly, without stopping the boil:
1 pound spiral OR other pasta
Cook the pasta until *al dente*, or tooth-tender, about 8 minutes. Remove, drain, and plunge the pasta into cold water to remove excess starch. Return it to your hot kettle and set aside to become warm again.

While the pasta is cooking, heat in a large heavy-bottomed skillet:

1 tablespoon extra-virgin olive oil

Sauté in it till tender:

1/4 cup diced red bell pepper
1/2 cup diced green bell pepper
3 cups chopped broccoli florets
   and their peeled, diced stems
1 medium-sized onion, diced

ADDITIONAL OIL

In a small saucepan, heat together:

6 tablespoons extra-virgin olive oil
1 garlic clove, smashed

COMBINING

Warm a large ceramic platter in the oven. Toss the warm reserved pasta lightly with:

the hot olive oil from which the
   garlic clove has been removed

Then add and toss lightly together again:

the sautéed vegetables
1 heaping tablespoon finely chopped
   fresh basil
sea salt to taste
a lot of freshly ground black pepper
a little finely grated lemon rind
   (optional)

Sprinkle with:

chopped fresh parsley

SERVING

Pour the pasta onto your heated platter and serve with grated Parmesan cheese passed in a separate bowl, freshly baked bread, and fruit for dessert.

Broccoli makes a fine soup.

Cream of Broccoli Soup

SERVES 4

In a large porcelainized pot, place:

2 tablespoons sunflower seed oil

Sauté in it until limp:

2 shallots, finely chopped,
   OR 1 medium-sized onion, chopped

Peel and cut into small cubes to equal 1 1/2 cups:

1 large potato

Chop coarsely:

1 pound blanched broccoli florets

Add to the cooked shallot or onion:

the potato cubes
the chopped broccoli florets
1 or more large garlic cloves, minced
2 cups Vegetable Stock (see page 43)
   or water

Cover, bring to a boil, reduce the heat (place the pot on a wok collar if you have one), and simmer for about 15 minutes, or until the potatoes are tender. Whiz in a blender on low speed until nicely puréed.

Return the soup to the pot along with:

2 cups milk
1/2 teaspoon sea salt
freshly ground black pepper
freshly grated nutmeg

Heat but do not boil.

Serve at once garnished with a dollop of yogurt in each bowl.

Stir-fried vegetables retain their nutrients because they're cooked so quickly. Seasoned with a few sprinkles of toasted sesame seed oil, broccoli becomes even tastier.
As with any stir-fry, be sure to have all the ingredients ready before cooking begins.

Broccoli Stir-Fry

SERVES 4

PREPARATION

Heat a big pot of water to boiling. Cut into florets:

1/2 pound broccoli

You should have 2 heaping cupfuls. Pop the broccoli into your boiling water for a few seconds. This will dislodge any little pests hanging on to their favorite treat. Remove from the water and drain well. Cut into small cubes:

1 small zucchini

You should have 3 cups. Then dice:

1 medium onion OR 2 leeks

COOKING

Set your wok on its collar and pour in:

1 tablespoon extra-virgin olive oil

Heat the oil briefly, then add and stir-fry for about 10 seconds:

2 teaspoons minced garlic
1 teaspoon minced fresh gingerroot
OR 1 heaping teaspoon powdered ginger

Then add:

the diced onions
the broccoli florets
the cubed zucchini
2 tablespoons Bragg's Liquid Aminos (see page 63) OR Vegetable Stock (see page 43)

Cover the wok and steam for about 3 minutes over medium heat. Remove the cover, increase the heat to high, and toss the vegetables for 5 minutes longer or till tender.

SERVING

Sprinkle with:

1 teaspoon toasted sesame seed oil
1 heaping tablespoon toasted sesame seeds

Serve immediately with barley, rice, or another cooked grain, sliced tomatoes, and a green leafy salad.

NOTE: Toasting sesame seeds is easy and takes only a few seconds. Pour a handful into an unoiled skillet and place over medium heat. Let the seeds brown, shaking the pan often.

Witches say coleflores eaten
reguler by a childless wyfe
alwayes resulten praenansy.
—A WYF'S BOK OF GARDYNING, 1709

Cauliflower

C arolus Linnaeus, that great classifier of flora and fauna, lumped two members of the Cruciferae family together in one genus and species, where they have remained ever since. For many years the plant we now call cauliflower was known as cauliflower broccoli, and broccoli was known as asparagus-broccoli or sprouting-broccoli.

The mustard family, of which these two are important members, "has been particularly significant for its vegetables," says Charles B. Heiser Jr. in *Seed to Civilization*. In fact, a single species, *Brassica oleracea*, Botrytis group, native to the Mediterranean region started it all.

"The magic of cultivation," reveals writer Maguelonne Toussaint-Samat in *A History of Food*, "has now created some 400 varieties: there are green cabbages, red cabbages, white cabbages, pointed or wrinkle-leaved Italian cabbages, round, frost-resistant North European cabbages, kohl-rabi with its edible roots, oilseed rape, broccoli grown for its spears of flower-heads, Brussels sprouts grown ever since the seventeenth century for the little buds sprouting from the stem, and the cauliflowers that resemble a bridal bouquet and were popular in ancient Greece and known to the Romans. . . ."

But historians seem to differ. Some report that the first primitive forms of cauliflower were cultivated more than 2,000 years ago east of the Mediterranean (one writer even suggesting it was the handiwork of a Babylonian in the Tigris-Euphrates valley), and that it only arrived in Europe during the Middle Ages when Moorish armies invaded Spain. Toussaint-Samat, however, states that "The cabbage is the oldest of the edible varieties of vegetables which provided inspiration for the gatherers [meaning early hunter-gatherer societies] in their plant-hunting and . . . culinary creativity," and that the wild cabbage, *B. oleracea*, was a small plant that "grew in all European coastal areas, absorbing fortifying mineral salts, and can still be found on the coasts of the English Channel."

She further states that Neolithic Near Eastern peoples, the Hebrews and Egyptians, didn't eat cabbage because it's "an old inhabitant of Europe. The first recorded mention of it is in a treatise on plants allegedly written by Eudemus of Athens, which distinguished between three kinds of cultivated cabbage. The Greeks and Romans believed that if you ate cabbage during a banquet it would keep you from getting drunk."

At any rate, cauliflower was soon beloved for things other than preventing drunkenness (says chef Bert Greene, "perfect cauliflower was often pressed into the décolletage of an unmarried Spanish maiden to call attention to her natural endowments") and dubbed *cavoli a fiore* (the cabbage that blooms like a flower). Harold McGee tells us that it "was known in Europe in the 16th century and introduced to England early in the 17th, probably from Cyprus." James Trager in *The Food Chronology* suggests that carrots, cabbages, parsnips, and turnips, as well as cauliflower, were introduced into England by Flemish weavers fleeing the persecution of Spain's Philip II around 1558.

Wherever and whenever its origins, by the time it arrived in America the cauliflower, according to Mark Twain, was "just cabbage with a college education"! Though Americans have always been great meat eaters, not everybody in pre-Revolutionary days disdained vegetables. Indeed, certain vegetables considered to be modern discoveries may have been more common in the 18th century than in the 20th. "We are accustomed to think of broccoli as a twentieth-century revelation," say Waverly Root and Richard De Rochemont in *Eating in America*, "but John Randolph, in *A Treatise on Gardening by a Citizen of Virgina*, written just before the Revolution, speaks of it as if it were well known in his time: 'The stems will eat like Asparagus, and the heads like Cauliflower'"—two other already familiar vegetables.

For tips on growing cauliflower, see page 213.

According to Lavon J. Dunne's *Nutrition Almanac*, cauliflower is a rich source of calcium. A cupful provides 16 International Units of vitamin A, 0.8 milligram of vitamin B_1, 0.6 milligram of vitamin B_2, 71 milligrams of vitamin C, 28 milligrams of calcium, 46 milligrams of phosphorus, 0.6 milligram of iron, 1.98 grams of protein, and 24 calories.

Toussaint-Samat reports that cauliflower is rich in vitamins B and K (which helps the blood clot), and its vitamin C content is greater than that of orange juice. "It contains a number of mineral salts, calcium, magnesium and potassium, and is good for the bones, the skin, the hair and the nails." Jean Carper says it reduces the risk of colon and stomach cancer.

Louis XIV reputedly liked his cauliflower simmered in stock, seasoned with nutmeg, and served with fresh butter. And Jeanne Bécu, the comtesse du Barry installed on April 23, 1769, by Louis XV as his *maitresse-en-titre*, became associated on French menus with the vegetable; consommé du Barry is a combination of veal and oxtail soup with *chouxfleur.*

For ordinary mortals (perhaps we should say normal mortals), fresh, raw cauliflowerettes plunged into a dip and eaten at once are unsurpassed.

Cauliflower Cottage Cheese Dip

MAKES 1 CUP

In a small bowl, mix together:
- **1/2 cup cottage cheese**
- **1/2 cup yogurt**
- **1 teaspoon finely chopped fresh parsley**
- **1 teaspoon finely chopped scallions**
- **1/2 teaspoon freshly minced oregano**
- **1/2 teaspoon freshly minced thyme**
- **sea salt to taste**

Cauliflower Tofu Dip

MAKES 1 CUP

Whiz together in a blender till smooth:
- **4 ounces soft tofu**
- **1/4 cup yogurt**
- **1/2 cup well-packed fresh cress**
- **2 tablespoons freshly squeezed lemon juice**
- **1 tablespoon shoyu (naturally fermented soy sauce)**
- **1 small onion, quartered**
- **freshly ground black pepper**

If cauliflower must be cooked, it must be barely tender.

And if you're fortunate enough to pick or purchase organically grown produce, you may find a little green worm or two climbing about on the white branches of the cauliflower forest. These visitors are easily seen and done away with by plucking them off with the blade of a small, sharp knife. But see how it's done for broccoli.

Cooking Cauliflower: The Florets

Rinse a head of cauliflower.

Bring a big pot of water to a boil. Add:
- **1 tablespoon distilled white vinegar**

Break off the florets and drop them into the rapidly boiling water. As soon as they're barely tender, plunge them into cold water to halt cooking. Remove and drain well. Then use in any manner you please.

If an entire cauliflower head is desired rather than florets, here's the procedure.

Cooking Cauliflower: The Whole Head

Rinse a head of cauliflower. Remove most of its core; then hollow it out a bit, using the small end of a melon scooper.

In a large pot, bring to a boil:
- **enough water to cover the cauliflower head (about 3 quarts)**
- **1 tablespoon white distilled vinegar**

Place in the head, florets downward, and simmer for about 10 minutes.

As soon as it's barely tender, plunge the head into a large bowl of very cold water. Remove and drain well. It's now ready to be sauced, chilled, or used in any way you please.

This buttery sauce made with cheese and dill is fatty but quick, easy, and—naturally—tasty.

Dill Cheese Sauce

MAKES 2 CUPS

In a small saucepan over medium heat, melt:
3 tablespoons butter
Whisk in:
3 tablespoons unbleached white flour
Cook for several seconds, whisking. While you're still whisking add:
2 cups milk

Cook and whisk till the sauce thickens. Then add:
1/2 cup freshly grated Parmesan cheese
When the cheese has melted, stir in:
2 teaspoons freshly chopped dill weed, stems omitted

Pour enough sauce over your cooked cauliflower to please you, and serve immediately.

NOTE: If you worry about fat, an alternative is to eliminate the butter and thicken the 2 cups of milk with 2 tablespoons of cornstarch. The taste will suffer, but your health may be worth it.

If a truly classic, butter-rich white sauce is required, béchamel is the one.

Classic Béchamel Sauce

MAKES 2 CUPS

Bring to a scald:
2 cups milk

In a saucepan, melt:
3 tablespoons butter
Sauté in the melted butter until soft:
1 tablespoon minced onion
Add, mix well, and cook over low heat, stirring, for 3 minutes:
1/4 cup more butter

Remove the pan from the heat and add:
the 2 cups scalded milk
Whisk until thick and smooth.

Add:
1/4 teaspoon sea salt
freshly ground white pepper
Simmer over low heat for about 10 minutes.

Strain through a fine sieve. Keep the sauce covered if you're not going to use it immediately.

The addition of cheese intensifies béchamel considerably, at which time it's called mornay.

To 2 cups of béchamel sauce (above), add:
2 tablespoons freshly grated Parmesan cheese
2 tablespoons freshly grated Gruyère cheese
2 tablespoons butter
Whisk gently over moderate heat until the cheeses and butter are incorporated.

Classic mornay creates a fine company dish when the big heads of cauliflower are in season and creamy white.

Cauliflower Gratin

SERVES 8

Rinse and divide into florets:
2 cauliflower heads
Bring a large pot of salted water to a boil and drop in the florets. Simmer until just tender, 10 to 15 minutes. Drain well in a colander. Remove to a heated, buttered casserole dish.

To 4 cups of mornay sauce (see note, page 220), add:
1 chopped (canned) pimiento
some finely chopped green bell pepper

In a small skillet, melt:
1/4 cup butter
Sauté in it till golden:
1/2 cup bread crumbs

Spoon the mornay sauce over the cauliflower florets and top with bread crumbs. Sprinkle with:
freshly chopped parsley

Serve immediately.

Nasturtiums

Midsummer finds nasturtium blossoms transforming the lush, green landscape of Simply Grande Gardens into a bright mélange of yellows, oranges, and reds. Native to Central and South America, the plants arrived in New England the long way around—via Europe, where introduction occurred in the 16th century.

Early immigrants brought many a flower with them, some for medicinal reasons, others for edibility, some for sheer delight. The nasturtium, with its peppery leaves and hint of honeyed blossoms, surely came on the last two counts.

The Fragrant Garden, a book by Louise Beebe Wilder originally published in 1932 and titled *The Fragrant Path,* revealed that "the name Nasturtium, an old Latin word used by Pliny, was derived by him from *narsus,* the nose, and *tortus,* twisted, in reference to the supposed contortions of the nose caused by the hot pungent odour and taste of these flowers."

She must refer to Pliny the Elder, a Roman savant and author of an encyclopedic work of uneven accuracy that was an authority on scientific matters up to the Middle Ages. Since Pliny died in 79 A.D., one wonders who added Nastortiomstohis to his *Natural History.*

By 1629 one of England's great gardeners and garden book writers, John Parkinson, was saying of the nasturtium that it "is of so great beauty and sweetnesse withall that my Garden of delight cannot bee unfurnished of it." And again, "the whole flower hath a fine small sent very pleasing, which being placed in the middle of some Carnations or Gilloflowers (for they are in flower at the same time) make a delicate Tussimussie, as they call it, or Nosegay, both for sight and sent."

"What a delicious place must Parkinson's garden at 'Long Acre' have been," exclaimed Wilder, "a very treasure trove of interest and beauty, for we know that he grew the greater number of the thousand odd kinds of 'pleasant flowers' that he describes in his grand book, the grandest garden book ever written, *Paradisi in Sole, Paradisus Terrestris* [1629]. . . . To read it today," she continued, "is to join in converse with one who knew and loved his plants well and spoke of them in simple and eloquent language. . . . He wrote, as someone has said of the early herbalists, as one who, as it were, 'walked in holy places and spoke with something of the fragrance of a garden in their very speech.'"

Parkinson is buried in the cathedral of St. Martin's-in-the-Fields, the register giving the date as August 6, 1650. The present Charing Cross and Covent Garden area in London have swallowed the site of his garden.

But nasturtiums remain.

Tropaeolum minus, the dwarf variety, and *T. majus,* a climber, provided Peruvians—and still provide us—with tangy leaves, flowers, and seeds. If you're lucky enough to have a garden, or know someone who does, the green rounded leaves, bits of tender stem, and brilliant flowers can be added to canapés, or used

---

THE CAPER, Tom Stobart tells us in *Herbs, Spices, and Flavourings,* is "a small bush with tough oval leaves. The flowers, the size of a wild rose, are white or pink with four petals and a tassel of long purple stamens." But "Flowers that open in the morning, are gone by the afternoon and the famous quotation from Ecclesiastes, 'The flower shall wither, beauty shall fade away', may well refer to the caper which grows, amongst other places, wild in the Holy Land." Used as a condiment for thousands of years, capers grow wild around the Mediterrandan basin and in North Africa, "well down into the Sahara."

Caper cultivation is "rather difficult," says Stobart, "and gathering them requires much hard work. Ideally, the buds may be picked every morning just as they reach the proper size. After being wilted in the air for a day, they are put in casks of strong salted white vinegar or are dry-salted.

"The taste of fresh caper buds is not promising," he promises, "and the characteristic flavour comes only after they have been pickled, due to the development of an organic acid—capric acid—which, when strong, smells unpleasantly of billy-goats. . . . Although there are many caper substitutes (broom buds, marsh marigold buds, caper spurge [possibly poisonous] and so on), most lack this essential flavour," he concludes. "But pickled green nasturtium seeds are excellent."

in appetizers for a piquant touch. A few blossoms strewn on top of a just-tossed green salad are a picture. "In the Orient," J. I. Rodale tells us, flower petals "are sometimes added to tea, as are jasmine flowers."

> **For tips on growing nasturtiums, see page 60.**

Seeds can be pickled for use as a caper substitute and make fine additions to vinaigrettes, white sauces, and yogurt dips. (The capers found in grocery stores are the preserved buds of the white flower of a spiny Mediterranean shrub; see the sidebar.)

This recipe is from
THE NEW MAINE COOKING.

J. A.'s Nasturtium Capers

THE SEEDS

When they're green and fat, pick:
3 cups nasturtium seedpods
Rinse them and drain.

THE BRINE

In a glass jar, combine:
1/2 cup canning OR kosher salt
1 quart cold water
Add:
the nasturtium seeds
If the seeds float, weight them down with anything but metal. (A ceramic bowl would do, as would a plate with a water-filled glass on it.) Let soak for 24 hours.

THE RINSE

Remove the seeds from the brine, drain, pour them into a big bowl, and cover with:

1 quart cold water
Soak for 1 hour. Drain.

THE PICKLING SOLUTION

In an enameled saucepan, place:
the drained capers
1 quart distilled white vinegar
Bring to a boil.

PROCESSING

Drain the capers again, saving the vinegar. Return the vinegar to the heat and allow it to resume boiling.

Place the capers into hot, sterilized, 1/2-pint jars (the size usually reserved for jellies). Pour boiling vinegar to within 1/2 inch of the tops.

Seal and process the jars in a boiling-water bath for 10 minutes. (If canning is new to you, see page 38 or the recipe for Great Cucumber Pickles on page 152.)

STORING

Once you've removed the jars from their water bath, let them cool, check to be sure all have sealed properly, then wipe and store them in a cool, dark place for at least 6 weeks before using.

For its high and grateful Taste it is ever plac'd in the middle
of the Grand Sallet, at our Great Mens Tables, and Praetor Feasts,
as the Grace of the whole Board. But Caution is to be given
of a small red worm often lurking in these stalks.
—JOHN EVELYN, ACETARIA: A DISCOURSE OF SALLETS, 1699

Celery

Celery, is a member of the Umbelliferae family, whose other members include carrots, parsnips, and parsley. An annual or biennial marsh plant, it was apparently native to Europe from Sweden south to North Africa, and eastward to the Himalayas.

Known and described by the ancients, it was not cultivated except for medicinal purposes until the 17th century . . . at least according to historians J. I. Rodale and Benjamin Watson.

In its wild form celery is a stubby, tough, fibrous weed. Bert Greene reports that original stalks still blossom "in salt marshes along the coastline of southern France. Bees love its tiny white flowers and in fact gave the plant its Latin name, *Apium graveolens,* which means 'heavy with bees.'

"From wild celery early horticulturists bred two separate and distinct strains," he continues. "*Apium graveolens dulce* (sweet only in comparison with its bitter forebear) is the crunchy green stalk that is every dieter's staff of life. *Apium graveolens rapaceum* (so dubbed because it must be literally ripped from the garden by force) is a bulbous white root that is the indispensable ingredient in one of the world's classiest hors d'oeuvres, *céleri rémoulade.*"

Certain food historians claim that both celery and celery root (or celeriac) were developed by the gardeners of Cyrus the First of Persia—reputedly a vegetarian—around the year 2000 B.C. Reay Tannahill, however, suggests that until about 2200 B.C. Egyptians were "trying to domesticate a wide variety of animals," after which they "turned more of their attention to the large areas of marshland preserved for hunting, fowling, fishing, and the gathering of wild fruits and . . . vegetables," such as papyrus stalks, the lotus root, and wild celery.

In ancient Greece celery was used like laurel to crown the heads of athletes, and it was used in funeral wreaths in Plutarch's time. When the T'ang dynasty came to power in the early seventh century A.D. in China, the king of Nepal sent gifts of spinach plants, a "vinegar leaf vegetable," and what appears to have been garden celery. Previously, of course, Confucius, who died in 479 B.C., had left behind more than 300 traditional songs of the Chou dynasty, giving a picture of Chinese agriculture. At least 44 food plants were mentioned, including celery. The Old Testament mentions only 29.

Celery didn't become a table vegetable in Europe until the Middle Ages—the 16th century at least, says Watson, having gradually become "cultivated for table use in Italian and French gardens." He adds that it was often referred to as "smallage" by early writers.

Composed of 95 percent water, celery is a good source of potassium. It's relatively high in sodium, minerals, and vitamin A; and it's low in calories, with a cupful containing only 20. Interestingly, it's also considered, along with cabbage, to contain an anti-ulcer factor.

The famous French writer Colette was on the mark when she used celery for dieting. Maurice Goudeket, her widower, told cookbook author Bert Greene that "When she had to have her photograph taken with the members of the French Academy for the first time, she went on a rare diet to lose five pounds. For a week she ate nothing but celery. Celery with water. Celery with salt and pepper. But only celery for seven days. Never once complaining

---

GARDENING NOTES

CELERY AND CELERIAC

CHOOSING SEEDS:

Celery has thick crisp stalks with a rich flavor. An easy-to-grow variety is 'Ventura'.

Celeriac is a long-season, swollen-root celery, good for winter storage.

There are 75,000 seeds per ounce. The tiniest package should do.

CULTIVATION: Celery and celeriac are both long-season vegetables that must be sown indoors in flats kept warm for germination, and planted outdoors when the soil and air are warm. Set plants 6 to 8 inches apart in rows 10 to 12 inches apart. Mulch with thick hay to keep the soil moist, prevent weeds, and blanch the lower stalks. Remove side shots from celeriac as it grows.

PESTS AND DISEASES: Aphids can cause celery mosaic (mottled leaves, twisted stems, dwarfing). Control them with insecticidal soap. Leaf blights can be prevented by crop rotation.

HARVESTING: Cut off the roots and poor-quality outer leaf stalks in the field. Dunk the plants in cold water, then store at high humidity and near-freezing temperatures.

even when I was served my normal meals. Later, after she had lost the weight, she confided that one day she had cheated. There had been a small red caterpillar at the heart of a celery stalk, but she was so hungry for meat, she ate it too!"

Celery, of course, is fine raw or cooked. Some of the uses to which it has been put are humorous. In Rome a stalk of celery was thought to cure a hangover—as well as constipation. A recipe correcting the latter is still extant. "Cookery-books seem to have been numerous in antiquity," say translators Barbara Flower and Elisabeth Rosenbaum, "but only one has come down to us, and that is in Latin." A compilation from various sources, it bears the name of Apicius and is preserved in two ninth-century manuscripts.

Crisp celery stalks stuffed with ricotta-herb filling are splendid for snacks, lunch, or hors d'oeuvres. Use the inner, tender stalks complete with leaves.

Cheese- and Herb-Stuffed Celery Stalks

Rinse and dry well:
  10–12 celery stalks

In a small bowl, mix together:
  1 cup low-fat ricotta cheese
  1 tablespoon finely chopped fresh cilantro
  1 tablespoon finely chopped fresh basil
  1 tablespoon finely chopped fresh chives
  1 small garlic clove, minced
  freshly ground black pepper
  sea salt to taste (optional)
Using a spatula or cake decorator, spread the filling in the stalks.

If you must cook celery, this recipe is satisfying, although fresh, sliced celery hearts tossed into a salad show it off to perfection. Of course, mixed-vegetable soups are always enhanced by the addition of leaves and outer, stringier stalks, well diced.

For the recipe below, use only the very tenderest stalks.

Braised Celery

SERVES 4

Wash, trim, and cut into 3-inch lengths:
  1 1/2 pounds celery hearts and tender inner stalks
Layer in a medium-sized heavy porcelainized pot.

Mix together, heat to boiling, and pour over the celery:
  1/2 cup Vegetable Stock (see page 43)
  3 tablespoons freshly squeezed lemon juice
  2 tablespoons extra-virgin olive oil
  1 tablespoon refined white sugar
  1/2 teaspoon sea salt

Cover tightly and simmer till fork-tender, about 20 minutes.

Drain the liquid into a small saucepan, and remove the celery to a hot serving bowl. Bring the liquid to a boil and reduce it to 1/2 cup.

Pour the liquid over the celery and serve at once with potatoes, cooked carrots or beets, and perhaps a nut loaf or bean burgers.

Celery soup is a longtime favorite. Combined with potatoes, it's delicious served hot in winter, chilled in summer. A 'Kennebec' potato would be a good ingredient; a 'Corolla' would make the soup faintly yellow.

Simplest Celery Soup

SERVES 2–4

In a big, heavy pot, heat:
**1 tablespoon sunflower seed oil
OR extra-virgin olive oil**
Sauté in it till soft:
1 large onion, chopped to equal 1 cup
Dice:
2 celery stalks to equal 1 cup

Peel and cube:
1 very large potato to equal 2 cups

To the sautéed onion, add:
**2 cups Vegetable Stock (see page 43)
OR 1 3/4 cups water plus
1/4 cup Bragg's Liquid Aminos
(see page 63)
the diced celery
the cubed potato**
Simmer till tender, perhaps 15 minutes.

Whiz in a blender on low speed, then higher, until a smooth purée has formed. (Place a towel over the blender top as you purée to prevent burning.)

Then add:
1/2 cup milk
You can adjust your soup's consistency by adding more or less milk.

Add:
**freshly ground black or white pepper
(optional)**

Serve hot or chilled. Garnish with freshly chopped cilantro, chives, or parsley.

Tomatillos

E arly New England women often planted flowers in their kitchen gardens among salad greens and medicinal herbs. One decorative inhabitant was the brilliant orange Chinese lantern *(Physalis alkekengi)*, cherished for dried flower arrangements and, of course, perennially a delight for children.

Today the tomatillo, *P. pruinosa*, a close relative hailing originally from South and Central America (where it added zest to Mexican cooking), has come north. With a tart flavor it's about the size of a walnut, and is enclosed in a parchment-like skin that must be stripped away to expose the rather sticky fruit inside.

Ripening in early September in New England, where they self-seed easily, tomatillos grow on somewhat straggly, bushy plants. When they're ready for harvest, they turn from green to golden yellow, may drop off the branches as they ripen, and reach perfection as their outer skins turn to gossamer. Inside its papery, straw-colored husk, the berry feels full and round.

A close relative, the ground or husk cherry has "an indescribable nutty flavor that kids love for raw snacks," enthuses the Fedco Seed catalog. "Grown-up kids will often go back for more, too." But there's a warning: "Don't eat them green—they can be a powerful emetic."

Benjamin Watson, in *Taylor's Guide to Heirloom Vegetables*, reports that "Left to their own devices, the tomatillo and all its relatives will self-sow readily from dropped fruit. Plant researcher Edgar Anderson once observed that, in western Mexico, the husk tomato grows semiwild as a tolerated weed in fields of maize.

GARDENING NOTES

TOMATILLO

SEEDS: The only varieties available are heirlooms from Mexico where tomatillos grow as tolerated weeds. The two common types are 'Toma Verde', and 'Purple de Milpa'. The green one comes earliest. The smaller purple one is good for storage and drying for winter salsa. Both have the delightful papery husks, like Chinese lanterns, surrounding the fruits, that characterize the species.

CULTURE: Start seedlings early (with tomatoes), about 6 weeks before e xpected last frost date. Plant seeds _-inch deep and keep soil warm until germination. Repot from flats if necessary. Tomatillos require no special soil. Space plants 2 feet apart if you are OK with a tangled mass of tomatillo plants, or plant 3 feet apart and place cages to support vigorous growth.

Plants grow vigorously. Prune them by pinching off the tips of branches helps to keep to a manageable size. As for tomatoes, this may increase the size of fruit and earliness of setting.

Water regularly in dry weather, and mulch to conserve moisture once the soil heats up.

PESTS AND DISEASES: Same as for tomatoes, but Colorado potato beetles and hornworms are not usually major pests.

HARVESTING: Pick the fruit when it has entirely filled out the husk, enough to split it, or when the husk turns dry and straw-colored. Remove the husk and wash off the sticky coating of the fruits in water.

He adds that larger-fruited tomatillos were commonly grown in central Mexico and these improved types are doubtless either the same or fairly recent parents of our present garden varieties."

Tomatillos make a tremendous green salsa, Watson adds, when "lightly roasted to bring out their flavor, then chopped up with chilies, salt, lime juice, and fresh cilantro." This, he advises, can be frozen for winter: "Cook it down with ground, roasted nuts and seeds to make a piquant mole (moh-*leh*) sauce for grilled fish."

The *toma verde*, or *tomatillo verde*—the common type most often grown by home gardeners—has a very dense pulp and tiny seeds perfect for sauces and salsas that liven up any bean or grain burger, tofu dish, tempeh patty, and, of course, anything Mexican from enchiladas to tamales to turkey *con mole*.

Smooth Tomatillo Salsa

MAKES ABOUT 2 1/2 CUPS

In a porcelainized saucepan, heat:
    2 tablespoons extra-virgin olive oil
Add:
    1 medium onion, finely chopped
    1/4 cup finely chopped almonds
    OR walnuts
Cook, stirring, till the onion is limp and the almonds are slightly browned.

Meanwhile, husk, rinse, and chop:
    2 cups (or more) fresh, yellow-ripe
      tomatillos
Whiz the chopped tomatillos in a blender till smooth.
Then add to the onion-nut mixture.

Stir in:
    1 4-ounce can diced green chilis,
      seeds and pith removed
    1 tablespoon fresh cilantro
    OR 1 teaspoon ground coriander
    1 1/2 cups Vegetable Stock
      (see page 43) OR 1 1/4 cups water
      and 1/4 cup Bragg's Liquid
      Aminos (see page 63

Bring to a boil, uncovered. Then simmer until the sauce is reduced and thick, stirring occasionally.

Chill and use as a condiment.

NOTE: For a hotter salsa, add cayenne powder to taste.

———————————

Using the foregoing sauce, you can make a green mole to serve with cooked, leftover turkey, chicken, or tempeh.

Entrée with Mole Verde

SERVES 4–6

Slice thinly:
    2 pounds cooked turkey,
    OR chicken, OR tempeh
Place the slices in a large, wide skillet.

Pour over:
    2 1/2 cups Smooth Tomatillo Salsa
      (at left)
Cover and place over low heat. When the mixture begins to bubble, simmer for 5 to 10 minutes. Add to taste:
    sea salt

Arrange the meat or tempeh slices and sauce on a platter with a rim. Garnish with:

chopped lettuce leaves
pickled chilis (optional)

Serve with:

1 cup sour cream
Rice or pasta accompany this well, along with a tossed leafy salad and tortillas.

Roasting tomatillos markedly changes the flavor of a salsa.

Roasted Tomatillo Salsa

MAKES 2 CUPS

Husk and rinse:

1 pound yellow-ripe tomatillos
Preheat your broiler. Place the tomatillos on a baking sheet in a single layer about 6 inches below the heat, and broil until they're dark and soft on one side (perhaps 2 to 3 minutes); then turn and broil the other side. Let them cool completely.

Once they're cool, scrape the roasted tomatillos and their juice into a blender. Add:

3 hot, fresh green chili peppers, seeded and chopped
1 garlic clove, minced
Whiz to a purée, leaving some chunks. Place the mixture in a bowl and stir in:

1/4 cup cold water
1 small onion, finely chopped
1/4 cup chopped fresh cilantro
1 teaspoon sea salt
3/4 teaspoon refined white sugar

Let the salsa rest before serving. If you prefer a thinner salsa, add:

2–4 tablespoons more water

Tomatillos add piquancy to any late-summer salad.

Marinated Tomatillo Salad

SERVES 4–6

THE VEGETABLES

Remove the husks, rinse, and slice into a serving bowl:

8 fresh, yellow-ripe tomatillos
Slice and add:

2 medium-sized tomatoes
1 medium-sized cucumber
Slice thinly and add:

1 small red onion

THE VINAIGRETTE

In a small bowl, whisk together:

2 tablespoons white wine vinegar
6 tablespoons extra-virgin olive oil
1 teaspoon refined white sugar
OR maple syrup
1/2 teaspoon dried basil
OR 1 teaspoon finely chopped fresh basil
1/4 teaspoon sea salt
1/8 teaspoon freshly ground black pepper

COMBINING

Pour the vinegar-oil mixture over the vegetables. Cover and chill for at least 30 minutes or up to 2 hours before serving.

Late Greens
Arugula and Mizuna

S eptember, October and November are prime times for these strongly flavored greens, arugula and mizuna.

ARUGULA

Called *ruchetta* or *rucola* in Italy, sometimes rocket-salad or *tiro*, arugula *(Eruca vesicaria* ssp. *sativa)* is a plant that has long been cultivated or gathered from the wild in most Mediterranean countries. The taste is peppery and nutty, but it becomes muted through cooking. According to Bert Greene, the ancients considered that eating arugula brought good luck. Certainly the cream-colored, purple-veined small flowers make good garnishes.

GARDENING NOTES

GREENS

Arugula, Amaranth, Cress,
Escarole, Endive, Italian Dandelion,
Mâche, Raab, Radicchio, Sorrel

CHOOSING SEEDS: These are delightful (mostly European) additions to salads that can change your whole approach to eating leafy greens. The idea is to experiment, so get your taste buds going with a variety of seed catalogs. And be prepared for surprises—there are more interesting leafy greens than just these. In all cases, small packets go a long way—there are about 18,000 endive seeds per ounce, for instance.

CULTIVATION: Plant like lettuce (see page 000), either indoors for seedlings (radicchio and sorrel) if you want to get a head start on the season, or by direct-seeding into the garden. If you're direct-seeding, plant in rows 10 inches apart, or plant one row and plan to transplant into a bed by thinning the seedlings. Collineal-hoe between the rows until plants are well established.

When plants are about 2 inches tall, thin the row to an 8- to 10-inch spacing between plants for all the above, except arugula and cress, which can be left in the row unthinned. Replant the seedlings into new rows to make a bed. New rows should be 10 inches apart so that when the plants mature, they'll choke out weeds. Choose a rainy day to do the replanting, or have a dribbling

---

hose close by as you work. Pinch off the top of the seedling so that only a little bit of a shoot remains to be supported by all the root you've dug up. Bury the root and soak with water.

Sorrel is a perennial. Once established, it'll be one of your first (and last) salad greens in the growing season.

All these greens are frost tolerant and thus are specially good for late-season salads. Some bolt easily from spring plantings, so they're best for summer planting and fall harvest anyway.

PESTS: Arugula, mizuna, mustard, and raab are bothered by flea beetles, so plant them as fall crops. Otherwise, there are few pest problems with any of these greens, though deer like to nibble on most of them.

HARVESTING: Snip arugula, amaranth, cress, endive, escarole, dandelion, mâche, and raab with scissors, or pinch off individual leaves or sprigs. More will grow from leaf stem buds.

For endive and escarole, cut out the heart down to 1 inch above ground level. Don't worry; it'll come back in a week or two. Continue such harvests till the season ends or the leaves turn bitter.

Harvest radicchio when the heart of the plant feels very firm to the touch and is about 4 inches across. Twist the plant off its root, then pull off and discard all outer leaves. Keep the lovely pink and white inner leaves for your salads.

Frances Mayes, in her charming *Under the Tuscan Sun*, gives a recipe for *bruschette*—slices of bread dipped quickly in olive oil, then grilled or broiled and rubbed with a clove of garlic. "In summer, topped with chopped tomatoes and basil, it appears frequently as a first course or snack. Winter's robust *bruschette* are fun to prepare at the fireplace."

She shares an arugula topping—a variation, she says, on the standard basil pesto and equally good with pasta. This one doesn't turn black, as do basil versions. We've revised her recipe here.

Bruschette con Pesto di Rucola

MAKES ABOUT 1 CUP

THE BRUSCHETTE

Cut into quarters:
  slices of sturdy bread
Prepare as described by Frances Mayes, above.

THE SPREAD

In a food processor or blender, combine till smooth:
  a large handful of arugula
  1/4 teaspoon sea salt
  freshly ground black pepper
  2 small garlic cloves
  1/4 cup pine nuts OR walnuts
  1/4 cup extra-virgin olive oil
Blend together to make a thick paste. Add:
  1/2 cup grated Parmesan cheese

SERVING

Spread on the grilled *bruschette*.

Reputation notwithstanding, soufflés are actually easy to make and, with arugula, tasty.

Arugula Soufflé

SERVES 4

Preheat the oven to 425°F.

In a large bowl, mash together until smooth:
  1/4 pound feta cheese
  the yolks of 4 large eggs
Beat in:
  1/2 cup ricotta cheese
Stir in:
  1 well-packed cup arugula leaves, chopped small
  1/8 teaspoon sea salt
  1/8 teaspoon cayenne powder

In another bowl, beat until stiff:
  4 egg whites
  1/4 teaspoon cream of tartar
Fold the whites into the egg-cheese-arugula mixture.

Pour the batter into a lightly buttered 2-quart soufflé dish and bake till it's puffed, about 30 minutes.

Serve instantly. Soufflés always fall. Sliced tomatoes, cucumbers, and leafy greens drizzled with a balsamic vinaigrette are good accompaniments.

MIZUNA

A favorite green for soups, stir-fries, and salads in the Orient is thick and feathery *Brassica campestris* var. *japonica*. According to Geri Harrington in *Grow Your Own Chinese Vegetables,* mizuna "is an Oriental green that seems to have no common English name; potherb mustard is as close as I can come, and that is a name which is also sometimes used for other greens." Although technically a member of the mustard family, it lacks the pungency "of either the common or Chinese mustards," she continues. Furthermore, "Mizuna is so widely grown in Japan that in China it is called Japanese greens."

Attacked by flea beatles in spring, it's perfect for late-fall salads in New England when beetles have departed and lettuces and other tender greens are past their prime. In fact, fall improves its flavor.

For more tips on growing mizuna, see page 231.

Mizuna is rich in vitamins and minerals. It's an essential ingredient in mesclun—that catchall term for any assortment of greens, plus edible flowers or herbs. The term *mesclun*, states *The All New All Purpose Joy of Cooking,* "comes from the Provençal word for 'mixture,'" and the idea results from the "practice common throughout Europe of gathering a variety of young field greens and mixing them in a salad."

Again according to *The All New All Purpose Joy of Cooking,* the ideal "is to create a balance between strong-flavored greens, such as arugula or mizuna, and more subtle greens, such as baby lettuces."

Mizuna is fine when tossed with flowers and a light dressing flavored with sesame oil. It can be stir-fried in sesame oil with ginger and soy sauce, used in clear soups, or added at the last minute to minestrone.

Mizuna makes a fine cream soup, garnished with a sprinkling of chives.

Creamed Mizuna-Potato Soup

SERVES 6

In a medium-sized pot over a medium flame, heat till warm:

1/4 cup water

Add and cook, covered, till tender:

1 medium onion, chopped
2 sliced garlic cloves
1/8 teaspoon freshly grated nutmeg

Stir often. Add:

4 1/2 cups Vegetable Stock (see page 43)
1 pound peeled, coarsely chopped potatoes

Cook till the potatoes are tender, perhaps 20 minutes.

In a blender, purée the onion-garlic-potato mixture until it's smooth.

Return it to your medium-sized pot and stir in:

1/2 cup milk OR heavy cream
1 teaspoon sea salt
freshly ground black pepper

Simmer briefly.

Chop finely to equal:

3 cups mizuna

Add the mizuna to the hot soup and mix well.

Pour into warmed bowls and sprinkle on top:

finely chopped fresh dill, parsley, OR chives

Serve immediately with fresh bread.

To be happy for a week, get married;
to be happy for a month, kill a pig;
and to be happy for a lifetime, plant a garden.
—OLD CHINESE PROVERB

Chinese Cabbage and the Chois

Sally DeVore and Thelma White assert that the Great Wall of China was built by men who ate little besides rice and cabbage. In fact, they say in their *Appetites of Man*, "Of all of nature's bounty, the lowly cabbage is probably the most universally consumed vegetable in the world."

Cabbage—*Brassica oleracea*, Capitata group—has been a New England staple from the beginning of European settlement. Familiar to everyone, the big, smooth-leaved heads can be round, cone shaped, or flat headed. They also appear in handsome green or red colors. Savoy, that distinctive crinkle-leaved type, has dark green outer leaves with a medium green-yellow heart.

But Chinese cabbages—doubtless the type DeVore and White extol—the heading type, *Brassica rapa pekinensis*, and the nonheading *B. r. chinensis* groups—are relative newcomers to the West. According to Geri Harrington in *Grow Your Own Chinese Vegetables*, seed catalogs occasionally lump Chinese cabbages together "at the end of the common cabbage section (although they are not true cabbages)."

Cylindrical or barrel-shaped *pekinensis* is known by many names, from celery cabbage to michihli, wong bok, tientsin, napa, shantung, and wom-buk. The Chinese call it *pe tsai*, which means "white vegetable"; the Japanese name is *hakusai*.

"Somewhat resembling lettuce (especially cos) . . . but with leaves very strongly veined, this fast-growing vegetable was introduced to Europe only in the nineteenth century" says *The Botanica*—probably in 1837, when it arrived in Paris. Apparently cultivated for more than 1,500 years in the Orient, Chinese cabbage is one of our most ancient vegetables. Says Harrington, "Botanists can't determine

ORIENTAL GREENS

CHOOSING SEEDS: Oriental gardeners have developed a different set of greens, mostly from Brassica rapa. They include at least the following:

Chinese cabbage: There are closed or open lettucy types.

Bok choi and other chois: Dark green leaves with thick white stalks.

Tatsoi: Rosettes of spoon-shaped dark green leaves.

Mizuna or kyona: Huge bunches of pencil-thin stalks and serrated leaves.

Mustard: Peppery taste for salads.

Chrysanthemum: Grown for aromatic leaves and edible flowers.

CULTIVATION: All of the above germinate in cool soils. If any bolt and go to seed, their progeny will be the first to germinate in your garden the following year. If you want early Oriental greens, you must cover the bed with a tear-free floating row cover, tucking in the edges to prevent insect damage. For fall crops, this is less of a problem.

For an extra-early-spring crop, sow in flats. Plant out early, spacing the plants so that they can spread to full size (6 to 18 inches apart). For late-season plantings, sow seeds in early August, 1/4 inch deep in rows 16 inches apart. Collineal-hoe to keep the weeds back.

If seeds come up very thick, you can thin one row per bed and replant to fill the bed, as for lettuce. Choose a rainy day to do the job, or keep a dribbling hose handy for soaking the seedlings once they're planted.

PESTS: Black flea beetles can destroy an early crop of Oriental greens—thus the need for a perfect floating row cover. Chinese cabbages attract earwigs.

HARVESTING
Chinese cabbage: Wait until the head has filled out so that it's firm. Then cut off the entire head at the base.

The chois: Thin the bed by pulling out the plants with the biggest stalks and leaves. Leave smaller plants to grow bigger.

where it originated because it has been cultivated for thousands of years; it is now found from Newfoundland to southern China. They think that the Celts brought it to the British Isles, but it was grown in the Far East long before that time. Most of the varieties we grow in the United States—where it has been cultivated since 1900—come from Germany or Holland, but in the past few years new varieties have been coming in from Japan and China."

The nonheading group (*B. rapa*, Chinensis group) is called Chinese mustard cabbage or bok choi, and produces excellent eating in fall when nearly everything else has succumbed to frost. Closely related to gai choi (*B. juncea*), pak choi, and tat soi (a roseate form of pak choi), bok choi is sometimes called Chinese white mustard cabbage, while gai choi is called Chinese green mustard cabbage. American seed catalogs sometimes describe bok choi as a "loose-leaf Chinese cabbage." It's very popular throughout Europe, especially in France, where it has been cultivated since the 1800s.

Bok choi is rich in vitamin C and minerals as well as fiber. With its white stalks framed by green leaves, it makes a lovely, simple coleslaw.

Simple Bok Choi Coleslaw

SERVES 4

Shred finely:
1 pound bok choi
Toss to taste with:
some finely grated fresh gingerroot
a sprinkling of shoyu
(naturally fermented soy sauce)
a sprinkling of toasted sesame oil
some rice wine vinegar
a little refined white sugar
OR maple syrup

Serve with rice, tofu in any of its forms, and other vegetables.

Bok choi is sometimes described as "two vegetables in one." Its leaves are cooked like spinach, its ribs like asparagus. If you're using both in a stir-fry, the ribs (cut into 1-inch pieces) go in first for a minute or two, then the leaves (cut into large pieces) for just a minute.

Tender inner leaves added to soup at the last minute are simmered just long enough to get slightly limp.

And, says Geri Harrington, "if you wish to cook the vegetable as a side dish, with roast chicken for example, separate the leaves from the ribs, cut the ribs into 1-inch pieces, and simmer for five minutes in boiling salted water. Then add the leaves, torn into large pieces, and cook

three minutes more. Drain well and serve with melted butter with a sprinkling of minced fresh Chinese parsley"—cilantro. Olive oil is a healthy butter substitute.

Bok Choi Stir-Fry

SERVES 2–4

Separate the leaves from the heart of:
1 pound bok choi
Wash well and trim off a small slice at each leaf base. Lay the leaves flat on a chopping board and remove the tough edges, leaving a little border of green on the white stems. Cut the stems into 2-inch lengths.

Place a wok on its collar and heat it.
Add:
2 tablespoons extra-virgin olive oil
Swirl to coat the wok.
Add:
1 garlic clove, bruised
3 slices fresh gingerroot
Fry for a few seconds till just golden.
Add and stir-fry for 1 minute:
the prepared bok choi
Then add:
1/4 cup water
1 teaspoon white refined sugar
1 teaspoon sea salt
Cover and simmer for 2 minutes. Uncover and stir-fry again till most of the liquid has evaporated. Turn off the heat and sprinkle with:
1 teaspoon toasted sesame oil
Toss to distribute the oil. Remove to a serving platter, discarding the garlic and ginger.

Serve at once with rice and other vegetables.

Koreans make a variety of quick sauerkraut called kimchee, which can be used in any sauerkraut recipe.

Kimchee

THE CABBAGE

Coarsely chop into a large bowl:
   1 head Chinese cabbage
Sprinkle with:
   2 tablespoons kosher
   OR canning salt
Mix well and let rest for 30 minutes, stirring twice. Then transfer the cabbage to a large stainless-steel, ceramic, or porcelainized pot and cover with:
   cold water
Stir briefly and drain. Repeat. Return the cabbage to the bowl and sprinkle with:
   1 tablespoon kosher
   OR canning salt

ADDITIONS

To the cabbage bowl, add:
   3 green onions, chopped coarsely
   1 garlic clove, minced
   1/2 teaspoon hot pepper sauce
Stir well, press down firmly, and add:
   water to barely cover

FERMENTATION

Allow the cabbage mixture to ferment at cool room temperature for a few days, covered well to keep out dust (enfolding the pot in a tightly closed plastic garbage bag works well).

SERVING AND STORING

When the flavor is satisfactory, use your kimchee at once, or store it in the refrigerator, where it will keep for 10 days.

While big-bodied Chinese cabbage—pekinensis—is superb simply sliced with other greens into a salad, it's also fine when quickly cooked, as in the following stir-fry. Added as one of the last ingredients, its cooking time is brief and crispness is retained. It's also nutritious: A cupful contains 2,100 International Units of vitamin A, 74 milligrams of calcium, 13 milligrams of magnesium, 176 milligrams of potassium, and 31.5 milligrams of vitamin C. This recipe eliminates highly saturated peanut oil, which is usually suggested.

Chinese Cabbage, Chinese Style

SERVES 4

THE CABBAGE

Trim and discard the tough leaf portions from:
   1 large (1 pound) Chinese cabbage
Slice into bite-sized pieces.

THE WOK

Place a wok on its ring, heat it, and add:
   1/4 cup rapeseed oil
   OR sunflower seed oil
Fry in the oil for a few seconds:
   1 large garlic clove, minced
   1/2 teaspoon (or more) finely grated
      fresh gingerroot
Add and stir-fry for 1 minute:
   the sliced cabbage

THE SAUCE

In a small bowl, quickly whisk together:
   1/4–1/2 cup water
   1 tablespoon fish sauce
   OR light soy sauce
   2 teaspoons cornstarch

COMBINING

Pour the cornstarch sauce over the cabbage and cook till the sauce is just thickened—a matter of seconds. Remove from the wok and sprinkle with:

toasted sesame oil

SERVING

Toss well and serve immediately with rice or other grain. A garnish of toasted sesame seeds would be a nice note.

"Sauerkraut ... or the principle of pickled cabbage, was brought to Europe by the Tartars from China," states Harold McGee in ON FOOD AND COOKING. Brine is the
pickling liquid. The ratio of salt turns the sugar in the vegetables to lactic acid and results in souring. A rule of thumb is 6 tablespoons of salt per 10 pounds of vegetables.

Fermentation temperature is important: Below 68°F, fermentation slows; above 72°, spoilage may occur.

Using Chinese cabbage produces a sauerkraut both similar to and different from the typical New England sample— a historic method for storing summer's largesse.

Chinese Cabbage Sauerkraut

MAKES A 1-GALLON CROCK

UTENSILS

A 1-gallon ceramic crock is perfect for making sauerkraut, although a wide-mouthed glass container would work just as well. Also necessary is a plate, nearly as large as the container's mouth, and a small glass jar with a plastic cap to be filled with water and used as a weight.

THE CABBAGE

Quarter:

2–4 Chinese cabbage heads

Cut out their cores and shred them finely. Weigh out enough to equal a little more than 5 pounds. Measure out:

3 tablespoons kosher OR canning salt

PACKING

In a large container, such as a stainless-steel bowl, thoroughly mix the 5 pounds of sliced cabbage with the 3 tablespoons of salt. The Ball Company's *Blue Book* recommends that you allow the mixture to sit for several minutes to wilt slightly; "this allows packing without excessive breaking or bruising of the shreds." Pack the salted cabbage into the crock, gently tamping with clean hands or a small jar to eliminate trapped air and start the juice flowing.

FERMENTING

Cover with a sterile cloth (well-washed muslin works well), tucking the edges down against the inside of the crock. Fill the small glass jar with water and adjust the cap.

Weight the cabbage with a plate, place the water-filled capped jar on it to keep it submerged, and store at room temperature (68° to 72°F) to ferment.

If brine hasn't covered the cabbage in 24 hours, adjust it to rise above the cabbage by adding:

1 1/2 teaspoons kosher salt per 1 cup cold water

By day 2 a scum may form on top of the brine. Using a scalded ladle or soup spoon, skim this carefully off; replace the scummy cloth with a sterile one. Wash and scald the plate before putting it back. Weight it with the scalded small water-filled jar. Repeat this daily.

Bubbles will rise to the top during fermentation. In 2 to 4 weeks, when fermentation has stopped, the kraut will be clear, pale in color, and tart. Remove the cloth and weighted plate, wipe around inside the crock's headroom, place a freshly scalded plate on top to keep the kraut below the brine's surface, and cover the whole with a close-fitting lid.

STORING

Store in a cool place (38°F) and serve as desired by using a glass or ceramic cup to dip out only what you need for a meal. Be sure enough brine is left to keep the kraut covered. Keep the container closed tightly.

NOTE 1: If the brine gets slimy during fermentation from too much warmth, throw it out. Begin a new batch in cooler weather.

NOTE 2: If you lack a cold cellar in which to store your crock of kraut, canning is the next best thing to do with it. The *Blue Book* gives directions:

Bring the sauerkraut to a simmer (185° to 210°F). Do not boil.

Pack the hot kraut into hot jars, leaving 1/2 inch of head space. Cover with hot liquid, again leaving 1/2 inch of head space. Remove air bubbles and adust the caps.

Process pints for 15 minutes, quarts for 20 minutes, in a boiling-water bath. (See the complete directions in the Great Cucumber Pickles recipe on page 152.)

OCTOBER

Red and Green # Head Cabbages

S pherical, solid, arrayed in Christmas colors of green and red—what could be more regal than the so-called common cabbage?

A member of the mustard family, this Brassica was once native to the Mediterranean region. "In such conditions it is very difficult to retain water, and the cabbage developed the waxy cuticle and thick, water-storing leaves charcteristic of desert plants," says Harold McGee. Such conditions also make for hardiness.

In its wild state *Brassica oleracea* was small, resembled rape or kale, and contained a high degree of mustard oil with an unpleasant taste. Nevertheless, from this single species descended all of the cole crops. "Selection with emphasis on different parts of the plant eventually produced the diversity of cultivated varieties we now enjoy," asserts Charles Heiser in *Seed to Civilization*.

Lore about the cabbage abounds. Although some writers insist that the ancients never knew the head cabbage of today, "The first recorded mention of it," writes Maguelonne Toussaint-Samat in *A History of Food*, "is in a treatise on plants allegedly written by Eudemus of Athens, which distinguished between three kinds of cultivated cabbage. The Greeks and Romans believed that if you ate cabbage during a banquet it would keep you from getting drunk and a legend attributes its origin to the sworn enemy of Dionysus, King Lycurgus of the Edones, a Thracian people. Dionysus, it is said, sweeping triumphantly through Europe with his train, reached Thrace with his gifts of wine and found Lycurgus opposing him. Armed only with an ox goad, the king captured the entire intoxicated army except for Dionysus himself. The god dived into the sea and took refuge in the caves of Thetis. Whereupon Rhea, goddess of the Earth, sent Lycurgus mad, and he cut his son Dryas to pieces, thinking he was a vine stock. The Edones overpowered him, tortured him and had him torn apart. Cabbages grew from the sand where his tears had fallen."

Quite a tale. Continuing with Maguelonne Toussaint-Samat: "From classical times to the present day, cabbage has not been regarded as a sophisticated vegetable. Horace liked it, but he ate it with plenty of pickled pork, and in any case he affected a taste for all things rustic. The genuine countrymen of his time who ate cabbage daily had nothing but salt and thyme to go with it. . . . Diogenes, famous for his philosophy and his boorish manners, lived in a tub and had low standards of personal hygiene. For reasons of economy and idealism combined he ate nothing but cabbbage and drank only water, cupped in his hands. Cabbage had been recommended by Pythagoras. But another philosopher, Aristippus of Cyrene, a pupil of Socrates and founder of the Hedonist school, was tireless in his search after subtle and refined pleasures, and was entirely opposed to the idea of Diogenes. Cabbage, he claimed, was a melancholy food which dulled sensations and so cut life itself short; Diogenes was mad, but would never be an old madman. To this Diogenes replied that if Aristippus ate more cabbage he would not fawn on the great (for the hedonist was a 'parasite' at the court of Dionysius, tyrant of Syracuse). In fact Diogenes lived to the good old age of 90, while Aristippus was only just over 40 when he died."

In *On Food and Cooking* Harold McGee remarks that the cabbage, cultivated for about 2,500 years, was introduced to Britain in its domesticated form by the Romans. Toussaint-Samat adds that the Romans liked their vegetables large, and according to Pliny (who felt it would be a big job to list all its praises) "enlarged the cabbage to the point where it was too big for the tables of the poor. The Emperor Tiberius, who did have a large enough table, had to be stern before his son Drusus would eat it." One should remember that Drusus was a friend of Apicius who—again according to Pliny—preferred *cauliculi*, cabbage shoots. *Cauliculi*, called *krambosparagos* (cabbage asparagus) by the Greeks, were sold in bunches at market.

It's fascinating old history. At any rate, the cabbage has been a favorite of Brits and Americans since colonial days, doubtless for enjoyment but also from need. By the end of the 18th century, Toussaint-Samat says, English ships setting out on long voyages "included many crates of cabbages among their provisions for the anti-scorbutic virtues of . . . vitamin C. . . . During Captain Cook's first expedition in 1769 a violent storm injured some 40 members of the *Adventurer*'s crew. The ship's doctor saved the victims from gangrene by applying compresses of cabbage leaves to their wounds." Regarding it as one of the secrets of the success of his expeditions, Cook included it among his shipboard provisions.

According to *Appetites of Man*, "Every culture eats cabbage, raw, cooked, or preserved. It contains a good deal of Vitamin C . . . as much as in a comparable quantity of citrus fruits. Unlike that in most foods, the Vitamin C in cabbage is not destroyed by cooking." It's also rich in phosphorus, potassium, and vitamins

CABBAGE AND BRUSSELS SPROUTS

CHOOSING SEEDS: Find varieties that appeal to you in your favorite seed catalogs.

Cabbage: You have lots of choices—early or late, open (savoy) or head, green or red.

Brussels sprouts: These look like tiny cabbages growing in the leaf nodes up and down the stem. Choose long-season variety for late-fall harvest.

There are 5,000 to 7,500 seeds per ounce. A 5-gram packet should sow 100 row feet.

CULTIVATION: Cabbages and brussels sprouts should be started indoors in plug flats about 2 months before your last frost. Plant out just after the last frost, spacing the plants about 36 inches apart. Wrap the stems with strips of brown paper bags to keep cutworms at bay. Have the end of a dribbling hose handy, and place it at the base of every seedling while you plant the next one.

All cabbages like fertile soil with plenty of moisture throughout the season. Mulch with hay, or plant in 4-inch holes in 6-mil black plastic sheeting to keep the soil and roots moist. Irrigate if necessary.

PESTS: Prevent cutworm damage to seedlings by wrapping seedling stems (see above). Beware black flea beetles in springtime. There are two ways to control them: You can use floating row covers, sealed all around the edges with dirt, or you can dust with rotenone.

Cabbage caterpillars are the pest in midsummer. A useful organic pesticide is Dipel. Or you can pluck off the caterpillars (if you can see them). Interplanting cabbages with tomatoes keeps the cabbage white butterflies (caterpillar parents) off the plants.

HARVESTING:

Cabbage: Harvest the entire head. For winter storage, wait until a month of frosts has gone by. Then pull the entire plant, keeping the root intact for winter storage upright in damp shavings at temperatures just above freezing.

Brussels sprouts: Harvest the first sprouts when mature. With a sharp knife, slice sprouts off the stem from the bottom few spirals. Sprouts near the top can survive moderate frosts. Before frosts to 20°F, take a hatchet to the base of the stem, cut it loose, and take it into the kitchen to remove the sprouts.

preserved by fermentation. Jean Carper's *Food Pharmacy* reports that cabbage may lower the risk of cancer, prevent and heal ulcers, stimulate the immune system, kill bacteria and viruses, and foster growth. A wonder drug! And, she adds, don't forget that "cabbage includes not only the typical head cabbage common in the United States, but also bok choy . . . and . . . Chinese cabbage."

The derivation of our word coleslaw comes from the Dutch kool (cabbage) and sla (salad). It's permanently popular in any of its manifestations.

Quick Coleslaw
SERVES 4–6

Pick or purchase:
1 1-pound green cabbage
Cut it in half, then into quarters, core it, and slice very thinly.

In a big bowl, mix together:
8 cups of the matchsticked cabbage
1/2 cup thinly sliced onions
1/2 cup finely sliced green peppers
1/2 teaspoon celery seeds
2 tablespoons sea salt
freshly ground black pepper
2 teaspoons refined white sugar
1/4 cup balsamic vinegar

Marinate overnight. The salt will cause moisture to drain from the mixture while its flavors meld. Enjoy it the next day with any meal that needs perking up.

The following recipe from a Scottish friend shows how delicious ruby-red cabbage can be. Maple syrup is a good substitute for sugar. Note that distilled white vinegar makes for greater piquancy; wine or cider vinegar, less.

Red Cabbage Delicious
SERVES 6

In a heavy stainless-steel or porcelainized pot, simmer for 30 minutes:
1 green pepper, seeded and diced
1 medium-sized red cabbage, shredded
1/2 cup water

Add:
sea salt to taste
a lot of freshly ground black pepper
1/2 cup vinegar
1/2 cup maple syrup
1 tablespoon celery seeds
1 tablespoon white mustard seeds

Cover and simmer over low heat for about 2 hours. Add more water to prevent sticking, if necessary, and stir occasionally.

Serve hot or cold.

Cabbage rolls, once considered exotic fare in New England, are now deliciously common. The version below uses beans and bulgur for stuffing rather than the proverbial lamb of the Mideast. Fine when hot, they're also perfect for snacking when cool.

Stuffed Cabbage Rolls

SERVES 4–6

THE STUFFING

Pick over, rinse, and cook in water to cover till tender:

2 cups garbanzo beans

When they're tender, drain well and purée in a blender. In a large bowl, place:

1 cup medium-grade bulgur
2 cups water

Let hydrate for half an hour. When the bulgur is moist and tender, squeeze it dry in a tea towel. When both beans and bulgur are ready, combine well in a bowl:

the puréed garbanzo beans
the drained and dried bulgur
1 medium tomato, chopped
1 medium Spanish onion,
chopped finely
1/2 cup finely chopped fresh parsley
1/4 teaspoon powdered cinnamon
1/4 teaspoon powdered cumin
1/2 teaspoon sea salt (or to taste)
freshly ground black pepper
2 tablespoons extra-virgin olive oil

If the resulting mixture is very dry (it should be the same consistency as hamburger), add some tomato juice or bean drainings to moisten it. If it's too wet, add a little white flour or rolled oats.

THE CABBAGE

Cut the stem off a cabbage head. Then stick a long-handled fork into the core and dip the head repeatedly into a big pot of boiling water. This will loosen the leaves three or four at a time.

Slice them off at the base as they get tender, and place them in a bowl. If they remain tough, place them in the boiling water a few moments longer until they become pliable.

When the leaves are cool enough to handle, lay one on your chopping block with its stem end toward you and slice out the tough base rib until the remainder will roll up easily. Very large leaves can be cut in half.

STUFFING THE LEAVES

Near the stem end, leaving a 1 1/2-inch margin on either side, place:

1 heaping tablespoon of the
bean-bulgur mixture

(Use more filling if the leaves are large.) Turn in one margin and roll up a little. Turn in the other and roll up entirely.

BAKING

Preheat the oven to 350°F. Place each roll seam-side down in a buttered 13- by 9-inch baking pan in a single layer. Over the closely stacked rolls, pour:

tomato juice to come halfway
up the rolls

Then add:

approximately 2 tablespoons red wine

Cover tightly and bake for about an hour, or until the cabbage is tender when pricked by a fork.

SERVING

Serve hot or cold with rice and a green leafy salad.

SAUERKRAUT

Maguelonne Toussaint-Samat's *History of Food*, filled as it is with ancient lore, remarks that cabbage preserved in brine—*choucroute* or sauerkraut—has been known since very ancient times. Its forerunners came in the form of acidic soups made from the young shoots, buds, and leaves of birch "eaten by the people of Northern Europe in Neolithic times, and those made of nettles, cardoons and sorrel . . . eaten until the sixteenth century. Choucroute made with cabbage goes back to the Germanic invasions. Germanic tribes from the steppes brought the recipe in their baggage, or at least applied their own procedures to the native cabbages they found." The principle of pickled cabbage "was brought to Europe by the Tartars from China," assures Harold McGee.

Historically sauerkraut was made in the home. In the 17th century, however, it became one of the first foods produced by the manufacturing industry, then just developing from such small-scale activities as oil and wine pressing, salting, and pickling.

Fall in Maine is an excellent time to visit the little town of Waldoboro. Originally settled by German immigrants, Waldoboro still produces succulent sauerkraut. Walking into a krauting shed is enough to make anybody salivate, and the sight of big wooden barrels oozing brine and sour scent makes the purchase of too many little tubfuls de rigueur.

Sauerkraut can be popped between slices of freshly made whole-wheat bread with cheese, tofu or tempeh, sliced chicken, tomatoes, and pickles for instant gratification.

This recipe has been adapted from the Ball Company's BLUE BOOK.

Sauerkraut

PREPARATION

Remove the outer leaves and any undesirable portions from the firm, mature heads of:

3–4 large cabbages

Wash and drain. Cut into halves or quarters and remove the cores. Place a large stainless-steel bowl on a scale. Using a shredder or sharp knife, cut the cabbage into shreds as thick as a dime and place them in the stainless bowl until you weigh out 15 pounds.

PACKING

In a large stainless-steel or ceramic container, thoroughly mix together:

5 pounds of the shredded cabbage
3 tablespoons kosher OR canning salt

Let stand several minutes to wilt slightly. (This allows packing without excessive breaking or bruising.) Then pack firmly and evenly into a large, clean pickling container of ceramic or glass. Old-fashioned crocks are perfect. Using a wooden spoon or clean hands, press down firmly until juice comes to the surface.

Repeat the shredding, salting, and packing until the container is filled to within 3 or 4 inches of the top.

FERMENTING

Cover with a clean, thin, white cloth (such as muslin), tucking the edges down against the inside of the container. Weight under the brine with an old, clean plate. Let the container sit at a room temperature of 68° to 72°F.

Formation of gas bubbles indicates that fermentation is taking place. It's usually completed in 5 to 6 weeks. Store in a cool place, well covered to prevent spoilage; sauerkraut can also be canned, as follows.

When sauerkraut is fresh, canning ensures long-term storage. Seven quart jars usually fit into a canner nicely, so do seven at a time.

Canning Sauerkraut

MAKES 7 SMALL-MOUTHED QUART JARS

In a large stainless-steel or porcelainized pot, bring to a simmer:

7 quarts sauerkraut

Do not boil.

Pack the hot kraut into sparkling-clean hot jars, leaving 1/2 inch of headroom. Cover with hot liquid from the sauerkraut, and remove air bubbles by probing into each jar with a clean chopstick.

Meanwhile, in a small saucepan of hot water, heat metal bands and lids to just under boiling. When they're hot, drop them into a sieve and drain.

Wipe the rims of your sauerkraut-filled jars. Place the hot lids and bands on the jars, screwing the bands down tightly.

Place your hot, filled jars on a rack in a big kettle of hot water. Add more hot water if necessary to come at least 1 inch above the jar tops. Cover, bring to a boil, and process pints in this boiling-water bath for 15 minutes, quarts for 20 minutes. Measure processing time from when a rolling boil begins.

When time is up, remove the jars with tongs and place to cool on a towel-covered counter to prevent breakage.

When the jars are completely cool, remove the metal bands, check to see that each jar is safely sealed—the metal lid will feel slightly concave when you press it—rinse gently, wipe dry, and label.

STORING

Store in a cool, dark place.

Cookbooks and written recipes are a fairly new invention. And they little resemble the sometimes rude directives offered in years past. In THE FORME OF CURY, a 1390 description of dishes prepared for King Richard II and his barons, there appears this: "Take chickens and ram them together, serve them broken. . . ." Or, "Take rabbits and smite them to pieces. . . ."

If you're a little more gentle, wonderful things can occur with chickens and rabbits and sauerkraut. Jugged hare—with its low-fat meat—is a sample. Chicken or turkey can obviously be substituted.

Jugged Hare or Chicken with Sauerkraut

SERVES 4–6

THE SAUERKRAUT

Drain:

6 cups sauerkraut

Let it soak in a bowl of cold water for 15 minutes (or more, depending on your taste buds). Change the water two or three times. Then drain and squeeze out as much water as possible with your hands. (Be aware that this loses nutrients.)

In a 3-quart stovetop casserole dish, place:
**2 tablespoons butter
OR extra-virgin olive oil
1 cup sliced onions
1/2 cup sliced carrots
the drained, squeezed sauerkraut**
Cover and simmer for about 15 minutes.

THE HERBS

Tie into a small cheesecloth bag a bouquet garni of:
**4–5 parsley sprigs with stems
1 bay leaf
6 peppercorns
10 juniper berries**
(If you lack berries, substitute 1/2 cup of gin later.) Bury the bouquet in the sauerkraut.

Then add:
1 cup white wine OR dry vermouth

**enough Vegetable Stock
(see page 43) to barely rise through
sauerkraut**
Set the sauerkraut to simmer, covered, on top of the stove or in an oven for approximately 3 hours. The liquid should be mostly absorbed by the kraut.

THE HARE

Near the end of the second hour, cut up into neat pieces:
1 hare OR chicken
Brown these nicely and thoroughly in butter and olive oil in a heavy skillet.

Pack the pieces into the midst of the sauerkraut, which is bubbling gently, and continue simmering for another hour or two—till the meat is very tender, most of the liquid in the kraut has been absorbed, and all the flavors have melded.

Before serving, add more salt (only if necessary), a little more wine (and gin, if juniper berries were unavailable), and some freshly chopped parsley.

Kale and Collards

Greens that come into their own in late summer, fall, and even winter are kale and collards.

Members of the cabbage family, they're leafy, nonheading greens "that probably represent the earliest cultivated forms of the European wild cabbage," according to Benjamin Watson in *Taylor's Guide to Heirloom Vegetables*.

Says Professor Heiser in *Seed to Civilization: The Story of Food*, "Human selection has produced varieties valued for their leaves (kale and cabbage), specialized buds (Brussels sprouts), flowering shoots (cauliflower and broccoli), and enlarged stems (kohlrabi)."

KALE

The cole crop ancestors were native to the Mediterranean region, and one of the varieties we now enjoy—especially as New England leans into a fall season replete with full moon and impending frosts—is kale, properly called *Brassica oleracea*, Acephala group.

Kale is possibly the form in which cabbage was known to the Greeks and Romans. During the Dark Ages in Europe, when the last months of winter often produced sick, hungry people and animals, peasants could still manage to make a meal of bread and ale, with perhaps a bit of salt pork or, more probably, stewed winter cabbage, onions, or kale.

Cole crops traveled early to New England from Europe, and Benjamin Watson lists a number of heirloom varieties, referring mostly to Fearing Burr's book *The Field and Garden Vegetables of America,* published in 1863, as well as to the English translation edition of Vilmorin-Andrieux's *The Vegetable Garden,* which appeared in 1885.

'Dwarf Blue Curled Scotch', Watson says, is identical to the 'Dwarf Green Curled Scotch' mentioned by Burr. The leaves are blue green and finely curled "and do not yellow even in severe cold." It survives well in Maine; in fact, it tastes sweeter and better after a frost, and if properly mulched can be harvested through part of the winter—at least into December.

'Lacinato', a unique Italian heirloom, is "one of the most ornamental kinds," probably the same variety that Vilmorin-Andrieux described in 1885 as 'Cavalo Nero' or 'Tuscan Black Palm'. Its dark, blue-green, straplike leaves look almost black at a distance, curl back at their edges, and are heavily blistered over their surface. The flavor, says Watson, "is sweet and mild, particularly after frosts."

'Pentland Brig' is an English variety, the result of a cross between the smooth-leaved 'Thousand-Headed' and curly-leaved types. Where plants can overwinter, he advises, "broccoli-like sprouts can also be harvested for eating."

Maine gardeners suspect "overwintering" applies only to England, not New England, although we can always try.

'Red Russian', also called 'Ragged Jack', "was introduced to Canada by Russian traders." Its flat, smooth, gray-green leaves have wavy margins that resemble oak leaves, while leaf stems and veins are reddish purple. "In cold weather," says Watson, "the leaves turn entirely reddish purple. Burr describes this variety as 'Buda Kale' in 1863, and Vilmorin-Andrieux briefly mentions 'Ragged Jack' in 1885."

Another type is the 'Thousand-Headed', which, according to Vilmorin-Andrieux, originated in western France, "and is not as cold-hardy as other kales."

For his last, and most unusual sample, Watson mentions a variety called *longata,* listed in 1885 by Vilmorin-Andrieux under the name 'Tree Cabbage' or 'Jersey Kale'. *Longata* is otherwise known as the 'Walking Stick'. Strictly speaking, Watson says, it's "neither a heading cabbage nor a kale." Grown in the Channel

Islands for over 200 years, the plant's incredible stem can reach 5 to 7 feet high and produce "a kale- or cabbage-leaved head at the top." But it's not the top that's of interest: In fall the stem can be cut, dried, and polished to make an attractive walking stick!

Walking or running, kale is deliciously nutritious. A cupful contains 5,963 International Units of vitamin A, 80.4 milligrams of vitamin C, 8 International Units of vitamin E, 90 milligrams of calcium, and 299 milligrams of potassium; it's also considered a cancer preventive as well as a good souce of iron. And it has the highest protein content of any of the green vegetables.

GARDENING NOTES

KALE AND COLLARDS

CHOOSING SEEDS:

Kale: Color and style are the name of the game: white, green, and pink, curly or frilly, "flowering" rosettes of leaves, or tall. Have fun with kale. Plant it ornamentally. Kale is also among the tastiest of fall treats, and is common as a garnish for restaurant servings.

Collards: All green. Base your choice on the earliness of first harvest or bolt resistance.

There are 7,500 seeds per ounce. A 5-gram package should suffice.

CULTIVATION: For early crops, sow seeds in flats like cabbage, then replant as seedlings. Like other cabbage family members, kale and collards are heavy feeders.

In the garden, plant seeds in rows 2 to 3 months before your expected fall frost date. Sow 1/4 to 1/2 inch deep, in rows 18 inches apart. Thin to 8 to 12 inches apart. Weed with a collinear hoe, especially around seedlings.

PESTS: Kale isn't as pest ridden as other cabbage family crops, but it's wise to cover beds with floating row covers in spring to exclude flea beetles. If necessary, you can control cabbage worm with Dipel. Collards get chewed up by pests in summer, so they're best grown for fall harvest.

HARVESTING: Snip off the biggest and best leaves all summer and through the fall. The taste improves in cold weather until hard frosts finally kill off what's left of the plant.

Because it shrinks when cooked (1 pound raw turns into about 2 cups cooked), it's important to expect that a great heap of kale will produce only a small result—especially once its stems are removed. This recipe is suggestive only: Adjust the seasonings to your taste, and remember that with something as tasty as kale, failure is impossible.

Curried Kale and Apples

SERVES 2

Pick or purchase:
   1 pound kale
Choose young leaves if possible, omitting stems. If kale is older, fold leaves in half along the center rib, and slice out stalks. Rinse well. Chop moderately fine to equal 3/4 pound.

In a wok or deep, heavy pan, heat:
   3 tablespoons extra-virgin olive oil
Add:
   2 tablespoons Madras hot curry powder
   1/2 teaspoon sea salt (optional)
   freshly ground black pepper
Sauté in it till limp:
   1 medium onion, chopped fine

Add and toss well:
   your 3/4 pound chopped kale
   2 peeled, cored and chopped apples
   1/2 cup water (if necessary)
Steam about 15 minutes over medium heat, or till the kale is limp but not mushy.

Serve with potatoes, rice, or barley. Mesclun salad, and carrots steamed in milk make colorful companions.

NOTE: In lieu of curry powder, substitute:
   2 cloves garlic, minced
   1 tablespoon freshly grated gingerroot
   1 teaspoon powdered cumin
   2 teaspoons powdered turmeric
   3 teaspoons ground coriander

Colcannon is the traditional Irish way of enjoying kale.

Colcannon

SERVES 2

Finely chop:
   1 pound freshly picked and washed kale
Place in a pot with about 1/2 inch of water and steam till tender, turning once or twice.

In a large pot, cook till tender:
   1 pound well-washed potatoes
   2 medium-sized carrots
When tender, mash.

In the meantime, slice thinly the white parts of:
   2 leeks
Place slices into a small pot and cover with:
   milk
Simmer till soft.

Mash the leek-milk mixture into the mashed potato-carrot blend.

Add kale and mix together. Season with:
   sea salt (optional)
   fresh ground black OR white pepper

Serve hot. Butter melting into the hot mound, of course, makes the dish divine.

COLLARDS

The word *collard* is a corruption of *colewort*. Romans and Greeks attributed therapeutic powers to this member of the cabbage family, *Brassica oleracea*, Acephala group. In fact, Julius Caesar is rumored to have eaten a plateful after a heavy banquet to ward off indigestion . . . and we all know what Roman banquets were like!

Someone has suggested that the first mention of collards in America was in 1669. As with other members of the cabbage family, these greens are high in calcium (218 milligrams per cupful) and beta-carotene—also known as vegetable vitamin A, because it converts in the body to vitamin A. One cup also has 43 milligrams of vitamin C, 275 milligrams of potassium, and other good things.

Leaves should be almost full sized when picked for cooking, but not yet tough or woody. For salads, half-grown leaves are best.

As with Swiss chard, collards and egg custard are a friendly combination. One pound of collard greens should produce 1 1/2 cups of chopped stems and 2 cups of chopped leaves. Prepare and cook as directed in the recipe for Swiss Chard Custard on page 171.

Because of their high nutritional value collards turn a plain dish of rice into something rich, savory—and healthy.

Green Rice

SERVES 2–3

Bring to a boil:
2 cups Vegetable Stock (see page 43)

Add and stir together once:
1 cup white basmati rice
1 tablespoon extra-virgin olive oil
1/2 teaspoon sea salt
freshly ground black pepper

Add, 1/2 cup by 1/2 cup, stirring constantly:
3 cups loosely packed chopped collard leaves
Cover, bring to a boil, reduce the heat, and cook till the rice is done—20 to 30 minutes.

Serve with other in-season vegetables such as carrots, beets, corn, or fennel.

NOTE: Other kinds of rice can be substituted, but remember that the cooking time may be longer and result in overcooked collard leaves.

Collard greens and lentils make a nutritious soup for fall, and the combination of hot pepper, lemon tang, and cold yogurt enlivens taste buds.

Collard Lentil Soup

SERVES 2–3

Pick over and wash in cold water:
1 cup red lentils
In a large pot, bring to a boil:
1 quart Vegetable Stock
(see page 43)

Add, reduce the heat, cover, and simmer for 15 to 20 minutes:
the lentils
1/2 cup thinly sliced leeks
1/2 cup diced carrots
1/4 cup diced celery

1 small potato, diced to equal 3/4 cup
1 small hot chili pepper (optional)

Into a skillet, pour:
1 tablespoon extra-virgin olive oil
Add and cook till wilted:
1/2 cup chopped onions
Add and stir for 1 minute:
2–3 minced garlic cloves

Roll into a "sausage" and slice into 1/2-inch strips:
collard leaves to equal 4 cups

When the lentil-vegetable mix is tender, stir in:

the 4 cups sliced collard leaves
the wilted onion-garlic mix
1/2–1 teaspoon freshly squeezed lemon juice
Simmer, covered, for another 10 minutes or till the vegetables are tender but not mushy. Add:
1 teaspoon sea salt
freshly ground black pepper
a few drops of hot pepper sauce to taste (if chili was omitted)

Serve in warmed bowls with a dollop of yogurt on top.

Apples

The apple as we know it has been understood—and favored!—from prehistory. But only in the Old World.

Evidence indicates that *Pyrus malus,* precursor to all modern varieties, originated in the Caucasus region of Europe—the result of cross-breeding between Asiatic and European crab apples, which, according to Peter Wynne in *Apples: History, Folklore, Horticulture, and Gastronomy,* are "found today in their original forms in that region."

The famous Greek poet Homer, who lived sometime between the 12th and 7th centuries B.C., provides what is perhaps the earliest mention of apples. In his classic tale *The Odyssey,* apple trees grow in the gardens of King Alcinous and Laertes, father of Odysseus.

Greek mythology also provides us with the story of the golden apples of the Hesperides. It seems that under the reign of Cronus, or Time, Night gave birth to Aegle, Erytheis, Hespera, and Hestia or Arethusa: the Hesperides. They lived in a wonderful garden beyond the river-ocean, at the extreme western limits of the world, where they personified the clouds gilded by the setting sun and guarded the golden apples that grew there.

But nothing is ever straightforward. Since the Greeks used the same word to mean both "apple" and "flock of sheep," "it has been wondered," says *The New Larousse Encyclopedia of Mythology,* "if the Hesperides were not rather guardians of the celestial flocks which in Indo-European mythology symbolised clouds."

Oh well. Romans as well as Greeks were great apple lovers. Pliny, in his *Historia Naturalis*, completed in A.D. 77, described many varieties, and cultivation was sophisticated. By the fourth century 37 varieties were listed. During the Dark Ages in Europe, however, much agricultural knowledge reverted to mere dreaming. You might say it returned to the Hesperides. Still, by the 1500s at least some members of the British gentry practiced grafting, and by the 1600s the French had perfected techniques of trellising as well as dwarfing.

It wasn't long, of course, before settlers brought the fabulous fruit to America. John Josselyn visited America twice. In *An Account of Two Voyages to New England* (published in 1675) he says that Governours Garden was "where the first Apple-Trees in the Countrey were planted," and that the south side of Boston was "adorned with Gardens and Orchards."

The first apple tree in the old province of Maine probably arrived from England in a tub. Thomas Gorges, deputy governor of the province, reputedly planted it about 1640 on his homestead farm in Georgeana, now York. (Johnny Appleseed wasn't history's only seed scatterer.)

As ancient gardeners understood, while grafting produces a tree identical to its parent, those derived from apple seeds don't "run true." Instead, new and sometimes fabulous creations arise. By 1872 such wildings had resulted in more than 1,000 varieties listed in Downing's *Fruits and Fruit Trees of America*. And although today the number is perhaps only 10 percent of what it used to be, old favorites still endure in many a back pasture, along a stone fence. Blue Pearmain was a famous one. Gravenstein, Porter, Red Astrachan, Tolman Sweet, Wolf River, and the Snow Apple were others.

Grandma always said, "An apple a day keeps the doctor away." Maybe she was right: One apple contains 81 calories, 74 International Units of vitamin A, 1 International Unit of vitamin E, 10 milligrams of calcium, 159 milligrams of potassium, and other vitamins and minerals. Jean Carper reports possible therapeutic benefits for the heart, lowered blood cholesterol and blood pressure, stabilized blood sugar, and dampened appetite; apples are also packed with chemicals that block cancer in animals. Apple juice, she says, kills infectious viruses.

What nibbling they've provided! What sauce and pies! What cider! And what rhymes:

> To eat an apple going to bed
> Will make the doctor beg his bread.

Raw apples add zest to any salad, particularly a fall salad when celery and walnuts are at hand.

Apple Celery Salad

SERVES 6

Pick or purchase:
5–6 big, ripe, red apples
Wash them carefully, core them, and cut to measure 4 cups apple cubes.

Toss these in a bowl containing:
freshly squeezed lemon juice
This will prevent browning.

Chop to measure:
2 cups chopped celery stalks

Pour the apple cubes into a sieve, if necessary, and drain.

In a big bowl, combine:
the 4 cups cubed apples
the 2 cups chopped celery
2/3 cup chopped walnut meats
Add:
enough salad dressing to hold
lightly together

Serve immediately on:
lettuce leaves

The best salad dressing is made with eggs and oil. It is, of course, not healthy to consume raw eggs (for fear of salmonella) or too much fat. But the result is toothsome. Purchase eggs from a hennery you can trust. This recipe first appeared in Jean Ann's NEW MAINE COOKING.

J. A.'s Favorite Salad Dressing

MAKES 1 1/2 CUPS

Place in a blender and whiz until light:
1 egg (wash it well before cracking)
1 teaspoon sea salt
3 tablespoons freshly squeezed
lemon juice
3 tablespoons vinegar of your choice
Add in a very thin stream while whizzing:
1 cup chilled extra-virgin olive oil

When the mixture is thick and creamy, stir in:
finely chopped fresh chives, basil,
cilantro, parsley, OR any other
herb

Baked apples are as luscious today as they were when settlers first brought them to Maine. This recipe first appeared in Jean Ann's NEW MAINE COOKING.

Baked Apples with Brandy

SERVES 6

Preheat the oven to 350°F.

Wash well and core carefully using a melon ball scoop, leaving enough flesh at the bottom to prevent leakage during baking:

6 huge Northern Spy apples

Into each cored apple, place:

1 tablespoon raisins
1 tablespoon sunflower seeds
a pinch of powdered cinnamon
some freshly grated nutmeg
1 tablespoon brandy

Place the stuffed apples in a shallow lasagne or cake pan, and pour around them:

2 cups water

Cover and bake for 30 minutes, or till the apples are soft but definitely not mushy.

Serve topped with whipped cream if your cholesterol levels are down; or try whipped soft tofu or low-fat cottage cheese sweetened with maple syrup.

Apple pie served with some grated extra-sharp Cheddar cheese melted on top is an old favorite. Oddly enough, and in contradiction to many recipes, don't use oil, lard, margarine, or butter in the crust of this pie.

Fall Apple Pie

MAKES 1 9-INCH DOUBLE-CRUST PIE

THE CRUST

Sift together into a bowl:

4 cups unbleached white flour
OR 2 cups white flour and 2 cups
  whole-wheat pastry flour
1 tablespoon refined white sugar
1 teaspoon sea salt

Using a pastry cutter or two forks, cut into dry ingredients until the mixture resembles coarse meal:

1 3/4 cups solid vegetable shortening

In a small bowl, beat together with a fork:

1/2 cup cold water
1 tablespoon distilled white vinegar
OR cider vinegar
1 large egg

Combine the two mixtures, stirring with your fork till moistened.

Divide into two portions and, with your hands, shape each portion into a flat, round patty ready for rolling. Wrap the patties in waxed paper or plastic, and chill in the refrigerator for at least half an hour.

THE APPLES

Pick or purchase:

5–6 large, tart apples

Wash well, peel (optional), core, and slice them thinly to produce 4 cups sliced apples. Toss these in freshly squeezed lemon juice to prevent browning. In a large bowl, combine:

1 cup refined white sugar
1/2 teaspoon powdered ginger
1 teaspoon powdered cinnamon
1/4 teaspoon freshly grated nutmeg
1/4 teaspoon sea salt
2 tablespoons white flour

Drain the apple slices in a sieve, if necessary, then toss them quickly with this sugar-spice mix.

CONSTRUCTING THE PIE

Preheat the oven to 425°F. Remove the pastry patties from the refrigerator. Lightly flour both sides of one patty, place it on a lightly floured board or pastry cloth, and roll out to a 1/4-inch thickness. Drape this over a 9- or 10-inch inverted pie pan and trim the edges to measure 1 inch larger all around. Line the pie pan with the dough and trim the edges to be even with the pan.

Place your sugared and spiced apple slices on the pastry, mounding high in the center. Dot with:

2 tablespoons butter, cut into bits (optional)

Roll out the second patty for the top crust. Rub a little water on the bottom pastry rim and drape the top crust evenly but loosely over the apples. Trim the edges of the two crusts, then press them together with the tines of a fork. Prick or cut slits for escaping steam in the top pastry. A big *A* in fork pricks looks nice. Brush the crust with milk or cream, and sprinkle very lightly with sugar.

BAKING AND SERVING

Bake for 40 to 45 minutes. If you can control yourself, serve when at least partially cool. Use leftover pastry for cinnamon roll-ups.

Apple pancakes, called griddle cakes, made hearty breakfasts in the old days. (Blueberries can obviously be substituted for apples!)

Apple Pancakes

MAKES 14–16

THE DRY INGREDIENTS

Sift together twice into a medium-sized bowl:

3/4 cup unbleached white flour
3/4 cup whole-wheat pastry flour
1 1/4 teaspoons double-acting baking powder (see page 28)
3/4 teaspoon sea salt
1 teaspoon powdered cinnamon
1/4 cup refined white sugar

THE WET INGREDIENTS

In another bowl, combine:

1 egg, well beaten

1 cup milk at room temperature
1/4 cup melted butter
OR sunflower seed oil
1 cup shredded apples

Add the dry ingredients to the wet, stirring only until moistened.

COOKING

Pour out by 1/4 cupfuls onto a hot (375°F), greased griddle. Cook until pinpoint-sized air bubbles appear on top and the underside is browned. Turn and cook on the other side.

SERVING

Serve right away with maple syrup, fresh fruit, and lots of smiling.

Nothing could be simpler to make or more in tune with New England than a crisp dessert combination of apples and cranberries.

Apple-Cranberry Crisp

SERVES 4

THE FRUIT

Preheat the oven to 375°F.

Wash carefully:

4 cups fresh cranberries
3 big, sweet apples

Core and slice the apples thinly, but don't peel. Dip into freshly squeezed lemon juice to prevent browning. Drain in a sieve.

In a large bowl, combine:

the cranberries
the apples
2 tablespoons brown sugar
1 teaspoon powdered cinnamon
a little grated nutmeg
1 tablespoon unbleached white flour

Spoon into a shallow, 6-cup baking pan.

THE CRISP

In the same bowl, combine:

scant 1/4 cup unbleached white flour
2 tablespoons brown sugar
3/4 cup rolled oats
1/2 cup finely chopped walnuts

Stir in:

3 tablespoons melted butter
OR sunflower seed oil

Mix well together, then sprinkle over the apple-cranberry mix.

BAKING

Bake for 40 minutes or till lightly browned. Let the crisp stand for 10 minutes before serving with or without a topping of whipped cream, whipped cottage cheese, whipped tofu sweetened with maple syrup, or vanilla ice cream.

Quick breads, especially those made with apples, are moist and slightly heavy—as is appropriate. The batter for this one is very stiff.

Apple Bread

MAKES 1 LOAF

Preheat the oven to 350°F. In the bowl of an electric mixer, cream together until light and fluffy:

1/4 cup softened butter
2/3 cup refined white sugar

Beat in:

2 eggs, already beaten lightly

Into a medium-sized bowl, sift together:

2 cups unbleached white flour
1 teaspoon double-acting baking
  powder (see page 28)
1 teaspoon baking soda
1 teaspoon sea salt (optional)

Grate to produce:

2 cups coarsely grated raw apples
1 tablespoon grated lemon peel

Add the grated apple and lemon peel to the egg mixture alternately with the sifted dry ingredients. Stir in:

2/3 cup chopped walnut meats

Scoop into a greased and floured 8- by 5- by 3-inch loaf pan and bake for 50 to 60 minutes. When a toothpick inserted into the middle comes out clean and the top of the loaf is golden, remove it from the oven and turn it out on a rack. Slice when cool.

A historic New England dish that often accompanied roast pork when early-winter hog butchering was in progress combined fall apples and onions with molasses from the Caribbean brought back by the coasting trade.

There's really no recipe for this: Every cook used ingredients on hand in whatever amount was possible. Some folks wanted it sweet as candy, others liked merely a hint of sweetener. Adjust the molasses to suit yourself.

Fried Apples and Molasses

SERVES 4

Cut in half and slice thinly:

1 big onion

Place the slices in a large skillet (often called a "spider" by Mainers) with about:

1 tablespoon butter

Pick or purchase:

4–5 big, tart, cooking apples

Wash the apples well, cut in half, core, and slice thinly. Add them to the skillet along with:

1/4 cup dark molasses
sea salt to taste
freshly ground black pepper

Cook over medium heat, stirring often, until the apples and onions are soft but not too mushy.

Serve hot with potatoes, baked beans, fowl or fish, and a green leafy salad.

Several methods are available for preserving apple goodness through the winter. One, of course, is to make applesauce and can it —a simple procedure. But if home canning is new to you, it's best to study the Ball Company's BLUE BOOK for good directions before you begin (see page 38).

Most canners will hold seven quart jars or eight pints.

Canned Applesauce

Wash well, quarter, and core:
  cooking apples
Simmer them, covered, in a small amount of water till they're tender. Press them through a stainless-steel sieve or food mill to remove the peel, seeds, and core.

Sweeten to taste with:
  1/4 cup refined white sugar
    per 4 apples
Reheat to a boil.

Pour the applesauce, boiling hot, into clean, hot jars, leaving 1/2 inch of headroom. Remove air bubbles by poking into each jar along the sides with a chopstick.

Meanwhile, in a small saucepan of hot water, heat metal bands and lids to just under boiling. When they're hot, drop them into a sieve and drain.

Wipe off the rims of your applesauce-filled jars. Place the hot lids and bands on the jars, screwing the bands down tightly.

Place the hot, filled jars on a rack in a big pot of hot water. Add more hot water if necessary to come at least 1 inch above the jar tops. Cover, bring to a boil, and process both pints and quarts for 20 minutes in this boiling-water bath. Measure the processing time from when a rolling boil begins.

When time is up, remove the jars with tongs and let them cool on a rack or towel-covered counter to prevent breakage.

When the jars are completely cool, remove the metal bands, check to see that each jar is safely sealed—the metal lid will feel slightly concave when you press it—rinse gently, wipe dry, and label.

Store in a cool, dark place.

Early New Englanders pickled crab apples to serve as garnishes with winter roasts. Red-hot cinnamon candies have been added in later years to color the apples a deeper red. Their use, of course, is entirely optional. And again, if home canning is new to you, it's best to study the Ball Company's BLUE BOOK for good directions before you begin (see page 38).

Pickled Crab Apples

MAKES 4–6 PINTS

Pick or purchase:
  2 1/2 pounds crab apples

Wash them well, wiping off the fuzzy blossom ends. Do not remove the stems. Run a large sterilized needle through each apple to prevent it from bursting while it cooks.

Into a small cheesecloth bag, tie:

3 2-inch cinnamon sticks

1 tablespoon whole cloves

1 1/2 tablespoons whole allspice

In a 6-quart pot, combine:

3 cups white refined sugar

1 1/2 cups distilled white vinegar

1 1/2 cups water

1/2 cup corn syrup

1/4 cup red-hot cinnamon candies (optional)

the bag of spices

Bring to a boil over medium-high heat, stirring until the sugar is dissolved. Cover the pot and reduce the heat to medium low. Simmer for 10 minutes.

Add and simmer until just tender, about 10 minutes:

the crab apples

Carefully pack the apples into clean, hot, pint jars, leaving 1/2 inch of headroom. Discard the spice bag. Pour hot pickling syrup over the apples, maintaining the 1/2 inch of headroom. Remove air bubbles by poking carefully into each jar along the sides with a chopstick.

Meanwhile, in a small saucepan of hot water, heat metal bands and lids to just under boiling. When they're hot, drop them into a sieve and drain.

Wipe off the rims of your apple-filled jars. Place the hot lids and bands on the jars, screwing the bands down tightly.

Place the hot, filled jars on a rack in a big pot of hot water. Add more hot water if necessary to come at least 1 inch above the jar tops. Cover, bring to a boil, and process for 15 minutes in this boiling-water bath. Measure the processing time

from when a rolling boil begins.

When time is up, remove the jars with tongs and let them cool on a rack or towel-covered counter to prevent breakage.

When the jars are completely cool, remove the metal bands, check to see that each jar is safely sealed—the metal lid will feel slightly concave when you press it—rinse gently, wipe dry, and label.

Store in a cool, dark place.

Gathering and pressing your own apples assures a fine cider. Cooked down, this cider can transform itself into a rather odd, but wonderful, jelly. Winter cider has more "body" to it than the first autumn squeezings, usually of aromatic McIntosh. It consists of several varieties of apples, resulting in richer flavor and more pectin, a necessary ingredient if jelly is to set well. Because you need varieties that contain a lot of pectin in order to gel properly, a mix of only 1 part ripe, very flavorful apples such as McIntosh, and 3 parts tart, wild apples and crab apples is recommended.

Wash them well, then have someone at an orchard grind and press them. One bushel will produce 3 gallons of cider —enough to drink and make jelly with.

Winter Cider Jelly

MAKES ABOUT 1 1/2 CUPS

Obtain:

1 gallon freshly pressed, late-autumn cider

Because apple cider ripens quickly, rush your gallon of fresh juice home and pour it immediately into a stainless-steel or porcelainized pot. Place over high heat and boil it down rapidly until "sheeting" occurs.

Test by placing a teaspoonful of cider in the refrigerator to see if it thickens as it cools. Because apples vary as to pectin content, it may not set as expected. (Don't keep boiling and hoping. Simply use a packet of low-methoxyl pectin and follow instructions.)

When the jelly is thick, dark, and setting readily, spoon it into carefully washed, hot canning jars, screw down the lids, then seal by turning each jar on its head for a few moments. The high heat will kill harmful bacteria.

Store in a cool, dark place. Spread over corn bread to oohs and aahs.

APPLE WINES

The Boston Puritans planted orchards immediately. And while tradition holds that Thomas Gorges, deputy governor of the old province of Maine, planted the first apple tree in a tub on his homestead farm in York around 1640, everyone knows that it takes more than one tree to make an orchard—or a barrel of cider, for that matter. It wasn't till two and a half centuries passed that Maine grew enough apples to send more than half of its commercial crop back to England.

In the meantime, though, those early pioneers had planted thousands of little home orchards on new land, mostly for cider making. And the practice continued until a temperance tide inundated the state in the second quarter of the 19th century. Then many old cider orchards were cut down or grafted with fruit better for simple eating.

Which began the era of luscious nibbling.

But though "hard cider," or cyser, days are mostly forgotten, and the words have lost their pairing with deep-cellar snickering, today's hard cider has turned simply, and with sophistication, into apple wine.

Producing a fine wine demands care and attention to detail for the short period of time involved in actual ingredient collection, preparation, mixing, fermenting, racking, and bottling. The enemies of successful wine making are wild yeasts and acetic bacteria. Acetic bacteria can convert alcohol to acetic acid, thereby turning wine to vinegar. Airborne yeasts and other bacteria must also be kept at bay. Therefore, cleanliness is of the utmost importance. All bottles and equipment have to be clean—chemically as well as visually. Sterilization is the key.

While wines can be made from almost anything—from herbs to fruit to flowers —apple wine demands firm, ripe apples, never battered windfalls or any that have partially decayed. Immature apples are low in sugar, a fact that makes them too starchy and acidic for good results. But by using a combination of apples that are higher in acid, sugars, and flavors, a well-balanced wine can be achieved. Crab apples contain more tannin than most varieties and are therefore beneficial as additives.

The following directions make a strong, yet delicately flavored wine with a fine bouquet. It's drinkable within 6 months but improves with age.

Items such as ascorbic acid, wine yeasts, Campden tablets, air locks, cork stoppers, cork floggers, food-safe plastic containers, and plastic hoses are available in natural food stores, or beer and wine supply shops. Note that the following system breaks all accepted rules in that the fruit is not sterilized, either with boiling water or with sulfite (Campden tablets), but the recipe doesn't seem to fail! Also, if you'd like a really dry wine, reduce the sugar by 1/2 pound.

Apple Wine 1

MAKES 1–2 GALLONS

GATHERING

Pick or purchase:

18–24 pounds of sound, ripe, mixed apples

One possible mixture would be 10 percent Northern Spy for high acidity, 10 percent McIntosh for aroma, 50 percent Baldwin for medium acid content, 5 percent Red Astrachan or any crab apple for tannin, and 25 percent Delicious as a kind of base.

PREPARING

Wash the apples well. If they come from a heavily sprayed orchard, cut off and discard the stem and blossom ends. Chop the apples into small pieces. This can be done with a hand food chopper, food processor, or whatever is most convenient. Chunk size doesn't really matter, although really large pieces should be avoided.

FERMENTATION 1

Place the chopped apples—pulp—into a clean fermenting container fitted with a cover. This can be a 2- to 4-gallon container of food-safe plastic, crockery minus cracks, glass, or stainless steel.

Using a long-handled plastic or wooden spoon, add and stir well:

1 gallon cold water
1 package sauternes wine yeast

Cover the fermenting container with a clean cloth and place in a large plastic garbage bag. Gather the plastic over the top and fasten with an elastic band. This ensures that dust, insects, and stray animals will stay out. Let the container sit (in its plastic bag) in a warm place. Stir vigorously from the bottom at least twice a day using a long-handled plastic or wooden spoon to keep floating fruit moist. Cover again each time.

Allow fermentation to continue for about 1 week, or until the first rapid bubbling stops.

FERMENTATION 2
AND INSERTING THE AIR LOCK

Using a layer of muslin or several layers of cheesecloth draped over a stainless-steel colander, strain the juice from the pulp into a second fermenting container. Again, this must be a clean, 2- to 4-gallon container made of food-safe plastic, crockery, glass, or stainless steel. This one needs a tight-fitting cover into which an air lock can be inserted. Press as much juice as you can out of the pulp by squeezing, and add it to the rest. Measure the juice.

For every gallon, add:

3 pounds refined white sugar

Cover the container and insert an air lock—a convoluted plastic or glass device with compartments, which can be partially filled with a small amount of sterilized water or a sterilizing solution such as that obtained from Campden tablets. (Rinsing all equipment in a Campden solution is a good idea. One tablespoon of Clorox added to a gallon of water works just as well, but you must remember to rinse, rinse, rinse afterward to get rid of the scent.) This allows carbon dioxide to escape while preventing oxygen from entering. It also acts as a barrier to the vinegar fly, which carries bacteria on its feet, as well as to airborne bacteria present all around. Seal the air lock by pouring enough boiled and cooled water, or Campden solution, into the lock to rise halfway up its convolutions.

Store the container for the next 2 to 3 weeks at an even room temperature. As the days pass, bubbling will become visibly quieter as most of the sugars are consumed by the yeast. Let fermentation continue till little bubbles no longer rise to the surface if the container is moved.

RACKING

At this point sediment will have fallen to the bottom of the container. This is spent yeast, which must be removed. Because wine can become oxidized and spoiled if exposed to air, rapid siphoning is best.

Using about 4 feet of 1/2-inch plastic tubing, which you've sterilized in Campden or Clorox solution, siphon the wine into 1-gallon glass jugs that can be fitted with a stopper-containing air lock. The easiest way to siphon is to stand your fermenter on a table or shelf and your jugs or bottles on the floor below. Place one end of the tube into the wine *above* the sediment. Suck at the other end till liquid comes down the tube, then pop it quickly into your clean jug or bottle and let it flow, being sure to leave all sediment behind.

You may add a lean 1/4 teaspoon of ascorbic acid (pure vitamin C) to each jug to eliminate problems of oxidation.

Cap each jug with an air lock and leave in a cool place. Rack again as more sediment forms, and again, if necessary, till the wine remains clear for a week or so. If you find it necessary to rack the wine more than once due to a lot of sediment, it may be necessary to top up your jug each time to eliminate air space. This can be done with cool, boiled water. With each racking, always refill the fermentation lock with clean water.

BOTTLING

Rinse wine or champagne bottles with Campden or Clorox solution and dry them in a warm oven.

Once the wine has cleared—usually 2 to 4 months—fermentation has totally ceased and it's safe to bottle. If you're using a fermentation lock that has twin chambers, watch for the water level to even out in both. This is a good indication that no more activitiy is going on. Siphon the wine into your sterilized bottles to within 1 inch of top.

OPTION

Within 24 hours before bottling you may again add a very lean 1/4 teaspoon of ascorbic acid, or 1 Campden tablet, per gallon of finished wine. A tiny amount of sulfite will remain in the wine if you use Campden; you need to tell imbibing friends, because some may be dangerously allergic to it.

CORKING

Soften new straight-sided corks in boiling water. Cork the bottles tightly. Blow them home with a cork flogger.

STORING

Label and store bottles on their sides in a cool, dark place (or wrap them with paper) and let them age.

This recipe is one of the easiest apple wines make, since the juice has already been extracted in the form of cider. Late-in-the-season cider is preferable because its sugar content is higher. This wine is best if left to mature in its bottles for 6 months, but it's also drinkable immediately.

If a spiced wine appeals to you, add some ginger, cinnamon, or any other spice during the first stage of fermentation, or during one of the rackings.

Campden tablets, sodium metabisulfite, will kill any wild yeast. A tiny amount will remain in your wine. Since some people have allergic reactions to sulfites, be sure to tell drinkers that you've used it.

Apple Wine 2

MAKES 1 GALLON

GATHERING

Purchase or have pressed:
1 gallon fresh apple cider
If you purchase it, be sure it contains no preservatives. Add:

1 Campden tablet, crushed
Let the cider sit for a day or two, tightly capped to exclude air.

ADDING AND COMBINING

In a 2-gallon fermenting container made of food-safe plastic, glass, or stainless steel with a cap capable of holding an air lock, place:
2 1/2–3 pounds refined white sugar
Pour your cider over the sugar and, using a long-handled wooden or plastic spoon, stir to dissolve. Add:
1 packet champagne yeast
**1 teaspoon yeast nutrient
    (see page 266)**
**1/3 pound chopped light raisins
    (optional)**

FERMENTING AND
INSERTING THE AIR LOCK

For complete instructions, see Apple Wine 1, page 263.

Cover the fermenting container and insert the air lock. Store at room temperature (50° to 60°F) until little bubbles no longer rise to the surface if the container is moved.

RACKING

When it's clear, in about 4 weeks, apple wine can be rapidly siphoned into a sterilized, 1-gallon glass jug. But because it oxidizes easily, add to it 24 hours (or less) before racking:
a lean 1/4 teaspoon ascorbic acid

Then rack (see Apple Wine 1). There should be plenty of liquid; you won't likely need to top up with sterilized water. Cap the jug with an air lock stopper and leave in a cool place. Rack again if more sediment forms till the wine remains clear for a week or so.

NUTRIENT FOR WINE: A healthy fermentation leads to better wine. Yeast nutrient acts as "food" for the yeast to grow on. Packets of nutrient are available at wine supply stores, but any pharmacist can prepare it to this formula for 1 gallon of mead or 2 gallons of wine:

> 80 grains tartaric acid
> 60 grains ammonium sulfate
> 8 grains magnesium sulfate
> 55 grains citric acid
> 30 grains potassium phosphate

The juice of a freshly squeezed lemon would prove almost as beneficial.

BOTTLING

Once the wine is clear, it's ready for bottling. Within 24 hours before bottling, add:

a lean 1/4 teaspoon ascorbic acid

Wash wine or champagne bottles with detergent and hot water, rinse them thoroughly, and dry them in a warm oven. Or rinse with Campden solution. Siphon the clear wine into the sterilized bottles to within 1 inch of the top.

CORKING

Soften new straight-sided corks in boiling water. Cork your bottles tightly by blowing them home with a cork flogger.

STORING

Label and store bottles on their sides in a cool, dark place (or wrap them with paper).

When honey is used to replace sugar in a wine must, the fermented result is called mead—possibly the oldest fermented drink known to roistering humans.

Cyser is mead made with apple juice, apples, or cider. It can be sweet, medium, or dry, depending on the amount of honey you use.

This recipe ages well, though it's also drinkable within a few months of bottling. If it's bottled before all the sugars are fermented, a sparkling mead results. If you choose the sparkling route, be sure to use champagne bottles for storage, because they're designed to withstand pressure.

For direction details, refer to Apple Wine 1 on page 263. A Campden tablet, sodium metabisulfite, will kill any wild yeast that might spoil your cyser, but be sure to tell your drinking friends: They might be dangerously allergic to it.

Cyser

MAKES ABOUT 1 GALLON

GATHERING

Purchase or have pressed:

1 gallon fresh apple cider

Be sure it contains no preservatives. Pour it into a big porcelainized or stainless-steel pot and add:

3 pounds honey

Boil for 15 minutes. Skim off the foam. Cool.

ADDING AND COMBINING 1

When the cider is cool, pour it into a 2-gallon fermenting container made of food-safe plastic onto which a tight-fitting lid can be applied. To sterilize the mixture, add:

1 Campden tablet, crushed

Cover and let the mixture sit for 24 hours. Then add:

> **the freshly squeezed juice of**
> **1 lemon and 2 oranges**

ADDING AND COMBINING 2

In a well-capped jar, shake together vigorously:

> **1 package champagne yeast**
> **(5–7 grams)**
> **1 teaspoon yeast nutrient**
> **(see page 266)**
> **1 1/2 cups orange juice at room**
> **temperature**

Let stand for 1 to 3 hours, till bubbly.

FERMENTING AND INSERTING THE AIR LOCK

Pour the champagne yeast mixture into the cider-honey "must." Using a long-handled wooden or plastic spoon, stir well. Cover the fermenting container, insert the air lock, and ferment at room temperature (50° to 60°F) for 5 days.

RACKING 1

Siphon the cider-honey mixture into a secondary 2-gallon fermenting container. Insert an air lock and ferment for 10 more days.

RACKING 2

Rack again into an air locked fermenting container.

RACKING 3

Rack into a 1-gallon, air locked fermenting container until fermentation is complete. Remember: If you bottle the cyser before all the sugars are fermented, a sparkling mead will result. Use your judgment.

BOTTLING

After the wine has cleared, rinse champagne bottles with Campden solution. Siphon the wine into the sterilized bottles to within 1 inch of the top.

CORKING

Use plastic corks, or soften new straight-sided corks in boiling water, blowing them home with a cork flogger.

STORING

Label and store bottles on their sides in a cool, dark place for 1 month, then move them to cellar temperature for aging.

VINEGAR

"An apple a day keeps the doctor away" ran the old-time adage. In colonial times doctors were usually far away—if they existed at all—and even then they'd be more apt to bleed or cup a patient than provide real help. Mothers with herb gardens were really the safest healers available. And orchards were a big repository of anti-infection edibles.

Although vinegar (acetic acid) is what you want to avoid when making wine, it has always been necessary as a preserver and taste enhancer. As a health promoter, it has been recommended by grandmothers for a long time—and not without precedent: Hippocrates prescribed vinegar as a respiratory aid. No doubt about it, reports Jean Carper in *The Food Pharmacy*, "Modern scientific investigations find apples a versatile and potent package of natural drugs that deserve their reputation for keeping doctors away."

Says Frank Romanowski in *Making Vinegar at Home*, "It is interesting to observe that the more uses found for this product the less it is made at home." But making it at home is as easy, if as time consuming, as it ever was.

Two fermentations are involved. The first is the alcoholic fermentation by yeast that produces a hard cider or apple wine, as in the foregoing recipes. Once apple wine is available, a second fermentation is introduced by the addition of certain bacteria, called in the old days "mother"—a substance found in all unpasteurized vinegars. This process is known as the French Orleans method. The vinegar is then aged, like wine, in a barrel. When such aging is allowed, vinegar loses its initial sharp bite. In fact, it's superior.

This old-time recipe for making vinegar with fresh apple cider rather than wine is simplicity itself.

Cider Vinegar

Purchase or have freshly squeezed to produce:

2–3 gallons fresh apple cider

Strain through several layers of cheesecloth or muslin into a large, clean crock. (Rinse the crock with a solution of 1 tablespoon of Clorox per gallon of water to sterilize it, and then rinse, rinse, rinse. A Campden tablet also works well.)

Leave ample headroom for the expansion of fermentation: about 25 percent of the container.

Stretch several layers of cheesecloth, sheeting material, or a tea towel over the crock, and tie it tightly with string. This is to keep dust, animals, and insects out while allowing air to circulate.

Let the cider ferment in a cool, dark place for 4 to 6 months.

After 4 months, remove the cover. You'll find a gelatinous mass of acetobacter floating in the container; this is called the mother. (Mother can be saved to produce more vinegar. Pour apple juice —or any other fruit juice or wine—into a crock, add the mother, and let it work.)

Taste your vinegar. Acid content varies with homemade brews. If it's strong enough for you, strain it through several layers of cheesecloth, pour it into bottles, and seal with caps or corks. If it's too weak, let it sit longer, testing every week or so until it's strong enough. If the taste is still too weak after fermentation has totally ceased, add commercially made vinegar to it. If it's too strong, dilute with a little water.

Hot and spicy vinegars are useful for leafy salads served with bean dishes, bean burgers, or other "heavy" winter fare.

Chili Pepper Vinegar

MAKES 1 QUART

Wearing rubber gloves, wash and cut two or three slits in:

4 hot chili peppers

Place them in a sterilized widemouthed quart canning jar.

Pour over the peppers:

4 cups apple cider vinegar

Cover tightly and let rest for 3 weeks.

Remove the peppers and refrigerate.

Crushing leaves and heating vinegar speeds up the process of herbal vinegar making: Warm vinegar decomposes leaves, and extracts the oils quicker.

Basil Garlic Vinegar

MAKES 3 QUARTS

In a 4-quart stainless-steel or porcelainized pot, place:

a handful of fresh basil leaves, bruised with your fingers

Add:

2 1/2 quarts cider vinegar

Turn the heat to high and bring to a boil. Remove immediately from the heat, pour into a clean crock or porcelainized pot, and add:

6–8 big, peeled garlic cloves

Cover and let steep for 2 weeks.

Strain the basil and garlic from the vinegar. Place another handful of fresh leaves in the crock or pot, pour back the vinegar, and let steep for 10 more days.

Test for flavor. If it's strong enough to suit you, strain into three sterilized 1-quart bottles, add a sprig of fresh basil to each bottle, and cap tightly.

Herbal vinegars were one of the accoutrements of colonial days, and Mother's herb garden provided all the necessary flavorings.

Favorite flavorings today are tarragon, dill, rosemary, mints, cucumber-flavored salad burnet, and combinations such as basil and tarragon, or basil and garlic.

It's especially pretty to have herbs floating in bottled vinegars. A handful can be added to each quart of vinegar, and the mixture allowed to rest for at least 2 weeks before use.

In general, the following directions work for nearly any herb.

Fresh Herbal Vinegar

MAKES THREE QUARTS

Pick or purchase:

a handful of herbs of your choice

Wash the leaves and pat them dry. Bruise them slightly and place in a widemouthed quart canning jar. Pour over them to cover:

best-quality cider vinegar

Cap the jar with a plastic cover and let it stand in a warm place for 10 days, shaking gently but well once daily.

Test for taste. If a stronger herbal flavor is desired, strain out the leaves and replace with a fresh batch. Infuse for 1 week longer.

Test again. Then strain and pour into pretty bottles. Cap tightly. To decorate, place a sprig or two of fresh herb inside each bottle before capping.

Winter Onions

A long with the white potato, sweet potato, and Jerusalem artichoke, Native Americans were eating onions when Columbus arrived, report Waverly Root and Richard de Rochemont in *Eating in America: A History*. Some writers, they allege, try to deny America this plant, claiming that it was unknown until Europeans brought it over. However, Bernal Diaz, who accompanied Cortés in Mexico and who seems to have been an alert observer, remarked in about 1520 that wooden objects, such as arrow shafts made by Indians, smelled strongly of onion and garlic.

It's possible, these authors affirm, "that this effect could have been produced by . . . native American onion-flavored ramps, but it is unnecessary to seek such an explanation. The fact is that native onions did grow wild in America—the nodding onion and the prairie onion among others. Wild onions saved Pere Marquette from starvation in 1670. Wild leeks have always grown in the woods of the Northeast."

However history is translated, the onion has played an important role in human cuisine. The civilization of Sumer, dating from about 3000 B.C., enjoyed onions and garlic as well as leeks. The onion is native to a broad band stretching from Israel to India, says Harold McGee in *On Food and Cooking*. In fact, according to Numbers 11, it and its flavorful relatives were especially missed by the children of Israel after they left Egypt: "We remember the fish, which we did eat in Egypt freely, the cucumbers, and the melons, and the leeks, and the onions, and the garlic." Egyptian laborers who built the Great Pyramids at Giza ate onions. And onions almost certainly date back to prehistoric times in Europe.

Allium cepa, the big, popular globe variety, probably originated in either western or central Asia, agrees Benjamin Watson in *Taylor's Guide to Heirloom Vegetables*. "Long before European explorers arrived in America, most of the various shapes and colors of globe onions had become well established, and the cultivation of this important vegetable spread quickly with the arrival of settlers to the New World."

McGee waxes philosophical: "The concentric shells of onion tissue are the swollen bases of the previous year's leaves, and contain food reserves for the following year's growth, when the plant will flower. Ibsen's *Peer Gynt* and many others since have used the onion as an emblem of superficiality and emptiness; peel away the layers, they say, and you are left with nothing. A nice conceit, but not quite accurate: peel the leaf bases away and you are left with two stem buds, from which the second year's growth arises. At the center of the onion, then, is the beginning of a new life."

Although the onion isn't particularly nutritious (it contains some potassium, protein, and fiber), eaten raw or cooked it certainly increases the tastiness of food, and it's medicinally valuable. George Washington is reputed to have said, "My own remedy is always to eat, just before I step into bed, a hot roasted onion, if I have a cold." Historically it has been lauded as a cure or preventive for "virtually every ailment known to man," reports Jean Carper in *The Food Pharmacy*. In actuality, its therapeutic benefits include a boosting of beneficial HDL cholesterol, a lowering of total blood cholesterol, and a thinning of the blood. It's also reputed to retard blood clotting, regulate blood sugar, relieve bronchial congestion, and operate as a bacterial killer and a cancer block in animals. A cupful contains only 26 calories but has 13.4 milligrams of vitamin C, 40 milligrams of calcium, 16 milligrams of magnesium, and 248 milligrams of potassium.

Globe onions arrive in different costumes. Popular varieties include the mild Spanish, Bermuda, and red Italian, which are often eaten raw in salads. These milder varieties also sauté well and are excellent in stir-fries, although the reds lose their beauty when cooked.

Yellow and white onions are in general stronger. It's said that freezing onions for half an hour before cutting will reduce eye irritation. Slicing a big sample under running cold water also helps. But no matter how you slice it, onions are natural treasures.

GARDENING NOTES

ONIONS AND LEEKS

CHOOSING SEEDS AND SETS: The variety of the onion family is enormous. Be prepared to find perennial bunching onions (scallions) that sprout from roots each year after the ground thaws in spring. Or find huge sweet (Spanish) onions, or hard storage onions, or shallots, or the cutest mini onions. Some Egyptian onions grow bulblets at the tips of their leaf stalks! Onions come in a range of colors, from pink to white, yellow, and purple. All come as seeds for growing as seedlings or sowing directly into the garden. A few are sold as sets: baby dormant onions that can be planted directly. Leeks, which are long sweet onions, can only be obtained as seeds or seedlings.

There are 6,500 to 10,000 seeds per ounce. Buy new seeds each year.

CULTIVATION: Choose a very fertile part of the garden for your onion patch, preferably near the house so you'll weed it more often. Onions are day-length sensitive; they must be started early enough that they're growing vigorously by midsummer.

Start seedlings indoors in late winter, broadcasting seeds 1/2 inch apart in trays. Clip tops to 5 inches tall, then replant in the garden the width of a fat onion apart in rows 8 to 10 inches apart. Or direct-seed in rows as early as the ground can be worked. For sets, push them down into the soil until half buried. Plant leeks in rows 10 to 12 inches apart, and 5 to 6 inches apart in the row; use a dibble to make a hole 6 inches deep, then drop the seedling in, but don't firm the soil around it.

Weed consistently, using a collinear hoe between rows, being careful not to cut off onion seedlings with the hoe's sharp tip. Later, visit the bed and pull weeds by hand, especially those that grow adjacent to onion bulbs. To keep weeding to a minimum, mulch the bed with hay or leaves.

PESTS AND DISEASES: There are few onion pests, and few diseases. Seed-grown onions are more disease resistant than sets. Weeds are a problem for onions, and stunt development.

HARVESTING: Bunching onions grow new shoots throughout the growing season. Loosen the dirt around the bunch and pull several stalks, leaving two or three per plant for regrowth.

When storage or sweet onions begin to develop skins and their tops fall over, pull and sun-cure for at least a week. Onions grown from sets and mini onions tend to mature fast and can be harvested early. The best storage onions are the last to mature. To braid storage onions, wait until the stalks die and start to turn brown before pulling. Braid before the dead stalk dries out completely. Hang onions in braids or net bags in a dry place for storage through the fall and winter.

Leeks are hardy and can be left in the ground through first frosts. After harvest, wash off the soil and store through December in a cool garden shed or root cellar, with roots in moist sand, shavings, or peat. Do not pack tight.

Certain Mainers of the past placed thin onion slices on crusty bread sprinkled with vinegar, salt, and pepper. As long as the entire family joined in, this surely was a grand way to experience the strength and aroma of the combination.

Onion salad remains the simplest, and perhaps the best, route to pleasure. Mild red onions are preferred, and salting further reduces the fire. Try wrapping some of this salad in pita bread (at right)—a newcomer to New England.

Sweet Onion Salad

MAKES 2 CUPS

Thinly slice:

2 medium-sized red onions

You should have 2 cups. Place the slices in a stainless-steel colander over a bowl. Sprinkle with:

1 tablespoon sea salt

Toss with your hands to distribute the salt well. Let stand for 20 minutes to drain. Rinse quickly under cold water and pat dry with a towel.

Mix together:

3 tablespoons cider vinegar

1 teaspoon refined white sugar

Place the drained and dried onion slices in a serving dish. Pour the vinegar mixture over the onions and toss gently with:

1 cup loosely packed fresh cilantro, chopped

Sprinkle with:

1/2 teaspoon cayenne powder

Serve at room temperature.

Pita Bread

MAKES 24 SMALL OR 12 LARGE PITAS

Pour into a large bowl:

2 cups warm water (90°–110°F)

Sprinkle in:

2 tablespoons active dry yeast

Stir to dissolve.

Using a wooden spoon, stir into the yeast mixture thoroughly:

1/2 teaspoon refined white sugar

2 teaspoons sea salt

Gradually add:

5 cups unbleached white bread flour

Stir constantly until the dough is smooth.

Slowly work in:

up to 1/2 cup more unbleached white bread flour

Knead in the bowl till the dough is no longer sticky, then turn it out onto a well-floured bread board and continue kneading till it's smooth and elastic.

Shape into a rectangle and cut in half lengthwise. Divide into 24 portions for small pitas, 12 for large.

Shape each portion into a smooth ball. Place the balls on another floured board or counter and cover with a slightly damp towel.

Flour your bread board again as well as your rolling pin. Remove one ball at a time and gently press it flat with your fingers, keeping it round. Roll each ball from the center to the outer edge, giving it a quarter turn each time to form a perfect circle about 5 inches in diameter for small pitas, 8 1/2 inches for large ones—both 1/4 inch thick. Flip the disks over gently to smooth out any creases.

As you finish rolling each disk, place it on a floured surface and cover it with a clean, dry towel. Do not let its surface dry.

Let the pitas rise for 30 to 45 minutes.

Preheat the oven to 500°F.

Place an ungreased baking sheet in the oven to warm.

Arrange four small pitas or one large one on the hot baking sheet. Bake on the bottom rack of the oven until puffed and lightly browned on the bottom and almost white on top, about 3 1/2 minutes. The pitas should be soft and pliable. If desired, you can flip the pitas over after they've puffed and bake up to 1 minute more to brown the tops; be careful not to produce brittleness.

Remove the pitas from the oven and wrap them immediately in clean, dry towels until they're cool enough to handle. Repeat until all are baked.

Serve warm or at room temperature.

To store pitas, remove them from the towels and place in plastic bags. Pitas will develop a slight moisture and stay soft. Let them cool completely; then seal the bags and store in the refrigerator for a week, or in the freezer for up to 3 months.

To thaw, let the loaves stand, covered, at room temperature for about 15 minutes. To heat, wrap in foil and place in a preheated 300°F oven till warm and soft, 1 to 2 minutes.

NOTE 1: Occasionally, pitas won't puff. You can use them happily in bread pudding; drizzle them with olive oil, sprinkle with a favorite herb, and broil till hot and bubbly for treats; or top with tomato sauce, mushrooms, diced peppers, onions, and mozzarella cheese, and broil till bubbly for mini pizzas. They also make fine croutons (below).

NOTE 2: You can replace up to half of the white flour with whole-wheat bread flour.

Save all the scraps you cut off pita bread for croutons.

Pita Croutons

Preheat the oven to 375°F.

Spread in a baking pan:
    4 cups pita scraps
Pour over the scraps, then toss:
    1/2 cup extra-virgin olive oil
    3 garlic cloves, minced (optional)

Bake, stirring occasionally, till lightly browned and crisp—about 15 minutes.

Store in a capped glass jar in the refrigerator. Croutons can also be frozen.

This recipe, especially appropriate for cold winter evenings, uses what may appear to be an odd combination: onions and dried plums, otherwise known as prunes. Originally from THE NEW MAINE COOKING, it's too good not to repeat.

Simply Grande Baked Whole Onions with Dried Plums

SERVES 6

Preheat the oven to 400°F.

Peel:
    6 medium-sized onions

Cut a cross in the top of each one 1/4 inch deep.

Place them in a heavy, lightly oiled, shallow 7 1/2- by 11-inch pan with:
12 pitted prunes
3 lemon slices
1/2 cinnamon stick
Add:
1 cup water
Cover tightly. Bake for half an hour, adding more water if necessary.

In a small saucepan, make a basting sauce of:
1/4 cup maple syrup
1 teaspoon Dijon mustard
1 tablespoon red wine vinegar
a pinch of ground cloves
1/2 teaspoon sea salt
freshly ground black pepper
1 garlic clove, minced
1 teaspoon dark brown miso
1 teaspoon toasted sesame seed oil
Baste the onions with this often while they bake. Continue baking for another half hour, or until they become soft and the prunes get plump.

Serve as the side dish to any tasty winter meal.

NOTE: You may substitute a different oil for the toasted sesame, although it won't be as tasty. Other varieties of miso are available at health food stores. They're all savory and salty. Dark brown is choice.

Small so-called boiling onions, traditionally served at Thanksgiving feasts, get an added boost when transformed into sweet and sour versions.

Sweet and Sour Onions

SERVES 4

Peel:
1 pound small onions

Heat in a large, heavy skillet:
1 tablespoon extra-virgin olive oil
Add the onions and cook for 5 minutes over medium heat till lightly browned. Stir gently every few minutes to prevent burning.

Add:
1 cup water
2 tablespoons currants
1 tablespoon dark brown sugar
OR maple syrup
1/2 teaspoon fresh rosemary leaves, minced
1 small tomato, diced,
OR 2 tablespoons tomato paste
Cover and simmer till the onions are tender when pricked with a fork.

Add:
2 tablespoons red wine vinegar
Increase the heat and simmer till the liquid has evaporated to a thick glaze, perhaps 6 minutes.

Sprinkle with:
sea salt
freshly ground black pepper

Serve warm with rice, pasta, or potatoes, a leafy salad, and in-season vegetables.

Everyone loves fried onion rings—even if they're weight watching. Beer batter makes them especially tasty. Note that a highly saturated oil such as peanut oil will not burn quickly at the high temperatures demanded for deep-frying.

Fried Onion Rings

SERVES 2–4

ONION PREPARATION

Pick or purchase:

4 large white globe onions

Cut into 1/4-inch slices. Separate the rings and place them in a large bowl with:

1 1/2 cups milk
1 1/2 cups water

Let them soak for 1 hour, turning often. Remove and drain.

BATTER

In a medium-sized bowl, whisk together:

1 cup light beer
1 cup unbleached white flour
1/2 teaspoon sea salt
1/4 teaspoon celery seeds
1/8 teaspoon freshly ground black pepper
1/2 teaspoon refined white sugar
1/4 teaspoon cayenne
OR chili powder

FRYING

Into a deep, heavy pot, pour:

3–4 inches peanut oil

Heat to 365°F.

With a fork, pluck up several dry onion rings, dredge them in batter, and drop them into the oil. Fry until light brown and drain on paper towels. Sprinkle with:

sea salt to taste (optional)

Serve hot.

While the English were settling New England, the French were settling Quebec. This classic baked dish, called a soubise, features onions more than rice, although rice plays a part.

Onion Rice

SERVES 2

Preheat the oven to 325°F.

Into a medium-sized pot of boiling water, pour:

1/2 cup basmati rice

Bring to a boil, reduce the heat, simmer for 5 minutes, then drain through a sieve.

Peel and chop medium fine:

2 pounds onions

In a medium-sized casserole dish, heat:

1/2 cup extra-virgin olive oil

Sir in and mix well together:

the rice
the onions
1/2 teaspoon sea salt

Cover and bake for 45 to 60 minutes, or till the rice is completely tender and the onions are soft.

Serve hot with:

a dollop of yogurt on each serving

Sprinkle with:

1/2 teaspoon sea salt (optional)
freshly ground mixed red, white, and black pepper
minced fresh parsley

A green leafy salad and other in-season vegetables complement this well.

Onion soup is a long-standing French tradition. All kinds of onions can be incorporated—from big solid winter varieties to chives and scallions. While the hollow stalks of some onions can be called scallions, one type specifically grown as a scallion is the nonbulbing perennial *Allium fistulosum*, commonly known as the bunching or Welsh onion. Introduced to Britain as early as 1629, the Welsh onion has nothing to do with Wales; the plant is a native of Siberia and gets it name from the old German word *walsch*, meaning "foreign" or "alien." Then there are multiplier onions (*A. cepa*, Agregatum group), which form several underground bulbs from a single planted bulb and are better known as shallots.

Whatever your choices, be sure to clean your onions thoroughly before cooking; peel when necessary.

Many-Onion Soup

SERVES 4

In a large, heavy pot, heat:
1/4 cup extra-virgin olive oil
Add and cook, covered, over low heat, till tender and lightly colored—perhaps 20 minutes:
2 1/2 cups finely chopped yellow OR white onions
4 large leeks, white parts only, thinly sliced
1 cup bunching onions, finely chopped
6 garlic cloves, minced

Add:
4 cups Vegetable Stock (see page 43)

Bring to a boil, reduce the heat, partially cover, and cook for 20 minutes or until tender.

In a blender, whiz gently together:
the cooked onions and their liquid
Return the purée to your pot. Set it over medium heat and add:
1 cup cream
Bring just to a simmer.

Serve in individual bowls and garnish each one with:
croutons (see Pita Croutons on page 274, or below)
a lot of freshly minced chives

Baked Yeast Bread Croutons

Cut into 1/2-inch cubes:
4 slices white OR whole-wheat bread
Spread the cubes on a baking sheet and toast in the oven at 400°F, stirring occasionally, till crisp and brown. This will take about 10 minutes.

Sautéed Yeast Bread Croutons

In a large skillet, heat:
3 tablespoons butter
OR extra-virgin olive oil
Sauté in it:
1 big garlic clove, minced

Cut into 1/2-inch cubes:
4 slices white OR whole-wheat bread

Add the bread cubes to the garlic oil and sauté over medium heat, stirring and tossing till golden brown.

Drain on paper towels.

New Englanders historically had to deal with a lack of winter sustenance so—like the busy ant and chipmunk—they prepared by storing food away. Pickling was always a prime method.

If canning is new to you, refer to the Ball Company's BLUE BOOK for complete directions; see page 38.

Pickled Onions

MAKES 2 PINTS

THE ONIONS

In a large pot, bring to a boil:

2 quarts water

Drop in:

4 heaping cups unpeeled small onions

Simmer for 1 to 2 minutes, or just long enough to allow the skins to slip off easily when cool. Plunge the onions into cold water. Cut off their root and stem ends, and slip off their skins. Rinse.

Pour into a large bowl:

5 cups water
1/2 cup kosher OR canning salt

Stir till the salt is dissolved. Add the onions, cover, and let rest for 48 hours. Drain well. Dry by placing onions on a towel in a single layer and rolling them around with your hands.

THE PICKLING LIQUID

In a large pot, bring to a boil:

3 cups white distilled vinegar
1 tablespoon Pickling Spice Mix
(see page 151)

CANNING PREPARATIONS

Sterilize two widemouthed pint canning jars. This is easily done by bringing the jars to a boil in a large kettle and lifting them out with a wooden spoon or tongs. Place them on a towel-covered countertop to prevent breakage. In a small saucepan, heat metal canning bands and lids to just under boiling. When they're hot, drop them into a sieve and drain.

CANNING

Divide the onions equally between the two jars, using a slotted spoon. Pour over them to within 1/2 inch of the top:

the hot pickling liquid

Divide the spices between the jars. Remove air bubbles by poking down the inside edge of each jar with a chopstick. Wipe off the rims of your onion-filled jars. Place the hot lids and bands on the jars, screwing the bands down tightly.

Place the hot, filled jars on a rack in a big pot of hot water. Add more hot water if necessary to come at least 1 inch above the jar tops. Cover, bring to a boil, and process in this boiling-water bath for 10 minutes. Measure the processing time from when a rolling boil begins.

When time is up, remove the jars with tongs and let them cool on a rack or towel-covered counter to prevent breakage.

STORING

When the jars are completely cool, remove the metal bands, check to see that each jar is safely sealed—the metal lid will feel slightly concave when you press it—rinse gently, wipe dry, and label.

Wash the jars and store in a cool, dark place.

NOTE: For variation you can add one small, rinsed grape leaf, one small head of dill, and six peppercorns to each jar.

Winter Squash and Pumpkins

"The ancient New England standing Dish," said John Josselyn in *New-Englands Rarities Discovered*, published in 1672, is made from "Pompions, there be of several kinds, some proper to the Country, they are dryer than our English Pompions, and better tasted; you may eat them green. But the Houswives manner is to slice them when ripe, and cut them into dice, and so fill a pot with them of two or three Gallons, and stew them upon a gentle fire a whole day, and as they sink, they fill again with fresh Pompions, not putting any liquor to them; and when it is stewed enough, it will look like bak'd Apples; this they Dish, putting Butter to it, and a little Vinegar, (with some Spice, as Ginger, &c.) which makes it tart like an Apple, and so serve it up to be eaten with Fish or Flesh: It provoketh Urin extremely and is very windy."

Considering that Josselyn was compelled to add "that some kinds of squashes give the eaters worms, he does not appear to have felt kindly towards that vegetable family," remarks Ann Leighton in *Early American Gardens*.

Josselyn couldn't have been more wrong if he'd tried. "Common around the world is the use of squash and pumpkin seeds to expel worms, including tapeworms," says Jean Carper's 1988 report, *The Food Pharmacy*.

John was the younger son of Sir Thomas Josselyn, whose name headed the list of supporters mentioned in the historic charter of Sir Ferdinando Gorges for the province of Maine. Although Sir Thomas never visited New England, his elder son, Henry, spent most of his life here.

To visit Henry, John made two visits. The first began in July of 1638. Arriving in Boston, he sailed up the coast to Scarborough, where he remained for a year and a half. The second visit began in 1663. He stayed eight years.

"It is to Josselyn's two small but lively volumes," says Ann Leighton, "that we owe our most extensive knowledge of what plants the early settlers used locally or grew themselves."

Squash, of course, were native Americans. Along with beans and corn they formed a holy triumvirate. Reports Margaret Visser in *Much Depends on Dinner*, "in Iroquois myth they were represented as three inseparable sisters." When a squash emerged from the ground where it had been planted with corn and beans, "the corn grew straight and strong, the beans climbed the corn, and the squash plant trailed down the side of the hill and covered the flat land between the mounds." Squash, she adds, helped keep down weeds. If experience is any teacher, its prickly vines also kept away corn-loving raccoons.

According to botanist Charles Heiser, whose book *Seed to Civilization* recounts the impact of agriculture on human affairs, "Five different species of squash or pumpkin belonging to the genus Cucurbita were domesticated in the Americas." Some of these, he says, rank among our oldest known foods, "being recorded in archaeological deposits from 7000 B.C. in Mexico"—a date corrected to 3500 B.C. by professor Jared Diamond (see page 157). The name *squash*, advises organic gardener J. I. Rodale, is derived from a corruption of the Indian name for "gourds": *ascutasquash*. And the species of the genus, including "all squash, pumpkins, cushaws and gourds . . . have become so mixed and interwoven that it is almost impossible to sort them out." *Cucurbita pepo* is the pie pumpkin with a flesh that's thicker and nuttier than *C. maxima*, the jack-o'-lantern.

For tips on growing winter squash and pumpkins, see page 158.

Squash and pumpkins are starchy vegetables with a low water content. As *Jane Brody's Good Food Book* puts it, "Baked, they have about 130 calories per cup; boiled, about 90. They are very rich in vitamin A and potassium, and are a fairly good source of niacin, iron, and protein." Jean Carper adds that they also appear to be a multiple-cancer preventive, lowering "the risk of lung, esophageal, stomach, bladder, laryngeal, and prostate cancers."

Josselyn recommended Squontersquashes, "all of them pleasant food boyled and buttered and seasoned with Spice." And pumpkins sustained many an American colonist. As one put it in 1683: "We have pumpkins in the morning and pumpkins at noon. If it were not for pumpkins, we'd be undone soon."

What follows are scrumptious recipes, including one for baked buttercup squash, and a pumpkin pie that will "undo" anyone.

Stuffed Buttercups

SERVES 2 BIG EATERS OR 4 SMALL ONES

Wash, cut in half, then scoop the seeds from:

1 buttercup squash

Into a casserole dish (that has its own lid), pour about 1 1/2 cups of water, or until the casserole's bottom is wet to a depth of about 3/4 inch. Then add the squash halves, cut-side up.

Into each squash hollow, place approximately:

1 tablespoon sunflower seeds
1 tablespoon raisins
2 tablespoons chopped apples, dipped in lemon juice to prevent browning
2 tablespoons Maine maple syrup

Add:

a sprinkling of powdered cinnamon (optional)

Cover the dish tightly, then bake in a 325° to 350° oven until the squash is tender, about 1 hour.

Serve the squash hot when soft but not mushy. Potatoes in any guise, beans either marinated or hot, and a green leafy salad accompany this well.

Squash are so easy to cook, and so tasty to enjoy, that they deserve more notice. This recipe for the big, tan, hammer-shaped butternut needs only a few moments to prepare—and an oven.

Baked Butternut Squash

SERVES 6

Pick or purchase:
1 large butternut squash

Preheat the oven to 350°F.

Wash the squash, then peel it and cut to equal 4 cups of squash cubes

Wash, core, and chop:
1 large, tart, cooking apple
Dip into freshly squeezed lemon juice to prevent browning.

In a large bowl, combine:
the squash cubes
the chopped apple
1 orange, peeled and cut into
    small bits
1/4 cup cider
some freshly grated nutmeg

Spoon this mixture into a medium-sized casserole dish. Cover and bake for about 1 hour, or till the squash is tender.

Serve hot with crisp, pan-fried potatoes, a leafy salad or cooked greens, and fresh bread.

Delicata squash, also known as sweet potato squash, dates back to 1894, according to the 1999 Fedco Seed catalog. Not only are the small, ivory-colored fruits with dark green stripes lovely to look at, but their flavor is unsurpassed. Weighing in at 1 to 2 pounds, they're good immediately, or as winter keepers. In storage, advises Fedco, "green stripes turn a delicate orange and the cream background sometimes yellows."

Like the buttercup and butternut, delicata is a morsel to savor when baked. Even the skin is edible.

Delicious Delicata

SERVES 2

Preheat the oven to 325°F.

Pick or purchase:
1 delicata squash
Wash it nicely and split it in half. Scoop out the seeds.

Place the squash halves in a baking pan that contains:
1/2 inch water
Drizzle the halves with a little:
extra-virgin olive oil
Sprinkle with:
sea salt
freshly ground black
OR multicolored pepper

Cover and bake till tender—perhaps 30 minutes. Serve with rice or potatoes, a green salad, perhaps quickly sautéed tofu, and other vegetables.

Dried pumpkin and squash seeds are fun to munch on and provide a lot of fiber. They're called pepitas in Mexico.

Certain pumpkin varieties are grown more for their seeds than their flesh. One such is 'Lady Godiva', whose seeds are hull-less. If you're lucky enough to plant your own, or you live near an organic grower and are able to store a fairly large quantity, here's what to do.

Unsalted Pepitas

Right after fall harvest, break apart a pumpkin and scoop out the seeds with your hands. Place them in a food-safe plastic pail and add warm water to cover plus about 3 inches more.

Allow the seeds to rest in the water until the attached fibers weaken and the seeds sink to the bottom. At this point fiber will float to the top and can be skimmed off.

Strain out the seeds, scatter in a thin layer on a cookie sheet, and dry in a very low, 90°F oven. (Naturally, a food dryer works even better.)

Once they're dry, store the seeds in a tightly capped jar.

Seeds can be dried each time you cook squash or pumpkins—even though their hulls are tougher than those of 'Lady Godiva'. This batch is salted.

Salted Pepitas

Using a big spoon, scrape the innards out of a buttercup or butternut squash, or a pumpkin. Clean the squash strands off with your fingers. Rinse the seeds under cold, running water until they're reasonably clean.

Pour them onto a cookie sheet and sprinkle with sea salt or shoyu (naturally fermented soy sauce). Let them dry in a slow oven until crisp. You could also bake them for 15 or 20 minutes in a 350°F oven. Don't let them get too brown.

Store in a tightly capped jar at room temperature.

New England pumpkin pie, of course, simply can't be missed, especially with its connection to Thanksgiving celebrations.

"Pompion" Pie

MAKES 2 9-INCH PIES, OR 1 10-INCHER

THE CRUST

Sift together:

1 cup unbleached white flour
1 cup whole-wheat pastry flour
1/4 teaspoon sea salt

Add:

1/8–1/2 teaspoon well-washed, finely grated lemon rind (optional)

Cut in with a pastry cutter or two knives:

2/3 cup butter, softened to room temperature

Add:

6–8 tablespoons ice water

Mix quickly with a fork. Add more water, if necessary, till the dough clings together. Knead lightly and briefly. Shape the dough into a firm ball, handling lightly. Refrigerate for at least 1 hour before rolling out.

When you're ready, roll out the dough 1/8 inch thick on a bread board (or marble slab) that has been lightly coated with unbleached white flour. Fold and drape the pastry over a rolling pin, and place it loosely over an upside-down pie pan. Trim to measure 2 inches larger than the pan's edges. Fold the dough again and remove it, turn the pan over, and lay the dough within. Arrange it to fit, overlapping the rim slightly. Fold the edges under and flute.

OPTION

At this point you have a choice. If you freeze your dough, the resulting pastry will be even crisper, and last-minute preparation will be simple. (For long storage, remove the crust from its pan once it's frozen and store in a plastic freezer bag, carefully removing as much air as possible.)

If you continue without freezing, or if you use an already frozen piecrust, brush the inside and fluted rim with the white of a slightly beaten egg. This helps prevent sogginess and promotes browning on the rim. You're ready to fill.

THE FILLING (for a 9- or 10-inch pie, depending on egg size)

Preheat the oven to 450°F.

In a medium-sized bowl, beat together until light:

2 large OR 3 medium-sized eggs
1/3 cup brown sugar
1/3 cup refined white sugar

Add and stir well:

2 cups cooked and puréed pumpkin
1 teaspoon powdered ginger
OR 1/2 teaspoon freshly ground
  gingerroot
1 1/2 teaspoons powdered cinnamon
1/4 teaspoon ground cloves
1 teaspoon freshly grated nutmeg
1/4 teaspoon sea salt

Stir in:

3/4 cup heavy cream
3/4 cup light cream

Pour into your pastry shell and bake for 10 minutes. Reduce the heat to 325°F and continue baking for about 40 minutes, or until a knife inserted into the center of the filling comes out clean.

SERVING

Cool on a wire rack, and serve with a topping of whipped cream over which you scatter freshly chopped walnuts.

Leeks

Allium porrum, or the common leek, is a biennial herb of the onion genus of the lily family. Cultivated by the Greeks, it "was so much esteemed by the Romans that Nero is said to have eaten it regularly for several days each month to clear his voice."

In fact, according to J. I. Rodale, the Romans took it all across Europe.

Originally, says food historian Harold McGee, the onion grew naturally from Israel to India, and has been cultivated "since at least 3000 B.C." Much, much later the Welsh created a legend about it. During a victory by Cadwallader, the last Briton king, in A.D. 640, Welsh soldiers wore leeks in their hats to distinguish themselves from Saxons. Wales celebrates it to this day: The leek is the national emblem.

The English, of course, were aware of it. Poet Geoffrey Chaucer's Reeve in *The Canterbury Tales,* begun soon after 1386, was "a slender, choleric man" who referred to the leek while describing people old in years but young in desire:

> For in our wyl ther stiketh evere a nayl,
> To have an hoor heed and a grene tayl,
> As hath a leek; for thogh oure myght be goon
> Our syl desireth folie evere in oon.

By 1390 English salads had become recognizable, if a bit heavy on the onion family, with fresh herbs taking the place of lettuce. In fact, in *The Forms of Cury,* a manuscript containing recipes of dishes prepared for England's Richard II and his barons, leeks appear.

Leeks were not familiar to Europeans alone. In 206 B.C. they were common, along with garlic and scallions, during China's Han period; and by A.D. 1271, along with wild onions, apples, melons, mulberries, and jujubes, they had become major components of the Chinese diet.

For tips on growing leeks, see page 271.

The leek apparently has a little more nutritive value than onions: A cupful of chopped leek contains only 76 calories, but it has 118 International Units of vitamin A, 14.9 milligrams of vitamin C, 73 milligrams of calcium, 223 milligrams of potassium, as well as other vitamins and minerals.

The leek's great gift is in providing subtle flavor—so subtle, in fact, that in Greek and Roman times it was referred to as "poor man's asparagus." When braised, as in this recipe, you'll see why.

Braised Leeks

SERVES 2

THE LEEKS

Rinse well:

2 pounds leeks

Slice off the roots and most of the green leaves. This should result in about 1 pound of trimmed leeks 6 to 7 inches long. Slice each leek in half lengthwise. In a low-sided pot, combine:

1 cup Vegetable Stock (see page 43) OR water to which you have added 2 tablespoons Bragg's Liquid Aminos (see page 63)

1/4 teaspoon yellow mustard seeds

1 bay leaf

Lay in the leeks, cut-side down. Bring to a simmer over medium heat, cover, and simmer for 10 to 15 minutes or till very tender. Remove the lid and let cool. Then chill.

THE SAUCE

While the leeks are chilling, combine:

3 tablespoons of the leek stock

1 1/2 teaspoons Dijon mustard

SERVING

Using a spatula, lift the leeks out of their stock and place on a platter. Dribble the mustard sauce on top. Serve with potatoes, rice, or pasta and in-season vegetables. Green leafy salads are always necessary.

A tart offers a fine way to enjoy leeks.

Open-Faced Leek Tart

MAKES 1 10-INCH TART

THE CRUST

Into a medium-sized bowl, sift together:

2 cups unbleached white
    all-purpose flour

1/2 teaspoon sea salt

1/4 teaspoon refined white sugar

Remove from the refrigerator and allow to soften slightly:

14 tablespoons butter

Using two knives or a pastry cutter, cut into the flour mix until the dough resembles coarse cornmeal:

7 tablespoons of the cool
    and slightly soft butter

Add and work in briefly, leaving bigger chunks:

7 more tablespoons cool butter

Using a fork, add till the dough is evenly moistened:

1/3 cup ice water

Divide the dough into two balls and knead them very lightly on a lightly floured board. Form into two flattened balls and wrap in plastic. Let them rest in the refrigerator for at least 1 hour.

When you're ready to use them, remove them from the refrigerator and let them warm up until they're soft enough to be rolled out.

THE FILLING

Rinse well and trim off the roots and green leaves from:

about 3 pounds leeks

Cut the white parts in half lengthwise, then crosswise into 1/4-inch slices to equal 3 heaping cups.

In a heavy, medium-sized porcelainized saucepan, heat:

1/4 cup extra-virgin olive oil

Add and cook over medium heat for 10 minutes or until soft:

the 3 cups leeks

2 medium onions, sliced to equal
    1 cup

Increase the heat, add, and cook until almost dry:

1/2 cup dry white wine

When almost dry, reduce the heat and add:

1/2 cup cream
OR cottage cheese whipped smooth

sea salt to taste

freshly ground black
OR white pepper to taste

Cook for 2 to 3 minutes, then remove from the heat and gently stir in:

1/2 cup stuffed green olives, chopped

BAKING

Preheat the oven to 400°F.

Grease a cookie or 12-inch pizza sheet. On a lightly floured surface, roll out one pastry disk to 12 inches in diameter and 1/8 inch thick. Lay this on the cookie or pizza sheet. Sprinkle with:

1 tablespoon white flour

Spoon the filling onto the disk, keeping it away from the edges by about 2 inches.

Place on top:
4–5 anchovy fillets (optional)
Sprinkle with:
paprika
Fold the pastry edges over the filling by about 1 1/2 inches to form a rough, enfolding lip. Brush with:
1 small, beaten egg

Place on the bottom shelf of the oven and bake for 30 to 40 minutes or until golden. If the edges become too brown before the bottom cooks, cover the tart with foil.

SERVING

Let the tart cool slightly, then transfer it to a serving platter. Cut it into wedges and serve on warmed plates. A big salad completes your enjoyment.

Chilled leek and potato soup is, of course, a classic dish.

Vichyssoise

SERVES 4

Cut off the green tops and roots from:
2–3 leeks, depending on size
Wash well. Slice the white part thinly to equal 2 cups.

In a medium-sized saucepan, place:
1 tablespoon butter
OR sunflower seed oil

Sauté in it over medium heat until limp:
the 2 cups thinly sliced leeks

Add:
4 cups peeled, thinly sliced potatoes
3 cups mild Vegetable Stock
(see page 43)
a pinch of freshly grated nutmeg
Bring to a boil, reduce the heat, and simmer for about 30 minutes, or till the potatoes are tender.

Beginning on low speed (increase the speed as you go along), purée the cooked leeks and potatoes in a blender till smooth. (Place a towel over the blender top as you work to prevent burning.) Pour into a large serving bowl. Add and mix in, beginning with 1 cup:
about 2 cups milk
For thicker soup, use less milk; for thinner, add more.

Then add:
sea salt to taste
a lot of freshly ground white
OR black pepper
Cover and chill.

Serve sprinkled with:
freshly grated nutmeg
chopped chives, garlic chives,
OR parsley

Garlic

Ah, *Allium sativum*—garlic!—that aromatic member of the Liliaceae family revered by some, sniffed at suspiciously by others, but gaining in popularity with every breath.

In fact, the winds of change have been turning it into a—well, a hurricane. Says Richard Wolkomir in a *Smithsonian* magazine article, U.S. garlic consumption jumped from 0.6 pound a year in 1975 to 1.6 pounds in 1994. "Between 1975 and 1994," he adds, "annual U.S. garlic production . . . zoomed from 140 million pounds to 493 million. . . ." At the same time, "another 97.3 million pounds were imported"—and American production is increasing about 10 percent a year.

What's happening?

In Shakespearean times, certain Englishmen considered garlic an aphrodisiac, while Nicholas Culpeper, in his 1652 *Complete Herbal,* suggested more mundane uses. Garlic would heal "the bites of mad dogs and venomous creatures" (he didn't mention vampires), rid children of worms, purge the head, and help "the lethargy."

But garlic has an older history.

Sumerians of about 3000 B.C. were wont to lace their bean and grain diet with it. And ancient Egyptians admired it as medicine. According to Pliny, they ranked garlic next to the gods when swearing an oath; and Roman laborers and soldiers consumed lots of raw garlic, which was thought to give them strength.

By the third century B.C., says Reay Tannahill, Greek Athens had developed the original hors d'oeuvre trolley as reported by Lynceus in *The Centaur:* "the cook sets before you a large tray on which are five small plates." One held garlic.

Then there were Scythians, tribes ranging the fertile lands around the Caspian and Black Seas characterized by Hippocrates as "a fat and humorous people." They supplemented their meals with sturgeon, onions, beans—and garlic.

India, of course, produced a fabulously satisfying kabob: beef or mutton cut small, sprinkled with salt and pepper, dipped into oil and garlic, then roasted on a spit, with sweet herbs between every piece.

China used it similarly. "In early spring, after the land was plowed, there was held the rite of expiation, the sacrifice of a lamb which even then, almost three thousand years ago, was aromatically seasoned with garlic before being cooked on a bed of fragrant southernwood."

In fact, when Marco Polo passed through Yunnan in the 13th century, he found mutton, beef, buffalo, and poultry eaten raw by being chopped small and put into a garlic sauce. Was this the origin of steak tartare?

Garlic has even inspired poets! Banquets at the court of 10th-century Baghdad caliphs, says Tannahill, "were renowned not only for the extravagance of the dishes but for the . . . gastronomic erudition of the conversation." One guest recited verses written by Ibn al-Mu'tazz:

> Here capers grace a sauce vermilion
> Whose fragrant odors to the soul are blown . . .
> Here pungent garlic meets the eager sight
> And whets with savor sharp the appetite . . .

GARDENING NOTES

GARLIC

BULBS, NOT SEEDS: There are three types of garlic.

Softneck: For braiding, and for the strongest flavor. Expect one layer of medium cloves on the outside, and many small cloves in the middle.

Stiffneck: These larger bulbs are more winter hardy and have a milder taste; they're easy to peel. They have four to six large cloves and none in the middle.

Elephant: Huge cloves. This plant is related to leeks and, like them, has a very mild taste. The cloves are easy to peel.

CULTIVATION: Plant in fall, between the first frost and November. Choose a patch of very fertile soil.

Separate individual cloves (use only the largest softneck cloves). Plant them about 2 inches deep and 4 to 6 inches apart, in rows. Plant the little softneck cloves like beans for spring garlic greens. Cover beds with hay or other mulch. The roots will enlarge in winter, with little or no top growth.

In spring remove the mulch to let the tops grow up straight. But spread it out between rows to keep weeds down and moisture in.

PESTS AND DISEASES: None.

HARVESTING: In summer (mid-July through August), when the leaves have half yellowed, loosen the soil with a fork and lift the plants. String up in an airy place to dry. Softneck garlics should be braided soon after harvest. For others, cut the tops off straight across, 1/2 inch above the bulb.

Stiffneck garlics have 360-degree coils on top, which should be removed to allow the largest cloves to fill out. But if you let the coils uncurl, use the little topset bulblets that grow on top for stir-fries.

Garlic is good for you! One 4-calorie clove contains 16 milligrams of potassium along with traces of vitamins A, C, and other nutrients. "At the turn of the century, garlic ointments, compresses, and inhalants were 'the drug of choice' against tuberculosis," says Jean Carper in *The Food Pharmacy*. "In World War I, garlic was used to fight typhus and dysentery. In World War II, British physicians, treating battle wounds with garlic, reported total success in warding off septic poisoning and gangrene." Even Dr. Albert Schweitzer, famous for his jungle hospital at Lambarene, "employed garlic against typhus and cholera."

Today its reputation soars: Recent scientific studies suggest that allicin, a chemical compound found in garlic (especially raw garlic), may ward off colds, fight infections, stimulate the immune system, act as an expectorant and decongestant, and contain cancer-preventing substances. It's reputed to lower the blood pressure and combat clotting. "A mere half a raw garlic clove a day can rev up the blood-clot-dissolving activity that helps prevent heart attacks and strokes. Only a couple of raw garlic cloves daily can keep blood cholesterol down in heart patients," advises Carper.

Here's a recipe to turn you into a real garlic lover. The flavor is surprisingly mellow.

Country Garlic Soup

SERVES 2–4

Blanch under boiling water for 30 seconds, then rinse under cold water, drain, peel, and slice thinly:

20–24 big, new garlic cloves

In a large, heavy pot, heat:

2 tablespoons extra-virgin olive oil

Sauté in the oil till soft:

2 cups sliced onions
1 cup sliced green bell pepper

Add:

the prepared garlic cloves
3 cups peeled, seeded, sliced ripe
** tomatoes OR canned tomatoes**

Reduce the heat, cover the saucepan, and simmer for about 30 minutes, stirring often. Pour in:

2 cups hot water flavored with
** 2 tablespoons dark miso**
** OR Vegetable Stock (see page 43)**

Thicken to whatever consistency you fancy by adding:

2–3 slices of crustless white bread,
** cubed**

One cupful works well.

Season with:

freshly ground black pepper
1 tablespoon freshly chopped cilantro

Sprinkle with:

freshly grated Parmesan cheese

Serve hot in warmed bowls.

Another way to enjoy garlic is by baking it, then spreading the soft result on crusty fresh bread. Special pottery garlic bakers make the job easy.

Baked Garlic

1 HEAD PER PERSON

Preheat the oven to 350°F.

Slit the papery skin around the base—about 1/2 inch up—of:

1 whole, new garlic head per person

Peel off the outer papery skin. This will leave the garlic clove clusters intact, still covered by their own thin, inner skins.

Arrange the clusters in a baking dish just large enough to hold them comfortably together. Top each head with:

1 tablespoon extra-virgin olive oil
a sprinkling of sea salt
freshly ground black pepper

Pour into the pan around the heads:
enough water or Vegetable Stock
(see page 43) to moisten the
pan bottom

Bake for 1 hour or more on the middle shelf of your oven, basting every 10 minutes or so, till the cloves are golden brown and tender.

Serve as soon as the garlic is cool enough to handle. Each person squeezes soft garlic mush out of the cloves, spreading it on thick, crusty bread. It can also be whipped into mashed potatoes or served with nut loaves, bean burgers, and in dressings for leafy green salads.

Stir-Fried Garlic

Fresh-from-the-garden garlic tops are marvelous in stir-fries. Although regular garlic harvesting doesn't begin until the tops begin to yellow in late summer, stiffneck varieties produce hard round stems called scapes. Thrusting upward, each scape forms a "topset" of tiny cloves too small to be useful. These topsets, with a few inches of scape, need to be clipped off. Otherwise the size of the maturing bulb below will be reduced by an average of 30 percent.

But this necessity is a boon for the cook: Simply add chopped topsets to any stir-fry.

Garlic can be pickled. Once used up, the resulting vinegar is fine for dressings. (If canning is new to you, refer to the Ball Company's BLUE BOOK for complete directions; see page 38.)

Pickled Garlic

MAKES 2 CUPS

Slice off the stem end and peel to equal:
1 3/4 cups new garlic cloves
Bring a small pot of water to a boil, add the cloves, and blanch for 30 seconds. Remove and drain well.

In a small porcelainized or stainless-steel pan, combine:
1 1/2 cups rice vinegar
OR mild apple cider vinegar
2 tablespoons Pickling Spice Mix
(see page 151)
Bring to a boil.

Meanwhile, in a small saucepan of hot water, heat two metal bands and lids to just under boiling.

Place the blanched garlic neatly into two scalded 1/2-pint canning jars and pour your just-boiled pickling liquid over, leaving 1/2 inch of headroom at the top. Wipe off the rims. Remove air bubbles by poking into each jar along the sides with a chopstick.

Drain the hot bands and lids in a sieve. Then place the lids on the jars, screwing the bands down tightly.

Place the hot, filled jars on a rack in a big pot of hot water. Add more hot water if necessary to come at least 1 inch above the jar tops. Cover, bring to a boil, and process in this boiling-water bath for 5 minutes. Measure the processing time from when a rolling boil begins.

When time is up, remove the jars with tongs and let them cool on a rack or towel-covered counter to prevent breakage.

When they're completely cool, remove the metal bands, rinse the jars gently, wipe dry, label, and store in a cool, dark place.

———————

Another version of long-term garlic storage is easy—if strongly scented.

Frozen Garlic

In a meat grinder, chop up:
    as many skinned garlic cloves
      as you please
Scoop this into a small bowl and add:
    any resulting garlic juice
    some extra-virgin olive oil

Store in small jars, freeze, and use one jar at a time as needed.

———————

Garlic-scented oils are prime ingredients for adding to salads or cooking. Before adding cloves to oil, however, they must receive a vinegar bath to prevent botulism.

And note that the more cloves you add to your oil, the more flavorful it becomes.

Garlic-Flavored Oil

Cut off the root ends and remove the skins from:
    any number of garlic cloves

Place the cloves in a jar and cover with:
    rice or apple cider vinegar
Let sit for 24 hours. Drain.

Place several cloves in each bottle of:
    extra-virgin olive oil

WINTER

As it does all over the Northeast, winter comes early at the

Simply Grande Gardens. Snow sometimes arrives in October,

frosting red and yellow fall foliage with white,

making every gardener glad of potatoes and cabbages

and beets and onions safely stored in root cellars.

But the brussels sprouts still standing in the garden love it,

keeping ready for human enjoyment well into November.

Not only that, but avid gardeners still find pride in

cellar shelves stocked with bright jars of canned tomatoes,

yellow and green string beans, purple grape jelly,

plum conserve, and dill pickles: the end

to a perfect gardening season.

NOVEMBER

Brussels Sprouts

M arian Morash gives a fine description of brussels sprouts in *The Victory Garden Cookbook*. "The tiny 'cabbages' develop along a thick 20–22-inch-high stalk that grows straight up from the ground. The sprouts start at the bottom and circle around the stalk, interrupted occasionally by great fanning leaves which top off the plant as an umbrella of protection for the rosettes below."

The original wild cabbage, *Brassica oleracea*, is native to the Mediterranean seaboard. Head cabbage, brussels sprouts, cauliflower, kohlrabi, kale, and broccoli are all varieties of this one remarkable plant species.

The brussels sprout "apparently developed in northern Europe in about the 5th century," says Harold McGee in *On Food and Cooking*, "although the first clear record of its existence is from 1587." Benjamin Watson, author of *Taylor's Guide to Heirloom Vegetables*, differs slightly, saying, "the Brussels sprout was first cultivated around the 14th century in the vicinity of Brussels, Belgium, from kalelike forms of wild cabbage."

Bert Greene, author of *Greene on Greens*, presents still another version: "No one knows for certain how or when the Brussels sprout first came to Brussels, but most certainly it is a vegetable that flourishes best in Belgium's particularly rich and loamy soil." In fact, he says, "Sprouts have been a source of Flemish national pride for over eight centuries."

Unfortunately, the plant didn't make much of an impression in English or American gardens until the early 1800s, and not until 1820 was it was officially "recognized by the king of Belgium's seedsmen as that country's official green."

Sprouts, states McGee, became "a popular vegetable in Europe only after World War I."

However, as is the case when chasing history, Bert Greene reports that much earlier the "Romans called these tender buttons *bullata gemmifera* (diamond-makers) because consumption was rumored to enhance a diner's mental agility." And "Roman chefs imported them from the seacoasts of western Europe, where they grew wild."

For tips on growing brussels sprouts, see page 244.

Brussels sprouts make fine eating today. Like all the cole crops, they're nutritious. A cupful contains 24 calories, 778 International Units of vitamin A, 74 milligrams of vitamin C, 36 milligrams of calcium, and 20 milligrams of magnesium. Jean Carper says that sprouts are "packed with anticancer chemicals."

Simple Brussels Sprouts

SERVES 4

Trim and wash:
   1 pound sprouts (about 32)
Steam or blanch until barely tender, perhaps 10 to 12 minutes. Halve each sprout lengthwise.

In a medium-sized porcelainized pot, heat:
   6 tablespoons extra-virgin olive oil
Add the sprouts and toss gently till hot. Add:
   freshly sqeezed juice of 1/2 lemon (about 2 tablespoons)
   sea salt to taste
   freshly ground black pepper

Toss and serve immediately with potatoes and other in-season vegetables.

NOTE: Drizzle with a little maple syrup for a taste surprise.

Saving food for winter use after snow blankets the earth is a tempting activity for every squirrel—and New Englander. Pickling is an ancient way to store summer's bounty. And of course the use of acidic vinegar means the preserving of pickled produce can be done with a simple water bath when canning, rather than a pressure cooker. (For people new to it, the "bible" to study is the BLUE BOOK: GUIDE TO HOME CANNING, FREEZING, AND DEHYDRATION, latest edition, published by the Ball Corporation. See page 38.)

Big heads of dill seeds and fat garlic cloves are perfect additions to brussels sprouts.

Pickled Brussels Sprouts

MAKES 4 PINTS

Pick or purchase:
   2 1/2 pounds brussels sprouts
Trim the stems and remove any blemishes or floppy leaves. Rinse quickly. Place the sprouts in a big pot of boiling water and blanch till they're

barely tender, 5 to 10 minutes. Drain in a colander and set aside.

In a stainless-steel or porcelainized pot, combine and boil for 5 minutes:

2 1/2 cups water
2 1/2 cups 5 percent cider vinegar
3 tablespoons canning OR kosher salt
1–2 small, hot chili peppers

Pack the sprouts into four widemouthed pint jars that have been sterilized by boiling. Leave 1/2 inch of headroom. (Placing a towel underneath the jars will prevent breakage if countertops are cold. Be careful not to get burned.)

To each jar, add:

1 garlic clove
1/4 teaspoon white mustard seeds
1 fresh dill head

Pour hot vinegar solution over the sprouts to within 1/4 inch of the rim. Remove air bubbles by poking into each jar along the sides with a chopstick.

Meanwhile, in a small saucepan of hot water, heat metal bands and lids to just under boiling. When they're hot, drop them into a sieve and drain. Wipe off the rims of your sprout-filled jars. Place the hot lids and bands on the jars, screwing the bands down tightly.

Place your hot, filled jars on a rack in a big pot of hot water. Add more hot water if necessary to come at least 1 inch above the jar tops. Cover, bring to a boil, and process in this boiling-water bath for 15 minutes. Measure the processing time from when a rolling boil begins.

When time is up, remove the jars with tongs and let them cool on a rack or towel-covered counter to prevent breakage.

Let the jars cool completely. Then remove the metal bands, check to see that each jar is safely sealed—the metal lid will feel slightly concave when you press it—rinse gently, wipe dry, and label.

Store in a cool, dark place.

Sprouts and cauliflower make a good pickled pair. Note that vegetables differ in sizes, so the amounts you end up with may differ from what you expected. Not to worry. If you're new to home canning, see page 38.

Pickled Sprouts and Cauliflower

MAKES 5–6 PINTS

Pick or purchase:

2 pounds small brussels sprouts
2 1/2 pounds cauliflower

Rinse the sprouts quickly, trim their stems, and remove any blemishes or floppy leaves.

Wash the cauliflower quickly and separate into small, short-stemmed florets.

In a medium-sized saucepan, bring to a boil:

2 quarts water

Place the sprouts and cauliflower in a large bowl and sprinkle with:

1/4 cup kosher OR canning salt

Pour boiling water over the vegetables to cover. Cover the bowl with a tea towel and let it stand at room temperature for 2 hours.

In the meantime, sterilize widemouthed pint jars by boiling. Leave them in the boiling water to keep hot until needed.

Drain the sprouts and cauliflower and plunge them into cold water to rinse. Then drain them well.

In a stainless-steel or porcelainized pot, combine:

1 cup water
3 cups white wine vinegar
1/3 cup refined white sugar

Bring to a boil over high heat and boil for 5 minutes.

Place your sterilized jars on a counter. A towel underneath will prevent breakage. Be careful not to get burned.

In each hot jar, place:

1/8 teaspoon hot red pepper flakes
OR 1/4 teaspoon cayenne powder
1 teaspoon dried tarragon
1 teaspoon white mustard seeds

Pack the sprouts and cauliflower into the jars, leaving 1/2 inch of headroom. Pour hot vinegar solution over the veggies to within 1/4 inch of the rim. Remove air bubbles by poking into each jar along the sides with a chopstick.

Meanwhile, in a small saucepan of hot water, heat metal bands and lids to just under boiling. When they're hot, drop them into a sieve and drain. Wipe off the rims of your filled jars. Place the hot lids and bands on the jars, screwing the bands down tightly.

Place your hot, filled jars on a rack in a big pot of hot water. Add more hot water if necessary to come at least 1 inch above the jar tops. Cover, bring to a boil, and process in this boiling-water bath for 15 minutes. Measure the processing time from when a rolling boil begins.

When time is up, remove the jars with tongs and let them cool on a rack or towel-covered counter to prevent breakage. Let them cool completely. Then remove the metal bands, check to see that each jar is safely sealed—the metal lid will feel slightly concave when you press it—rinse gently, wipe dry, and label.

Store in a cool, dark place.

Winter-Keeping Carrots

According to historian Clarence Day in *A History of Maine Agriculture,* by the year 1606 King James I had divided an entire region of the New World measuring from 34 degrees to 45 degrees north latitude (that's from Cape Fear, North Carolina, to present-day Canso, Nova Scotia) between two English companies organized for colonization. They were called, as every schoolchild knows, the London and Plymouth Companies.

The London Company founded Jamestown. The Plymouth Company failed at Popham Beach, Maine.

In 1607 the Plymouth group built at Popham cabins, a storehouse, a church, a fort, and a "pretty Pynnace" of about 30 tons' burden named the *Virginia*. It was the first vessel launched in New England. They also "quarreled with the Indians;

their storehouse burned in the dead of winter; their aged president, George Popham, died; and in the spring their new leader, Raleigh Gilbert, returned to England "along with the rest of the faint-hearted colonists."

Faint-hearted indeed. "All our former hopes were frozen to death," was the mournful comment of Sir Ferdinando Gorges.

We can well imagine. What stranger, for instance, having just arrived from England and enjoyed a blissful Maine summer, could really imagine Maine's arctic winter? How could novices realize the shortness of Maine's growing season and the absolute necessity of storing crops where rot and mice couldn't destroy them?

Obviously they couldn't. Cold, scurvy, and starvation took their toll. Leaving England at the end of the 17th century, as far as eating is concerned these hopeful colonists would have been accustomed to "beef, mutton, fowls, pigs, rabbits and pigeons"—a diet "heavy on the meat," according to Henri Misson de Valbourg's 1690s memoir. The mutton would also have been "underdone and the beef salted for some days before being boiled and then served up besieged 'with five or six heaps of cabbage, carrots, turnips, or some other herbs or roots, well peppered and salted, and swimming in butter.'"

So much for cholesterol. But hurrah for the vegetables—especially the "herbs" and root varieties.

Turnips, radishes, carrots perhaps, and an undeveloped form of parsnip were among the root crops common in Europe during the first millennium A.D., we're assured. In fact, *Food in History* author Reay Tannahill says that "Root vegetables, protected by the soil from the worst ravages of the weather, must have been important from earliest times."

They certainly helped American colonists survive. By 1630 a dissertation of the Reverend Francis Higginson of Salem praised New England specimens by saying that turnips, parsnips, and carrots were bigger and sweeter "than is ordinary to be found in England."

They weren't always so. Introduced to England in 1558 by Flemish weavers fleeing the persecution of Spain's Philip II, "the familiar orange-rooted carrot that we know today is a recent innovation. Although ancient peoples from the Mediterranean Sea to the Orient undoubtedly knew about various forms of wild carrots and to some extent cultivated them as both food and medicine (carrots and ginseng are kissing cousins), not much was written about them specifically until the 16th century," says *Sturteront's Edible Plants of the World.*

In the wild, carrot roots vary in color from the dominant white to shades of yellow, orange, red, and the milder purple—pigmented by anthocyanin. The pretty meadow wildflower known as Queen Anne's lace is simply a wild form of *Daucus carota* and has white roots that are perfectly edible, though they contain a woody central core.

By 1763 the Dutch, apparently tired of having their pots and soups stained purple, developed three orange varieties: late half long, early half long, and early scarlet long. "But for today's sweet, orange-red, improved varieties, we can largely thank the French who early on became the most enthusiastic carrot-boosters," says Benjamin Watson. "In the latter half of the 19th century, the famous French seed house of Vilmorin developed many of the strains we still grow today."

Wild carrots, of course, were used by the Greeks and Romans—but mainly for medicinal purposes. The old Greeks had it right: Carrot color is due to beta-carotene pigment, the parent chemical to vitamin A and a substance noted for cancer-preventing properties. Carrots are very rich in vitamin A (a cupful contains 30,942 International Units), are a good source of potassium (356 milligrams), and contain 10 milligrams of vitamin C. Raw carrots reputedly depress blood cholesterol.

Not only that: They're tasty! Eaten raw or cooked, everybody loves them. Sliced thinly into disks, then simmered slowly in a little milk flavored with sprigs of rosemary, they can't be beaten.

GARDENING NOTES

CARROTS

CHOOSING SEEDS: Carrots come in three basic shapes: cylindrical with blunt ends (Nantes), tapered (Imperator), and short and fat (choose these if you have clay soils). Some are short season (50 days from seed to carrot); others are late season for winter storage (68 to 80 days). All are orange, but they vary somewhat in taste to the connoisseur.

There are 18,000 seeds to the ounce. Ten grams plants 100 row feet. Seeds lose their capacity to germinate over several years. Note that commercial gardeners use pelleted seeds to improve spacing.

CULTIVATION: Any good soil will grow carrots, but deep, loose loam with a good water-holding capacity is best. Carrots germinate slowly in cold soil, so be patient with early-spring planting. Keep planting in succession for a summer-long harvest. Plant storage carrots 100 days before your expected first frost date so that they mature just in time for harvest.

Plant 1/4 inch deep in 3-foot-wide beds, with rows 8 inches apart. This is ideal row spacing for collineal-hoeing. Do your first hoeing before the carrots emerge (carrot seedlings are slow). Water the bed if need be to ensure that the soil doesn't crust over before seedling emergence. Alternately, plant radishes in the same row—they'll break the crust to let the delicate carrot seedlings through. Keep hoeing every 10 days until carrots crowd out weed seedlings. Then pull weeds within the row, and thin carrots to 3/4- to 1-inch spacing. An overcrowded carrot bed will yield only disappointment.

Finally, hoe soil up to cover growing carrots and prevent green shoulders.

PESTS AND DISEASES: Carrot rust fly and wireworms can wreak havoc. To prevent them, provide fertile soil, and avoid planting carrots in newly plowed ground. If necessary, cover the bed with floating row covers early in the season to exclude the insects.

Blights can reduce yield and quality. To prevent this, rotate carrots with other crops.

HARVESTING: Dig down next to the row with a garden fork to loosen the soil. Pull a carrot and examine it. If it's bright orange and the right length for the variety, the bed is ready. You have 3 weeks to harvest. Remove the tops and store the carrots washed or unwashed in humid conditions: moist sand or shavings, or in perforated plastic bags or bins. Keep at near-freezing temperature.

For extra-sugary carrots, plant a bed in early August. In fall, leave the carrots in the ground and cover the bed with 6 to 12 inches of hay. Place a stake at each end of the bed. On a nice day in the middle of winter, take a snow shovel and garden fork. Find the bed between the stakes, remove the snow, then the hay, and dig the carrots out. Expect them to have grown under the hay! You'll never eat better-tasting carrots.

An extremely tasty way to cook carrots is with honey glazing—a sweet way to treat an already sweet vegetable.

Glazed Carrots

SERVES 3–4

Wash well, peel if necessary, and cut into 1/4-inch disks:

1 pound carrots

You should have 2 cups.

In a medium-sized, heavy porcelainized saucepan, melt:

2 tablespoons butter

Add and cook for 1 minute:

1 small onion, finely chopped

Add and simmer for 15 minutes, covered:

the prepared carrots
1/2 cup water

Pour over the carrots:

2 tablespoons honey

Sprinkle with:

freshly grated nutmeg

Increase the heat and cook, stirring constantly, until a syrup forms. (If the carrots are well done, remove them from the pot and reduce the liquid. Then pour it over the carrots.)

Serve sprinkled with:
a little sea salt
Potatoes, pasta, or rice are good accompaniments, along with a green leafy salad, pickled beets, and other vegetables.

————————————

Although most people are accustomed to carrots as additions to soups, what follows is a soup featuring the carrot itself. This was introduced in THE NEW MAINE COOKING and is too good to forget.

Jean Ann's Carrot Nut Soup

SERVES 4–6

Pour into a large, heavy-bottomed saucepan:
3 tablespoons sunflower seed oil
OR extra-virgin olive oil
Heat it and add:
3/4 cup chopped onion
2 cups grated carrots, tightly packed
Sauté until the onion is transparent.

Add:
1/2 cup peeled, chopped apples
2 tablespoons tomato purée
2 1/2 cups water
1 teaspoon sea salt (optional)
1/4 cup barley
Bring to a boil. Lower the heat and simmer for 45 minutes.

Add and simmer for about 5 minutes, or until the raisins are plump:
1/2 cup raisins OR currants
1/2 cup cashew pieces
1/2 cup milk (optional)

Serve hot, garnished with yogurt and sprinkled with finely chopped fresh parsley or cilantro. Fresh rolls are perfect with this.

————————————

Leftover cooked carrots are easily scooped into quick breads, not to mention muffins. Grapefruit-Rhubarb Marmalade (see page 73) makes a good accomplice.

Carrot Quick Bread

MAKES 1 LOAF

Preheat the oven to 350°F.

Grease and flour a 9- by 5-inch loaf pan.

Sift together twice:
1 cup unbleached white flour
1/2 cup whole-wheat flour
1 teaspoon baking soda
1 1/2 teaspoons powdered cinnamon
1/2 teaspoon sea salt

In the large bowl of an electric mixer, at high speed, beat:
2 large eggs
Reduce the speed, then add and beat in:
1 cup refined white sugar
1/2 cup sunflower seed oil
1 cup mashed cooked carrots
On low speed, mix in:
the flour mixture
Stir in:
1/2 cup chopped walnut meats

Pour the batter into your greased and floured loaf pan and bake for about 60 minutes. Cool for 10 minutes in the pan, then turn out onto a rack to cool completely.

Food fads come and go. Versions of the carrot cake arrived in the 1970s and, despite being a fad, continue to please. The following recipe came to Maine from California via a gal named Monica, who called it a wedding cake.

California Wedding Cake

Preheat the oven to 325°F.

Sift together into a large bowl:

3 cups whole-wheat pastry flour
2 cups raw sugar
1 teaspoon baking soda
1 teaspoon double-acting baking powder (see page 28)
1/2 teaspoon sea salt

In a small bowl, beat:

4 large eggs

Add and beat together:

2 cups sunflower seed oil

Pour the oil-egg mixture into the dry ingredients and mix well. Add and mix well:

3 cups grated carrots
1/2 cup chopped walnuts
1/2 cup currants
1/2 cup chopped dates
1 cup sliced bananas
1 cup fresh pineapple, cut into small chunks
1 teaspoon natural vanilla
1 teaspoon powdered cinnamon

Grease a shallow, rectangular, 12- by 9-inch cake pan, and an 8- by 9-inch pan. Pour the cake batter into both pans and bake for 1 hour on the middle rack of your oven. Remove from the oven and let both cakes cool in their pans for 45 minutes.

Beat together:

2 cups powdered sugar
24 ounces cream cheese

Remove both cakes from their pans. Arrange the larger cake on a suitable tray. Spread smoothly with the icing mixture. Place the smaller cake on top and spread it likewise. Coat the sides, and decorate in any way you fancy.

NOTE: For a simple flat cake, use a single larger pan.

A much simpler carrot cake, and one dating from the 1700s, appears in a booklet called FANNY PIERSON CRANE, HER RECEIPTS 1796. We've updated it here.

Fanny Pierson Crane's Carrot Tea Cake

Preheat the oven to 350°F.

In a large bowl, mix together:

3/4 cup plus 2 tablespoons sunflower seed oil
2 cups refined white sugar
4 eggs, lightly beaten
2 cups finely grated raw carrots

Add:

2 cups unbleached white flour
1 teaspoon sea salt
1 teaspoon baking soda
1 tablespoon powdered cinnamon
1 teaspoon freshly grated nutmeg

Bake in a size-2 springform pan for 1 hour. Or use a well-greased bundt pan.

Dust with sugar and, when cool, slice very thin.

Today many Americans lack that old-fashioned, chilly, dark root cellar in which to store summer's largesse. Home canning is the next best way to store vegetables such as carrots. And of course those you grow yourself or purchase from a farm garden make the tastiest winter treats.

What follows is a recipe for basic carrot canning, taken from the Ball Company's BLUE BOOK: THE GUIDE TO HOME CANNING AND FREEZING (see page 38). Carrot canning requires a pressure cooker.

Canned Carrots

MAKES 7 1-QUART JARS

Select:

carrots 1–1 1/4 inches in diameter
Wash and scrape. Wash again. Slice into disks.

Bring a large pot of water to a boil and add the carrot disks. Return to a boil, reduce the heat, and simmer for 5 minutes.

Pack the carrots into hot quart jars that have been sterilized by boiling. (Placing a towel underneath the jars will prevent breakage if countertops are cold. Be careful not to get burned.) Leave 1 inch of headroom. To each jar, add:

1 teaspoon sea salt
Cover with:

boiling water
Be sure to leave 1 inch of headroom.

Using a chopstick, probe inside each jar to release any air bubbles.

Meanwhile, in a small saucepan of hot water, heat metal bands and lids to just under boiling. When they're hot, drop them into a sieve and drain.

Wipe off the rims of your carrot-filled jars. Place the hot lids and bands on the jars, screwing the bands down tightly.

Place your hot, filled jars on a rack in a big pressure canner that contains 2 to 3 inches of hot water. (Be sure to carefully read the directions for your pressure cooker before using it.) Place the canner over high heat and lock on the cover per the manufacturer's instructions. Leave the vent open until steam escapes steadily for 10 minutes; then close the vent, bring the pressure up to 10 pounds, and keep it steady by adjusting your stove's heat—30 minutes for quarts at 10 pounds of pressure. Watch carefully. Measure the processing time from when the pressure reaches 10 pounds.

When time is up, remove the canner from the heat and allow the pressure to fall to zero. Be certain the pressure is all the way down. Wait for 5 minutes, then open the vent. Unfasten the cover and slide it toward you, allowing steam to escape, then hold it tipped away from your face to prevent any possible burn. Place on a shelf. Let the jars rest for 10 minutes before removing them with tongs. Place them on a rack or towel-covered counter to cool and prevent breakage. Do not allow the jars to touch each other.

Let the jars cool completely, perhaps overnight. When they're completely cool, unscrew the metal bands, check to see that each jar is safely sealed—the metal lid will feel slightly concave when you press it—rinse gently, wipe dry, and label.

Store in a cool, dark place. Always test a jar's seal before using it.

Midwinter Beets

A 1935 cookbook titled *Recipes of All Nations,* compiled and edited by Countess Morphy, remarks that "the History of Cookery is part of the history of civilization."

That seems reasonable enough. Then she adds, "My motive in writing this book is to help the modern housewife who takes an intelligent interest in cooking to have excellent, varied and inexpensive food in her own home. Ordinary food is apt to be monotonous."

We don't know about the countess, but ordinary New England cooking has never been monotonous! In the early days, as described by a manuscript found in the letter book of Governor William Bradford of Plymouth Plantation and titled *A Descriptive and Historical Account of New England in Verse,* we learn that:

> All sorts of roots and herbes in gardens grow,
> Parsnips, carrots, turnips, or what you'll sow,
> Onioins, melons, cucumbers, radishes,
> Skirrets, beets, coleworts, and fair cabbages.

In those early years of settlement a Puritan mother's herb garden was a necessary component for colonists living in areas with no doctors. And, as reported by historian Howard S. Russell in *A Long, Deep Furrow: Three Centuries of Farming in New England,* the first garden vegetables to become important in the new colonies were the roots.

The ruby root as we know it apparently originated in Germany. Says Benjamin Watson, "no written reference to the red, turnip-rooted vegetable we know . . . exists before the 16th century." It was initially preferred in a less vibrant shade—yellow white, in fact.

And therein lies an amusing story, for the ability to metabolize that bright red pigment (betacyanin) is controlled by a single genetic locus. Says Harold McGee, only "those people who have inherited two recessive genes pass it in their urine!"

For tips on growing beets, see page 117.

A cupful of *Beta vulgaris,* family Chenopodiaceae—really a biennial herb—contains 28 International Units of vitamin A, 15 milligrams of vitamin C, 22 milligrams of calcium, 440 milligrams of potassium, as well as other vitamins and minerals.

By 1935 the good Countess Morphy had become adventurous. She served up *Salata* under a section called "Greece." "This," she said, "consists of uncooked shredded white cabbage, beets, beans, small black olives, and capers, with a dressing of 4 tablespoons of vinegar, 3 of oil, a little mustard, salt, and pepper, well mixed and poured over the salad."

Jean Ann's own NEW MAINE COOKING first offered this recipe.

Hot Beet Salad with Tarragon

SERVES 2–4

Cook enough beets to measure:
4 cups when sliced
When they're cool enough to handle, slip off the skins. Slice the still-hot beets into a hot bowl.

Add:
1/4 cup extra-virgin olive oil
2 teaspoons finely chopped
fresh tarragon
1/4 teaspoon maple syrup

Toss gently. Serve with potatoes, rice, big salads, and other vegetables.

THE NEW MAINE COOKING contains a recipe for pickled beets—which remains a splendid way of preserving that deep, ruby-red color and vitamin A. Due to their long, cylindrical shape, 'Formanovas' are perfect for this process, and because of the high acid content of vinegar, a plain hot-water bath will do for processing, rather than the more formidable pressure cooking.

J. A.'s Pickled Ruby-Red Beets

MAKES 2 QUARTS

Wash well and cook until barely tender:
enough beets to result in 8 cups of
1/4-inch-thick slices

Make a syrup of:
4 cups 5 percent cider vinegar
4 cups refined white sugar
Heat to boiling.

Place the cooked, sliced beets into clean, hot, widemouthed quart canning jars, leaving a bit more than 1/2 inch of headroom.

To each quart jar, add:
1 teaspoon canning OR kosher salt

Cover with the boiling syrup, leaving 1/2 inch of headroom. Remove air bubbles by poking gently into each jar along the sides with a chopstick.

Meanwhile, in a small pan of hot water, heat metal bands and lids to just under boiling. When they're hot, drop them into a sieve and drain.

Wipe off the rims of your beet-filled jars. Place the hot lids and bands on the jars, screwing the bands down tightly.

Place your hot, filled jars on a rack in a big pot of hot water. Add more hot water if necessary to come at least 1 inch above the jar tops. Cover, bring to a boil, and process in this boiling-water bath for 30 minutes. Measure the processing time from when a rolling boil begins.

When time is up, remove the jars with tongs and let them cool on a rack or towel-covered counter to prevent breakage.

Let the jars cool completely. Then remove the metal bands, check to see that each jar is safely sealed—the metal lid will feel slightly concave when you press it—rinse gently, wipe dry, and label. Store in a cool, dark place.

Another recipe for midwinter beets is equally pleasing and makes a tasty, hot dinner dish. The 'Lutz Greenleaf' variety produces superb keepers, so these are the beets of choice.

And do note: Leftovers can be whizzed in a blender with milk or cream plus a sprinkling of tarragon to make a thick, fuchsia-colored soup that's about as nonmonotonous as possible. Countess Morphy should have paid attention!

Baked Beets

SERVES 6

Preheat the oven to 350°F.

Peel and slice thinly:
4–5 large beets
Also slice thinly:
2–3 large onions

Lightly oil a lasagne dish and place in it a layer of sliced beets. Place a layer of onions over the beets. Sprinkle with:
a little sea salt
freshly ground black pepper
Repeat until all the beets and onions are used up.

Pour over the vegetables:
3/4 cup water OR seasoned
  Vegetable Stock (see page 43)
Drizzle with:
a little extra-virgin olive oil

Cover and bake for about 40 minutes, or till the beets are tender. Check by pricking with a fork.

Serve hot with mashed potatoes, greens, and other vegetables.

There are as many varieties of borscht as there are Russians. This recipe remains a favorite.

J. A.'s Midwinter Beet Stew

SERVES 6

Wash well, pop into a big pot, cover with water, and cook until tender (perhaps 45 minutes):
5 medium-sized beets

When the beets are fork-tender, place them in cold water until they're cool enough to handle, then slip off their skins. Dice enough to measure 1 quart.

Combine in a heavy-bottomed saucepan:
2 large onions, chopped
1 well-washed, unpeeled potato,
  cubed
1/2 head red cabbbage,
  finely shredded
2 cups stewed tomatoes
Simmer till the vegetables are tender and blended—at least an hour. Add water if necessary to maintain a consistency of your choosing.

When the vegetables are tender, add and heat thoroughly:
the cooked, diced beets
1 sprig dill weed
OR 1 teaspoon dill seeds
1 tablespoon soy flour
OR unbleached white flour
1 teaspoon sea salt (optional)
a lot of freshly ground black pepper
2 or more garlic cloves, minced

Serve in heated bowls with a dollop of thick yogurt or sour cream on top. Sprinkle with more freshly chopped dill.

Beet burgers are a surprising possibility. If your patty mixture is too wet, you can add rolled oats or more flour to dry it slightly.

Beet Burgers

SERVES 4–6

Wash well, peel, and grate to equal:
   2 scant cups grated beets
Do the same to equal:
   2 scant cups grated carrots
Peel and chop finely:
   1 medium-sized onion
Place all the vegetables in a big bowl.

Grind or chop to equal:
   1 cup finely chopped walnuts

In a big skillet, brown lightly:
   the chopped walnuts
   1/2 cup sesame seeds
Mix these into the beet-carrot mixture.

Add to the above and mix well:
   1 cup cooked basmati OR other rice
   1 cup grated Cheddar cheese

3–4 large garlic cloves, minced
1/4 cup finely and freshly
   chopped parsley

Using a fork, whip together in a small bowl:
   2 large eggs
   2 tablespoons shoyu
      (naturally fermented soy sauce)
   1/4 cup extra-virgin olive oil
Pour into the beet-carrot bowl. Add and mix well:
   3 tablespoons whole-wheat
      pastry flour
   freshly ground black pepper
   sea salt (optional)

In a big skillet over medium heat, warm:
   2–3 tablespoons olive oil
Form the beet mixture into 3-inch patties, or drop by heaping tablespoonfuls into the hot oil, and sauté until golden.

Serve on big buns with a tossed salad and cooked (possibly marinated) beans such as navy, black, or adzuki.

Celeriac

There are few references to celeriac in the literature. *Any* literature. At least in America.

In Europe, however, this member of the Umbelliferae family linked to parsnips *(Pastinaca sativa)*, carrots *(Daucus carota)*, and parsley *(Petroselinum crispum)* has long been revered. A curious little booklet called *The Healthy Life Cook Book,* published in London in 1915, says, "This is a large, hard white root, somewhat resembling a turnip in appearance, with a slight celery flavour. It is generally only stocked by 'high-class' greengrocers."

Which may be surprising, considering its history.

Bert Greene, in *Greene on Greens,* tells us that celery "in its wildest guise is a stubby, tough, fibrous weed that holds no possibilities whatsoever for any stockpot."

Early horticulturists, however, "bred two separate and distinct strains" from the original. Both "have proven the test of palatability for almost four thousand years."

Apium graveolens dulce is the crunchy green stalk with which we are familiar. *A. g. rapaceum* is the large, turniplike root with a slight celery flavor of which we are suspicious.

According to historians, both celery and celeriac were developed by the gardeners of Persia's King Cyrus the First around 2000 B.C. Ancient Egyptians, Greeks, and Romans considered celery a gift from the gods. Says Greene, "Egyptian physicians divided celery's medicinal properties sexually: the strong stalks that grew upward from the ground were judged to be a cure for all masculine dysfunctions from bed-wetting to impotence, while the hairy, tuberous root that swelled beneath the earth's surface was prescribed for female disorders."

Very interesting.

According to J. I. Rodale, the end of the 16th century saw celeriac being culti- vated for food by Europeans. And, says cookbook writer Marian Morash in her *Victory Garden Cookbook,* it used to be a fairly common vegetable in America. "The 1824 Beecher cookbook mentioned it, as did Mrs. Rorer in 1886. In those days, however, celeriac was invariably boiled up and then drenched in cream sauce."

By 1915 *The Healthy Life Cook Book* had a different inspiration. "It is nicest cut in slices and fried in fat or oil until a golden brown."

During World War II celeriac was widely cultivated in England because it was less trouble than regular celery, would grow in shallow soil, and could be stored for winter use.

It does fine in New England.

For tips on growing celeriac, see page 225.

Low in vitamin C, celeriac is "richest in calcium and phosphorus, providing 467 milligrams of calcium and 71 of phosphorus per 100 grams; 0.8 milligram of iron; 3 grams of protein; and a total of 38 calories." In half a cup. At least according to J. I. Rodale's 1967 calculations.

When meeting celeriac for the first time it's important to choose roots that are round, firm, and not withered. Be prepared for a lot of waste. A 1 3/4-pound giant, for instance, will produce only 6 cups of julienned strips after trimming.

Since, like apples, the pale inner flesh darkens on contact with air, slices should be dropped immediately into a mixture of cold water and lemon juice. Julienned strips about an inch long are perfect.

*The Simply Grande kitchen use slices
of celeriac in winter soups for a faint celery
taste, but we believe it's best eaten raw.*

Basic Celeriac Preparation

Scrub well, then cut off the hairy roots
and top of:

1 large celeriac

Cut off the outer skin as thinly as
possible, removing all blemishes.
Slice into fine julienned strips.

Place the strips in a bowl containing:

2 quarts cold water
freshly squeezed juice of 1/2 lemon

When you're ready to use celeriac in any
of the following recipes, remove it from
the bowl and pat dry.

---

*The combination of fall apples,
celeriac, and late-growing cilantro
is an amiable one.*

Apple Celeriac Salad in Mustard Sauce with Cilantro

SERVES 4

THE SAUCE

In a blender or a medium-sized bowl,
whisk well together:

3 tablespoons finely chopped onion
1 tablespoon Dijon mustard
1 scant teaspoon refined white sugar
1/2 cup sunflower seed oil
1/2 cup extra-virgin olive oil

**2 tablespoons basil-flavored
red wine vinegar**
sea salt to taste
freshly ground black pepper

COMBINING

In a large bowl, place:

**4 cups prepared julienned celeriac,
cut into 1-inch lengths**
**2 large apples, peeled, cored, and cut
into chunks**

Pour the vinaigrette over the celeriac
and apples. Chill for 1 hour (at least).

Add and mix lightly:

1/2 cup freshly chopped cilantro
1/4–1/2 cup thick yogurt
OR sour cream

SERVING

Place individual servings, drained, on a
bed of crisp lettuce or cooked, cooled
basmati rice.

NOTE: Sprinkling walnut halves or
pecans on top at the last minute is nice.

Cooked Celeriac with English Cream Sauce

SERVES 2

THE CELERIAC

Prepare and slice (see Basic Celeriac
Preparation at left) to equal 4 cups
julienned strips:

1 large celeriac

Into a large saucepan, pour:

1 tablespoon extra-virgin olive oil

Add and brown lightly:

1 tablespoon minced shallot
OR finely chopped onion

Add and simmer till tender—about 10 minutes:

the 4 cups drained celeriac strips
2 cups Vegetable Stock (see page 43)
OR water

Remove the celeriac from the liquid with a slotted spoon, place it in a serving bowl, and keep warm.

THE SAUCE

In a smaller saucepan, reheat the liquid and reduce it to 1/2 cup by boiling. Stir in:

1/4 cup heavy cream

Return to a boil and remove from the heat.

In a small bowl, lightly beat:

1 egg yolk

Very carefully mix 2 tablespoons of the hot cream mixture into the yolk. Then whisk the mixture into the remaining hot liquid. Cook, stirring constantly, until thick. Add:

sea salt to taste (optional)
freshly ground black pepper

SERVING

To serve, spoon the sauce over the warm celeriac. Sprinkle with:

a lot of chopped parsley

Offer pan-fried potatoes, a winter salad of broccoli and cauliflower, and greens.

Famous Céleri-rave Rémoulade, or "celery root in mustard sauce," is a fine way to present celeriac as an hors d'oeuvre.

Céleri-rave Rémoulade

SERVES 2–4

Dig or purchase:

1–2 celeriac roots (to measure about 1 pound)

Peel and cut into matchsticks to equal 3 to 3 1/2 cups.

Into a 2-quart bowl, pour:

1 1/2 teaspoons sea salt
1 1/2 teaspoons freshly squeezed lemon juice

Add and toss to cover (to prevent browning):

the celeriac matchsticks

Let rest for at least 30 minutes. Then rinse the celeriac in cold water, drain, dry in a towel, and set aside.

Whiz in a blender until smooth:

1/4 cup Dijon mustard
3 tablespoons boiling water
1/3–1/2 cup extra-virgin olive oil
2 tablespoons rice wine vinegar
sea salt to taste
freshly ground black pepper

Pour the sauce into a bowl and stir in:

the prepared celeriac root

Marinate for 2 to 3 hours.

Serve as an appetizer on a bed of:

washed, dried, and trimmed watercress

Turnips and Rutabagas

At the time of the American Revolution a soon-to-be famous English earl, Lord Thomas William Coke of Holkham, was developing the four-course system of agriculture in County Norfolk. Said many later admirers, it was due to his intelligent and dedicated attention to all things agricultural that England was saved from starvation when Napoleon came knocking at the door. He had, in fact, begun turning Norfolk into the breadbasket of the United Kingdom.

Coke was friendly to American interests. Parading in countryman's clothing to shock the royal court, he put forward the motion that independence be recognized. Carried by a majority of one in the House of Commons, the war was formally ended.

Americans, naturally, flocked to visit. Coke also traveled. From the Dutch he probably learned to grow turnips for cattle fodder in fields formerly left fallow. The resulting overwintering of cattle and sheep increased dairy products and meat; their droppings improved field fertility, which further increased crop productivity; and so it went. His huge estate, once agriculturally impoverished, became both agriculturally and financially wealthy.

New England colonists brought turnips to the New World with them. In 1634 William Wood described provisions to be taken for the sea journey, as well as "the quantity necessary to ensure enough food for a year and a half after landing." He added that "The ground afford very good kitchin Gardens, for Turneps . . . and whatever grows well in England."

In fact, turnips, parsnips, and carrots were considered "both bigger and sweeter than is ordinarily to be found in England," boasted Pastor Higginson of Salem, seconded by Governor William Bradford of the Plymouth Plantation, who also praised them.

The turnip and its sibling the rutabaga are members of the cabbage family. Rutabagas are thought to have resulted from a cross between a cabbage and a turnip made by Swiss botanist Gaspard Bauhin in the 17th century. "The birth was neither heralded nor honored," says Bert Greene in *Greene on Greens*, "but it should have been. For half the northern countries of the world live on rutabagas half of every year, and this vegetable, thriving in cool air, keeps the denizens of Scandinavian countries a heck of a lot healthier than they would be without its mineral-high presence." In fact, for centuries the rutabaga has been variously known in vegetable circles as Russian turnip, Canadian turnip, Bulgarian turnip, and Swedish turnip or swede.

"According to food pundits," Greene assures us, "the rutabaga did not arrive in the United States until 1806. How it came here no one seems to know for sure, but despite its northerly association in the Old World, its first official appearance in the new one was in a seed catalogue that advertised it as 'South of the Border Turnip'!"

Turnips themselves have a long history. According to evidence found in the caves at Choukoutien near Peking, Greene continues, "turnip was not merely eaten raw by its first consumers; it was roasted with meat (on flat stones in the fire) or wrapped up with fern ends or wild onions and steamed in flat wet leaves. . . . Several millennia later (as the cave paintings near the village of Aurignac, France, show) . . . they were boiled in watertight pots of clay."

Sumerians of the Fertile Crescent some 5,000 years ago enjoyed barley, wheat, and millet; chickpeas, lentils, and beans; onions, garlic, leeks; cucumbers; fresh green lettuce, cress, mustard, and—turnips.

When ancient Greeks and Romans inherited the vegetable, Greene says, "its kitchen status was so elevated that devotees literally held forums to theorize on the ideal culinary fabrication. In Rome (according to the *Pantropheon*) . . . optimum cookery took several hours and the roots were steamed successively with cumin, rue, and benzoin [a resin]; then pounded in a mortar with honey, vinegar, gravy, boiled grapes, . . . a little oil; and then simmered well before they were served."

Romans, naturally, introduced turnip cultivation into other parts of Europe. According to John Midgley's *The Goodness of Potatoes and Root Vegetables*, the latter "were grown by monks in their kitchen gardens throughout the Dark and early Middle Ages to provide sustenance through the 200 or so meatless days of the year and were a crucial part of the medieval and later European diet. Writing in 1719, a Monsieur Misson remarked upon the Englishman's passion for roast and boiled beef served with 'heaps of cabbage, carrots, turnips or some other herbs or roots, well peppered and salted, and swimming in butter'."

A cupful of rutabaga contains 64 calories, 3 International Units of vitamin A, 60 milligrams of vitamin C, 92 milligrams of calcium, 335 milligrams of potassium, and other vitamins and minerals. A cupful of turnip, with 39 calories, contains only a trace of vitamin A, 47 milligrams of vitamin C, 348 milligrams of potassium, and other nutrients.

Please note that Jean Carper, in *Food: Your Miracle Medicine*, reports rutabagas and turnips as gaseous. She suggests: "Add a little garlic and/or ginger. . . . Both are reputed in folk medicine to be antiflatulent."

Researchers at India's G. B. Pant University have recently pronounced the tradition of adding spices to legumes and vegetables to be based on "sound principles."

TURNIPS, RUTABAGAS, AND KOHLRABI

CHOOSING SEEDS: Few choices are available for any of these cabbage family root crops, all of which have swollen bases to the stem.

Turnip: White flesh, with delicious greens in spring. There are short-season and long-season varieties. The long-season kind are good for storage.

Rutabaga: Yellow flesh, gargantuan. 'Laurentian' seems to be the current favorite. They're good for storage.

Kohlrabi: The swollen base is suspended above ground level. Most are short season. One ('Gigante') is a late-season variety good for storage.

There are 9,000 seeds per ounce; 1/4 ounce will sow 100 row feet.

CULTIVATION: Sow outside in early spring for long-season varieties, and through midsummer for short-season types. Sow in rows 18 inches apart. Collineal-hoe as seedlings emerge. Thin in row to 3 or 4 inches apart. Keep rows weeded.

PESTS: All are susceptible to flea beetle and cabbage root maggot damage early in the season. Cover them completely with new floating row covers to keep the flying insects off. Sprinkle later, if necessary, with rotenone or pyrethrum.

HARVESTING:

Turnip: Thin the plants in the row by harvesting the leaves for a spring treat, as you would the more familiar beet greens. Leave the remaining roots at a spacing of 3 to 4 inches to grow big for summer or fall harvest and winter storage.

Rutabaga: Keep it growing as long as possible into early fall. Harvest the entire plant and cut off the root, and leaves from the stem, which provides a useful handle.

Kohlrabi: Pull it all: ball, leaf, and root. Chop off the root and leaves, and cut the ball into slices or chunks.

Because the rutabaga is slightly higher in nutritional value than the turnip, and because it's a reputed anticancer agent, this recipe combines it with that old favorite, the potato.

Rutabaga Potato Fluff
SERVES 4

Peel thinly and set aside:
1/2 pound potatoes

Cut into quarters or eighths and peel thinly:
1 pound rutabagas
Chop the rutabaga bits into potato-sized pieces and place them in a heavy pot along with:
1 1/2–2 cups water
Cover and bring to a boil for about 10 minutes.

Add the potatoes, return to a boil, then reduce the heat to a gentle simmer. Cook slowly for perhaps 45 minutes or until the vegetables are soft. Be careful not to burn them. If any water remains, pour it off.

Mash the potatoes and rutabagas thoroughly with a hand masher, adding:
2 tablespoons butter (optional)
1/4 cup milk OR cream
1–2 teaspoons maple syrup
plenty of freshly ground black pepper
freshly grated nutmeg
1 teaspoon (or more, depending on taste) powdered ginger
sea salt to taste

Serve in a warmed casserole dish with finely chopped fresh parsley sprinkled thickly on top. Quickly sautéed slices of marinated firm tofu or tempeh and a green leafy salad would complement it well.

Rutabagas and apples, which arrive in autumn at the same time, are lovely when combined with port. The resulting recipe produces tender but firm cubes of rutabaga in a port-flavored apple sauce.

Rutabaga, Apple, and Port
SERVES 4–6

Peel and cut into 1/2-inch cubes to measure 4 cups:
1 large rutabaga
Steam the cubes in a colander over boiling water until they're barely tender but still crisp (about 8 minutes).

Peel, core, and cut into small slices to measure 4 cups:
3 large, tart, winter-keeping apples
Dip the apple slices into freshly squeezed lemon juice to prevent browning and increase tartness.

Place the rutabaga and apples into a large stainless-steel skillet. Then add:
1/4 well-washed lemon rind grated
1/2 cup port
1 teaspoon caraway seeds
1/4 teaspoon sea salt
freshly grated nutmeg

Cover and steam until the apples are sauced and the port is reduced. It won't take long. Stir gently once or twice.

Serve as an elegant side dish to any meal.

NOTE: You may substitute potatoes for half the rutabaga.

Simply cooked is possibly the best way to enjoy this ancient root vegetable—as Thomas Jefferson advised. This recipe is based on Jefferson's.

Thomas Jefferson's Turnip

SERVES 4

Wash carefully:

1 turnip

Peel it, chop into medium-sized bits, and boil in a modicum of water until tender. Drain and mash well.

Add:

a little milk (optional)

Season with:

a walnut-sized bit of butter

sea salt to taste

freshly ground black OR white pepper OR a mix of black, white, and red

Return the turnip to medium heat and let it dry slightly. Then scoop it out onto a hot platter and serve immediately. Garnish with:

freshly chopped parsley

An intriguing addition would be:

a drizzle of freshly squeezed lemon juice

Oriental cuisine has always been fond of pickles. During the first century A.D., Gavius Apicius, man-about-town in Rome and ostentatious bon vivant, is reported to have preserved turnips with myrtle berries, honey, and vinegar. Here's a Chinese version.

Chinese Pickled Turnip and Carrots

Cut into small, bite-sized pieces and place in a bowl:

1 small white turnip

1/2 carrot

Add:

10 thin slices fresh gingerroot

1 red chili pepper, diced

1 red pepper, diced

4 teaspoons sea salt

Mix well and let stand for 6 hours.

Lightly rinse the vegetables, drain, and return them to the bowl. Add and mix well:

5 tablespoons refined white sugar

5 tablespoons apple cider vinegar

Let rest for 6 hours, refrigerated. Serve as a condiment.

The Near East also has a version of pickled turnips. These must be made 3 days before serving to assure that pickled taste.

Pickled Turnips and Beets

MAKES 2 QUARTS

Wash well:

2 1/2–3 pounds medium-sized white turnips

Slice off their tops and bottoms, and remove any brown spots. Cut into halves, if small, or into quarters if large. Place in a large bowl.

Sprinkle with:
 sea salt

Let stand for 6 to 8 hours at room temperature, draining off excess water frequently.

Wash well, pop into a big pot, cover with water, and cook till tender:
 2 pounds small whole beets

When they're fork-tender, place them in cold water until they're cool enough to handle, then slip off their skins.

Sterilize two widemouthed quart canning jars.

Place some turnip chunks in each jar and add to each one:
 2 beets
 several black peppercorns

In a small bowl, combine:
 1 1/2 cups lukewarm water
 1 1/2 cups distilled white vinegar
 2 teaspoons sea salt
Pour this liquid over the beets and turnips, leaving 1/2 inch of headroom at the top of the jars. Seal with plastic caps and set aside in a cool place for 3 days. Turn the jars upside down occasionally to disperse color.

Refrigerate on day 3. Serve with any meal, especially with pita bread (see page 273).

The Great Uncommon Common

Potato

S trictly speaking, root vegetables such as parsnips, beets, carrots, rutabagas, turnips, radishes, and celeriac are the swollen subterranean stems of plants from which leaves sprout. Each vegetable, therefore, is actually the root of a single plant.

Sweet potatoes, yams, taro, cassava, Jerusalem artichokes, and our common/uncommon potato (*Solanum tuberosum*), on the other hand, are defined as "underground structures consisting of a solid, thickened, rounded outgrowth of a stem or rhizome, bearing eyes or buds from which new plants may arise." As every good gardener knows, a single tuber can produce several plants.

Early humans were not unaware. "Even on the fringes of the American ice sheet," assures writer John Midgley in *The Goodness of Potatoes and Root Vegetables*, the forerunners of cassava, yams, and potatoes allowed early foragers to dig up nutritious food. The hardy potato, belonging to the same group of plants as nightshade, easily became an essential starchy staple. In Peru its hardiness at cold Andean altitudes made it the equivalent of corn, the "staple grown at lower levels by other Indian civilizations."

By 1530, when the Spanish conquistador Gonzalo Jiménez de Quesada arrived, Peruvian Indians had already been cultivating potatoes—called *papas*—since sometime between 3700 and 3000 B.C. Apparently small in size, they were mistaken by the intruders for a kind of truffle and called *tartuffo*—a name that persisted with variations in parts of Europe for some time.

According to food chronicler James Trager, potatoes arrived in Spain from Quito in 1539, Pedro de Cieza of the Pizarro expedition describing them as somewhat similar to chestnuts. But the first written reference appeared in a 1553 account called the *Chronica del Peru* by Pedro de Leon (Pedro Creca), published at Seville. There the potato was termed a *battata* as well as a *papa*.

Nomenclature is interesting if confusing. According to John Midgley, invading Europeans noted how Caribbean islanders relied on two tubers: "the cassava, from which a very durable bread was made, and the sweet potato, the tuber of a tropical convolvulus. The Spaniards adopted their word for the latter—batatas—and named the true potato after it when they first encountered specimens on reaching Peru."

Soon they were using the tubers as basic rations aboard ships. They also began cultivation at home. "Potatoes were introduced into Italy and other European countries from Spain, although Sir Francis Drake was responsible for their introduction to England, having acquired a consignment in the Colombian port of Cartagena," says Midgley.

Trager, on the other hand, reports that certain accounts name Sir John Hawkins as bringing the tuber to England. But, he adds, "the potato from Bogota may be a sweet potato."

At any rate, the spud was soon the starch of choice in many parts of the world, notably central and northern Europe, Russia, the British Isles, Ireland, and, of course, the United States. Its journey from South America to North America was roundabout. Sent to Spain by de la Vega or some other conquistador, the Peruvian vegetable had been shipped to Virginia in 1622 "included among a list of plants and seeds ordered shipped to Governor Endecott in 1628," according to historian Howard S. Russell in *A Long, Deep Furrow: Three Centuries of Farming in New England*. Nothing, however, seemed to come of it.

In Pennsylvania a rich merchant is said to have tried potatoes in his garden in or about 1685. And at a Harvard commencement in 1707 potatoes appeared on the menu, perhaps from Bermuda.

But the spud was truly introduced to North America by Scots-Irish settlers. The first potatoes "of historic consequence," says Russell, "arrived with five shiploads of families of Scottish blood from Londonderry, Ireland." Some of the immigrants, he says, spent the winter in Portland, Maine; a few settled permanently at Cape Elizabeth and about Casco Bay. "Sixteen families were granted land in the Merrimack Valley in southern N.H., and on April 11, 1719, began a settlement there now called Londonderry. The next year, 1720, more came to settle on the

Maine coast. They planted potatoes at Wells, while others sat down about the mouth of the Kennebec."

According to another Maine historian, Clarence Day, by 1718 German and Huguenot settlers were arriving; the Scots-Irish came that fall. Some of them stayed in and about Falmouth, settling principally at Cape Elizabeth, but most went to New Hampshire the following summer, where they founded Londonderry. That state's historian is explicit: They "introduced the culture of potatoes which were first planted in the garden of Nathaniel Walker of Andover."

Says Clarence Day, "ever since known as Irish potatoes," spuds were "but little regarded" by the English. "One of the immigrants gave some seed potatoes to an English neighbor, who planted them and then waited for them to set balls which he thought were the edible parts. These potato balls the good wife tried to cook in various ways but gave up in disgust. Not until the garden was plowed the following spring were the tubers found."

As in Ireland, potatoes quickly became a staple in Maine. In fact, Maine long produced more potatoes for both human and livestock consumption than all its grain crops combined, reports Clarence Day.

But in 1845 a succession of crop failures throughout Europe caused by wind-borne spores of the potato blight fungus exacerbated by a particularly cold, wet summer destroyed three-quarters of the European potato crop, killing more than a quarter million people in the great Irish Potato Famine and setting off waves of emigration to America. Maine, too, experienced problems.

Wrote the Reverend Samuel Deane in *The New England Farmer,* "No longer than about the year 1740, we had but one sort, a small reddish colored potato, of so rank a taste that it was scarcely eatable. Soon after this the white kidney potato appeared, as good table potatoes as I have known since; unless the red rough coated potato be excepted, which was introduced soon after. Since then we have had the Spanish potato, extremely prolific, but fit only for cattle and swine: Then the bunker potato; the small round potato, white and good tasted: A long red potato: A potato part red and part white, brought from Ireland in the late war: A large white potato, a great bearer, known by the name of the flour potato: Orange potato, so called from its color: Purple potato: Cranberry potato: and winter white. The last is as pleasant tasted as any that is cultivated, and exceeded by none, unless it be the yellow rough coat."

By 1840 "The most prolific variety was the Long Red, also known as La Plata, Spanish, and Merino. It was grown chiefly as feed for livestock, although it was a good table potato late in the spring. The principal potato grown for the home table and for market was the Chenango, known also as Philadelphia and Mercer." It was "somewhat earlier than the common orange potato that it replaced." "Other varieties from about 1840 were the Pink Eye, Christie, Cowhorn, Irish Buckster, Perkins Early, Quoddy Blue, White Bluenose, and Peachblow."

POTATOES

CHOOSING SEEDS: Potatoes do have seeds, but you won't be buying them. Instead, buy bags of "seed potatoes." There are hundreds of varieties available in the United States. Most have white flesh; some have yellow, blue, or pink. Most have brown skins; others are pink, purple, blue, or speckled. Some are big, some small; some oval, some fingerling; some early, some late. Try a variety. If your soil is alkaline (with a pH higher than 7), choose varieties that are scab resistant.

Twenty-five pounds will plant about 200 row feet and produce 100 to 300 pounds, depending on the variety.

CULTIVATION: Ideally, the soil should be slightly acidic, light, and well drained. But potatoes grow in almost any soil. Prepare by rototilling. Do not add manure the same year that potatoes are grown. You can plant anytime from after the last frost till mid-July.

A day or two before planting, cut the seed potatoes so that each piece is about the weight of a large egg, and has at least one "eye" (bud) on it. There are three ways to grow potatoes:

1. Dig trenches 6 to 8 inches deep and 3 feet apart. Lay the potatoes in the bottom of the trench 9 or 10 inches apart and cover with compost or soil. When shoots appear, hoe soil into the trench to make the ground level. Two to 3 weeks later, hill the soil high over the trench from the area between rows. Irrigate to prevent scab and to increase the harvest.

2. Lay the cut seed potatoes on the ground. Cover with 6 to 12 inches of hay or other organic mulch. When shoots emerge, hill with more mulch.

3. Lay a sheet of 6-mil black plastic over the tilled bed. With a posthole digger, cut holes through at 12-inch spacing in rows 24 inches apart. Lift out 4 inches of soil and pop the potato into the hole. Drop the soil back down. These last two methods require no weeding or irrigation.

PESTS AND DISEASES: The Colorado potato beetle (CPB) is the worst pest. Walk along the rows, knocking them off the plants into a can. Then you can either drown or squish them. Repeat every few days for 4 weeks. Their orange eggs—left on the undersides of some leaves—will hatch into soft brown bugs that will eat your potato plants bare. Either knock them off into a can to share the fate of their parents or spray them with Bt, a bacterial insecticide, mixed with 5 percent rotenone to get the larger larvae and adults.

To prevent virus buildup, rotate potato plantings with other crops (but not peppers, tomatoes, or eggplant, which are all members of the same family).

HARVESTING: Once plants have blossomed, you can reach carefully under the soil (or mulch or plastic) for new potatoes. If you're careful, the plant will survive to grow the rest bigger.

For mature harvest, wait until the plants die back. Choose a cool, dry day and dig carefully with a fork, or pull back the mulch or plastic to expose the "nests" of potatoes. Lift them and leave them to dry for a few hours—or, if your soil is muddy, take them for a hosing, then dry them. Discard green ones. Pick out scabby or damaged potatoes to eat first. The rest are ready for storage.

But "The long Reds and the Chenangoes were the lords of the potato field," according to a Mr. Holmes in the 1828 issues of *The New England Farmer and Mechanics Journal*. "Varieties grown to some extent in 1860 were the Carter, Cowhorn, Christie, Bearse, and Butman."

Blight today is still a possibility. Potato choices have narrowed. But some old-time favorites remain—'Kennebec', 'Green Mountain', 'Norland'—along with newer, often colorful arrivals.

Starch, an essential component of the human diet, is present in most traditional cuisines around the world. Throughout Asia it historically comes in the form of rice. In the Americas it's corn. In the Mediterranean and Middle East it's wheat, often shaped into bread. In the many tropical countries of both hemispheres tubers like yams, sweet potatoes, and casava take over.

Potatoes have become a starchy staple of North America. A cupful, minus the skin, contains 114 calories and 117 milligrams of calcium. Rich in vitamin C (30 milligrams), they're also high in potassium (611 milligrams), which is concentrated in and around the skins (782 milligrams with the skin left on). They're an excellent source of fiber. Potatos also contain antioxidant properties that may be important in cancer prevention.

And spuds are extremely versatile. "The hundreds of potato varieties are classified as either 'new' or 'main crop,'" according to John Midgley. "The former are harvested while the leaves are still green and are smaller and sweeter with very thin, flaky skins." These, and later varieties such as 'Caribe', are waxy and perfect for salads where it's necessary to retain form. Others are mealy and wonderful for mashing. Still others are big and round for baking. There are even tiny varieties called fingerlings. Needless to say, with fingerlings especially, it's useless to try peeling. In fact, since most of a potato's nutrients lie just under the skin, it's important not to peel before cooking.

Simply cooked potatoes are best, either boiled or baked. This is a classic version.

Baked Potatoes

Preheat the oven to 400° to 450°F.

Scrub well:

1 large 'Kennebec' OR 'Russet Burbank' potato per person

Place on the middle shelf of the oven and bake for 20 minutes. Pierce with a fork to prevent explosions! Then bake until tender, perhaps 40 minutes in all. Cooking time depends on potato size and variety.

To serve, cut a cross in the top. Squeeze the sides to push up the flesh. Spoon on sour cream if you're not counting calories, low-fat yogurt if you are. Sprinkle with any of the following:

**chopped red onion
OR chives
minced raw broccoli with
    freshly grated Cheddar cheese
finely chopped fresh herbs such as
    parsley, cilantro, or dill weed
freshly grated Parmesan cheese
chopped hard-boiled egg and hot
    pepper
finely chopped green bell pepper and
    bits of a small, red, seeded tomato**

Twice-baked potatoes are a favorite.

Baked Stuffed Potatoes

Bake large, mealy potatoes at left.

When they're cool enough to handle, cut each potato in half lengthwise. Scoop the flesh into a warm bowl, leaving the half skins whole.

Blend the flesh with:

**grated extra-sharp Cheddar cheese
a little yogurt
chopped chives (optional but lovely)
some freshly ground black pepper
sea salt (optional)**

When the mixture is smooth, heap it back into the skins. Sprinkle with:

freshly grated Parmesan cheese

Pop back into the oven and bake till browned on top, perhaps 20 minutes.

Potato skins are not only nutritious; they're tasty.

Potato Skins

Bake large potatoes as above.

When they're tender, cut each potato in half lengthwise and scoop out the insides, leaving 3/8 inch of flesh on the skin all around.

Cut the skins into strips. Top each strip with grated extra-sharp Cheddar cheese. Sprinkle with a little olive oil.

Place about 6 inches beneath broiler coils, and broil till the cheese is melted and the skin is getting crisp.

French fries are surely one of the most popular ways to enjoy potatoes. They can be oven-fried rather than deep-fried.

Oven Fries

Preheat the oven to 450°F.

Peel and cut lengthwise into 3/8-inch-wide strips:

4–5 medium-sized potatoes

Drop the strips into a big bowl of cold water and add:

juice of 1/2 lemon

Let rest for 10 minutes. Drain and pat dry on a towel.

Toss with:

2 tablespoons extra-virgin olive oil
OR sunflower seed oil

Spread on a cookie sheet and bake at 450°F, turning several times with a spatula, until golden—30 to 40 minutes, depending on the type of potato. Drain briefly on paper towels.

Scoop the fries onto a platter and sprinkle with:

1/2 teaspoon sea salt

A sprinkling of freshly chopped parsley or cilantro is always beneficial.

With all the potato varieties out there, and with an artist's palette of colors to choose from, blue soup is naturally on the menu. The midseason 'All Blue', with its dark purple skin and bright purple flesh, is the variety of choice.

All Blue Potato Soup

SERVES 6

Dig from the garden or purchase:

6–8 medium-sized blue potatoes
(about 2 pounds)

Wash well and cut into cubes.

In a large pot, bring to a boil:

6 cups savory Vegetable Stock
(see page 43)

Add the potato cubes. When the stock begins to boil again, reduce the heat, cover, and simmer till the potatoes are soft—30 to 40 minutes.

In a small skillet, heat:

1 tablespoon extra-virgin olive oil

Add:

1/2 cup diced celery
1/2 cup finely chopped onion
1 large garlic clove, minced

Sauté over medium heat till the onion is translucent and the celery is tender. Remove from the heat and set aside.

Whiz the cooked potatoes in a blender for a few moments until smooth and thick. Return them to the pot, add the onion-celery mix, and simmer for 10 minutes more, or until heated through.

Add:

1/2 teaspoon sea salt (optional)
freshly ground multicolored pepper
1 tablespoon freshly chopped parsley

Adjust to taste.

Serve in warm bowls garnished with:

1 tablespoon yogurt per bowl
some freshly chopped chervil
(optional)

Fresh rolls and a green leafy salad are perfect accompaniments.

Dried Beans

During a New England winter, dried beans come into their own. Easily stored, they've been a staple since migrating peoples, spreading south and eastward after crossing the Bering Strait, discovered them growing in Central America and, it is supposed, carried them northeast to our rockbound coast and Atlantic provinces. Jared Diamond suggests they arrived sometime around A.D. 1000.

One bit of evidence comes from Roger Williams, who "talked farming with his Indian friends in Rhode Island," as reported by Howard S. Russell in *A Long, Deep Furrow: Three Centuries of Farming in New England.* Native Americans told him that in the beginning the crow had brought their ancestors "a graine of corne in one Eare, and an Indian or French Beane in another from the great God Kantantowit's field in the Southwest, from whence come all their Corne and Beanes."

Migrations of people all over the continents of North and South America occurred thousands of years before Spanish conquistadores came to plunder. But as Benjamin Watson puts it, "So ubiquitous is the cultivation of beans around the world today that it comes as something of a surprise to realize that the common or kidney bean, *Phaseolus vulgaris,* was not 'discovered' by Europeans until the time of Columbus. Common, lima, runner, and tepary beans, all members of the large genus *Phaseolus,* are all native to the Americas." In fact, "The oldest archaeological evidence of common beans comes from Tehuacan in Mexico, where radiocarbon dating suggests they were grown as early as 7000 B.C." The latest dating methods, according to Jared Diamond, of course, bring the date forward to about 3500 B.C.

But almost certainly "ancient farmers harvested and consumed dried beans, not only because the 'stringless' bean had not yet been developed, but because dried beans could be stored and used over an extended period of time as an excellent and nutritious food."

It's this dry, mature stage that makes the bean so fascinating to seed savers and collectors. Four main color groups—white, black, red, and brown—form the basic background for the seed coat, or testa, says Watson. "But all sorts of complex patterns and markings, from streaks to splotches to rings around the hilium, or 'eye,' of the bean, distinguish many heirloom varieties from one another and make them living works of art."

Closer to us in time and place, Governor William Bradford of Plymouth Plantation (as recorded in *A Descriptive and Historical Account of New England in Verse,* a manuscript found in his letter book) recounted another migration of vegetable-carrying peoples—that from the Old World, which mentioned crops that could be grown in the New:

All sorts of grain which in our land doth yield

Was higher brought, and sown in every field;
as wheat and rye, barley, oats, beans and pease.

We're talking, of course, about Pilgrims and Puritans. As Clarence Day put it in *A History of Maine Agriculture, 1604–1860,* "The first permanent [European] settlers had gardens and tiny patches of corn and small grains that they cultivated entirely by hand." Planted among the corn, naturally, were beans—just as their Native American friends had taught them. The French explorer Samuel de Champlain observed "Indian corn which they raise in gardens. Planting three or four kernels in one place, they then heap up about it a quantity of earth with the shells of the signoc (or horseshoe crab). . . . Then three feet distant they plant as much more, and thus in succession. With this corn they put in each hill three or four Brazilian beans which are of different colors. When they grow up they interlace with the corn."

"Among the Iroquois and Shawnee," writes Professor David Tucker in *Kitchen Gardening in America,* "women gardened together as a group." In every seventh hill of corn, climbing beans of two main species—lima and common—were later added. Included "were the kidney of Andean origin and the navy, black, red, and pinto of Mesoamerica."

Howard Russell reveals that, although corn was the main food adopted by Europeans from Native Americans, a second food "was beans cooked soft in pork or beef pot liquor . . . and eaten hot or allowed to jell. . . . Beans boiled with corn kernels into Indian succotash made a popular combination." It was intelligent thinking: Corn and beans produce a protein as complete as that of meat by combining amino acids.

Tucker says that probate court records reveal "that Indian beans had replaced the English pea in food storage and therefore probably in the supper dish" by the early 18th century.

By 1820 farming operations in New England were incredibly self-sufficient, as exemplified by that of Major Hannibal Hamlin of Waterford, Maine. "We changed into money, at Portland, chiefly butter, cheese, a fatted hog, oats, beans, and nothing else that I can think of."

For tips on growing beans, see page 134.

Dried beans, as all early Americans understood, are storehouses of nutrients. A cupful of cooked red kidney beans, for instance, contains 14.4 grams of protein, 10 International Units of vitamin A, 70 milligrams of calcium, 629 milligrams of potassium, vitamins B_1 and B_2, as well as other nutrients. Black beans contain 44.6 grams of protein in a cupful, along with 60 International Units of vitamin A, 270 milligrams of calcium, 2,076 milligrams of potassium, and some of the B and other vitamins. One cupful of cooked navy beans contains 14.8 grams of protein,

95 milligrams of calcium, 790 milligrams of potassium, 281 milligrams of phosphorus, 1.8 milligrams of zinc, and additional nutrients.

Not only that, Jean Carper reports, but black beans, kidney beans, pinto beans, navy and white beans, black-eyed peas, garbanzos, and many other beans may produce the following benefits: "A cup of cooked dried beans every day . . . should send your bad LDL cholesterol down, control insulin and blood sugar, lower blood pressure—and keep you regular and your intestinal tract functioning in ways that may prevent gastrointestinal troubles like hemorrhoids and possibly bowel cancer."

Baked beans, so common on Saturday-nights all over New England, continue to please and satisfy. Here's a version made with handsome yellow eyes and maple syrup.

Saturday-Night Baked Beans with Maple Syrup

FRIDAY NIGHT

Pick over carefully, and remove any stones from:

3 cups yellow eye dried beans

Rinse, then soak overnight in a big bowl with about three times as much water.

SATURDAY MORNING

Discard the soaking water, then place the hydrated beans into a big pot with just enough fresh water to barely cover them. Bring to a boil. Reduce the heat and simmer till the skins begin to peel when you blow on them. When they're ready, drain, and pour them into a large, ceramic bean pot. Add:

1 medium-sized onion, sliced thin
2 medium-sized, tart winter apples, cored and sliced, OR a handful of dried apple slices
a lot of freshly ground black pepper
1 heaping teaspoon dry mustard
1 heaping teaspoon powdered ginger
1/2 cup maple syrup
1/4 cup extra-virgin olive oil (optional)
enough boiling water to barely cover

BAKING

Place in a preheated 300°F oven and bake all day, adding hot water as necessary to keep the beans covered but not swimming.

SERVING

Serve with coleslaw and steamed brown bread.

NOTE 1: Don't add salt to cooking beans. Salt toughens the skins. Add salt only when the beans are as thoroughly cooked as you want them to be.

NOTE 2: Yellow eyes cook much faster than red kidney beans. And "new" beans—that is, from last summer's crop—cook faster than "old" ones.

Certain varieties of black beans can be grown in the North Country. They cook quickly and make delicious soups. Black turtle is a very old variety originally from South America. Although it wants 85 to 105 days for maturity, resulting in worried New England farmers, the soup it produces must not be missed.

Black Bean Soup

SERVES 6–8

THE DAY BEFORE

Pick over carefully, removing any leftover stones or mud from:

2 pounds black beans

Rinse well and place in a large bowl. Cover with cold water, add 3 inches more, and let the beans soak overnight.

COOKING DAY

Drain the beans, rinse, and set aside. Into a large pot over low heat, pour:

1/4 cup extra-virgin olive oil

Heat the oil and add:

3 cups chopped onions

Using the broad blade of a knife, smash:

8–10 garlic cloves

Remove the skins and add to the onions. Cook until the onions are just wilted. Then add:

the soaked, drained beans
5 quarts water
2 tablespoons powdered cumin
1 tablespoon crumbled dried oregano
2 bay leaves
1 tablespoon freshly ground
    black pepper
a few hot pepper seeds
OR 1/8 teaspoon cayenne powder
3 tablespoons freshly chopped
    cilantro
3 tablespoons freshly chopped parsley

Bring the mixture to a boil, then reduce the heat and simmer, uncovered, till the beans are very tender—about 2 hours. The liquid should be reduced by about three-quarters. Stir in:

3 tablespoons freshly chopped parsley
3 tablespoons freshly chopped
    cilantro
1 1/2 teaspoons sea salt
2 red bell peppers, chopped
1 medium-sized carrot, diced
1/4 cup dry sherry (optional)
1 tablespoon dark brown maple syrup
1 tablespoon freshly squeezed
    lemon juice

Simmer for another 30 minutes.

SERVING

Serve with a dollop of yogurt or sour cream in each bowl, and garnish with:

freshly chopped cilantro

Fresh rolls and a big green salad are always necessary with soups!

Dried beans come in hundreds of varieties and colors. Simmered on top of the stove with herbs and garlic till just tender, they can be served hot with grains from rice to barley (producing a complete protein); cold sprinkled on any green leafy salad; or simply as a tasty side dish with potatoes, pasta, and other vegetables.

Cooked this way, they're also ready for later use in soups, loaves, or any other dish such as Succotash (see page 207).

Note that 1 cup of dry beans yields about 2 cups of cooked, depending on the bean. For this recipe, use red kidney, white navy, black, pinto, or cranberry.

To hydrate the beans without soaking them overnight, use the quick boiling-water method described below.

Stovetop Beans

SERVES 4

PREPARATION

Sort carefully by pouring from hand to hand, removing any little stones, dirt lumps, and moldy or imperfect beans from:

**2 cups beans of your choice
(see above)**

Wash them well and drain in a colander. In a large pot, bring to a boil:

6 cups water

Pour the beans into the rapidly boiling water without stopping the boil. Cook for 2 minutes. Remove them from the heat, cover, and allow the beans to soak for 2 hours before proceeding.

COOKING

Drain the beans. Pour them into a heavy pot with:

**enough boiling water to cover
2–3 garlic cloves, minced**

**1 small onion, chopped
2 bay leaves
2 teaspoons freshly chopped oregano
OR 1 teaspoon crumbled dried
   oregano
1 teaspoon dried basil, crumbled
1 teaspoon dried thyme
1/2 teaspoon cayenne powder
   (optional)
a lot of freshly ground black pepper
1 teaspoon sea salt (optional)**

Simmer till the beans are tender, 2 to 3 hours. Add more hot water as necessary, and keep it level with the beans. When the beans are tender, remove the cover and let the liquid simmer till it's thick and reduced by half.

STORING

Store, covered, in the refrigerator.

SERVING

Serve hot or cold as a side dish, in loaves and burgers, or mashed as refried beans in tacos, burritos, and enchiladas.

Perhaps the best thing about cooked beans is the variety of transformations possible with them. Burgers might be the easiest and, arguably, the tastiest.

Bean Burgers

MAKES 10

In a nonaluminum meat grinder, grind through the fine cutter:

**2 cups leftover cooked, well-drained
   beans
1 cup leftover cooked rice OR barley
1 large onion**

In a large bowl, mix together:

**the bean-grain-onion combo
3 garlic cloves, minced**

1 teaspoon sea salt
freshly ground black pepper
1 teaspoon dried thyme
1 teaspoon crumbled dried oregano
1 teaspoon crumbled dried basil
1 tablespoon nutritional yeast
(optional)

Add to bind it all together:
1 lightly beaten large egg

The consistency should be similar to that of meat burgers. If it's too dry, add some olive oil. If it's too wet, add some wheat germ, and/or rolled oats, and/or sunflower seeds whizzed in a blender until powdered.

Form into patties and pan-fry over moderate heat, using sunflower seed oil, until both sides are dark and crisp, the inside remaining rather soft.

Serve on light buns (below) piled with lettuce or alfalfa sprouts, a slice of mild onion, a slice of tomato, strips of bell pepper, a slice of cheese, and anything else to make it complete.

Burgers naturally need buns. And because beans are "heavy," the buns need to be light. This recipe originally appeared in Jean Ann's NEW MAINE COOKING.

Bean Burger Buns

MAKES 12

In a 2-cup measuring cup, soften together:
1/4 cup warm water
1 tablespoon dry baking yeast
1 teaspoon maple syrup

When the yeast bubbles, add:
1 egg, lightly beaten
1/4 cup extra-virgin olive oil
3/4 cup milk

Pour into a large bowl and add:
3 cups whole-wheat bread flour
1 teaspoon vitamin C powder
(optional)
1 tablespoon nutritional yeast powder
(optional)

The result will be a ball of rather sticky dough.

Turn the dough out onto a lightly floured board, grease your hands with butter, and knead until the dough is smooth and elastic—perhaps 5 minutes.

Shape into flat, round buns 3 inches in diameter by doing the following: Roll the dough into a 10-inch "sausage." Slice down the middle lengthwise to produce two "sausages." Slice across each thin "sausage" five times to make 12 pieces. Form into balls by holding the dough in your fingertips and pulling it down from topside to underside. This results in a smooth top and a bottom that's rather puckered and uneven. Flatten each ball with your palm.

Place each ball, seam-side down, onto a large, greased cookie sheet, allowing space between each. Brush the tops with cold water. Sprinkle with:
sesame seeds

Cover with a damp cloth and set in a warm place to rise until doubled—30 minutes to 1 hour.

Preheat the oven to 375°F. When the buns have risen, place them in the oven and bake for 15 to 20 minutes, till they're browned and crusty.

Use immediately, or store the buns in a bread box or ventilated plastic bag.

*Mexico, original home of Phaseolus,
has produced some of the world's
tastiest, most nutritious food.
Burritos are a prime example.
Flour tortillas stuffed with refried
beans are superb, and of themselves
provide complete protein.*

*Refried beans, usually heated with
animal fat, can be heated with extra-
virgin olive oil and are just as tasty.
Quick-cooking pinto beans are perfect
for this recipe.*

Bean Burritos

MAKES 8

Preheat the oven to 200°F.

THE REFRIED BEANS

Into a large, heavy, iron skillet, pour:

3 tablespoons extra-virgin olive oil

Heat and add:

1 cup finely chopped onion
2–3 big garlic cloves, minced

Sauté until tender. Add:

1–2 teaspoons sea salt (optional)
**4 cups cooked beans (as in Stovetop
Beans, page 328)**

Mash with a potato masher and cook
over low heat, stirring frequently, for
perhaps 10 minutes or until rather dry.
Remove from the heat.

THE BURRITOS

Lay out:

8 9-inch flour tortillas

On the center of each tortilla, place:

2/3 cup of the refried beans
1 tablespoon finely chopped onion

Sprinkle over:

1/2 teaspoon taco sauce
OR Hot Tomatillo Salsa (see page 230)
**1 1/2 teaspoons grated extra-sharp
Cheddar cheese**

ASSEMBLING

Fold the stuffed tortillas into oblongs
and place them on an ungreased cookie
pan, seam-side down. Heat for 15 to 20
minutes in your 200°F oven, or until the
cheese is melted.

SERVING

Spoon additional taco sauce on top
of the burritos if you please. Hot
Tomatillo Salsa would be excellent. A
big green leafy salad will complete your
enjoyment

BIBLIOGRAPHY

PLEASE NOTE: Nutritional information was obtained from the following sources:

Brody, Jane. *Jane Brody's Good Food Book: Living the High-Carbohydrate Way*. New York: W. W. Norton, 1985.

Carper, Jean. *Food: Your Miracle Medicine*. New York: HarperCollins, 1993.

———. *The Food Pharmacy*. New York: Bantam Books, 1988.

Dunne, Lavon J. *Nutrition Almanac*, 3rd ed. New York: McGraw Hill, 1990.

McGee, Harold. *On Food and Cooking: The Science and Lore of the Kitchen*. New York: Charles Scribner's Sons, 1984.

Rodale, J. I., ed. *How to Grow Vegetables and Fruits by the Organic Method*. Emmaus, Penn.: Rodale Books, 1961.

Weiss, Suzanne E., ed. *Foods That Harm, Foods That Heal*. Pleasantville, N.Y.: Reader's Digest, 1997.

American Farmer and Gardener, Sept. 6, 1836.

Angier, Bradford. *Feasting Free on Wild Edibles*. Harrisburg, Penn.: Stackpole Books, 1972.

Angier, Natalie. *Woman: An Intimate Geography*. New York: Anchor Books, 2000.

Apicius. *The Roman Cookery Book*, trans. by Barbara Flower and Elisabeth Rosenbaum. London: Peter Nevill, Ltd., 1958.

———. *Ars Magirica*, Book 3.

Audiger. *La maison réglée*. Paris, 1692.

Belknap, Jeremy. *History of New Hampshire*, vol. 2.

The Ball Company's *Blue Book: Guide to Home Canning, Freezing, and Dehydration*. Alltrista Corporation (Consumer Products Company, Dept. PK40, P.O. Box 2005, Muncie, IN 47307-0005).

Baxter, James P. *Sir Ferdinando Gorges and His Province of Maine*, vol. 2. Boston, 1890.

Botanica: The Illustrated A–Z of Over 10,000 Garden Plants for Asian Gardens and How to Cultivate Them. Introduced by William Warren. 2nd ed. Singapore: Periplus Editions, 1998.

Bradford, Governor William. *A Descriptive and Historical Account of New England in Verse*. Boston Historical Society.

Bremness, Lesley. ed. *Herbs*. Pleasantville, N.Y.: Reader's Digest, 1990.

Brown, William E. "A Guide to Growing Potatoes." *Kitchen Garden* 18, Jan. 1999.

Burr, Fearing, Jr. *Field and Garden Vegetables of America*. 1863. Reprint Chillicothe, Ill.: The American Botanist, Booksellers, 1994.

Callery, Emma. *The Complete Book of Herbs: A Practical Guide to Cultivating, Drying, and Cooking with More Than 50 Herbs*. Pennsylvania: Courage Books, 1994.

Campbell, Susan. *Charleston Kedding: A History of Kitchen Gardening*. London: Ebury Press, 1996.

Champlain, Samuel de. *Voyages, 1613*, trans. by H. H. Langhton and W. F. Ganong. In H. P. Biggar, ed., *Works of Samuel de Champlain*, vol. 1. Toronto: Champlain Society, 1929.

Culinary Herbs. A Plants and Gardens Handbook. *Brooklyn Botanic Garden Record* 38, no. 2, 1988.

Culpeper, Nicholas. *The English Physitian Enlarged.* London: George Sawbridge, 1681.

Daniel, Florence. *The Healthy Life Cookbook.* London: C. W. Daniel, Ltd., 1915.

Day, Clarence Albert. *A History of Maine Agriculture 1604–1860.* University of Maine Studies, Second Series, no. 68. Orono, Maine: University Press, 1954.

Deane, Reverend Samuel. *The New England Farmer, or Georgical Dictionary.* Worcester, Mass., 1790.

DeSoto, Hernando. *The Discovery and Conquest of Terra Florida,* trans. by Luis Hernandez de Beidma (London: Hakluyt Society, 1851). In *Sturtevant's Edible Plants.*

DeVore, Sally, and Thelma White. *Appetites of Man.* New York: Anchor Books, 1978.

Diamond, Jared. *Guns, Germs, and Steel: The Fates of Human Societies.* New York: W. W. Norton, 1999.

Downing, Pat. *The Fruits and Fruit Trees of America.*

Duncan, Wilbur Howard, and Foote, Leonard E. *Wildflowers of the Southeastrn United States.* University of Georgia Press, 1975.

Evelyn, John. *Kalendarium Hortense.* London, 1666.

———. *Acetaria: A Discourse of Sallets.* London, 1699.

———. *The Compleat Gardner. By the famous Monsr. De La Quintinye, Chief director of all the Gardens of the French King . . . Made English by John Evelyn Esquire.* London, 1699.

Faust, Clifford M. *Rhubarb: The Wondrous Drug.* Princeton, N.J.: Princeton University Press, 1992.

Fedco Seeds, Co-op Seed Packers, catalog (P.O. Box 520, Waterville, ME) Begun by C. R. Lawn, 1978.

Foley, Daniel J., ed. *Herbs for Use and for Delight: An Anthology from The Herbalist.* A publication of the Herb Society of America. New York: Dover Publications, 1974.

Fox, Nicols. *Spoiled: The Dangerous Truth about a Food Chain Gone Haywire.* New York: Basic Books, 1997.

Gerard, John. *The Herball, or general historie of plantes.* London, 1597.

Gibbon, Euell. "Euell Gibbon's Dill Crock." *Organic Gardening and Farming.*

Grant, Anne. *Memoirs of an American Lady,* vol. 1. London: Longman, 1808.

Greene, Bert. *Greene on Greens.* New York: Workman Publishing, 1984.

Hamlin, Cyrus. *My Life and Times,* 5th ed. Boston.

Harrington, Geri. *Grow Your Own Chinese Vegetables.* Pownal, Vt.: Garden Way Publishing, 1978.

Hatfield, Audrey Wynne. *How to Enjoy Your Weeds.* London: Frederick Muller, Ltd., 1969.

Hedrick, U. P., ed. *Sturtevant's Edible Plants of the World.* New York: Dover Publications, 1972.

Heiser, Charles B., Jr. *Seed to Civilization: The Story of Food.* Cambridge, Mass.: Harvard University Press, 1990.

Herbrandsan, Dec. *Shaker Herbs and their Medicinal Uses.* Albany, N.Y. Shaker Heritage Society, 1985.

Higginson, I. *New England's Plantation, or a Short and True Description of the Commodities and Discommodities of that Countrye, Written by a reverend Divine now there resident.* 1630.

Hopper, Vincent F. *Chaucer's Canterbury Tales (Selected).* Brooklyn, N.Y.: Barron's Educational Series, 1948.

Hupping, Carol, and the staff of the Rodale Food Center. *Stocking Up,* 3rd ed. New York: Simon and Schuster, 1990.

Hyll, Thomas. *The Gardener's Labyrinth.* 1577.

Imlay, G. *A Topographical Description of the Western Territory of North America.* London: Debrett, 1792.

Thomas Jefferson: The Garden and Farm Books, ed. by Robert C. Baron. Golden, Colo.: Fulcrum, 1987.

Thomas Jefferson's Garden Book, 1766–1824, with Relevant Extracts from His Other Writings, ed. by Edwin Morris Betts. Philadelphia: The American Philosophical Society, 1944.

Josselyn, John. *New-Englands Rarities Discovered.* 1672.

———. *Account of Two Voyages to New England.* London: 1673. Second edition, London: G. Widdowes, 1675. Reprint, Boston: Wm. Veazie, 1865.

Juvenal II. *The Sixteen Satires,* trans. by Peter Green. Harmondsworth, 1968.

Kline, Roger A., Robert F. Becker, and Lynne N. Belluscio. *The Heirloom Vegetable Garden: Gardening in the 19th Century.* Ithaca, N.Y.: Cornell Cooperative Extension Information Bulletin 177.

Larsen, Henning. "An Old Icelandic Medical Miscellany." MS Royal Irish Academy, 23 D 43. Oslo J. Dybwad, 1931.

Leighton, Ann. *Early American Gardens.* Boston: Houghton Mifflin, 1966.

Lescarbot, M. *The History of New France,* 3rd ed. 1617. Trans. by W. L. Grant. Toronto: Champlain Society, 1914.

The Maine Times, Nov. 4, 1994.

Mayes, Frances. *Under the Tuscan Sun.* New York: Broadway Books, 1997.

McGee, Harold. *The Curious Cook.* New York: Collier Books, MacMillan Publishing, 1990.

McIntosh, Charles. *The Book of the Garden.* 2 vols. Edinburgh and London, 1855.

Midgley, John. *The Goodness of Potatoes and Root Vegetables.* New York: Random House, 1992.

Misson de Valbourg, Henri. *M. Misson's Memoirs and Observations in his Travels over England,* 1690s. Trans. by Mr. Ozell. London, 1719.

Morash, Marian. *The Victory Garden Cookbook.* New York: Alfred A. Knopf, 1982.

Morphy, Countess, ed. *Recipes of All Nations.* New York: Wm. H. Wise, 1935.

Mowat, Farley. *Westviking: The Ancient Norse in Greenland and North America.* Minerva Press, 1965.

Nearing, Helen, and Scott Nearing. *The Maple Sugar Book.* New York: Schocken Books, 1950.

The New Encyclopaedia Britannica, 15th ed. 1988.

The New Larousse Encyclopedia of Mythology. London: Hamlyn, 1968.

Norman, Jill. *Salad Herbs: How to Grow and Use Them in the Kitchen.* New York: Bantam Books, 1989.

Parker. *History of Londonderry, New Hampshire.*

John Parkinson. *Theatrum Botanicum.* 1640.

Peterson, Lee Allen. *A Field Guide to Edible Wild Plants: Eastern and Central North America.* Boston: Houghton Mifflin, 1977.

Peterson, Roger Tory. A *Field Guide to the Northeastern and North Central North America.* Boston: Houghton Mifflin, 1968.

Pliny the Elder. *Natural History (Historia Naturalis).*

Pollard, Jean Ann. *The New Maine Cooking.* 1987. Reprint, Camden, Maine: DownEast Books, 1996.

Richardson, Joan. *Wild Edible Plants of New England: A Field Guide.* Yarmouh, Maine: DeLorme Publishing, 1981.

Rohde, Eleanor Sinclair. *A Garden of Herbs,* 1936. Reprint, New York: Dover Publications.

Rombauer, Irma S., Marion Rombauer Becker, and Ethan Becker. *The All New All Purpose Joy of Cooking.* New York: Scribner, 1997.

Romanowski, Frank, and Gail Canon. *Making Vinegar at Home.* Northampton, Mass.: Beer and Winemaking Supplies, Inc., 1985.

Root, Waverly, and Richard de Rochemont. *Eating in America.* New York: The Ecco Press, 1995.

Rush, Benjamin. *An Account of the Sugar Maple-Tree of the United States.* Philadelphia: Aitken, 1792.

Russell, Howard S. *A Long, Deep Furrow: Three Centuries of Farming in New England.* Hanover, N.H., and London: University Press of New England, 1982.

Salaman, R. N. "Why 'Jerusalem' Artichoke?" *Journal of the Royal Horticultural Society* 65 (1940).

Siegler, Madeleine H. *Growing Herbs in New England.* Winthrop, Maine: 1980. Self-published.

Simmons, Amelia. *American Cookery, or the Art of Dressing Viands, Fish, Poultry, and Vegetables, and the Best Modes of Making Pastes, Puffs, Pies, Tarts, Puddings, Custards, & Preserves, and All Kinds of Cakes, from the imperial Plumb to plain Cake adapted to This Country & All Grades of Life.* 1796.

Smartt, J. "Evolution of American *Phaseolus* Beans Under Domestication." In P. J. Ucko and G. W. Dimbleby, eds., *The Domestication and Exploitation of Plants and Animals.* Chicago: Aldine Publishing, 1959.

Smith, Andrew F. *The Tomato in America: Early History, Culture, and Cookery.* Columbia: University of South Carolina Press, 1994.

Smith, Captain John. *Description of Virginia and proceedings of the colony.* 1612. In Tyler, ed., *Narratives of Early Virginia.* New York: 1959.

Sokolov, Raymond. *Why We Eat What We Eat.* New York: Simon and Schuster, 1991.

Spayde, Jon. *Japanese Cooking: A Complete Guide to the Simple and Elegant Art of Japanese Cuisine.* Chartwell Books, 1984.

Spurling, Hilary. *Elinor Fettiplace's Receipt Book: Elizabethan Country House Cooking.* New York: Elizabeth Sifton Books, Viking, 1986.

Stackpole, Everett S. *History of New Hampshire.* New York: American Historical Society, 1916.

Stobart, Tom. *Herbs, Spices, and Flavourings.* Reprint, London: Penguin Books, 1979.

Stoner, Carol Hopping, ed. *Stocking Up.* Emmaus, Penn.: Rodale Press, 1977.

Super, John C. *Food, Conquest, and Colonization in Sixteenth-Century Spanish America.* Albuquerque: University of New Mexico Press, 1988.

Tannahill, Reay. *Food in History.* New York: Stein and Day, 1973.

Tatum, Billy Joe. *Billy Joe Tatum's Wild Foods Field Guide and Cookbook.* New York: Workman Publishing, 1976.

Thomas, Robert B. *The Farmer's Almanack, 1803 and 1805.*

Toussaint-Samat, Maguelonne. *History of Food.* Oxford, U.K.: Blackwell Publishers, 1992. Trans. from the French by Anthea Bell.

Trager, James. *The Food Chronology: A Food Lover's Compendium of Events and Anecdotes, from Prehistory to the Present.* New York: Henry Holt, 1995.

Tucker, David M. *Kitchen Gardening in America.* Iowa State University Press, 1993.

Ulrich, Laurel Thatcher. *Good Wives: Image and Reality in the Lives of Women in Northern New England 1650–1750.* New York: Alfred A. Knopf, 1982.

Vilmorin-Andrieux. *The Vegetable Garden.* Trans. by W. Miller. 1885. Reprint, Berkeley, Calif.: Ten Speed Press, 1981.

Visser, Margaret. *Much Depends on Dinner.* New York: Collier Books, 1986.

Watson, Benjamin. *Taylor's Guide to Heirloom Vegetables.* Boston: Houghton Mifflin, 1996.

Weld, Isaac. *Travels through the States of North America and the Provinces of Lower Canada.* London: Stockdale, 1799.

Wilder, Louise Beebe. *The Fragrant Garden.* Originally *The Fragrant Path*, 1932. Reprint, New York: Dover, 1974.

Wolkomir, Richard. "Without Garlic, Life Would Be Just Plain Tasteless." *Smithsonian*, Dec. 1995.

Wood, William. *New Englands Prospect.* London, 1634.

Wright, Clifford A. *A Mediterranean Feast.* New York: Wm. Morrow, 1999.

Wynne, Peter. *Apples: History, Folklore, Horticulture, and Gastronomy.* New York: Hawthorn Books, 1975.

INDEX